Four Biblical Heroines
and the Case for
Female Authorship

FOUR BIBLICAL HEROINES AND THE CASE FOR FEMALE AUTHORSHIP

An Analysis of the Women of *Ruth*, *Esther* and *Genesis* 38

HILLEL I. MILLGRAM

McFarland & Company, Inc., Publishers

Jefferson, North Carolina, and London

LIBRARY OF CONGRESS CATALOGUING-IN-PUBLICATION DATA

Millgram, Hillel I., 1931–
Four biblical heroines and the case for female authorship :
an analysis of the women of Ruth, Esther and Genesis 38 / Hillel I. Millgram.
p.   cm.
Includes bibliographical references and index.

ISBN-13: 978-0-7864-3081-9
softcover : 50# alkaline paper ∞

1. Bible. O.T. Ruth — Criticism, interpretation, etc.
2. Bible. O.T. Esther — Criticism, interpretation, etc.
3. Bible. O.T. Genesis XXXVIII — Criticism, interpretation, etc.
4. Ruth (Biblical figure)   5. Naomi (Biblical figure)
6. Esther, Queen of Persia.   7. Tamar, daughter-in-law of Judah.
8. Women in the Bible.   I. Title.
BS1315.52.M55 2008   222'.0922082 — dc22   2007027949

British Library cataloguing data are available

On the cover: Ruth and Naomi stained glass window,
Saint James Anglican Church, Halifax, Nova Scotia
(artist Sue Obata in association with Satler Studio of West LaHave, Nova Scotia)

Manufactured in the United States of America

*McFarland & Company, Inc., Publishers
Box 611, Jefferson, North Carolina 28640
www.mcfarlandpub.com*

For Deborah Esther

Proverbs 31:10

Contents

Preface and Acknowledgments ix

Abbreviations Used in the Text xiii

Introduction 1

PART I. IN THE BEGINNING

1. A Woman's Tale: An Introduction to the Book of Ruth 17
2. The Exiles 31
3. Amid the Alien Corn 43
4. The Winning of Boaz 53
5. At Bethlehem's Gate 61
6. What Means This Tale? 68
7. Tamar 76

PART II. STRANGERS IN A STRANGE LAND: ESTHER, A TRAGI-COMEDY IN THREE ACTS

8. Understanding Esther: An Introduction 93

Act I: The Women in His Life

9. Party Time in Old Persia, or Lessons on How to Run an Empire 105
10. The Substitute 111

Act II: The War Against the Jews

11. Prologue: The Night of the Assassins 121
12. The Man Who Would Not Bow 124
13. The War Commences 133

Act III: Fighting for Their Lives

14. In the Valley of the Shadow: Looking into the Abyss 141
15. Interlude: The Theater of the Absurd 150

16. Esther Triumphant   158
17. Reversing the Engine   161
18. Judgment Day   171
19. Thou Shalt Not Forget!   178

Conclusion

20. The Dark Vision   188
21. The Hidden Hand   196

PART III. SUMMING UP

22. Thinking Outside the Box   207

Appendix I. From Whom Did Boaz Buy the Field?   221
Appendix II. Can Judah and Tamar Be Fitted into the Joseph Narrative?   224
Appendix III. It's Greek to Me: The Greek Versions of Esther   227
Appendix IV. Mordecai's Decree: A Technical Interlude   230
Appendix V. But Could She Read? The Question of Literacy in Ancient Israel   233
Timeline: Putting Things in Perspective   240
Glossary of Terms, Place Names, and Persons   243
Selected Bibliography   251
Biblical Verses Index   255
General Index   257

Preface and Acknowledgments

This is a book about the Bible. Or to be more exact, a book about three selected biblical narratives: the Book of Ruth, the Book of Esther and the 38th chapter of the Book of Genesis. It proposes that, amazingly, the authors of these narratives saw their world much the same way as we see it — as secular. Living at a time when God's involvement with His world was axiomatic, their inability to perceive the presence of God compelled them to develop a radical new theology to explain why, in a world made by God, humans cannot perceive Him. Simultaneously these same authors were grappling with gender issues and were involved in a process of radically revising the views of the Ancient Near East as to the place of woman in society. Lastly this book proposes that two, and possibly all three, of these narratives were authored by women.

The genesis of this book perhaps calls for a word of explanation. Its gestation proved to be not so much a standard scholarly project as a voyage of discovery. It began, simply enough, as a comparative study of two biblical Books, Esther and Ruth, which shared the unusual element of having female protagonists rather than male. It quickly morphed into something else entirely: a leap into the unknown. I set forth to explore a region I thought I at least partially understood, only to find myself in terra incognita, grappling with unanticipated issues and arriving at unexpected conclusions.

Often on voyages such as these, the outcome is so far from the original goal as to defy assimilation. So Columbus, setting forth to find a sea route to the Indies, discovered the Americas, yet unable to let go of his preconceptions continued to insist to his dying day that he had arrived at the offshore islands of Asia. Some adventurers, perhaps less sure of themselves, stumbling upon the unexpected, find within themselves the capacity to stretch their minds, admit the possibility of the previously inconceivable, and adjust their thinking to radically new possibilities.

I have attempted to follow the latter route, altering the framework of my thinking so as to embrace unexpected facts rather than try to explain them away on the basis of outmoded paradigms. This revision in my thinking did not take place overnight; it was a process, at times vigorously resisted, that lasted for several years. At countless points I revised my opinions — sometimes as a result of cogent criticism, sometimes after reading books and articles previously unknown to me, most often by finding myself in some blind alley and being forced to retrace my steps and to rethink matters from a different perspective. What emerged from this difficult gestation is the present book.

There have been not a few, perhaps more than enough, books on the Bible published over the last few years. As bookshelves get ever more crowded and before readers' eyes dull, I should try to explain in what way, besides the above proposals, this book differs from the others.

It differs in being a bit more old-fashioned than most. It takes the form of a classical commentary on a biblical work, reproducing the full texts of the narratives in question (apart from the human interest of the stories, this has the advantage of an enforced fidelity to the text, compelling me to follow the circumstances and the sequences of the narratives exactly as the authors of these texts determined, lead where they will; and they lead, I think, to a truer understanding of the significance of these unusual tales than if I had imposed my own plan by picking and choosing what suited me). On the other hand, the book has little to say about anthropologically oriented archaeology, ethnicity and "ethnic markers," minimalism (either for or against), and many other of the scientific procedures and currently contentious theories associated with biblical studies in these days. In fact, in many respects this book could have been written a half a century ago. Except that it wasn't. If it breaks new ground it does so with tools that have been around for some time, some of them since ancient times.

It differs in being more ambitious than many. It sets out to explain not just the paradox of biblical narratives in which the main protagonist, God, is conspicuous only by His absence, but also that of women displacing men as heroes — and this in a world dominated by men who had every interest in monopolizing the limelight. It moreover attempts to fathom what the connection can ever be between these two anomalies. Most scholars focus, at the most, on one of these issues; many prefer to avoid both of them. The questions raised lead out into some of the dark and murky waters in which we find ourselves increasingly immersed in our times. It is always easier to remain with the traditional — the tried and true questions where the ground is seemingly firm under one's feet.

It differs in being written not for scholars but for the intelligent layman and laywoman. The phrase of the Preacher, *of making many books there is no end*,[1] is one with special applicability to scholarly books and articles about the Bible; the landscape is so crowded with scholarly trees and shrubs as to form a virtually impenetrable forest. Yet when one looks for well researched works accessible to the general public of non-specialists the thickets thin dramatically. Here and there one can find wonderful books — Norman Podhoretz's *The Prophets* and Leon Kass' *The Beginning of Wisdom: Reading Genesis* are two recent works that spring to mind — but they are like oases in a wilderness, emphasizing by their presence how much is missing. Grounded in serious research, this book is designed to be accessible to the average reader and to appeal to religious and non-religious readers alike.

And lastly, it differs in seeing the Books of the Bible both as ancient texts reflecting the primary concerns of well-nigh forgotten times, yet insisting that their issues remain our issues, that the persons who people the pages of the Bible are ourselves in more than a metaphorical sense, and that the wisdom attained by their struggles can in truth be, as the ancient Psalmist puts it, *a lamp unto our feet and a light unto our path*.[2]

[1]Ecclesiastes 12:12.
[2]Psalms 119:105.

Voltaire is reputed to have remarked: "History never repeats itself; man always does." Some of the greatest of the classical historians, Thucydides for one, made this principle the ideational basis of their works. This conviction also undergirds this book. If we have felt increasingly threatened over the past several decades in our previously unquestioned assumptions, not the least in the realm of gender, and at sea in a world seemingly devoid of God and of values, it may be reassuring to know that the human species has lived through similar challenges before. More, that there have been remarkable persons who have come up with answers that some of us might find applicable to those topics that so trouble us today. Some of these answers can be found in the pages of the Bible that are the focus of this book.

Looking back over the arduous revision of the way I was brought up and taught to understand the Bible and the place of gender in the world, I have come to realize the debt I owe to so many for making it possible for me to travel the path of discovery. Without them I would never have made it, ending up, like Columbus, in denial.

First, I must thank several teachers, sadly no longer with us, who not only trained me rigorously in the disciplines that have proved vital in writing this work, but who also taught me to avoid the orthodoxy of the herd and to think "out of the box": Professor Hans Kohn in the field of intellectual history, Professor Emery Neff in comparative literature, and an especial vote of thanks to the late Professor Shalom Spiegel, who not only introduced me to the serious study of the Bible but also kindled in me a lifelong love of Scripture and an appreciation of its complexity and depth.

No book is written without the author first reading the works of many others. The many authors to whom I am greatly indebted are mostly detailed in the Selected Bibliography. However I feel it necessary to acknowledge a special debt to Professor Robert Alter for having spearheaded the ongoing revision of the way the Bible is seen and studied: the shift away from the methodology and assumptions of source criticism to a literary analysis of the received text. Though I quote him sparingly, his shadow looms large over all aspects of this book.

Among the many persons who took it upon themselves to read sections of this work in the various stages of its preparation, and whose comments have done so much to correct both errors of commission and omission, I must single out for especial thanks Professor Judith Porter for steering me to the sociological sources and insights that underpin the conclusion of the book, and Rabbi Yitzhak Rubin for the meticulous scrutiny he brought to bear on the manuscript and the detailed suggestions drawn from his vast store of Rabbinic lore that proved so helpful. A special debt is owed to my eldest son, Professor Elijah Millgram, whose specialist knowledge saved me from many philosophical follies, and whose skillful editing of the manuscript has made me sound in many places a better writer than I am.

Most of all I am grateful to my wife, Deborah, to whom this book is dedicated. A lifetime companion, her encouragement, trueness of judgment and language skills have benefited me in more ways than I can recount. She has lived with Ruth, Tamar and Esther as well as with me for three years, and much of the finished product is as much hers as mine. Without her this book would not have come into being.

Lastly, I am grateful to the editors and publishers of those works from which I have cited extracts, and to the staffs of the National Library in Jerusalem, the

Bodleian in Oxford and the Library of Congress in Washington, DC, for their unstinting help and unfailing courtesy during the many hours I spent working in these wonderful institutions.

In conclusion, the avowal once made by Thomas Gifford sums up my sentiments exactly: "Whatever may be wrong with the piece of work you are holding is my doing; whatever is right I gladly share with these."[3]

Hillel I. Millgram
Jerusalem, Fall 2007

---

[3]Gifford, *The Assassini*, p. x.

Abbreviations Used in the Text

The Hebrew Bible and Its Ancient Versions

AT   Alpha Text (of Esther)
LXX   Septuagint
MT   Masoretic Text
OL   Old Latin translation
Q   Dead Sea Scrolls (Qumran)
Syr.   Peshita (Syriac)
Targ.   Targum
Vul.   Vulgate

English Bible Versions

AV   Authorized Version (King James Bible)
NIV   New International Version (1978)
NJPS   New Jewish Publication Society (1985)
OJPS   Old Jewish Publication Society (1917)
RSV   Revised Standard Version (1952)

Commentaries (with Name of the Biblical Book Following the Abbreviation)

AB   Anchor Bible
ICC   International Critical Commentary
JPSBC   Jewish Publication Society Bible Commentary
JPSTC   Jewish Publication Society Torah Commentary

Other Commonly Used Abbreviations

BCE   Before the common era
CE   Of the common era
NT   New Testament
OT   Old Testament

A religion which does not affirm that God is hidden is not true; and every religion which fails to declare why is not illuminating.... "Verily, Thou art a God that hidest Thyself" (Isaiah 45:15).
　　　　　　　　　　　　— Blaise Pascal, *Pensées*

For mankind is ever the same and nothing is lost out of nature, though everything is altered.
　　　　　　　　　　　　— John Dryden, *Fables, Ancient and Modern*

Introduction

I found Him in the shining of the stars,
I marked Him in the flowering of His fields,
But in His ways with men I find Him not.
— Alfred Lord Tennyson,
The Idylls of the King

Three Strange Tales

Four women whose lives have gone disastrously wrong: separated by hundreds of years from each other, they all share the fate of living in worlds shaped by men and for men. They have all seen men wreak havoc with their lives, and they share the grim choice: to submit to a diminished existence, or take their lives into their own hands and to make something of the ruin they have been handed. Their stories are the tales of how they accept the challenge. Each in her own way, against all odds, and at great personal risk, succeeds in rebuilding her life on her own terms, winning through to a successful conclusion. Their names are Naomi, Ruth, Tamar and Esther, and the record of their lives is to be found in the Bible.

What are they doing there? When we think of biblical women our attention is usually drawn to women paired with men: Sarah with Abraham, Rebecca with Isaac, Rachel and Leah with Jacob and Bathsheba with David. In these pairs, the man is always dominant, the woman in his shadow, under his care and protection. But our four women are alone and adrift. Far from protecting them, the men in their lives have betrayed them.

When one places these tales in the context of the Ancient Near East, the historical setting in which the epic events related in the Bible played themselves out, the stories assume an aspect that is almost bizarre. In the male-dominated world of the Ancient Near East, men were the subjects of history, women its objects. Against this background, how can we explain narratives featuring women rather than men as the heroes? And considering the man-centered nature of most of biblical narrative, how could such tales ever have been incorporated in the Bible?

The stories of these four women are unusual in another manner: they are all secular stories. And this phenomenon is so extraordinary in its biblical setting as to demand elucidation.

It goes almost without saying that the biblical narratives — from those that recount the beginnings of the world and of humanity, the birth of Israel, and the epic stretching from Israel's liberation from Egyptian bondage and the Settlement in the Promised Land, the establishment of the monarchy and on to the tragic destruction of Jerusalem and the exile of the People of

Israel[1]— share one dominant characteristic: the central figure in the narrative is God. It is He who acts and speaks and, through His actions and words, drives the plot forward. In comparison to God, all the other actors in this gigantic drama are no more than bit players, on stage for at most a few brief chapters, only to vanish and be replaced by others. For instance, God creates the universe, places Adam and Eve in the garden of Eden, gives them their marching orders and, when disobeyed, expels them; God then brings a flood upon mankind, saves Noah, and enters into a covenant with him and his descendants; God subsequently chooses Abraham to be the father of His chosen people, leads him, tests him and constantly speaks with him. The central figure of God provides the cohesion that unites the variegated and disparate scenes into one vast, unified drama.

Against this background, the tales of the four women that we are about to examine stand out starkly, in that God *does not* set the agenda, and *does not* tell people what to do. God does not appear on the stage, and in one of the stories is not even mentioned. In all of them, people do what they do and act as they act solely on the basis of their own dispositions and motivations, entirely like the characters in most of the modern novels and short stories with which we are familiar. It is in this sense that I am calling these tales secular. What are secular stories doing in the Bible?

A third issue confronts us, one that flows directly from the two anomalies we have just raised: what can the connection between women heroes and secular stories be? Why is it that the very narratives that so atypically feature women as their central figures are also seemingly devoid of the presence of God?

These three issues — women emerging as hero-figures out of a world dominated by men, godless tales incorporated into the biblical Saga of God's ways with humankind and the strange coincidence that the very tales that center on women are simultaneously the ones where God is absent — are the subject of this book.

I propose to show that these texts are not isolated phenomena, but rather that they form a tradition. They share and develop an innovative view of religion, and they underwrite their central theological claim by working out a position that will be of interest even to persons not directly concerned with religious and theological matters — to anticipate: that the duration and pace of human life make phenomena on larger temporal scales almost entirely invisible to us. I also intend to demonstrate that women are the protagonists in these tales because they are being presented as role models for a revisionist evaluation of the proper role of women in the world. Lastly I intend to propose that the use of female protagonists raises the question of whether the authors were themselves women. These aims form the agenda of the book.

While this book is meant to serve as a nonpartisan introduction to the works it introduces, I do have an agenda of my own as well, and in the interests of making it clear to the reader where I am advancing novel views, I mean to be up front about it.

About Myself

Before we go any further, I think it is only fair that you know something about the person who is setting this agenda. I personally am a religious person. This, however, does not mean that I am writing solely for a religious audience. The book is meant to be available to a secular audience as well, and my own religious beliefs are at no point introduced into the argument.

---

[1]Genesis, the narrative sections of Exodus, Numbers and Deuteronomy, and the Books of Joshua, Judges, Samuel, Kings and Chronicles.

My aim is to analyze a series of biblical texts that have held a place of honor in the annals of Western civilization, and through their explication to uncover both the motivations that brought them into being and their intended message. Briefly, this is not a proselytizing work.

Being a Jew, I am a descendent, both physically and spiritually, of the ancient Israelites out of whose community the authors of the Bible sprang. They being my distant ancestors, it is understandable that the text speaks to me. But two thousand years have passed since the Bible ceased to be the exclusive possession of the Jewish people. The Bible is now the common possession of all humanity, and is one of the foundations of the Western world. As such this book is not intended for an exclusively Jewish audience, but rather for all those who see in the Bible a part of the heritage of humanity in general, and of the West in particular. It is in this light that this book has been written.

And now, having introduced myself, it is time to begin putting this pledge into practice, and to introduce the meta-subject of this book. The book provides necessary background on a "need to know" basis as it progresses. Where the use of some technical terms becomes unavoidable, or even when the use of common terms may be ambiguous in the specific context in which they are found, care will be taken to explain their use.

What Is the Bible?

This is a book about the Bible; or to be more exact, about selected parts of the Hebrew Bible.[2] Before analyzing in depth the biblical tales we have highlighted, it is only proper that we be clear in our minds what exactly we mean when we speak of the Bible, and precisely how we intend approaching it.

The Hebrew Bible is the creation of a people known as the Children of Israel,[3] or in shorthand, the Israelites, who were the ancestors of the present-day Jews. The thirty-nine Books that became the Bible we currently possess were composed over a period of close to a thousand years. They are the end result of the sustained efforts of this unusual people to reach an understanding of itself, of its place in the world and of its tortuous, and often tortured, relationship with its God. The insights reached during this millennial undertaking, known subsequently as the Biblical Age, and embedded in the Books of the Hebrew Bible, have not only shaped Judaism and its daughter religions, Christianity and Islam, but have determined the form and direction of civilization in the modern world.

The Bible contains literary works composed in different periods and under vastly divergent conditions, and these comprise radically different literary forms. There are surges of exhortation alternating with vehement denunciation; dry legal codes side by side with philosophical speculation; odes of joy and sadness, comedy and tragedy, phrased either in poetry or prose, and sometimes both intermingled, side by side with long stretches of narrative. These last include stories, biographies, reportage and, most of all — history. It is within this last category, narrative prose, that we find the works on which we will be concentrating our attention: the Book of Ruth, the Book of Esther and the 38th chapter of the Book of Genesis.

How did these works come into being? Obviously, someone wrote them. As we examine

[2]So called because it is mostly written in the Hebrew language (a few parts are written in Aramaic, a sister language to Hebrew). To Christians the Hebrew Bible is known as the Old Testament (OT), to differentiate it from the New Testament (NT), which is written in Greek. The Hebrew Bible is the Holy Scriptures of the Jews. It, together with the New Testament, forms the Holy Scriptures of Christianity.

[3]That is, the descendents of Israel, the third of the Patriarchs (see Glossary), who is also known by the name of Jacob (see Genesis 32:23–33).

them we will attempt to determine when each was written and, if possible, by whom. At this stage let us simply state that our working hypothesis is that each was written in much the same way stories and novels are written today: an author sitting down, composing his or her narrative and putting it on paper.[4] As in no case do we think that the authors of our works were contemporaneous with the events narrated, they obviously relied on sources, oral or written. But the literary form of the final composition, the way it was structured and, of course, its moral or message were original to the author.[5]

Once written, the next concern of an author, then as now, was to get the book into circulation. Millennia before the invention of the printing press, this was a very difficult matter. All books were hand-written and were, in this aspect, identical with the original manuscript. The author would write out one or more copies (or if wealthy, could hire a scribe — a kind of professional secretary — to do it) and would then circulate the copies among friends and acquaintances. These would, in turn, pass the book on to their friends. If any of these should take a special liking to the book they could have a private copy written out for personal use. No one ever thought in terms of copyright in those days; a book once circulated was the property of the public.

As long as a book remained popular with the reading public it remained "in print," new copies being made as old ones wore out. If not, a book would go "out of print," no new copies replacing the natural attrition of wear and tear, accidents, wars and fires. Most books in the ancient world suffered this fate: vanishing from public view, they were known only by name, or sometimes from quotes. Such was the fate of a number of very important books that had wide circulation in biblical times. While accident obviously played an important part in the survival process, the more copies in circulation, the higher the book's life expectancy. The works that are the subject of our inquiry, Ruth, Esther and Genesis 38, seem to have been bestsellers from the start, and to have remained so as century followed century. Through the vicissitudes of the years, down to the invention of the printing press, enough people and groups cared about these books to ensure their preservation.

The laborious hand-copying process ended about 500 years ago with the printing press. In Venice, in 1524–1525, Daniel Bomberg printed what was to become the universally accepted edition of the Hebrew Bible.[6] With one exception, all Hebrew Bibles today are copies of this original edition.[7]

---

[4]In the Biblical Era people wrote with pen and ink on sheets of papyrus or parchment (see Glossary). These sheets were then sewn together to form scrolls which were kept rolled in cabinets or chests, and unrolled to be read. When the word "book" is used in the Bible it refers to these scrolls. (Books in the modern sense of the term — sets of sheets bound at one side and read by turning from one page to the next — were only introduced into common use during Roman times.) The Torah scrolls still used in Synagogues to this day have preserved the form that biblical Books originally had. The present-day Torah, being five Books (Genesis, Exodus, Leviticus, Numbers and Deuteronomy) "bound together" as one, is obviously far larger than the typical Book of biblical times.

[5]The extent to which the contents of the Books of the Bible are the result of human insight and discovery, or derive from divine inspiration has been a subject of vehement dispute within religions that look to the Bible for their authority and justification. We make no claim to resolve these questions.

[6]Actually he published his first Hebrew Bible in the years 1516–17, but it didn't sell. Not being a Jew (Daniel Bomberg was a devout Catholic), he hadn't realized that his main market, the Jews, wouldn't buy a Bible without the marginal Masoretic notes (see **Masorite** in the Glossary). Realizing his mistake, he corrected this error in the second (1524–25) edition and had a bestseller.

[7]The manuscript used by Bomberg was the text of Jacob ben Chayyim, based on manuscripts from the 13th and 14th centuries CE. There is an even earlier manuscript, the ben Asher text, which is several centuries older and is preserved in the Public Library of Leningrad (now St. Petersburg) and hence sometimes known as the Leningrad Manuscript. This formed the basis of the *Biblia Hebraica* (begun under the editorship of Rudolf

Endless recopying has its dangers. Being human, even the most devoted and careful scribes make mistakes. Sometimes scribes' eyes would wander, and they would skip words, or even entire sentences. Sometimes they would misread a word and replace it with something that looked superficially similar but was quite different in meaning. Despite the best of precautions and proof-reading, errors would slip through. And these errors would be copied in turn. After centuries of constant recopying, a situation was created in which several versions of Ruth and Genesis, and possibly Esther as well, were in circulation simultaneously. At this time Genesis had been canonized, while Ruth and Esther were universally accepted as Scripture, that is, Holy Writ.[8] The circumstance of having different versions of Holy Books became intolerable to the religious authorities in Jerusalem. So, taking the best copies available in the Temple Archives, and by a process of careful comparison, they issued authorized versions of these works, the most error-free editions they could achieve. This is the Masoretic Text (MT)[9] of the Bible, which has been standard to this day.

But the story does not end here. Good as these efforts were — and they were very good — problems still remain. There are phrases, and at times whole sentences, that don't seem to make sense. And there are places where quite obviously something is missing. This is where the ancient versions can help us.

More than two thousand years ago Jewish communities living in different areas of the world lost their traditional facility with the Hebrew language. No longer speaking Hebrew in their daily lives, more and more Jews lost the ability to read it. And so it became necessary to provide a translation of the Bible into the various languages these communities of Jews spoke and understood. The first such translation, into Greek, was made in Alexandria, Egypt, during the reign of Ptolemy II Philadelphus (283–245 BCE). This translation, known as the Septuagint (LXX),[10] is recognized today as an excellent translation, but it was often made from different versions of the various Books of the Bible than those used by the Masorites. Comparing and editing the MT in the light of LXX can prove an enormous help in clearing up difficulties.

As the years went by, translations into other languages were made: into Aramaic, called the Targum (Targ.),[11] into Syriac (an Eastern form of Aramaic) called the Peshitta (Syr.), and into Latin, called the Vulgate (Vulg.).[12] All these exhibit differences from the MT and invite comparison.

While one must exercise extreme caution in the use of these alternate versions, with care they can help us to a better understanding. My translation of Ruth, Esther and Genesis 38 is almost entirely based on the MT (about ninety-nine percent). It is by far the best version we have. But in certain cases, when I feel the ancient versions can be of help, I have not hesitated

Kittel and completed by Paul Kahle). This text has increasingly begun to take the place of the previously used ben Chayyim text as the standard version of the Masoretic Text (MT).

[8]Canonization simply means the formal recognition and acceptance of a given Book as holy or "inspired" by an authorized body. Works so recognized became as a consequence Sacred Scripture, writings that were author-itative and binding. Genesis was canonized c. 445 BCE; Ruth and Esther, as parts of the Ketubim (Writings — see Glossary) sometime after 70 CE, but had popularly been accepted as Scripture long before the formal seal of approval was given. The issues are further discussed in the introductions to the various Books.

[9]See **Masorite** in the Glossary.

[10]The Greek word means "seventy," an abbreviation of the full title: *The Translation of the Seventy Elders.* This refers to the story that seventy-two scholars, summoned from Jerusalem, made the translation of the Torah ("The Five Books of Moses"), the first part of the Hebrew Bible. The remainder of the Hebrew Bible (The Prophets and The Writings) was translated later, in stages.

[11]In reality there were several different translations made into Aramaic. *Targum* is the Aramaic word for trans-lation.

[12]We are referring here to the translation made by St. Jerome from the original Hebrew.

to proceed on their basis, hoping thereby to come somewhat closer to the author's original intent. In order to play fair with the reader I always indicate in a footnote when I have departed from the Masoretic Text, and on what basis; and I include the MT reading for comparison. That way it is possible for the reader to come to an independent conclusion, deciding whether to go along with my version or to prefer the MT.[13]

A Word on Translation

This volume contains the full text of Ruth, Esther and Genesis 38. As such, it can be used as a companion to and commentary on these works. You may be used to reading the Bible in the King James Translation, or in one of the more modern versions. While the King James Translation is easily the greatest rendition of the Bible into English, the archaic language of this version no longer facilitates understanding, but instead acts as a barrier to most people.[14] On the other hand I feel that many of the modern translations, in striving to be relevant, are too free in their renderings, often imposing on the text contemporary agendas that distort the original meaning. Some modern translations I simply find wooden. All this, in addition to the considerations listed above, has led me to translate the text anew.

I have tried to make the translation simple and to keep it in contemporary English. The translation is literal; I have stayed as close to the Hebrew original as possible, avoiding euphemism and paraphrase, while conforming to proper English usage. In a word, I have tried to render just what the text says while avoiding stilted and convoluted English. This not only facilitates ease of reading but also, to my way of thinking, best conveys the feel of the simple and lucid style of the original text.[15]

---

[13]Unlike many scholars, I am extremely hesitant to second-guess the received text, substituting my own conviction for what lies before us. As a basic rule I do not approve of emending the text; that is, altering the text on one's own authority in order to make "better sense" of it. My approach is to try to make sense of what we have, and make no changes except on the authority of alternate versions. Therefore, any alterations that I have made in the MT have been on the basis of ancient versions of the text. There are three exceptions to this rule, cases where I could get no meaning from the Hebrew and no help from the ancient versions. In desperation I have been forced to offer my own understanding of the text, and indicate this as such in the footnotes.

[14]In fact, the language used was already archaic in 1611, when the Authorized Version (which is the official title of the "King James Translation") was published. "Thee's" and "thou's" had long since ceased to be used in everyday speech. The Bishops' Committee that was responsible for the translation made the conscious choice to use "old-fashioned" language in order to give its Bible a tone of solemn antiquity. The committee felt everyday language would "cheapen" the text.

[15]A word about the way we refer to God in our translation of the biblical text. The Bible routinely uses two separate ways of referring to the deity: the general term *elohim*, which simply means "deity" and is virtually universally rendered as "God," and what is termed as "the Tetragrammaton," the four-letter personal name of God. This is often rendered by modern scholars as "Yahweh," or "Yahveh," or sometimes without vowels as "YHVH." These are current attempts to reconstruct God's personal name (a previous attempted reconstruction was "Jehovah"). But since biblical Hebrew was written with a consonantal alphabet (there are no vowels), and because we really have no idea how the consonants were pronounced in those days, all reconstructions are highly speculative. Jews ceased pronouncing God's name more than two thousand years ago, out of a sense that it was improper to address God by name. Instead they substituted the title *Lord*, a convention adopted by the Bishops' Committee that issued the Authorized English Translation of the Bible (known as the King James Bible). This convention has been used in most subsequent translations down to the present day. We have continued this tradition in our translation. There is a further point to be considered, one succinctly expressed by Norman Podhoretz: "I prefer LORD because YHVH ['Yahweh'] in English willy-nilly makes God seem a tribal deity (which is in fact what some scholars — wrongly, I believe — think He was to the earliest of His Israelite devotees)" (Podhoretz, *The Prophets*, p. 12). Like him, I only allow this putative reconstruction into this book when I am quoting someone else as, for example, in Chapter 6, note 11.

A Word about Footnotes

I have already mentioned that this book has been designed for the general reader, and thus is not written in the format typical of academic literature. So what is all that small print doing on the bottom of the pages?

It is true that notes are a scholar's tool, their primary purpose being to facilitate peer review. Meticulous documentation of every fact and opinion with its scholarly source allows specialists to check up on each other to see how well they have done their homework, whether they are accurately reflecting the views of those upon whom they rely, and therefore how seriously one can take their results. None of this is appropriate for a work that is not destined for the world of biblical scholarship, but rather for the intelligent and interested layman. In this book the notes serve different purposes entirely.

The purposes are three. The first we have already mentioned: to play fair by letting the reader know whenever the translation departs from the Masoretic Text. As most readers will have little or no command of Hebrew, they will have no way of knowing when their guide has departed from the accepted MT. These notes are just a way of keeping the translation transparent, and of not relying on different versions without the reader's knowledge.

The second purpose is plain common courtesy. Whenever there is a direct quotation from a work it is polite to give the author credit. So whenever an author is mentioned or quoted directly that author is given his or her due.

But the overwhelming majority of notes serve the purpose of optional enrichment. Some readers work on the principle that the shortest distance between two points is a straight line. Anything extraneous to the matter at hand is an annoyance, to be avoided at all cost. Others, myself included, far from finding digressions distracting, discover in them half the reward of reading: detours that open new vistas, expand horizons and deepen understanding. Most of the notes, those with more than one or two lines, fall into this category of short side excursions.

Assuming that at least some of my readers will have the same kind of temperament as myself, while others will prefer to get on with the task at hand, I have arranged to remove most side issues from the main body of the text and put them into the notes (and into a selected series of appendices). Some of these will give a deeper understanding of the subject under discussion; sometimes they will give a view of some related field or issue. The several notes that you have encountered so far are a taste of what you can expect. Those who prefer to stay with the main text will find that it is fully self-contained. But for those inclined to explore side issues, the doors have been left open.

How Should One Read the Bible?

SHOULD THE BIBLE BE VIEWED AS LITERATURE?

One of the barriers to a profitable and enjoyable reading of the Bible nowadays lies not so much in its language or its unfamiliar contexts as in our sense of diffidence. We begin by viewing the Bible as an exalted "Holy Book," and this raises expectations of all sorts of in our minds. We feel, perhaps unconsciously, that it must be held at arm's length, and approached with awe and reverence — an attitude that hinders direct and personal contact with the text. Yet when the various Books that became the Bible were written and first read they were not Scripture. They were literature, and part and parcel of the literature of the time. Centuries were to pass before a consensus developed that led to their canonization as Holy Writ. Unless we approach these works through the eyes of those who read them shortly after they first saw the light of day, we will not only lose their impact and import, but will miss what it was about them that led to their eventual canonization.

What I am suggesting is that we start by approaching Ruth, Esther and Genesis 38 as works of literature. By this I mean that not only should we be prepared to take very seriously *what* is being said in these works, but also *how* it is being presented to us. In most cases the way the message is packaged influences, and often determines, its meaning. And this packaging, despite its apparent simplicity, often proves to be elaborate and sophisticated. The authors of the works that we will be discussing were not amateurs in the art of writing.

But in raising the issue of "The Bible as Literature," as it is often termed in introductory college courses, we are exposing ourselves to the pointed, *and valid*, criticism of D.F. Rauber:

> Many readers ... have recollections that the art of the biblical writers is always being discussed. In most cases, however, the payment of literary tribute to the authors is almost ritualistic: a slight bow is made in the direction of the Muse, a few generalizations are shuffled off, and then attention turns to what is really important.[16]

After giving several examples of these "generalities" Rauber continues:

> The objection to this kind of literary evaluation is not that it is condensed and offhand, but that it is so simplistic that it gives a radically wrong impression of the work.... And the reason is simply that the commentators do not study the story very seriously as an art product.[17]

I do take very seriously this criticism of earlier biblical scholarship. Only in recent years has a school of modern scholars begun the task of recovering an appreciation of the craft with which biblical authors constructed their works. Their deliberate choice of every word and the painstaking design of each sentence served two distinct ends. The first was to gain an audience, and the second was to convey a message to that audience. No one would take a mediocre writer seriously; brilliant writing was the only path to a respectful hearing.

We must never allow ourselves to lose sight of the simple truth that every Book of the Bible was, in its time, a bestseller. As we are using the term, "bestseller" describes books with staying power; books that continued to be valued and read decade after decade, century after century. If they hadn't been they would never have survived to be canonized and become part of the Bible. And the artistic excellence of the Books that eventually made it into the Bible was no small part of the reason they were so popular.

But while artistic excellence could earn popularity, and thus was a critical factor in ensuring a book's survival over the course of the centuries, it by itself was no guaranteed entry ticket to the biblical canon. Canonization was determined by content: only those books whose message was deemed of transcendent value and of enduring worth were considered. These messages could be widely divergent, even seemingly heterodox (compare Ecclesiastes with Psalms, for example, or Isaiah with Job), but in each case the decision rested on the conviction that the Book addressed some aspect of the essential human condition, and that as its message had remained relevant despite the many changes that time had wrought, so it would continue to apply in ages yet to come. What is surprising is how often, in the Books that became part of the Bible, the essential message was enhanced by the artistic excellence of the work in which it was embedded, and how often the surest path to an understanding of what the author was trying to convey is to be found through an appreciation of the artistry by which it is being presented. For this reason we will give close attention to the way in which each work is structured,

[16]Rauber, "Literary Values in the Bible," p. 27.
[17]*Ibid.*, pp. 28–29.

and to matters such as choice of vocabulary or calculated turns of phrase. By identifying the means through which our authors elected to express themselves, we will put ourselves in a position to infer their ends.

IS THE BIBLE HARD TO UNDERSTAND?

There has been a tendency in recent years to see the Bible as a repository of secrets concealed from the average reader, who lacks the keys to decipher the codes in which they are embedded. This has led to a proliferation of books that purport to reveal the key to these "Bible codes." This approach reveals a misunderstanding of the intentions of the Bible and its methods.[18] The Bible is not an esoteric work, nor does it pretend to be one. On the contrary, the Bible continually insists that it is transparent and easily accessible. Meir Sternberg refers us to Moses' declaration in his valedictory speech, where we are being given instructions as to how to read the Bible[19]:

> For this commandment which I command you this day is not too baffling for you, neither is it far off. It is not in the heavens, so that one should say: "Who will go up for us to the heavens to get it for us and declare it to us, that we may do it?" Neither is it beyond the sea, so that one should say: "Who will cross the sea for us to get it for us and declare it to us, that we may do it?" But the word is very near to you, in your mouth and in your heart, that you may do it (Deuteronomy 30:11–14).

This is followed by the injunction:

> You shall read this Teaching[20] before all Israel in their hearing. Assemble the people, men and women and little ones, and the stranger that is within your gates, that they may hear and that they may learn (Deuteronomy 31:11–12).[21]

If this injunction was put into practice, and there is every reason to assume that it was, every seven years during the Festival of Tabernacles (Sukkot) there was a public reading of Scripture. The point is that everyone — men and women, young and old — were expected to understand what was being read to them. Scripture was written so as to be accessible to everyone.

The Bible was meant to serve as the national charter or constitution of the people of Israel, and to contain its national heritage. The nation's very sense of identity and its continuity depended upon it. As such, the Bible had to make sense to the people it was designed to serve, and to establish a common ground between all ages, classes and genders. The way the Bible attempted to achieve these goals was through what Meir Sternberg calls "foolproof composition, whereby the discourse strives to be open and bring home its essentials to all its readers."[22] In a word, the central rule of biblical composition is transparency.

This transparency is accomplished through adhering to two basic principles. In the Bible

---

[18]Despite being a composite of many different Books written at different times, all the works that make up the Bible share in common a basic methodology, a series of literary conventions and an overarching purpose that bind these disparate Books into an overall unity. This makes it possible to treat the Bible as if it were a unitary work. These unifying modalities will be dealt with as we proceed.

[19]Sternberg, *The Poetics of Biblical Narrative*, p. 49.

[20] The Hebrew word used is "*Torah.*"

[21]The public reading of this Torah or Teaching (by which is meant the very earliest parts of the Bible) before the entire population was not unique to the days of Moses. It was repeated to our certain knowledge in the days of Joshua (Joshua 8:34–35), in 622 BCE during the reign of King Josiah (2 Kings 23:2), and in 445 BCE, after the Babylonian Exile (Nehemiah 8).

[22]Sternberg, *The Poetics of Biblical Narrative*, p. 50.

the narrator always tells the truth; he is absolutely and straightforwardly reliable. The reader is never lied to and is never led by the nose to false conclusions; he can never go far wrong even if he does little more than follow the statements made and the incidents enacted.[23] But the Bible rarely tells the whole story; large gaps are left for the reader to fill in. Questions are raised for the perceptive reader by what is *not* said. In other words, reading the Bible is like conducting a dialogue between oneself and the biblical author. And it is in this dialogue that the richness and the subtleties of the Bible begin to emerge. What one will get out of the Bible will largely depend on what one brings to it, and on how much effort one is willing to invest. Bring little and invest little, and you won't go far wrong. Bring more and invest much, and the Bible will open up before you with unexpected richness. One of the main purposes of this book is to enable appreciation not only of the surface text but also of some of the deeper levels of insight and meaning.

CONVENTIONS AND CONTEXT

Having set forth the basic approach that we will be using, as well as some of the ground rules that determine how the text works, what remains to be considered are remaining barriers that might impede our understanding of these biblical tales. First and foremost among these is the fact that we will be reading an ancient work. The Bible, like all ancient works, was written for the readers of those days, with their specific backgrounds and attitudes in mind. We are not that ancient audience, and so we lack much of the context assumed by the authors. Moreover, we look at matters from a different perspective than that of the original target audience. What for them was timely is for us often incomprehensible.

An example will make the issue clearer. A modern author can take the socio-economic and political configuration of America for granted. He can assume that his readers are familiar with the general outlines of the way the United States governs itself. He does not need to spell out that the president is elected to a four-year term of office, that Congress is composed of the House of Representatives and the Senate, and that the United States is currently composed of fifty states. Similarly he can assume that his audience has a working knowledge of how the American economic system works: of how one purchases groceries and uses a credit card. He knows the names of some of the larger producers of consumer goods and what unions are. Only when one comes down to specific situations is it necessary for an author to elaborate. In much the same way biblical authors could assume a background knowledge of the economic, social and legal conditions of their times on the part of their readers.

Modern readers, separated from the biblical period by thousands of years, lack this background knowledge. As a result, situations depicted in the Bible often are inherently incomprehensible to us. Worse, we often try to fill in the gaps with erroneous assumptions and so misread what to people in the Biblical Age was perfectly clear and comprehensible.

Over the past century much progress has been made in reconstructing ancient societies. We are far from having a complete picture of life in the various periods of the Biblical Age, but we have learned enough to enable us to understand in large part the tales we will be discussing. Thus one of my main tasks will be to explain the background that was common knowledge at the time and which the authors did not need to rehearse. Of course we will not attempt to fill in the whole known background — an impossible task within the confines of a single book — but only that which is absolutely essential to understanding both the specific tales and the main points that they are

---

[23]"The Bible always tells the truth in that its narrator is absolutely and straightforwardly reliable ... in context his remain accounts of the truth communicated on the highest authority.... But follow the biblical narrator ever so uncritically, and by no great exertion you will be making tolerable sense of the world you are in, the action that unfolds, the protagonists on stage, and the point of it all" (*ibid.*, p. 51).

trying to make. This will be done in the introductory chapters to the Book of Ruth, where the focus will be on aspects of the social and legal system of pre-monarchic Israel, and in the introduction to the Book of Esther, where we will concentrate on the Persian world and how it worked. (A separate background chapter to the Tale of Tamar [Genesis 38] is unnecessary, as the legal and social background necessary to understand Tamar is sufficiently similar to that for Ruth.)

Beyond taking relevant background for granted, the biblical authors could also assume that the literary conventions of the time were known to their audiences. All mature literatures possess patterns and forms of writing that act as signals to readers. They don't have to be explained because readers have absorbed them and know how to interpret them. Once again here are some modern examples: when we see a story opening with the words, "Once upon a time..." we at once recognize that what follows will be a work of fiction — a legend, fairy tale or something similar — and not a report of actual events. In much the same way, when reading detective fiction, we confidently expect the villain to be discovered — and not among the obvious suspects (where they are usually to be found in real life), but among those whom we would least suspect. These are conventions that constitute those literary genres. The Books of the Bible are the products of a mature literature with well-established conventions held in common by writers and readers alike. So it is important that we be aware of some of them so that we may be alert to their signals.

The first is *repetition*. When a key word or phrase is repeated it is sending a strong signal.[24] Sometimes the signal is one of emphasis. Biblical Hebrew lacks the tools we usually employ for emphasis: italics, punctuation, exclamation marks, capitalization and so on. Its only means of emphasis is repetition.

Sometimes the signal is one of allusion: we are being reminded of the use of the same word or phrase in another context, either in the same Book or in another Book of the Bible, and we are being invited to compare or contrast the present setting with a different one for purposes of illumination. The comparison may help us better understand an ambiguous situation, or to see it in a different light. Sometimes repetition is used to draw attention to a key word or phrase that tells us what the story is really all about. The ancients were sensitive to these hints. As we proceed we will see how helpful these can be.

A second biblical convention has to do with how narratives are written. In Western literature we are used to stories that rely on description. We have a very clear mental picture in our minds of Sherlock Holmes; his face, his hat, his bearing, his idiosyncrasies. We are also told at great length what the characters in our books think and how they feel. Indeed some books focus almost exclusively on the inner lives of the heroes — an almost uninterrupted stream of consciousness. By contrast, biblical literature contains virtually no description and no exploration of the thoughts and feelings of the persons portrayed. We have no idea whether Boaz is tall or short, fat or thin, handsome or plain. We are told that Esther is stunningly beautiful (a fact necessary to the advancement of the plot), but nothing about the color of her eyes or her hair. We are almost never informed as to what people are thinking or feeling.[25] Instead the Bible focuses almost exclusively on what persons say and what they do: on speech and action.

---

[24]Sometimes it is not a specific word that is repeated but a *root*. Hebrew words are mostly based on three-letter roots which, depending on their different grammatical constructions, can have different meanings. Native Hebrew speakers are very sensitive to the roots of words and can recognize them with ease even when in different forms and contexts. In translation they often appear as totally different words. In cases such as these we will have to point them out to the modern reader who is working from a translation.

[25]Only rarely are we given snippets of the kind of information that appears in virtually every other sentence in Western literature: an ambiguous remark seems to inform us that David was a redhead (1 Samuel 17:42) and, as we shall see, we will be informed as to Judah's motivation for refusing to give his son Shelah to Tamar (Genesis 38:11) — see Chapter 7, note 19 — but their very rarity makes them stand out as dramatic exceptions to the general rule.

This convention of a descriptively sparse narrative form which finds its focus in the recorded acts and words of its protagonists is actually a reflection of one of the deepest insights of the Bible: that knowledge possessed by human beings is limited and imperfect. We infer from what we see and hear — actions and words — what others are thinking and what motivates them. But we never can be certain, and our knowledge of the world is shrouded in ambiguity. Human knowledge is at best partial, and the biblical narratives consciously mirror the ambiguity of human understanding. Almost always, we are left to connect the dots, and we can never be certain that the way we have put the pieces together is the right one.

FACT OR FICTION?

The last question that remains to be addressed under the rubric of "How Should One Read the Bible?" is that of factuality. The narratives that we will be considering are presented as historical occurrences. Are they to be read as factual accounts or are we to treat them as fiction?

This question conceals two hidden assumptions. The first is that the question is usually taken to imply that the truth or value of these narratives depends upon their factual historicity, and should they be deemed fiction they lose any value that they may possess. But this notion is mistaken. We are confronting two separate problems. The assessment of the message of the work is independent of the historicity of the story, which is merely the vehicle used to convey it. This can be made clearer through the use of an example: the force of the message of Dostoyevsky's novel *Crime and Punishment* — that abandoning the moral framework of good and evil for an amoral life of self-interest is an enterprise that has built-in costs, and that the price one has to pay may be more than the enterprise is worth — has nothing to do with the historicity of the story. No one would seriously consider dismissing *Crime and Punishment* because there never was such a person as Raskolnikov, the hero of the novel. In much the same way, the truth of the messages conveyed by the tales we will treat — radical reevaluations of the role of women in society and of how God relates to humanity — is independent of whether or not there ever lived persons by the name of Ruth and Boaz.

The second mistaken assumption is that the question — did these events really happen as they were depicted or were they invented? — is applicable to the texts that we will be discussing. The problem resides in that this query is anachronistic, one that presupposes a modern view of history. The discipline of history, as it has developed and assumed its present form over the past several centuries, is concerned with *what* happened and *how* it happened. The biblical view of history is concerned with a different issue: *what does it mean?* So in this sense, asking what happened, and when and how it did, is, in biblical terms, asking the wrong question.

This much having been said, there is another level on which the question of historicity is a valid one. We have pointed out that the central figure of the Hebrew Bible, the One who unites all the thirty-nine Books into one comprehensive whole, is God. To the extent that it is a connected story it is His story; or to be more exact, the story of His relationship with humanity. The reason why so much of the Bible is structured as history and as biography (which is merely personal history) is the conviction that to come to an understanding of God's purposes, the study of the development and the vicissitudes of humanity, and especially of the People of Israel, is one of the surest routes.

As the Bible sees it, the purpose of the study of history is to draw lessons of universal import, applicable to women and men in all ages and in all climes. But such conclusions are only as reliable as are the sources from which they are drawn. If one is to get the conclusions right one first has to get the facts right. This implies that we should take seriously what we would think of as the basic historical data that the narrations contain.

When the occasions arise, we will go into questions of historicity on a case-by-case basis. Here it suffices to say that, as a general rule, the biblical authors choose their episodes with an eye to the lessons that they wish to draw. But once the subject is chosen, the authors take scrupulous care to get their facts straight. The biblical authors saw matters in terms of factual foundations shaped by realistic art. It was accepted literary practice in the biblical period, and later in the Greek world, that when the author knew, in general, the gist of what had been said or what had taken place, he would frame speeches for his protagonists, giving form and dramatic impact to the known contents. The noted historian J.B. Bury explains this style of historical writing in his analysis of the speeches in the works of the Greek historians. Of Thucydides, the greatest of the Greek historians, he states:

> The persons who play leading parts in the public affairs which he relates reveal their characters and personalities, so far as required, by their actions and speeches. The author, like a dramatist, remains in the background, only sometimes coming forward to introduce them with a description as brief as in a playbill.... His general rule was to take the general drift and intention of the speaker, and from this text compose what he might probably have said.... The speeches in general served two purposes. In the first place they were used by the author to explain the facts and elements of a situation, as well as underlying motives and ideas.... [Thus] he uses the actual expositions of politicians—genuine political documents so far as the main tenor went,—as the most useful means of explaining a situation.... The speeches had the second function ... of serving the objective dramatic method of indicating character.... The general plan was that the men, as well as the events, should speak or be made to speak for themselves, with little or no direct comment from the writer.[26]

Bury's account sums up one of the main techniques of the biblical historians as well.

So how can we answer our original question? It would seem that we are dealing with narratives based on historic fact. These have been sculpted into works of art through conscious choice of what to present and how to present it, in order to embody a message of enduring value. It is partially this sculpting, but mostly the embedded message, that gave these narratives their timeless worth, and which led them ultimately to become part of the heritage of our world.[27]

Some Final Remarks

Having delineated the scope of the task that lies before us and sketched the approaches that will be employed, all that remains now is to remind ourselves what we will be attempting and to put on record several reservations. I intend to probe in depth three unusual narratives: unusual first in the sense that despite emerging from a male-dominated culture, it is women who hold the leading roles in these tales, and second, in that despite being products of an intensely religious world view, God is conspicuous in them only by His absence. I will be attempting to discover what lies behind these anomalies, and why place was made for these tales in the Bible. In so doing we will be raising the issue of relevance to the modern world in which

---

[26]Bury, *The Ancient Greek Historians*, pp. 108–117.

[27]In none of our tales is the author a contemporary of the events portrayed; in other words we are dealing with history and not with reportage. Thus while the facts narrated appear to be more or less accurate, we must bear in mind that the author, writing from the vantage point of a later period not only betrays the point of view of his or her own age, but at times may unconsciously project parts of the social context of her or his own era back onto the time of the related events. We will see the sometimes startling effects of this phenomenon as we examine the individual tales.

we live. It is my contention that these extraordinary works speak to many of the concerns of our era. They embody reevaluations of how we have traditionally seen women's roles in society, and how we have understood the world in which we live.

Our search will not be simple. We will have to find our way through cultures and mores far removed from our experience, and bring ourselves to empathize with people whose patterns of thought and basic assumptions were very different from our own. We will have to disregard many modern preconceptions, and in doing so open our minds to the possibility that past eras may have had different answers to the issues that beset us — perhaps even superior answers — than those currently popular. And most challenging of all, we will be forced to think through problems that have baffled generations of highly intelligent readers. This last is inevitable because it comes with the territory. Once again, these tales were designed to be ambiguous; explanations were consciously omitted and gaps purposely left to force the reader to puzzle things through on his or her own. In this I will be right at hand to help steer you, the reader, through the various minefields that lie in our path and to smooth the rough patches. It promises to be an interesting ride, and one with a payoff that will well repay the effort.

Lastly, I wish to quote the qualification made by a noted and rather idiosyncratic scholar in the preface of his recent magnum opus, a reservation with which I find myself in deep sympathy:

> I do not expect the reader to be steadfastly grateful. Nobody likes to hear a rooted opinion challenged, and even less good reasons offered for a principle or policy once in force and now universally condemned.... Not that I am in favor of ... [here several very politically incorrect opinions are cited] ... or any other evil supposedly outgrown. I cite these examples as a hint that I have not consulted current prejudices. My own are enough to keep me busy as I aim at the historian's detachment and sympathy. For if, as Ranke said, every period stands justified in the sight of God, it deserves at least sympathy in the sight of Man.[28]

This said, we begin our quest by turning back the clock more than three thousand years, making the acquaintance of two remarkable women, and the little biblical Book that has preserved their tragedy, their struggle and their triumph down through the centuries and which rests in our hands today as part of the canon.

---

[28]Barzun, *From Dawn to Decadence*, p. xiv.

PART I

IN THE BEGINNING

Errors, like straws, upon the surface flow;
He who would search for pearls must dive below.
—John Dryden, *Prologues and Epilogues*

Invoked or not, God will be present.
—Attributed to the Delphic Oracle,
this epigraph is to be found engraved
over the lintel of C.G. Jung's house
in Küsnacht.

CHAPTER 1

A Woman's Tale: An Introduction to the Book of Ruth

I'll tell thee everything I can.
— Lewis Carroll, *Through the Looking Glass*

Ancient Israelite society was structured on patriarchal lines, as were all the societies of the Ancient Near East. This would lead us to expect that literature produced by such a culture would reserve the main roles for men. And such is the case in most of the works that have come down to us in the Bible. Yet surprisingly, in Ruth we find ourselves faced with heroines rather than heroes. Ruth is first and foremost the story of two women whose lives have been ruined, yet rally to successfully create new futures for themselves. In a word, this is a woman's tale.[1]

Getting a bit ahead of ourselves, by the time we have finished the Book of Ruth we will have learned that one of the main purposes of the narrative is to describe the unlikely series of events that ultimately made possible the birth of David, Israel's greatest king. Taking this purpose at face value, and keeping in mind the patriarchal makeup of Israelite society, why didn't the author so structure the story as to make Boaz, the man who marries Ruth, the hero?[2] He, after all, is the great-grandfather of David, and it is he who figures in the genealogy that forms the Epilogue of our Book. The entire story could have been told from his point of view: how he heard of the return from abroad of the widow of one of his relatives, accompanied by her daughter-in-law; how he met that daughter-in-law looking for work in one of his fields; how their relationship developed and the events that led to their marriage. Told this way, the resulting "Book of Boaz" would have been much more in keeping with the biblical mainstream than is the Book of Ruth. Seen in this light, Ruth — a tale focusing on the women rather than the men, and told moreover from a woman's point of view — is an anomaly. And this anomaly demands explanation.

But before we can begin to address this, one of our central issues, we need some background. We will have to consider the way the Book was written and the question of the historicity of what we are being told. Above all we will have to understand the context of the story,

---

[1]It seems amazing in retrospect, but before Phyllis Trible's groundbreaking study "Two Women in a Man's World" a little over thirty years ago, virtually everyone seemed oblivious to the now obvious feminine theme of the Book of Ruth.

[2]While the solitary male, Boaz, proves to be a forceful and dynamic personage in his own right, his role in the story is strictly supportive.

which is a society very different from the one we inhabit. The Book assumes that the reader is familiar with the way society worked, and the legal structures that underpinned it. Without this knowledge it is impossible to come to an informed understanding of the actions and the motivations of the characters that people this little tale.

The Book of Ruth is one of the shortest Books in the Bible. Among the narrative Books only Jonah is shorter.[3] This brevity comes at a price. The extreme conciseness forces the author to ruthlessly exclude anything that is not absolutely essential to advancing the story. Only the short genealogy in the appendix to the Book could possibly be considered superfluous.[4]

The result is that, despite the deceptively simple story line, the Book abounds in difficulties. Indeed, once one begins to probe beneath the surface one encounters issues with no apparent resolution. Every proposed solution raises in turn new problems, often more impenetrable than the original difficulty. H.H. Rowley, whose brilliant analysis has probably done more to make Ruth comprehensible than the work of any other scholar, freely admits to the limits of our understanding:

> The simple story of the book of Ruth abounds in problems for which no final solution can ever be found, since the materials for their solution are denied to us. On this village scene, so different in character from most of the scenes of those ungentle times, the curtain is half lifted. But only half.[5]

Part of the difficulty lies in the lack of background. One of the ways the author achieves brevity is to set the action on what amounts to an empty stage. The author leaves the readers to furnish the set themselves: to provide both the backdrop and the props from their own knowledge of the era. The author assumes that the opening statement of the Book, "Now it came to pass, in the days when the Judges ruled..." (1:1) which defines the historic period in which the events occur, and the subsequent statement focusing the narrative geographically at *Bethlehem in Judah*, are sufficient to allow the reader to fully understand the socioeconomic and legal background necessary to make sense out of the narrative. For the biblical readership who comprised the original audience, this assumption was probably justified. We, who live at a remove of something close to three millennia, find ourselves facing a strange world, one that our experience does little to equip us to understand. This vacuum defines one of our main tasks: to attempt to fill in for the modern reader, to the extent possible, the necessary setting. Much of the socioeconomic background of the period in question will be sketched in the opening pages of Chapter 2. Here, in Chapter 1, we will try to clarify some of the main social institutions and legal structures that underlie the action in the narrative: the way society was organized, land ownership, the laws of inheritance and the institution of the "*Redeemer*."

Our understanding of these institutions rests upon the data that we have been able to amass from other parts of the Bible, from the disciplines of archeology and comparative Ancient Near East studies, and from the vast outpouring of modern scholarship. Yet as Rowley admits, despite our progress in understanding, much remains unknown and, realistically speaking, much will undoubtedly remain unknown. On the other hand, although problems persist, the larger outline of the Book, and answers to many of the issues that have vexed us in the past, are now fairly clear.

---

[3]In number of verses Ruth contains 85, Jonah 48. All the other Books that contain fewer verses than Ruth are written in poetry. They are Obadiah (21), Haggai (38), Zephaniah (43), Nahum (47), Habakkuk (56), and Joel (73).

[4]Indeed there are numerous scholars who claim, for this reason among others, that it was not originally part of the Book but only was added on later.

[5]Rowley, "The Marriage of Ruth," p. 163.

A second consequence of the terse style of the author is the absence of explanation from the text. The author assumes that without any help the readers will be able to figure things out by themselves. It is a measure of the brilliance of the author's structuring of the narrative that in large part we are almost unconscious of this need. We fill most of the gaps automatically. But there are areas where, due to the differences in the life style of Ancient Israel from that of the modern world, the demands prove excessive. The exposition that accompanies the biblical text will attempt to remedy this failing.

Family and Clan

In ancient Israel, in the period from the Settlement of the Land until the rise of a centralized monarchy under Saul (roughly 1210–1020 BCE), the era known as the "Age of the Judges," and even through the reign of Saul[6] (until approximately the year 1000 BCE), a person's identity was defined by the family to which he belonged and to the larger clan of which it was a part. When King Saul watched David go out to battle Goliath and asked his general: "Whose son is that boy, Abner?" (1 Samuel 17:55), the question really meant no more than: "Who is he?" One's family background determined one's identity.

Blood kinship was all. Your life was lived in the context of your kinfolk. The inhabitants of your village or town were all relatives; the members of families from other towns and villages that made up the clan were also related to you, and only slightly more distantly, on the average, than those who were your immediate neighbors.[7] As there was no state and tribal demands were few and far between, the main societal responsibilities of your life were to your immediate family and to the rest of your kin — your more distant blood relatives. The form these responsibilities took was defined under the rubric of *Redemption*. If the need should arise, and the degree of relationship with one of your kin was sufficiently close, you would be called upon by your conscience and by social pressure to assume the role of "*Redeemer*."[8]

The most pressing role of the Redeemer was as the "*Redeemer of the Blood*." What this meant was that should someone kill one of your near relatives it became your responsibility to seek out the killer and kill him in turn.[9] The first and most pressing responsibility fell upon the brothers of the murdered individual. Should there be no brothers, or should the brothers be prevented by objective circumstances from avenging the death, the responsibility would pass to the next closest relative: the father of the slain, say, or an uncle or cousin. Needless to say, should a son of the slain be old enough, his would be the primary responsibility. It is important to note

---

[6]Saul was a transitional figure: he can with equal justice be defined as either the first king or the last of the Judges.

[7]The main difference between the terms "town" and "village" lies in the fact that towns were usually more populous and were fortified with a surrounding wall while villages were smaller and less defensible. From the data presented in the narrative, Bethlehem at this time could be defined as a town. Tekoa, not so far away, was, it would seem, a village.

[8]Although the Hebrew term *goel* is used at times to describe God (cf. Job 19:25, Psalms 19:15, Isaiah 41:14, etc.), in the Hebrew Bible it is not a synonym for "Messiah," nor has it here any metaphysical connotations. Its use in Ruth, and in other early biblical texts, refers exclusively to human beings who have assumed certain social duties and responsibilities in connection with their kin, as will be described in the coming paragraphs.

[9]Numbers 35:16–29. This applied only to what we call first-degree murder (premeditated murder), and not to homicide (accidental, unintended killing). Inasmuch as a *Redeemer* was a relative of the deceased, and might not be in any mood to make fine distinctions, legislation provided that the unintentional killer could flee to one of a number of Cities of Refuge. There he would stand trial: if judged innocent of first degree murder he could remain in the City of Refuge and be safe; if judged guilty, he would be turned over to the *Redeemer of the Blood* for execution.

that in this, as in all matters of Redemption, a kind of inverse square law operated. The more distant the relationship, the less urgent was the need to assume the role of the Redeemer.

The institution of Redeemer of the Blood was vital in that period. In an age in which there was no central authority, no organized police forces and no network of impartial criminal courts, one's only protection was one's family. The institution of the Redeemer of the Blood was meant to deter would-be killers by guaranteeing that they would be hunted down and killed by their victim's relatives. This was one of the most powerful deterrents possible to the committing of murder.[10]

In a few pages we shall return to a consideration of two other areas of a Redeemer's responsibility that are vital to the understanding of the Book of Ruth: the safeguarding of the family inheritance and the preservation of the family line. Here we conclude this section with the observation that the structure of the family, and therefore of society, was patriarchal. All aspects of Redemption were duties of males alone. No woman was considered obligated to hunt down and kill a murderer of one of her close relatives. Nor was it the duty of a woman to take upon herself any of the other obligations of a Redeemer. Some implications of this sociological fact for the Book of Ruth will become evident shortly.

The Laws of Inheritance

One of the more significant corollaries of the Patriarchal structure of Ancient Israelite society lies in the form taken by the rules of inheritance. Property passed from generation to generation exclusively through the male line. Only sons inherited from their fathers. The only exception to this otherwise universal rule was the case in which a man only fathered daughters. If there were no sons and there were daughters, the daughters inherited, and their male descendants inherited from them.[11]

The rules of inheritance were as follows: inheritance followed the direct line from father to sons (with the exception previously noted). Lacking sons and daughters, the deceased's brothers inherited from him. If he had no brothers, the next in line were his uncles (his father's brothers). Lacking these the inheritance went to the nearest surviving male blood relation.[12]

Readers of Jane Austen's *Pride and Prejudice* will recall a similar situation. The Bennet family's house and lands are entailed and, lacking sons, upon the father's death the property will pass to his nearest male relative, a rather stupid clergyman. This explains the urgent need of his five daughters to find prosperous husbands (unlike the more liberal Israelite law, English law made no provision for daughters). Upon their father's death, they and their mother would be turned out into the street. The novel accurately reflects the conditions of late 18th–early 19th century England.

These rules of entailment in ancient Israel applied exclusively to land. With regard to other forms of property (both real and movable) it would seem that women could inherit, and the owner had the right to apportion possessions, by means of a will, to whomever he or she saw

---

[10]In later years under the monarchy, when police and a court system did exist and where the institution had not died out, the *Redeemer of the Blood* was considered by the government an arm of the state, and his killing a legal execution in lieu of state action.

[11]Ancient Israel operated under precedent law. During the Wilderness period a man by the name of Zelophehad died leaving no sons. His five feisty daughters appealed for the inheritance, on the weighty grounds that alienating the prospective ancestral estate from the direct line of succession would in effect wipe out an entire family line in Israel. (More on the significance of this claim later.) Moses granted the justice of their claim, awarded them the estate due to be settled on their father, and amended the laws, making the precedent an established part of the rules of inheritance (Numbers 27:1–11).

[12]Numbers 27:8–11.

fit.[13] Only with regard to the inheritance of land was this freedom of assignment restricted. Upon the owner's death, land had to be disposed according to the strict laws of inheritance outlined above.

This leads us to a subject that becomes critical to understanding the Book of Ruth: the issue of land ownership.

The Inheritance of the Fathers

The laws determining ownership rested on the fundamental thesis that the land — all land — belongs to God. When the Psalmist proclaimed

> The earth is the Lord's....
> For He has founded it upon the seas,
> And established it upon the floods (Psalm 24:1–2),

he was not merely enthusiastically praising his deity, but stating a legal doctrine which everybody accepted: that since God had created the world, it was His to dispose of as He pleased.[14] It was His pleasure to give the Land of Israel to the Israelites, and as land in those days was the main form of wealth, to decree that the wealth was to be shared equally by the families of Israel. To reduce matters to their simplest form, at the time of the Settlement of the Land the country was divided among the tribes, and the tribal areas were parceled out, each family receiving its portion. Several chapters in Numbers and almost half of the Book of Joshua are taken up with this matter.[15] Furthermore, to counter the inevitable trend in human affairs that leads capital (in this case land) to concentrate in the hands of the few at the expense of the many, the land grants of the families were *entailed*, which means that the owner had no freedom of disposition. The land had to be passed on, from generation to generation, by the strict laws of inheritance. Thus the descendants of the original families would continue in the possession of the ancestral lands, the apparent intent being to prevent the development of a poor class of landless peasants dominated by the wealthy owners of vast estates.

Did this mean that there could be no sales of land? Of course land was sold. All sorts of circumstances could conspire to induce, or compel, a person to sell part or all of his land. But, and it is a crucial *but*, no sale was final. No entailed estate, and virtually all land was entailed, could permanently be alienated from its original family. Every owner had the right to *redeem* — that is, to repurchase — his land whenever he could manage to scrape together the cash to do so. The purchaser had no right of refusal; he had to resell the land upon demand:

> Now the land may not be sold in perpetuity, for the land is Mine; for you are strangers and settlers with Me. And in all the land of your possession you must provide for the redemption of the land.... A man ... that prospers, and acquires enough to redeem [his land] shall compute the years since its sale, refund the difference to the man to whom he sold it,[16] and return to his possession (Leviticus 25:23–24, 26–27).[17]

[13]With the proviso that the firstborn son had to receive a double portion of the estate, that is, twice as much as any of his younger brothers (Deuteronomy 21:15–17).

[14]RASHI (see Glossary) begins his comments on Genesis with the opinion that one of the logical inferences to be drawn from the fact that the Bible begins with an account of God's creation of the world is that this establishes His sovereignty over His creation, and gives Him the unquestioned right to dispose of His creation in any manner pleasing to Him.

[15]Numbers 32, 33:54, 34:1–35:8, Joshua 13–21. Note also Numbers 36.

[16]See further note 22 below for an understanding of the basis on which the repurchase price is calculated.

[17]"Thus the right of redemption is theologically grounded. The Israelites received their property by lot (Numbers 33:50–56, Joshua 14–19) — that is, from God. Given by God it is revocable only by God" (Milgrom, *AB Leviticus*, p. 2185).

"To summarize the preceding verses: An owner of land who has sold it under economic stress could redeem it at any time.... Implicit in the law is the fact that the purchaser could not refuse the right of redemption."[18]

But what if the owner was incapable of amassing the necessary funds to redeem his property? It would then become the responsibility of close blood relatives to assume the role of Redeemer and bring the land back into the family by repurchase.[19]

The technical term for an entailed estate was *nahalot avot* (the inheritance of the fathers)[20] or sometimes *nahalat avotenu* (the inheritance of our fathers). The roots of the families in their ancestral plots of land went deep, and the sense of responsibility to keep the land within the family was felt by all relatives. We can cite, as one example among many, the case of King Ahab and Naboth. Naboth's vineyard bordered on the king's palace and the king wished to acquire it. Naboth refused to sell, giving as his reason: "The Lord forbid that I should give you the inheritance of my fathers" (1 Kings 21:3). The king could neither force him to sell, nor confiscate the land under right of eminent domain (and this under one of the most autocratic regimes that the Kingdom of Israel had ever known). Only by murdering Naboth could the king lay his hands on the land. This was in the 9th century, 400 years at the least from the time that parcel of land had come into the possession of Naboth's ancestors. Such was the tenacity with which families clung to their inherited estates.

What if no one was able, or willing, to assume the role of Redeemer and reclaim the family land? The law provided a further fallback position, the Jubilee Year. Every fiftieth year all land returned to the possession of the original owners or, should they no longer be alive, their heirs.[21] The upshot of the matter is that the "Inheritance of the Fathers," which was entailed land, could never be sold in perpetuity. A "sale" was simply a long-term lease that gave the "purchaser" the right to farm the land and enjoy its benefits, and which could be terminated at will by the original owner, or his family, by redeeming the property.[22]

The Three Faces of the Redeemer

We return to the institution of Redemption that was so central to society and the role of law in the first centuries of Israel's existence. We have already dealt with one aspect of Redemption responsibility: that of the Redeemer of the Blood. It is now time to summarize two other aspects still more critical to the understanding of Ruth.

Our understanding of land ownership in Ancient Israel will make it possible to under-

---

[18]Levine, *JPSTC Leviticus*, p. 176.

[19]Leviticus 25:25. See the next section: The Three Faces of the Redeemer.

[20]Namely, one's ancestors.

[21]Leviticus 25:8–10. Another provision of the Jubilee Year was the freeing of slaves.

[22]Since "sales" of entailed landed estates were, legally speaking, leases, the value of these leases was calculated in terms of crop years. Since the property would automatically return to the original owner in the Jubilee, the price was computed on the value of the number of crops that would be realized before the land reverted to its true owner (Leviticus 25:14–16). There is a difference of opinion as to the *price of repurchase*. There is general agreement that the price was not the market value. No one would sell his land except under duress, and usually at fire-sale prices. The purchaser should not be allowed to make a windfall profit by demanding full market value. Some are of the opinion that the redemption price was simply a repayment of the sum the purchaser had laid out for the land. Others suggest that the value of the number of harvest seasons that had passed since the purchase was deducted from this price.

stand how the sense of family and clan responsibility translated itself into social institutions.

> If your brother becomes destitute,[23] and he sells part of his inheritance, then the Redeemer who is closest to him [in relationship] shall come and Redeem that which his brother has sold (Leviticus 25:25).

It was deemed imperative that ancestral land — most especially land in which one's ancestors were buried — not pass out of the family. Every member of the extended family keenly felt the responsibility to insure that land that had been alienated — that had been sold outside the family — be returned as soon as possible to the family's possession. The closer the relationship to the "true owner," the greater the sense of responsibility. Here the law specified that the responsibility fell first upon the closest relative, and only if he was (economically) unable to fulfill his obligation did the responsibility of assuming the role of Redeemer pass down to the next of kin, and so on.[24]

In addition there was the essential duty of not allowing any of the individual family lines within the clan to die out.[25] This last is the most vital of the Redemption duties associated with Ruth. The entire Book is premised upon the knowledge of this responsibility, known as the duty to "raise up the name of the dead upon his inheritance" (Ruth 4:10). It amounts to the following: if a man dies childless, leaving no heirs to inherit the family estate or to carry on the family name, then his brother (or lacking a brother, some other close relative) has the duty to marry the widow for the express purpose of producing an heir to carry on the family name. The first child born of this union will legally be the son and heir not of his biological father, but of the late husband of the widow.[26]

It is also important to understand that there are significant differences between the case in which there are surviving brothers and the case where there are none. When a brother survives the deceased we are dealing with a case of Levirate Marriage. The term "Levirate Marriage" comes from the Latin word for brother: thus "Brother Marriage" in plain English. The legislation in Deuteronomy 25 (see note 26) deals with this case alone. Here the widow is not free to marry whom she wills. She *must* marry her brother-in-law. Relations with any other man are treated as adultery. Only if the brother-in-law refuses to act as Redeemer and marry her — in which case he is forced to undergo a public ceremony in which his sister-in-law spits in his face, removes his shoe,[27] and publicly reviles him (Deuteronomy 25:7–10) — is

---

[23]More literally, *declines into destitution.*

[24]It is important to grasp the sociological assumption underlying all the laws relating to redemption. The clan, that close-knit brotherhood of blood relatives, all descendants from an original ancestor, was the building block on which society rested. "The Bible, in its earliest stages, presumes a tightly knit clan structure; the foremost goal of its legal system was the preservation of the clan" (Milgrom, *JPSTC Numbers*, p. 482).

[25]There are further responsibilities of *Redemption* that fell upon close kin — for example the case of a relative who is sold into slavery (usually for debt); one must buy him out and set him free (Numbers 35:47–55) — but these duties are irrelevant to our central concern: the Book of Ruth.

[26]This practice is alluded to in three separate instances in the Bible: in the narratives of Genesis 38 and the Book of Ruth where the workings of this practice are depicted, and Deuteronomy which legislates the rules that govern Levirate marriage, one of the specific forms this practice takes. The passage reads as follows:

> If brothers dwell together, and one of them dies childless, the wife of the deceased shall not be married to a stranger; her husband's brother shall go into her, and take her to him to wife, and perform the duty of a husband's brother to her. And it shall be that the first-born [son] that she bears shall succeed to the name of the dead brother, that his name be not blotted out of Israel (Deuteronomy 25:5–6).

[27]The removal of the shoe is apparently the symbolic act that attests to the transfer of the brother-in-law's authority over the widow from him to her. More on this matter in Chapter 5.

she released from obligation to the family and freed to remarry. In the case where there are no surviving brothers, the widow is bound by no restrictions. Similarly, the social stigma cast upon a more distant relation who declines to marry the widow is correspondingly lessened.[28]

At this point we should be sufficiently knowledgeable to understand the Book of Ruth.

Fact or Fiction: Is Ruth Historical?

This much having been said about the background of those early times, what can be said about the Book itself? Why was the Book written in the first place? When was it written? Did the events actually occur more or less as depicted, or are we being treated to a charming piece of historical fiction? Shelves of books have been written on these questions, and it is not our intention to become involved in often-abstruse scholarly arguments, disputes of scant interest to any but specialists in biblical studies. For our purposes it will be sufficient to summarize a consensus on these questions where there is one, and to advance what seems to me to be a commonsense approach where the scholarly differences of opinion seem unbridgeable.

During most of the nineteenth and twentieth centuries students of the Bible were of the opinion that the Book of Ruth was written toward the close of the Biblical Age, in the Persian period (538–330 BCE). Among the many arguments advanced for this position,[29] the most objectively based, and thus the most compelling, were linguistic. The Book seemed to contain words and grammatical forms that came into use only in the Persian Era.[30] The fact that the style of the Book of Ruth is typical of the early Biblical Age and that most of the vocabulary is likewise early,[31] was put down to "archaizing"—that is, the author intentionally writing in an outdated, archaic manner, copying the style of long-gone times. Every now and then, these scholars held, the author slipped up, accidentally using more modern terms. More than a half-century of scholarship has discredited this thesis. All of the so-called "Aramaisms"[32] have been shown to have been in use in the early Biblical Age, or in earlier forms of Hebrew that preceded

---

[28]The philosophical reasoning behind this complex of custom and law can be described as follows:
> The heart of marriage, especially but not only biblically speaking, is not primarily a matter of the heart; rather it is primarily about procreation and, even more, about the transmission of a way of life. Husband and wife, whether they know it or not, are incipiently father and mother, parents of children for whose moral and spiritual education they bear a sacred obligation — to ancestors, to community, to God.... Precisely because of their communal commitment to righteousness, they must not ... cease to be their brother's keepers.... In levirate marriage, all these central principles are defended. A man serves literally as his brother's keeper: he refuses to let his brother die without a trace.... Taking seriously the commandment "Be fruitful and multiply," levirate marriage elevates the importance of progeny above personal gratification, and hence, the importance of lineage and community above the individual. In accepting the duty [of the Redeemer] a man simultaneously shows reverence for his ancestors, respect for the meaning and purpose of marriage, and devotion to the future of his family and his people (Kass, *The Beginning of Wisdom*, pp. 530–31).

[29]For the commonly advanced argument that Ruth 4:7 implies a post–Exilic date see Chapter 5, note 22.

[30]These terms and usages were considered to be imports into Hebrew from the Aramaic language, a phenomenon typical of Late Hebrew; hence the term "Aramaisms," which scholars applied to these words.

[31]"Specifically, scholars argue that the Hebrew of Ruth more resembles the 'classical' language evident in, say, Genesis and Samuel than the 'late' Hebrew known from, say, Esther, Chronicles or Nehemiah. Further, they argue, the presence of 'archaic' linguistic elements in Ruth implies that the book's language is old, thus reflecting an early date of composition.... In sum, while the case is not conclusive, the linguistic evidence favors a pre-exilic date for the book" (Hubbard, *Ruth*, pp. 30–31, 33).

[32]See note 30 above.

the Bible.[33] The pendulum has swung back and a new consensus is now forming that accepts Ruth as an early work.[34]

The Book can be no earlier than the reign of King David, who is mentioned by name; the author assumes that readers will know who he is and be aware of his significance. It now seems likely that Ruth was part of the burst of literary creativity, called by some "The Solomonic Enlightenment," which followed the unification of the tribes of Israel into a united and centralized kingdom.[35] This would place the writing of Ruth a little over a century after the events depicted in the Book: say, in the last decade or two of the reign of David or, more probably, in the first couple of decades of the reign of his son Solomon. What this means is that we can take seriously the descriptions of what life was like in the days before the monarchy: at the time of writing there were still persons alive who could remember those days.[36]

Does that mean that because the background is probably authentic the story of Ruth is historical? Not necessarily. There is indeed a branch of literature known by the name of historical fiction: a fictional story set against an authentic historical background. The tale must be evaluated on its own merits. Looked at this way we can say with fair certainty that the story could be true: there is nothing in the story that contradicts established fact or that is inherently improbable. Indeed, one of the most charming aspects of the story is how human it is, how believable the characters are, and how easily we grasp their motives and empathize with them. The most compelling argument for the historicity of the events related in the Book is the element most difficult to believe: that the great King David traced his ancestry to a non–Israelite great-grandmother; to one, moreover, who was native to a country which was a sworn enemy of Israel, and with which Israel had been at war off and on for centuries. It is hard to see how

---

[33]Hebrew, as a language, long preceded the emergence of the Israelite people. It was the language spoken by the Canaanites, and was itself a development of an earlier language, called today proto–Canaanite, the precursor of all the Western Semitic languages. The language was fully mature with a well developed literature when the Israelites first adopted it from the Canaanites.

[34]As early as the 1950s Jacob Meyers, after a careful study of the language of Ruth, came to the conclusion that the Book belongs to the period of the early monarchy (Meyers, *The Linguistic and Literary Form of the Book of Ruth*, pp. 8–32). E.F. Campbell concurs:

> there are alleged Aramaisms throughout the text, which point to a time when the influence of the Aramaic language upon Hebrew became significant, and that presumably means after the Babylonian exile. As scholars have studied Ruth, the number of alleged Aramaisms has steadily declined.... When Wagner published his catalogue of Aramaisms in the Old Testament [1966] he listed only the two verbs in 1: 13 as vocabulary examples and could find no Aramaic grammatical constructions.... In sum, no linguistic datum points unerringly to a late date.... The language of Ruth is the language of the monarchic period ... the overall impression is one of close relationship to stories stemming from the tenth and ninth centuries.... On language alone one would be justified in leaning toward the earlier part of our spread 950–700 BCE (Campbell, *AB Ruth*, pp. 24, 26).

[35]This literary upsurge was merely one symptom of the seismic shift in sensibility and intellectual outlook that Gerhard von Rad calls "The Solomonic Enlightenment" (Rad, *Old Testament Theology*, pp. 48–56). Ronald M. Hals gives a good summary of the arguments for a late and for an early dating of the Book, arguing strongly that not only the style but also especially the underlying ideas in the Book lead to this early dating. Or as he phrases it: "the story has a theological purpose which pervades the entire book ... and this purpose seems best understandable in the time of the Solomonic Enlightenment" (Hals, *The Theology of the Book of Ruth*, p. 75). This matter will be explored further in the conclusion to this book, Chapter 22.

[36]A further point strongly implying an early date to the Book is that the entire story of Ruth is predicated on a clan-based society, and that the author assumes the readers know from their own experience the way such a society worked. The primacy of the clan began to disintegrate with the rise of the State and its attendant urbanization. One hundred and fifty years after the death of King Solomon, we find the early classical prophets describing — and denouncing — a radically different social structure. The clan-based world depicted in Ruth would have seemed as distant and difficult to comprehend to the contemporaries of Amos and Isaiah as the endless dueling of King Louis XIII's Three Musketeers with Cardinal Richelieu's Guards is to us.

such an embarrassing piece of genealogy could have been published and allowed to circulate in the days of David and his successor kings unless it was true and widely known.[37] While all this does not necessarily validate every detail of the narrative of Ruth, yet it seems reasonable to assume that the main lines of the story are indeed historical.

Was a Woman the Author of This Tale?

Leaving aside the question of historicity, we pass on to the contents of this short and elegantly written tale. Excluding the Prologue and the Epilogue (which together account for approximately ten percent of the verses),[38] the heart of the Book covers a period of no more than two months and concentrates on a series of carefully selected events in the lives of three persons, two of whom are women. It is they who are the focus of the drama. And with this singular fact we finally return to our original problem: how can we explain the appearance of a woman's tale in a literature and a society run by men and dominated by men's concerns?

Since the pioneering study by Phyllis Trible[39] that first firmly placed the issue of the feminine focus of the Book on the agenda, the problem has resisted a satisfactory solution. Discussion has tended to center on what is the hidden (or not so hidden) message of the Book as it stands,[40] and not so much on why the author chose to write the work in this particular way and not in some other. I would suggest that an obvious explanation for the feminine point of view exhibited by Ruth would be that the Book's author was a woman. This is an idea that has suggested itself to a number of scholars, yet most seem reluctant to endorse the thesis wholeheartedly. Carol Meyers has gone so far as to point out:

> As part of a canon that is almost entirely ascribed to male authorship, Ruth has rarely, even by feminist critics heralding it as a woman's story, been seen as the work of a woman writer. Virtually no one has forcibly maintained that a woman could conceivably have written it.[41]

Even before Phyllis Trible's article, Edward Campbell *"risked" "proposing"* a "wise woman" or some woman singer of epic events as its author in the context of his theory that Ruth originated as a story to be told orally by professional storytellers.[42] Athalya Brenner claims that Ruth is the type of literature where "the women are obviously seen as strong and constant characters; and

---

[37]One can find corroboration of David's ancestral connection to Moab in the report that, while on the run from Saul, David entrusted his parents to Moab for safekeeping. If he did have Moabite ancestry that meant that he had blood relations in Moab to whom he could turn. Kinship responsibilities were taken as seriously in Moab as in Israel. (See 1 Samuel 22:3–4.)

[38]The first five verses of Ruth briefly set the scene by informing us when and where the action takes place, and briefly sketches the events that lead up to the opening of the main narrative. The last five verses of the Book consist of a genealogy that places the tale into a wider historical perspective.

[39]Trible, "Two Women in a Man's World."

[40]Among the purposes discerned as flowing from the female focus of the Book are the championing of women's struggles to survive in a man's world (*ibid.*), as part of a genre of literature that exalts the type of woman who sacrifices her own interests in the service of the greater good of achieving the goals of a patriarchal society — the production of male heirs (Brenner, "Female Social Behavior," p. 272); the view that Ruth is really about the (divine) empowerment of powerless women (Laffey, *An Introduction to the Old Testament*, pp. 208–9), as protest literature against the policies of the male establishment (Andre LaCocque, *The Feminine Unconventional*); and as women's literature "as part of a social context in which women were not powerless and subservient" (Meyers, "Returning Home," p. 88).

[41]Meyers, "Returning Home," pp. 88–89.

[42]Campbell, *AB Ruth*, pp. 21, 23 (emphasis mine).

the male role is kept to a skeletal minimum." She holds that "it originated in female circles," yet in the end backs off with the words: "Proving female authorship ... would have been quite to my personal taste. However, this is not warranted by any further evidence in the texts themselves; and here we should let the matter rest, and regrettably so."[43] Carol Meyers, while admitting that "recent scholarship has convincingly reversed the notion that the production of literature in biblical antiquity was almost entirely the result of the compositional activities of men," and strongly contending that Ruth is "women's literature," yet tepidly concludes, "Still, even if the existence of female authors for certain biblical verses, chapters or even books can be accepted, the idea of female authorship seems problematic."[44]

Norman Gottwald and S.D. Goitein come closest to taking an unambiguous stand. Goitein states:

[I]t is probable that the Book of Ruth was, in fact, written by a woman — not a woman like the heroine, Ruth, but rather an old "wise woman." For the narrator's interest, and even more so her inner knowledge, are concentrated around Naomi.[45]

Gottwald, after pointedly insisting that

The assertive deeds of Naomi and Ruth are the driving force of the story.... Threat of death is turned to promise of life solely because these women do not wait passively for men to solve their problems but take the lead to make things happen.... Throughout the story, the women operate out of their own culture with their own values in mind.[46]

concludes that

It is not difficult to imagine that this story was framed by a woman confidently at home in her social world.[47]

I also do not find it difficult to imagine a woman as the author of the Book of Ruth, and while definitive proof as to the gender of the author is something that probably will always elude us, I am nonetheless adopting the thesis as a working hypothesis. It seems hard to conceive of a more reasonable explanation for the undoubtedly feminine perspective that pervades the work.

Life as It Was Really Lived

Taking all that has been said about the authenticity of background portrayed in Ruth, the broad historicity of the plot and the probable authorship and date of composition, what does Ruth tell us about how life was lived in biblical times by the average person? Granted the Bible is from first to last a religious work, whose aim is to clarify God's purpose for His world and for the humans who so briefly occupy it, it nonetheless remains a work compiled from many Books, Ruth among them, that were written by human beings in different times and places. The writers were all Israelites who were, quite naturally, concerned with God's relationship with them — His Covenant with the people of Israel — and the history of this relationship. Most of the Bible was undoubtedly written by men.[48] As a result it is hardly surprising that by and large

---

[43]Brenner, "Female Social Behavior," p. 273.

[44]Meyers, "Returning Home," p. 89.

[45]Goitein, "Women as Creators of Biblical Genres," p. 31, note 2.

[46]Gottwald, *The Hebrew Bible*, pp. 555–557.

[47]*Ibid.*, p. 557.

[48]In every case where a Book is "signed" — that is, the name of the author is known, as in the Books of the Classical Prophets — the authors are uniformly men.

the Bible reflects a man's view of the world — a preoccupation with politics and wars, and with the male figures that advanced the unique religious vision of Israel. There is nothing particularly wrong in this, except that it is all rather one-sided. When we try to use the biblical texts to gain an understanding of the world that gave them birth, there is a tendency to lose perspective. It wasn't, as some feminists are wont to claim, that women and their concerns were censored out; rather men wrote about what most concerned them.[49] The converse is of course also true. When women wrote, and they did (and probably more than we have hitherto realized), they would tend to ignore men's primary concerns and to focus on their own.

This issue can become clearer when we consider the Age of the Judges. Most of what we know of this era comes from the Book of Judges, a catalogue of wars, upheavals and crises covering about two centuries. This has led readers, and even scholars who should know better, to view these centuries as ones of *continual warfare* and *upheaval*. We have already quoted H.H. Rowley's reference to "those ungentle times."[50] To this we can add G.A. Cooke's "a half-barbarous age of struggle and disorder"[51] and J.J. Slotki's "those lawless times"[52] as examples of evaluations that sum up the consensus view. But this view is belied by the very chronology preserved in Judges: for that portion of the Book where figures are given,[53] every period of invasion, war, turmoil and oppression is concluded with the words "and the land had rest — years."[54] Simple arithmetic reveals that the years of peace outnumbered the bad years by a ratio of five to one. This brings us to the unconventional conclusion that it is the Book of Ruth that reflects the normal conditions of that age, while it is the Book of Judges that portrays the aberrations. Objectively, most of the two-century period was peaceful.

There is an old Chinese curse, reserved for particularly abhorred individuals: "May you live in an interesting time." The Book of Judges focuses on the "interesting times" of that era, and we can easily appreciate why the man (or possibly men) who wrote the Book was fascinated by them — they are interesting subjects, and works of history often focus on such events. It took a woman (if we are correct in our assumption that it was a woman who authored Ruth) to show us another side to the life of those times.

So what can we learn about life in the days of the Judges when wars weren't going on — that is, most of the time? For one thing, it wasn't "a man's world." How could it be, if fifty percent of the population was women? There were two worlds: there was a man's world and there was a woman's world, and they coexisted, side by side.

Having grown up in the waning years of the industrial age, our understanding of the way society is formed and functions has been conditioned by our upbringing. It is therefore only natural that, without reflection, we tend to project this understanding back onto bygone eras. But the biblical world was pre-industrial. Over ninety-five percent of all people were peasant farmers living in small villages. In the Biblical Age, as in virtually all subsistence economies,

---

[49]When women fitted into these concerns they found their place in the narrative. Deborah, prophet and Judge, initiator of a war of liberation and author of a superlative victory ode, very much fitted into the political, military and religious themes of the Book of Judges and therefore was accorded pride of place in two chapters of that bloody work. Likewise Jael the Kenite, whose assassination of the Canaanite general Sisera proved to be a major political-military turning point, gets better press than Barak, the victorious Israelite general (Judges 4–5).

[50]Rowley, "The Marriage of Ruth," p. 163.

[51]Cooke, *Ruth*, p. xi.

[52]Sloyki, "Ruth," p. 37.

[53]Judges 3:12.

[54]Judges 3:11, 30, 5:31, 8:28.

the primary economic unit was the family, which was for all practical purposes self-sufficient, producing not only the food that was consumed but almost all other necessities of life, such as clothing, housing, and even most tools of production. "Providing these essentials involved a carefully orchestrated division of labor among all family members, male and female, young and old. Clearly, the survival of the household as a whole depended upon the contribution of all its members."[55] The family rose with dawn. Domestic animals had to be watered, fed, and, if taken out to pasture, tended. Goats had to be milked. Food had to be prepared, water drawn from the well or cistern, thread spun, cloth woven, clothing sewn. The list must have seemed endless to the participants; this all in addition to the central job of farming the land.[56] All in all, life was hard and there was little time for leisure. More to the point in our context, women were an integral part of the work force. Carol Meyers estimates that "roughly 40 percent of the productive labor in agrarian communities in the highlands of Palestine was contributed by women."[57] Moreover, "the female's role in the household production system was no less important than the male's.... In such situations, households are typically characterized by internal gender balance rather than gender hierarchy."[58] In light of these economic and social realities it becomes necessary for us to radically revise our stereotyped notions of the relations between men and women in those days. This revision will make it easier to accept the assertiveness of the women in the Book of Ruth. In portraying women as the ones who determine the course of events in her tale the author is reflecting the realities of those days.

The Place of Ruth in the Bible

When one compares the Hebrew Bible, which serves as the Jewish Scriptures, with that part of the Christian Scriptures known as the Old Testament, we discover that while the contents are identical, the arrangement is different.[59] In the Christian Bible one finds Ruth immediately following Judges, while in the Hebrew Bible we find Ruth further along, grouped with four other short Books (Song of Songs, Lamentations, Ecclesiastes, and Esther) under the heading of "The Five Scrolls." This discrepancy requires a bit of explanation.

The arrangement of the Christian Bible derives from the Septuagint, the Greek translation of the Hebrew Bible made in the centuries just prior to the Common Era (see Glossary). The basis for its arrangement is historical sequence. Since the events in the Book of Ruth take place in the time of the Judges, it was deemed appropriate to append Ruth to the Book that tells about the period in which these events took place. Those who arranged the order of the Books in the Hebrew Bible were more concerned with the nature of the various Books and their contents than when the happenings portrayed took place. Therefore they divided the Hebrew Bible into three sections: the Torah (often known as the Five Books of Moses), the Prophets (which includes the Books of Joshua, Judges, Samuel, and Kings—a consecutive history of the Biblical Age after Moses, written from what was felt to be the prophetic point of view),[60] and

---

[55]Meyers, "Returning Home," p. 98.

[56]A description of some of what was involved in just the harvesting of the crops will be dealt with in the course of our discussion of Ruth itself.

[57]Meyers, "Women of the Neighborhood," p. 110.

[58]Meyers, "Returning Home," pp. 98–99.

[59]See Introduction, note 2. The version of the Hebrew Bible that we possess today is known as the Masoretic Text (see Glossary), abbreviated MT.

[60]As opposed to Chronicles, a parallel history written from a priestly point of view.

the Writings (Books deemed written under divine inspiration and felt to convey essential messages about life and its meaning). Ruth was assigned to this last category.[61]

By this point the reader should have sufficient background to enable an informed appreciation of the Book of Ruth, and the time has come to plunge directly into this marvelous little gem of a Book.[62] As to the purpose of the Book — why it was written in the first place — we will leave the discussion of this crucial question until we have completed Ruth and will be better able to appreciate the issues involved.

---

[61]The grouping with the four other Books in The Five Scrolls was for liturgical purposes: each of these Books is assigned for reading in the Synagogue on a specific Holiday. Ruth is read on the Holiday of *Shavuot* or Pentecost (while the Book of Esther, which will be dealt with later in the book, is read on the Holiday of *Purim*).

[62]"It is indeed a gem, but a gem in the sense of a gathered and concentrated power, a bright clarity beneath a somewhat deceptive setting of lyric grace and simplicity" (Rauber, "Literary Values in the Bible," p. 35).

CHAPTER 2

The Exiles

Our frailties are invincible, our virtues barren;
The battle goes sore against us to the going down of the sun.
— Robert Louis Stevenson, *Across the Plains*

The world of three thousand years ago, the era in which Ruth and Naomi lived, was radically different from the one in which we find ourselves today. While the inner nature of human beings has not significantly altered over the last ten thousand years or more, the external conditions that mold our perceptions and the way we respond to our condition have shifted to a degree difficult to conceive. While courage remains courage — as do love and devotion, hope and despondency, fear and hate — how these express themselves is dependent upon the world into which we are born, and what we learn to believe and expect from our parents and from those about us. This means that unless we gain some insight into the world in which Ruth and Naomi moved and acted, we will neither be able to understand what they did, nor to appreciate why they came to have such an influence on the future.

Our tale takes place in the Land of Israel and its close environs during a period known as the Age of the Judges, a period that stretched between the Conquest and Settlement of the Promised Land, and the rise of a monarchial form of government (roughly from about 1210 to 1020 BCE), a span amounting to roughly two centuries.[1] During this age the tribes that made up the People of Israel, while united by common language, culture and religion, as well as by a commonly held history and a strong tradition of common ancestry,[2] were nevertheless administered as politically autonomous units. Each tribe functioned as an independent primitive democracy, its affairs presided over by a council of "elders"[3] which represented the various clans that made up the tribe. Each of these clans was, in turn, run by its own council of "elders" who were themselves the representatives of the families that made up the clan. In times of crisis (usu-

---

[1]BCE, that is, Before the Common Era (see Glossary). The dating system used in this book follows that of Kenneth Andrew Kitchen in his encyclopedic work *On the Reliability of the Old Testament*.

[2]This last was of paramount importance as in those days the strongest bond felt by people was the bond of common blood. Thus the very definition of a people was the claim of a common ancestry; the descent from a primordial founder was the bond that defined a nation. Thus the bond that held the Romans together was that they traced their ancestry to Aeneas, the Trojan hero who was reputed to have founded Rome. Indeed the very definition of a Roman was a descendant of Aeneas. In the same manner the definition of an Israelite was a descendant of the Patriarchs: Abraham, Isaac and Jacob.

[3]See Glossary for an explanation of this term.

ally a foreign invasion) a charismatic leader would arise to unite some or all of the tribes into a common front, to defend the land and drive off their foes. These men and women were called "Judges" and gave this name to their era. With the defeat of the foes these leaders would be rewarded with the governorship of the tribes that they had rallied, a position that lasted for their lifetimes. Upon their deaths the temporary tribal unification would dissolve and the political situation would revert to its previous anarchy.[4]

Our story takes place in the southernmost of the tribes — Judah; specifically it is centered in the town of Bethlehem, about six miles directly south of Jerusalem. We have already called attention to the fact that in those days over ninety-five percent of the population of Israel were subsistence farmers, each family cultivating its own parcel of land and caring for its own livestock, and that most necessities were homegrown or home manufactured. What could not be produced in the home was made in the local village, but even the blacksmiths and wagon makers, to take but two examples, were themselves farmers and only part-time artisans. Though a rudimentary cash economy existed — for example sales of real estate were normally for money — barter usually sufficed for day-to-day needs. Life in the town or village was self-sufficient.

Families lived in independent two-story houses; the ground floor was used to store food and supplies, stable animals (usually one or two cows, a few sheep and goats, perhaps an ox and a donkey or two), prepare and cook food, and for household industries. The family, consisting of parents and their children, and possibly a few relatives (an unmarried brother or sister of one of the parents, an uncle or perhaps an aged grandparent), lived in the rooms on the upper floor.

In those days most people lived all their lives in the village or town of their birth. They would leave only to partake in an annual pilgrimage to a central shrine, an absence of no more than a week.[5] Sometimes, in periods of emergency, men of military age would be mustered to war, the survivors immediately returning once the crisis was past. Girls might marry a man from another village or town, more rarely from another tribe. Under these circumstances the girl would leave the village permanently to go and live with her husband. To undertake a trip for business or other purposes, while not unheard of, was a very rare, even extraordinary event. It is against this very enclosed and provincial background that we must view the decision of Elimelech, with which the Book of Ruth begins, to pull up roots and leave his home where he has lived all his life.

In our day, an age of rapid communications and constant mobility, people move all the time. It is increasingly rare for a person to end his life in the city where he was born. It takes a serious exercise of the imagination for us to realize how outlandish Elimelech's act was. It meant tearing himself loose from the entire web of relationships, duties, responsibilities and rights that went with his being part of the town and the clan. It meant severing his ties with his family and everyone he had ever known. It meant abandoning the safety net that he could count on in times of need. And if this were not enough, he meant to relocate not in some other part of the tribal area of Judah, or of the Land of Israel, but to leave for a foreign country (Moab), where the best he could hope for was the status of a *ger*, a landless resident alien.

What brought him to take this radical step? We are told that the proximate cause of his departure was famine. Famine was a phenomenon all too common in those days. Its usual cause

---

[4]The word that is traditionally rendered "Judge," the Hebrew term *shofet*, has as its basic meaning "ruler," "governor," "administrator." Thus these charismatic leaders were being accorded the title of "Ruler" or "Governor" with no connotation of judicial function except to the extent that every ruler in those days was ipso facto the chief justice of the land, and spent a given portion of his time hearing cases (note the position of King Solomon in 1 Kings 3:16–28). It was only centuries later that the term *shofet* gained the primary meaning of "judge."

[5]As in the case of Hannah and Elkanah (1 Samuel 1–2). Hannah was probably a younger contemporary of Ruth, separated from her by maybe twenty years of age.

was drought; the failure of the heavens to provide sufficient rainfall. The crops would wither and die. In a subsistence economy reserves would be limited and the possibility of importing food from elsewhere usually non-existent. By resolute scrimping one might get through until the new crops were harvested. But should the rains fail two years in a row the result was inevitably famine: people starving to death.

But there must be more to the story than famine. We are not told of others leaving, though of course there may have been a few. Most people hunkered down and roughed it out. Furthermore Elimelech was not relocating himself and his family as a temporary measure to wait out the bad times and return when things got better. His move was meant to be permanent. Why do I say this? Because he sold his land![6] Selling one's land was the equivalent of burning one's bridges. It would leave one with nothing to return to.[7]

The landless individual was at the very bottom of the social and economic heap in Ancient Israel, his only option being to hire himself out as an agricultural laborer — often as a share-cropper — *if* he could find work. The abject poverty of the landless will be revealed to us when we observe the desperate straits in which Naomi and Ruth find themselves upon their return to Bethlehem. The last thing one would do if intending to return would be to sell one's land.

But for one planning a permanent break, selling makes excellent sense. In the first place one no longer needs to hold on to the seed grain, the critical reserve necessary to make possible next year's planting. If the land is sold you will not be planting next year, and so you can use the grain for food. This alone will give you enough to cover you and your family for the journey, and to tide you over the period when you are looking for a place to live and to establish yourself. Furthermore, selling the land leaves you with cash in hand, the capital needed to establish yourself in your new home.

All things considered, the famine alone might explain Elimelech's need to leave and find something to eat for the family. It doesn't explain the decision to cut his ties and burn his bridges to all he has known — his town, his family and friends, everything he has built and accomplished up to that point in his life. It suggests a profound disillusionment, a deep embitterment and even a sense of desperation. We are not told of the failures, the crises and the entanglements — social as well as economic — that have led to this point. We are informed only of the decisive act; Elimelech pulls up stakes, leaves Bethlehem and Israel with his family to live in Moab, and there he settles. The clear implication is that he has decided to cut his losses, whatever they are, and to make a fresh start in a new land.[8]

While there will be no language barrier barring Elimelech's acclimatization — the Moabites

---

[6]We are not told this but it can be inferred. We are told that he had land (Chapter 4:3). Over a decade later we discover that the land is no longer in the family. In those days it was virtually impossible to sell land while not in possession but abroad, so it would seem that the only time he could have disposed of the land was prior to departure. While this is not a universally accepted point of view, I am far from alone in holding that Elimelech sold his land prior to his departure from Bethlehem. Among others who share this understanding of the events are Brichto ("Kin, Cult, Land and Afterlife," pp. 14–15) and Gordis ("Love, Marriage and Business in the Book of Ruth," pp. 255–56). This issue becomes important in the last chapter of Ruth, and will be examined in detail in Chapter 5, and in Appendix I: From Whom Did Boaz Buy the Field?

[7]It could be objected that the land would, in any case, revert to Elimelech at the Jubilee. But the sequence of events indicates that this would be far in the future (see Chapter 5, note 16). While his children might eventually have something to which to return, given the average life span of those days Elimelech, being already in middle age, had few personal prospects.

[8]There is an alternative possibility: that economic straits had forced Elimelech to sell his land prior to the crisis of the famine, and that the famine acted as the last straw, crystallizing his determination to wash his hands of his past and get out. Either way we seem to be dealing with a bitter and disillusioned man who feels that he has nothing to lose.

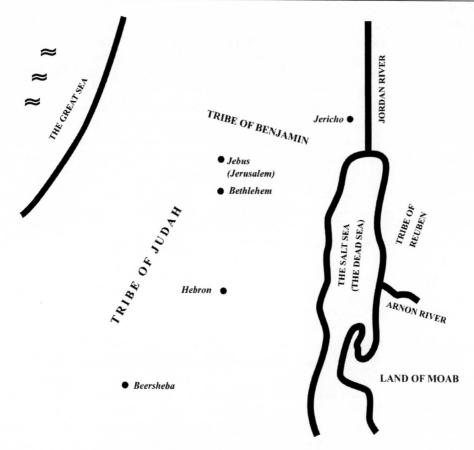

Map 1. Judah and environs during the eleventh century BCE.

speak a dialect of Hebrew, the language of the Israelites — there is a steep spiritual price to pay. In those days religion was national; every land had its own god. Even a traveler passing through a land would be expected to pay obeisance to the god of the country, in this case Chemosh; a settler would be expected to worship him routinely. For a polytheist, a believer in many gods, this would prove no hardship. There would be no obligation to cease the worship of the gods one has revered up to this point, only to add the god of the land to the list. But as an Israelite, Elimelech (whose very name means "My God is King") is a monotheist, whose central article of faith is that there is but one God, the Creator of heaven and earth. All other "gods" are no-gods, mere figments of their worshiper's erroneous imaginations. Worse: in those days Israelites were convinced that God, though universal, could only be worshiped properly on the soil of the Promised Land.[9] To settle in Moab would not only mean to become a worshiper of "other gods" (i.e., an idolater) but simultaneously to cut himself off from the God of his fathers. In his quest for a new start, Elimelech is committing himself and his family to a life of total alienation. And so, in his desire to better himself, he lays the ground for the tragedy to come.

---

[9]In those days to worship a deity meant to offer sacrifices to him. Sacrifices to the God of Israel could only be offered on holy soil. Leaving the Land of Israel would thus automatically make proper worship of the Lord impossible. David equates foreign exile with apostasy (1 Samuel 26:19) and so, for all practical purposes, it was.

Prologue: In Foreign Fields

Now it came to pass, in the days when the Judges ruled,[10] that there was a famine in the land. And a man from Bethlehem in Judah[11] went to live in the Land of Moab[12]; he, his wife and his two sons. Now the name of the man was Elimelech, and the name of his wife Naomi, and the name of his two sons Mahlon and Chilion — Ephrathites[13] from Bethlehem in Judah. And they came to the Land of Moab and they settled there. And Elimelech, Naomi's husband, died; and she was left, she and her two sons. These took for themselves Moabite wives: the name of one was Orpah and the name of the second Ruth, and they lived there about ten years. And [then] these two — Mahlon and Chilion — also died, so the woman was bereft of her two children and her husband (1:1–5).

In a simple, almost laconic manner the author opens the narrative; nothing is elaborated, nothing is explained. We are told the names of the protagonists, and the minimal facts of a saga that must have lasted at least twelve years: emigration, marriages and deaths. Not even the name of the town in which the family settled is deemed worthy of mention. We have already discussed in Chapter 1 the extreme terseness of the author's style and the price paid for this conciseness. Here we will try to partially mitigate this cost by filling in the outlines of this family's tragedy.

But first a parenthetical note: these opening lines were not written in a vacuum. This is not the first time that famine has induced a member of God's people to leave the land. The statement with which our Book opens, "Now it came to pass that there was a famine in the land," followed immediately by the announcement that a certain person leaves to live in a foreign country, recalls the virtually identical wording introducing an episode in the life of Abraham.[14] Isaac also is induced by famine to live in the Philistine principality of Gerar, and that episode also opens with very much the same words.[15] And who could forget the famine that led Jacob and his family to relocate in Egypt?[16] The author of our Book purposely frames the opening words to recall to readers these previous episodes. Now biblical authors almost always treat leaving the Promised Land in a negative light. Even when sanctioned by God[17] the move seems inevitably to lead to problematic consequences. Both Abraham and Isaac feel impelled to lie about the status of their wives, and are caught out and exposed as liars, which seriously compromises them. Jacob's sojourn in Egypt results in the enslavement of his descendants. Thus from biblical days onward these opening words, by association, prepare the reader to expect dire results.[18]

What went wrong in this case? We have already offered some reasons for assuming that Elimelech's aim was to make a fresh start in a new land. A grown man and his wife, both probably

---

[10]Literally: "in the days when the Judges judged." See footnote 4 above.

[11]That is, the town of Bethlehem that is located in the territory of the tribe of Judah in the south, and not the town of the same name located in the territory of the tribe of Zebulon in the north of the country.

[12]Literally: "in the fields of Moab," a common designation of Moab in the Bible, although usually in the singular (Genesis 36:35, Numbers 21:20, 1 Chronicles 1:46, 8:8). In the future this designation, whether in the singular or the plural, will be rendered as "the Land of Moab" (1:2, 6, 22, 2:6, 4:3).

[13]That is, of the clan of Ephrath; see Chapter 3, note 5.

[14]Genesis 12:10. The foreign land in that case was Egypt. Indeed there was another instance when Abraham left the Promised Land to dwell in another principality (in this case Gerar, Genesis 20) though no famine is mentioned.

[15]Genesis 26:1–6.

[16]Genesis 41:54–46:27.

[17]Both Isaac and Jacob had their moves approved by God (Genesis 26:2–5, 46:2–4).

[18]On a balancing note it is important to remember that all these narratives saw the moves of all the Patriarchs as necessary parts of a divine master plan aiming at a greater good. This would lead the biblical reader not only to expect the worse in the short run, but also to entertain the hope of an ultimate good to emerge from tragedy.

somewhere between twenty-five and thirty-five years of age — that is, in the prime of life — and their two sons, both probably in their early teens,[19] start out with money in their pockets, and hope in their hearts. Their destination, Moab, was not all that far away. One crosses the Jordan River, turns south along the eastern shore of the Dead Sea and crossing the Arnon River (see Map 1) passes out of the Land of Israel and enters Moab. Moab, the land of the Moabite people, had coalesced into a kingdom in the 13th century BCE, and despite a tradition of common ancestry with the Israelites had a long history of hostility with them.[20] At this period Moab fronted the lower half of the Dead Sea, its northern border being the Arnon River (the current Wadi Mojib) and its southern the Brook Zered (the current Wadi Hesa). It is a mountainous region clearly visible from Bethlehem. From the shore of the Dead Sea the land rises precipitously for several thousand feet to a fertile plateau about twenty-five miles wide in which grain is cultivated to this day. This productive region, the heartland of ancient Moab, is probably the destination of our immigrants.[21]

How long it takes before they find work and what kind of reception they face we are not told. At the best it couldn't have been easy. Life was usually bleak for one outside the web of blood-kin relationships. The extensive biblical legislation establishing basic rights for the *ger*, the resident-alien, and the continuing exhortations to give the *ger* an even break can give us an idea of how precarious such an existence could be. We have no evidence that equivalent legislation even existed in Moab. Nahum Sarna sums up the situation as follows: "Everywhere in the Near East the resident alien (Heb., *ger*) was without legal rights and protection and was wholly dependent upon the goodwill of the local community."[22]

Obviously our immigrants did not encounter uniform hostility. At least two families were willing to give their daughters to the newcomers as wives.[23] And they must have gotten some sort of foothold in Moab to last as long as they did. We even may permit ourselves the impression that they began to see light at the end of the tunnel. What seems to have done them in is the brutal fact of mortality: Elimelech dies. How, why, and after what length of time we are not told. It doesn't seem that it was soon after arrival; we are told that "they settled there." A year or two, perhaps more, pass and relationships with local families are established. Then "Elimelech, Naomi's husband, died; and she was left, she and her two sons." Note the wording: we are not told that Elimelech, father of Mahlon and Chilion, died. The focus has shifted to Naomi. Widow and mother of two orphans she may be, but the clear implication is that she is now the de facto head of the family. From what we learn of her later in the Book, she is very much a take-charge personality. I do not think we will be amiss in entertaining the strong suspicion that hers is the guiding hand behind the marriage of her two sons. Thus the first disaster is partially recouped. In

---

[19]A couple of years later we find them married. They must have been at least fifteen or sixteen when they married.

[20]The Bible records that Abraham's nephew, Lot, was the progenitor of the Moabite people (Genesis 19:30–38). Following the Exodus from Egypt, the records of the first contact between the Israelites and Moab depict the Moabites as exhibiting a very unfriendly attitude (Numbers 22–24, Judges 11:17). This soon degenerated into open warfare, Moab conquering central Israel and holding it subject for 18 years, until the Judge Ehud succeeded in assassinating the King of Moab and leading a successful insurrection against his occupying army (Judges 3:12–30).

[21]These were probably the "fields of Moab" to which our text refers (see note 12 above). The region is composed of numerous microclimates. Thus it would occasion no surprise to locals that Judah should be suffering drought and famine while a short distance away there is sufficient rainfall to ensure waving fields of grain.

[22]Sarna, *JPSTC Genesis*, p. 93.

[23]As a bride price (the amount paid to a father in order to obtain permission to marry his daughter) was a universal practice in the Ancient Near East, paying the sizable sums required to be able to marry Orpah and Ruth must have put a serious dent in the investment capital the family brought with them.

place of a family of two parents and two children we now have two families of husband and wife with a mother in the background. Life can go on, and it does, for about ten years.

But how? They get by, but the clear implication is that they are living from hand to mouth, subsisting on the young men's labor but unable to put anything aside. At the end of this decade we find their dependents destitute. And what of their reserves, the funds gained from the sale of Elimelech's land, the cash they were counting on to set themselves up? This too seems to have vanished. And there are no children! Nothing seems to have gone right. Then, to top it all off, Mahlon and Chilion, now full-grown men, fall victim to the family ill fortune. Together? Separately? Again we are not told. We are simply informed that "Machlon and Chilion also died, so the woman was bereft," that is deprived of "her two children and her husband."

By this time we have come to realize that this story is not about Elimelech at all, about his ambitions and his failures, but about someone who has received only casual mention, someone up to now almost hidden in the shadow of her men-folk. This, we now understand, is the story of Naomi. The prologue concluded, the real tale commences.

The Bitter Road to Bethlehem

Did Naomi agree with her husband in his decision to leave home and land? We are not told. If not, she has followed him loyally. Upon his untimely death she made no move to reverse the decision. Even if she had no hand in procuring wives for her sons, she obviously welcomed her new daughters-in-law with open arms and treated them with dignity and love; else how can we explain their devotion to her a decade later? Sweet is her name,[24] and that must have been a just description of her character. But there is more to Naomi than just a winning personality. As we shall discover, she has a keen appreciation of the circumstances in which she finds herself. If her sons were ever to fulfill their father's aim, and probably theirs as well, of making good in an alien land, their only hope was to marry into local families. That this would involve inevitable acceptance of an idolatrous religion must have been very hard on Naomi. She has remained, as we shall learn, loyal to the faith of her fathers. Yet all this she has resolutely put aside for the sake of her sons' futures. She has subordinated herself and her beliefs for the good of her men folk — in vain. Everything has collapsed, leaving her husbandless, childless and with no hope of future progeny. At this juncture, standing amid the ruins of everything she holds dear, Naomi takes charge of what is left of her life.

> Then she arose, she and her daughters-in-law, to return from the Land of Moab, for she had heard in the Land of Moab that the Lord had remembered His people and given them food.[25] So she went out from the place she was, and her two daughters-in-law with her; and they set out on the way to return to the Land of Judah (1:6–7).

Her men dead, her identity shriveled — at the start of the saga she was *wife* and *mother*, at its end she is no more than a *woman* bereft — nothing remains to hold her in Moab. The news of the famine having ended is hardly recent. We will find Bethlehem bustling and long prosperous. But while her men were alive this information was not relevant. They never had any intention of returning. Now, in her despondent condition, the old tidings assume a new importance. The economic upturn will make return possible. She makes her decision and at once puts it into action.

---

[24]In Hebrew, *Naomi* means either "my sweet one" or "my pleasant one." Similar names were in general use in the Ancient Near East.

[25]Literally *bread*. The term *bread*, "the staff of life," is often used in the Bible to signify food in general.

What is remarkable is that her two daughters-in-law, Orpah and Ruth, decide to come with her. Their husbands dead, the natural, indeed the logical course would be to return to their parents' homes. Yet they decide instead to accompany Naomi into a strange land where they will have all the disadvantages of being aliens. Such a decision speaks worlds about not only their natures but that of Naomi's. She, however, having their best interests in mind, cannot see them following her. Knowing from personal experience what awaits resident-aliens, Naomi attempts to dissuade them.

We must picture the scene. It was common in the Ancient Near East for a person setting out on a journey to be accompanied an indeterminate distance by those from whom he or she is taking leave.[26] It may be that Naomi was not fully aware that Orpah and Ruth intended to go all the way. Was the moment of realization a mile or so down the road, or did the matter not come to a head until they reached the border?

> Now Naomi said to her two daughters-in-law: "Go [back]; return, each of you, to her mother's house; may the Lord deal kindly[27] with you even as you have dealt with the dead and with me. May the Lord grant that you find rest,[28] each of you in the house of her husband." And she kissed them, and they lifted up their voices and wept (1:8–9).

This is a bitter moment for Naomi. The time has come to cut clean, to sever the bonds of love and devotion — in a way, the last living link to her now dead sons. In all fairness it is not right to hold on to her daughters-in-law. With her they have no future. Their best interests lie in Moab. Go home, she tells them. Find yourselves nice Moabite boys. Raise families and there find your fulfillment.

Note that she blesses them not in the name of Chemosh, god of Moab, but in the name of the Lord, the God of Israel, and this occasions no surprise on the part of Orpah and Ruth. Naomi has remained steadfast in her faith all these years. In all these years the girls have been kind and devoted to her sons and to her. She has repaid their kindness and devotion with her own. Now she will no longer be able to do so. So she prays that the God she worships, the God of Israel, will take her place. He is everywhere and can shower His love and devotion on them when she cannot. He can grant them homes and families when she cannot. And at this both she and the girls break down and cry unabashedly.

Then comes the shock. Instead of taking their tearful leave the girls refuse:

> But they said to her: "No! We will go back with you to your people" (1:10).

This avowal of devotion and commitment by the girls is a magnificent gift to Naomi. Beyond the emotional support of two beloved women whom she sees as virtual daughters, this is an unparalleled offer of economic support. Naomi is entering the autumn of her life. She is at the very best in her mid-forties, possibly even fifty years of age. That is old in those days. We are not told of her state of health. We never hear of her working. And at her age she has no prospects of remarrying. How will she live? And here are two young and, to all indications, healthy women offering to accompany her and, given the mores of the time, work to support her. Naomi could graciously accept this unsolicited offer and we would find no fault in her.

But Naomi will not even consider their sacrificing their futures for her sake. She rejects their offer categorically.

---

[26]For example Abraham, after hosting the three "strangers" courteously accompanies them "to send them on their way" (Genesis 18:16).

[27]Or "graciously."

[28]That is security, lack of anxiety, peace.

And Naomi said: "Turn back, my daughters. Why should you go with me? Have I yet sons in my womb who could be husbands for you? Turn back, my daughters, go! For I am too old to have a husband.[29] Even should I say: 'I have hope'; even if I were with a man this very night; even were I to bear [several] sons — would you wait for them till they were grown? For their sakes would you debar yourselves from marriage?[30] No,[31] my daughters! It is exceedingly bitter to me, for your sakes, that the hand of the Lord has gone forth against me." And they lifted up their voices, and wept again (1:11–14a).

Something emerges in Naomi's passionate plea that must be addressed before we stop to consider the specific content — namely, her bitterness over what has happened to her. Up to this point the text has been extremely reticent not only about Naomi's opinions but also about her feelings. We have, in passing, speculated over how she felt about her husband's decision to leave home and strike out for foreign climes, only to admit that we have no way of knowing. Up to this point Naomi has kept her opinions and her feelings to herself. Now, at this emotion-laden confrontation with her daughters (since she addresses them as her daughters it would be pedantic on our parts to continue to refer to them as her daughters-in-law), she lifts the veil and lets us see into her soul. Her reaction to the loss of her husband and her sons and of her hope of family, grandchildren and some modicum of prosperity is not resignation but bitterness. And it is even more than bitterness, as we shall soon have occasion to learn, it is anger. She holds God responsible for all that has happened to her. His hand has gone forth against her! She has remained faithful to Him in her heart all these long years and look what He has done to her! She does not reject her God or deny Him; but she is furious with Him.

Does she see the cumulative disasters that have befallen her family as punishment for leaving the Promised Land, for cutting themselves off from the proper ritual worship of their God, even for the possible idolatry (possible because not being told we cannot be certain) of her menfolk? She does not say, but it is possible that a lot of guilt lies behind her bitterness.

It is in the light of this overriding sense of bitterness and anger that we must read her exhortation to Orpah and Ruth. In effect she is saying to them: don't stay with me; I am a sinking ship. I am old and worn out. My life is a disaster. I have nothing left to offer. Get out while the getting is good. There may even be the implication that she is hexed — cursed. God's hand has gone forth against me, striking down my nearest and dearest. You may be next in line. Contact with me can be contagious. Save yourselves while you can.

Her appeal to her daughters consists of taking the common custom of the age, that of Levirate Marriage,[32] to its ridiculous extreme. What Naomi is saying is: Don't be silly. I am no good to you. I have no more sons to take the place of those who have died; I am not even pregnant. Anyway, I am past childbearing age. But even let us suppose that by some miracle I am still capable of becoming pregnant, and that this very night I slept with a man and became pregnant, would you be willing to wait 16 or 17 years until they are old enough to marry (which would make Ruth and Orpah almost Naomi's age)? Would you be ready to lock yourselves into a situation wherein you could not marry anyone else? This is ridiculous. Be sensible. I am old and worn out, and of no possible further use to you. Think of yourselves. Your future is still

---

[29]Literally, "I am too old to be with a man."

[30]Literally, "debar yourselves from being with a man."

[31]The Hebrew term used here, *al*, is a shortened form of the expression *al yehi ken*, "may it not be so!" and has the force of the current colloquial expressions "Enough already!" or "No way!"

[32]For a discussion of Levirate Marriage see Chapter 1, especially notes 26 and 28. True Ruth and Orpah, as childless widows, are candidates for Levirate Marriage had there been any surviving brothers of their dead husbands — but there are none.

before you. My life, bitter as it is, is behind me. Don't make it worse by linking yourselves to me, and being pulled down.

Of course Naomi is right, and after another burst of uncontrollable weeping the logic begins to sink in. Orpah makes her peace with the situation, kisses Naomi goodbye and departs.

Then Orpah kissed her mother-in-law [goodbye],[33] but Ruth clung to her (1:14b).

While Orpah's only response to Naomi's impassioned rhetoric is to weep, kiss her mother-in-law farewell and depart, it is Ruth who summons up the courage to trump Naomi's fervored eloquence with an even more powerful declaration, a decisive pronouncement that brooks no reply. When Naomi appeals to Ruth to follow Orpah's example, Ruth makes no attempt to respond to Naomi's arguments; she simply brushes them aside as irrelevant. Ruth's reply to Naomi is to ask her to stop wasting her breath. Ruth has made her decision and her commitment, and will not be deterred. Naomi has no power to stop her.

And she [Naomi] said: "Behold, your sister-in-law has returned to her people and to her gods. Return after your sister-in-law." But Ruth said: "Don't pressure me[34] to leave you, to turn back from following you[35]; for where you go I will go, and where you lodge I will lodge; your people shall be my people and your God my God. Where you die I will die, and there will I be buried. The Lord do so to me, and more also[36] if even death separates me from you!" So when she [Naomi] saw how determined she was to go with her she ceased to speak to her (1:15–18).

Much as been written about Ruth's declaration. It is not really a declaration of faith but rather one of total commitment. Because of Naomi, Ruth is prepared to take a leap into the unknown: to commit herself totally to a people and to a God of whom, as the Israelites themselves come to realize, she knows next to nothing.[37]

Let us think about this anomaly for a moment. What does Ruth know about Naomi's people, the Israelites? Probably not very much on an informational level. Life in those days was very provincial, and there were no newspapers. What did she know about Naomi's religion? Probably less than nothing. I say this because her very declaration hints at major misconceptions about the God Israel worships.[38] Objectively speaking, not only has she much to learn

---

[33]LXX adds "and returned to her people."

[34]The basic meaning of the Hebrew term *lifgoa b...* is "to strike down," so E.A. Speiser therefore renders the parallel expression in Genesis 23:8 as "to put pressure on him" (Speiser, *AB Genesis*, p. 170; see also Hubbard, *Ruth*, p. 114). This seems closer to the meaning than the more usual rendering of "entreat" or "urge."

[35]Literally "to turn around from behind you."

[36]This was a common form of oath in biblical times, invoking God to perform some sort of punishment (the phrase possibly being accompanied by a gesture indicating what sort of punishment), and asking Him to repeat it an unspecified number of times, if a specific action is not performed or if the invoker does not fulfill a certain commitment. In this case Ruth has unconditionally declared to Naomi that she will not part with her, adopting Naomi's people and God as her own. Now she reinforces her commitment by turning her declaration into an oath, calling down upon herself punishment from the God of Israel, to Whom she has just committed herself, should anything short of death part her from Naomi. There is no incongruity in Ruth, a non–Israelite, using this typical Israelite formula. It seems that this form of oath was common among the pagans of the region as well, except that they would not invoke God, but rather "the gods." Thus Jezebel to Elijah — "May *the gods* do so [to me], and more also"— if you are still alive twenty-four hours from now (1 Kings 19:2).

[37]Boaz will say as much to her not so long afterward (2:11–12).

[38]Ruth's declaration "your people shall be my people and your God my God" reads literally "your Gods." Is the plural form simply a poetic parallel to Naomi's statement that "your sister-in-law has returned to her people and to her gods" where the plural is used, or is Ruth's knowledge of the religion of Israel still so sketchy that she assumes that besides the Lord God of Israel, the main God, there must be numerous lesser deities also venerated by the Israelites, as in the case of the Moabites?

but, more to the point, much to unlearn. But all this is beside the point. Ruth's commitment is not of the head but of the heart. She looks up to her mother-in-law, and loves her with her whole being. Naomi has become her ideal. If Naomi is an Israelite, then what a wonderful people the Israelites must be. If Naomi's religion has created such a lovely soul, then how great and inspiring is its God. In her love for her mother-in-law and her desire to be like her we find the roots of her commitment to sever her ties to her people and her gods, to become part of Naomi's people, and to worship Naomi's God. What is precious to Naomi will be precious to her. Nothing will be able to deter Ruth from this commitment not to separate herself from Naomi's person; even Naomi herself will prove powerless, no matter what the reason, to separate them. It is through Ruth's eyes that we first begin to get a glimmering of the scope and the depth of Naomi's character.

Ruth's opening exhortation to Naomi — "stop pressuring me to leave you for my own good" — and her passionate avowal of devotion prove to be the last word. Naomi knows her daughter's personality by now. Once she makes up her mind, once she commits herself, she will not let go. There is no purpose in prolonging the conversation. Naomi accepts the inevitable. Two figures turn as one to trudge down the dusty road leading to Bethlehem.

The Homecoming of the Destitute

So the two of them went on till they came to Bethlehem. And it came to pass, when they entered Bethlehem the whole town was in an uproar over them; and [the women] said: "Can this be Naomi?" She said to them: "Don't call me Naomi,[39] call me Mara[40]; for the Almighty[41] has dealt very bitterly with me! I went out full and the Lord brought me back empty. Why call me Naomi when the Lord has afflicted me,[42] and the Almighty has brought calamity upon me?" (1:19–21).

Naomi's appearance at the town gate creates a sensation. It is broad daylight. Most men are away working in the fields, so it is the women of the town who accost the travelers. Ruth, the stranger, occasions no comment; all the attention centers on Naomi. Twelve to fifteen years have passed since last they saw her, and how she has changed! She barely seems the same person. "Is this Naomi?" they exclaim in shock. "What has happened to you?" is the implication. At this, all Naomi's bitterness overflows. In a cutting play on the meaning of her name (sweet, pleasant) she responds: "Don't call me Naomi, call me Mara [bitter]! Look at what God has done to me; what He has made of me. This is all His doing! When I left Bethlehem I was young. I had a husband and children. Our pockets were full, and our hearts hopeful. And God has taken everything from me: husband, children, money and hope. It is His doing that I return empty-handed. I may have deserved my name of 'sweet' when I left, but no longer. Now I am bitter, bitter, bitter — and it is God," she insists, "Who is the cause of the change in me."

The virulence of this outburst stills any possible response from the townspeople. This indeed is no longer the Naomi that they knew. But we, looking back over the chasm of the

---

[39]That is, "sweet," "pleasant."

[40]That is, "bitter."

[41]In Hebrew *Shadai*, an appellation for God most common in Patriarchal and pre-monarchial Israel. Beyond her emotional outburst, there is also bitter irony in Naomi's choice of this designation, *Shadai*. In Genesis, calling God "the Almighty" (*Shadai*) is always connected either to the promise of fertility or the preservation of life (17:1–2, 28:3, 35:11, 43:14, 48:3–4, 49:25). In effect Naomi is saying: "So where is my husband? So where are my children? So where are all your promised benefits? You have betrayed me!"

[42]Reading with LXX, Syr. and Vul. MS reads "testified against me."

years, note that Naomi's harangue is not factually true. This embittered old woman has not returned empty: she has returned with Ruth. And while, in her outburst of anger and discontent, she has momentarily forgotten Ruth hovering in the background, we haven't. Nor has the author. It is Ruth that will make all the difference.

> So thus Naomi returned — and Ruth the Moabitess, her daughter-in-law with her — who returned out of the Land of Moab. And they arrived in Bethlehem at the beginning of the barley harvest (1:22).[43]

We have come full circle: we began the chapter with a family leaving Bethlehem to settle in the Land of Moab, and conclude with its remnants returning from Moab to Bethlehem. We began with a famine, with no harvest, and end with a new harvest season commencing. The author, in a summary as terse as the opening, in closing a chapter of tragedy, is simultaneously opening the next one on a note of hope. Naomi is home; she has Ruth by her side, a woman whose sterling devotion and wondrous potential have been revealed to us on the road to Bethlehem. And the omens are good, the timing is right: they have returned just in time for the opening of the harvest season. We may agree with Naomi that God has done her dirty. But this same God is now opening new opportunities. Naomi has been dealt a rotten hand, but this is the hand she has been dealt, and this is the hand she will have to play. How she will play the hand she has been dealt will determine not only her destiny but that of her people as well.

---

[43]The barley crop reaches maturity in mid–April. The wheat crop, which is slower in maturing, only becomes ripe in June, a bit less than two months later. Thus no sooner is the barley harvest over than one must begin bringing in the wheat. The next three chapters, the focus of the Book for which everything up to now has been preparation, thus takes place in the late spring and early summer of the year.

CHAPTER 3

Amid the Alien Corn

> The voice I hear this passing night was heard
> In ancient days by emperor and clown:
> Perhaps the self-same song that found a path
> Through the sad heart of Ruth, when sick for home,
> She stood in tears amid the alien corn.
> — John Keats, *Ode to a Nightingale*

Naomi has returned to Bethlehem with her foreign daughter-in-law in tow, and now that the sensation occasioned by their appearance and Naomi's outburst has subsided, practical issues demand their attention. Where are they to stay? What are they to do? How will they support themselves? It is here that the tight focus of the author obtrudes and forestalls any clear answers. The author is remorseless in telling us only what we need to know to follow the plot. This is how she succeeds in keeping down to four short chapters what easily could have been a book-size drama. The price paid is that we are left guessing about numerous, and to our minds critical, pieces of information.

For example, what did Ruth look like? Harold Fisch ponders this issue:

Is Ruth beautiful? She is the heroine of ... [a] romantic story and yet the book of Ruth makes no reference to her physical charms. This is a little curious because the average reader has a clear impression that she is fair and graceful. Novelists too. Thus Eppie, the child heroine of George Eliot's *Silas Marner* who, in the manner of Ruth (and with deliberate echoing of the biblical text), turns her back on her natural family and determines to stay with her foster father, is, as everyone terms her, a pretty child — "a round fair thing with soft yellow rings all over its head." Ruth amid the alien corn also figures in the work of many visual artists and she is invariably beautiful. Yet nothing of this is said in the text. She is complimented on her loyalty, never on her appearance.[1]

Why should this be so? The impression given by the story is probably correct. As Fisch remarks: "Beauty in the Bible is an elusive quality. It affirms itself even when it is not directly invoked."[2] But why does the author refrain from invoking it? Perhaps because it is not essential. Ruth is a story revolving around character. We have already been shown Ruth's devotion and loyalty. We have been given a glimpse of her unshakeable will. As this chapter and the next unfold, we will be treated to a progressive revelation of a remarkable personality. It is *who* Ruth proves to be and *what* she does, not how she looks, that will determine the outcome of our drama. Commenting on her appearance would not only be introducing data that is irrelevant in the author's

---

[1]Fisch, *Poetry with a Purpose*, p. 15.

view, but might even distract from our focus on Ruth's character. The tight focus is all. It is this tight focus that leaves us guessing in so many areas.

We have already mentioned that Elimelech sold his land, the ancestral estate inherited from his fathers. Did his house go with the land or, being in the town, was it excluded from the sale? Has this house, if it exists, been standing vacant and derelict all these years? Is this where Naomi and Ruth take up their abode?

While the text itself gives no information one way or the other, we do not get the impression that they are rooming with someone; that some relative or friend has taken them in. Naomi does not seem to have the option of returning to her parent's home, the one place that would have to take her in. She is already old and her parents most probably long gone. What about brothers and sisters? We hear of none. It may be that Naomi is not a native of Bethlehem. We hear only of relatives of her husband but of none of her own. Perhaps this might explain the isolation and destitution we sense as the story unfolds. Blood kin, by the norms of those days, would have felt obligated to take her in and support her. But what if she is not a blood relation, only the ex-wife of a not-so-very-appreciated relative; one moreover who had cut himself off from kith and kin? Let us take this line of reasoning a step further: perhaps if she were alone, some relative of Elimelech might have felt compelled to go beyond the strict obligations of kinship and open his door to her. But she is not alone; she has a daughter-in-law with her, and a foreigner to boot. The combination may seem a bit too much. The bottom line seems to be that no one feels sufficiently obligated to act. Naomi and Ruth are on their own.[3]

As pressing as is the need for shelter,[4] even more so is the need for sustenance. How are they to eat? I do not think that if Naomi had turned to her late husband's kin and asked for help that they would have refused her. Begging is demeaning, but necessity knows no place for pride. It might have come to this had not another alternative presented itself.

Enter the Redeemer

> It happened that Naomi had a kinsman of her husband's, of the family[5] of Elimelech, a man of substance[6] whose name was Boaz. Now Ruth the Moabitess said to Naomi: "I am going out, if you please, to the fields to glean among the ears of grain behind whomsoever I find favor."[7] And she said to her "Go my daughter." So she set out, arrived, and gleaned in the field behind the reapers (2:1–3a).

[2] *Ibid.*

[3] Even Boaz, with whom this chapter opens, does not seem to have raised a finger to help.

[4] It being the beginning of the barley harvest (i.e., April) the weather was clement and it would have been possible to camp out in the open, though there is no indication that they were forced to this extreme. This is what makes the speculation that they found shelter in a derelict house, that of Elimelech or some other, seem attractive by comparison. Carol Meyers makes the suggestion that the women of the town may have joined together "to help them establish themselves." But where? (Meyers, "Women of the Neighborhood," p. 120).

[5] The Hebrew term *mishpaha*, usually translated as "family," had a wider meaning than it has today. In early biblical days it connoted the kinship groups of which tribes were made up (i.e., a clan). The clan referred to is that of the Ephrathites mentioned in 1:2. Each clan was made up of "extended families" (each called in Hebrew *bet-ab*). F.I. Anderson estimates that the tribes of Israel were made up of about sixty clans, each numbering in populous times about 10,000 members by a conservative estimate (Anderson, "Israelite Kinship Terminology," pp. 31–35).

[6] Literally, "a man of valor," Hebrew *gibor hayil*. In a military context this term denotes a warrior, a brave and exemplary soldier. In a civilian context, as here, it defines a man of wealth and high social status.

[7] Literally, "find favor in his eyes."

The contrast is telling: Naomi and Ruth do not know where their next meal is coming from but, we are told, Naomi has a rich in-law, a kinsman of her late husband. Here is one to whom she can turn in her need, to beg for assistance. He, on the other hand, as we shall discover, while perfectly aware of her plight, has made no offer of aid. Ruth here interposes. She, who with the exception of her impassioned avowal on the road to Bethlehem, has remained speechless and has almost vanished into the background, now takes the initiative out of Naomi's hands and speaks up. She informs Naomi that she will assume the responsibility for the support of the two of them (the "if you please" is simply a pro-forma phrase to soften the harsh fact that once again she has made a decision and will brook no denial).

Her opportunity lies in the fact that the barley harvest has just begun. This is a season when the poor, the widow, the orphan and the alien (*ger*) can find sustenance. Israelite law provided that these, the underclass of society, had the right to follow the reapers and glean (that is, to pick up whatever had been dropped during the harvesting). Furthermore, law provided that at least one furrow of every field was to be left untouched; this was set aside for the unfortunate to harvest.

> And when you reap the harvest of your land, do not reap all the way to the edge of the field, or gather the gleanings of the harvest. You shall not pick your vineyard bare, or gather the fallen fruit of the vineyard. You shall leave them for the poor and the alien [*ger*]; I, the Lord, am your God (Leviticus 19:9–10).

And again:

> When you reap your harvest[8] in your field and forget a sheaf in the field, do not go back to take it; it shall go to the alien, the orphan and the widow — in order that the Lord your God bless you in all the work of your hands (Deuteronomy 24:19).

As one who is a resident alien in Israel, and a poor widow to boot, Ruth obviously fits the legal criteria.

But things are not quite that simple. While laws may be on the books, their implementation lies in the hands of the local farmers, and compliance may be spotty. Ruth recognizes this. She is a stranger, and a non–Israelite as well. It is only natural to favor one's own. She runs the risk of not being allowed to implement her legal rights. She indicates as much when she speaks of the need to find an owner in whose eyes she finds favor; that is, where she will be welcomed rather than driven away. There are further dangers to which she does not allude, but which must have been very much in her mind and that of Naomi as well. Ruth is a very presentable young woman[9] with neither husband nor relatives to protect her. In other words she is totally vulnerable. Leaving town and going out into the countryside is virtually inviting molestation. So at the best Ruth will be on suffrage, and can expect only the poorest of pickings. At the worst she runs real bodily risk. It takes courage to even make the offer that she does.

Why doesn't Naomi go out to glean? As a penniless widow she certainly has the right, would be far better accepted, and would run little risk of molestation. We are not told. As an older woman perhaps she has health problems. Gleaning involves strenuous daylong physical work. She may not be up to it. Or perhaps the issue is one of pride. For the widow of a landowner to be gleaning on her former neighbors' plots would be humiliating in the extreme. But she might have been forced to it, age, health, and humiliation notwithstanding, had Ruth not

---

[8]Literally, "When you harvest your harvest."

[9]Though we are not directly informed, all indications are that she was at this time in her mid-twenties.

insisted on taking the initiative. Despite the problematic nature of Ruth's undertaking Naomi does not protest. Perhaps she is relieved that the burden is taken off her shoulders and Ruth is assuming the responsibility. Perhaps she has already learned that when Ruth makes up her mind, protest and argument are useless. Whatever the reason, Naomi simply acquiesces: "Go, my daughter." And Ruth, good as her word, at once puts her resolve into practice.

> Now it chanced that the portion of the field [where Ruth alighted] happened to belong to Boaz, who belonged to the family of Elimelech. And behold, Boaz arrived from Bethlehem, and said to the reapers: "The Lord be with you." And they said to him: 'The Lord bless you." Then Boaz said to his foreman[10]: "To whom does this young woman belong?"[11] And the foreman[12] answered "She is a Moabite girl[13] who came back with Naomi from the Land of Moab. And she said: 'Please let me glean, and gather among the sheaves after the reapers.' So she came, and has been standing from morning until now, [except] that she sat in the house a little [while]" (2:3–7).[14]

The text here, seemingly very straightforward, is actually quite subtle. A number of things are taking place just under the surface. Ruth sets out, and it just happens, we are informed, that the place where she asks permission to glean belongs to Boaz (who, we are reminded, belongs to the same clan as her late father-in-law, Elimelech, and is therefore a kinsman-in-law). We rendered the Hebrew in a rather redundant manner:

> "Now it chanced that the portion of the field happened to belong to Boaz...."

But that's the way the Hebrew is. In fact the redundancy is even more pronounced in the original, literally something like "now there chanced a chance" or perhaps "now there happened a happening." This redundant doubling not only emphasizes the surprising turn of events[15] but has the effect of suggesting a reversal of meaning. Used just once the verb would mean that it was a matter of pure chance that Ruth happened to light on Boaz's property, repeating the term raises the question in the reader's mind: was this really just chance? Is there more to this choice, and the encounter that will immediately ensue, than simply a stroke of luck? Why is the author insisting so strenuously that this is really nothing more than chance? Is something going on behind the scenes of which we are not aware?[16] This is one of the first indications of what we will discover to be the central theme of the Book: the hidden hand of God.[17]

The second point relates to Ruth's request. We have been talking freely about gleaning; it has come time to explain exactly what gleaning involves. For this we need to understand how grain was harvested in the Ancient Near East, and in Israel in particular. Grain was planted in

---

[10]Literally, "his young man who was in charge of the reapers."

[11]A person's identity in those days was connected with family and clan. So in asking what family and clan this woman belongs to Boaz is simply asking: "Who is she?" See Chapter 1.

[12]See note 10 above.

[13]Literally, "young woman," the same term as used by Boaz in his question.

[14]The Hebrew of the latter part of this verse is obscure. I have refrained from adopting the many proposed emendations (changes) of the text and have attempted to make some sense out of what we have in the MT. The assumptions that lie behind this rendering will be made clear below.

[15]As noted in the Introduction, the usual, and often the only means the biblical text has to emphasize something is by repetition. When a biblical author repeats himself he is usually doing so for emphasis. See Introduction, note 24.

[16]One is reminded of the Queen's comment to Hamlet: "The lady doth protest too much, methinks" (Shakespeare, *Hamlet*, III:2).

[17]Bezalel Porten, referring to the blessings of Boaz and the reapers (2:4 above), remarks: "not only does the divine hover *over* events (as in v. 3) but He is on the lips of great and small alike, of the 'man of valor' (c.f. v.1) as well as of his reapers" (Porten, "The Scroll of Ruth," p. 33).

rows or furrows.[18] When ripe, the stalks of grain would be cut by a row of reapers moving systematically from one end of the field to the other. Each reaper would grab several adjacent stalks with one hand; in his other hand he held a sickle and with this he would cut the seized stalks loose from the roots. With the hand holding the original stalks he would now grab several more and cut them, and so on until his hand could hold no more. This bunch he would put down and then begin the process again. Before beginning the next row he, or another member of the team, would gather these bunches together into bundles (called sheaves) and leave them at various collection points, often at the end of rows, to later be tied up and removed for transport to the threshing floor.[19]

Needless to say, even skilled reapers would tend to drop individual stalks during the cutting, and more would tend to be dropped in the gathering and tying-up process. Gleaners would follow the reapers and gather up the stalks dropped during the cutting. This was their right. But once the cutters had passed and the bunches were gathered into sheaves, what was dropped belonged to the owner. It was normal procedure for the staff to go back and collect any stalks of grain that fell down during the collecting and binding of the sheaves. All this was thoroughly understood in biblical times and needed no explanation; it is necessary background to understand what takes place when Ruth arrives at the field.

We are informed that sometime during the morning Boaz arrives to check on how things are going,[20] only to discover a young woman standing around who is a stranger to him. That he does not recognize her speaks volumes. He knows all about her, down to the last detail, as we shall shortly learn. That he has never set eyes upon her can only mean that, despite Naomi being the wife of his late close relative, he has felt no need to meet with her and welcome her back, much less to extend assistance. Had he done so he could not have avoided meeting Ruth. Boaz has been keeping his distance.

Upon his asking who she is, the foreman hastens to fill him in: "That's that Moabite girl who came back from Moab with Naomi. She requested that I allow her to glean after the reapers and also to gather among the sheaves. She has been standing around from early morning up to now, except for a little time she went to sit in the house [to get out of the sun?]." The clear implication is that the foreman didn't feel that it lay within his authority to grant permission, and that she has been waiting for the boss to show up.

Why does Ruth ask for permission (except as a matter of politeness)? Legally she is not required to do so to glean after the reapers. And to a request such as this the foreman probably would have said: "Sure, go ahead." But this is not what Ruth has requested. Simply to glean after the reapers would garner rather slim pickings. She has also requested permission to "gather among the sheaves." Here the pickings are much better, but this goes beyond her legal rights. This would be a privilege and an unusual one at that. Ruth is requesting to take what properly belongs to the owner. Only when we realize the audacity of this request do we finally begin to grasp Ruth's nature.

The traditional picture of Ruth is of a woman who is quiet, unassuming, modest and self-effacing: a pious model of love and devotion. This is also the conclusion reached by the majority of modern scholars. Up to a point it is true, but only up to a point. I think that the time has

---

[18]A furrow is literally the trench in the earth made by the plow in which the seeds are placed.

[19]We will discuss this subsequent stage of the harvesting process, threshing, when we get to it later in the chapter. See also note 36 below.

[20]It tells us something about the wealth and status of Boaz that he has the leisure to meander around checking up on his various holdings. This is harvest season when there is enormous pressure to get in the grain as quickly as possible. Every hand is needed. Farmers are working from morning to night alongside their wives, their children and any spare hands that they can mobilize. Boaz, on the other hand, can afford a foreman to take charge in his stead and oversee a hired staff of reapers. This is not a family farm and Boaz is far from a simple farmer.

come to challenge a two-dimensional picture that more properly belongs in a Sunday School col-
oring book. We have already learned that Ruth has a mind of her own, and once she has made
up her mind she has a will of iron. Here we discover that she possesses an audacity that is breathtaking. True, most of the time she is self-effacing. But this is when there are no issues at stake.
When it came to sticking with Naomi she was willing to abandon home, land, people and religion to become "a stranger in a strange land."[21] Now another "life or death" issue has arisen. Having grown up in the breadbasket of Moab, Ruth is a farm girl. She understands agricultural
realities. Working hard all day gleaning behind the reapers she will be able to gather enough to
feed herself. It will never be enough for two persons, and she is committed to providing for Naomi.
Only if she is permitted to gather what is dropped where the sheaves are collected, bundled, tied
and carted for transport — each separate activity generating further wastage — will she be able to
gather enough for two. Yet how does she, a poor stranger knowing no one, and a foreigner with
none of the legal rights of an Israelite, presume to make so outlandish a request? Behind her quiet
and unassuming demeanor this is an extremely gutsy female.

Boaz's reaction is surprising. Instead of telling her to get lost and chasing her away (his
undoubted prerogative), Boaz turns to Ruth who is standing there:

> Then Boaz said to Ruth: "Hear me well, my daughter![22] Do not go to glean in another field;
> indeed, do not leave this one. Stick close to my girls here. Keep your eyes on the field that they
> are reaping and follow after them. I will command the young men[23] not to molest you.[24] And if
> you get thirsty, go to the vessels and drink from what the young men have drawn." Then she fell
> on her face and bowed down to the ground and said to him: "Why have I found favor in your
> eyes, that you should take notice of me, when I am a foreigner?" Then Boaz answered and said to
> her: "It has been told me clearly[25] everything that you did for your mother-in-law after your hus-
> band's death: how you left your father and your mother, and the land of your birth, and have
> come to a people that you did not know before. May the Lord repay you for what you have done,
> and may your reward be full from the Lord, the God of Israel, under Whose wings you have
> come to take refuge." Then she said: "May I find favor in your eyes, my lord, for you have com-
> forted me, and because you have spoken to the heart of your maidservant; And as for me, would
> that I may be as one of your maid-servants"[26] (2:8–13).

---

[21]This is a phrase that Moses used to describe himself when he was an alien fugitive from justice in Midian
(Exodus 2:22).

[22]Literally, "Have you not heard, my daughter?" In biblical Hebrew a strong affirmation is often phrased as a
rhetorical question, demanding a "yes" as the answer. Note also his reference to her as "my daughter"—hardly
the way one addresses a stranger!

[23]Literally, "Have I not commanded the young men?" Boaz once again uses a rhetorical question to convey in
the strongest manner that this is what will be done. It seems that this is Boaz's style of discourse.

[24]Literally, "not to touch you."

[25]Literally, "It has been told, been told me"; the verb "to tell" is repeated twice for emphasis.

[26]This last phrase is highly problematic. MT reads literally, "And I will not be as one of your maidservants,"
creating problems for commentators, ancient and modern alike. What does this mean: a declaration of a status superior to Boaz's maidservants? This is totally out of harmony with everything Ruth has said to date. Most
commentators, ancient and modern, interpret this as saying that she is not as worthy as, or not even the equal
of, Boaz's maidservants. But this tortures the text, adding (implied) words and forcing the meaning. The plain
text says nothing of the sort. To make matters worse, the ancient versions (LXX, Vul., and Syr.) show *no negative*, reading "I am one of your maidservants" (Vul.) and "I will become one of your maidservants" (LXX and
Syr.). My suggestion, embodied in the translation, is to rely on the lack of a negative in the ancient versions,
and to assume a simple scribal copying error that led the term *lu* (would that) to be mistaken for the negative
lo. I hasten to say that I am far from the first to propose this change, and tentatively adopt it not only because
it makes good sense, and has serious implications for Ruth's character (that will be developed below) but also
because all the other interpretations seem to me to be so much worse.

This is an extraordinary exchange, and it behooves us to examine it closely. Boaz, a man in middle age, and probably old enough to be Ruth's father, takes her under his wing. His addressing her as "my daughter" not only recognizes the difference in their ages but emphasizes the paternalistic attitude toward her that he adopts. He not only grants her extraordinary request, but insists she remain on his property where he can protect her. We have referred to the dangers inherent in the position of a young unconnected woman out in the fields. Boaz is perfectly aware of these dangers and takes her under his protection. "Stick close to my women employees and you will be safe," he tells her. Furthermore, he will issue strict orders that none of the men so much as touch her. "And further," he says, "feel free to drink from the water jars provided for my employees whenever you are thirsty." All this is quite beyond anything Ruth has any right to expect.

Ruth's response is to prostrate herself face-down on the ground before him; common and perfectly acceptable Oriental courtesy, but a form only used under unusual, even extreme circumstances. "Why are you being so good to me," Ruth asks, "especially seeing that I am a foreigner?" Boaz's answer tells us several things, the first of which is that the "town telegraph" has been working overtime. He knows all about her. Boaz focuses on two aspects of the situation. First is how good she has been to her mother-in-law. Boaz, out of politeness, refers to Machlon as Ruth's late *husband*, but what he is really thinking about is the death of Naomi's *son*. In ancient Israel it was up to the sons to take care of the widowed mother. With the death of her sons Naomi is left adrift. Ruth, instead of being preoccupied with her own loss and looking after herself, has stepped into the breech and has acted in the place of Naomi's dead son. This is a loving concern of noble dimensions.[27] But more — Ruth's loving care has resulted in an act so unparalleled in the ordinary run of things that Boaz can think of only one precedent: Abraham, Father of the People of Israel. In summing up Ruth's act — leaving home and land, parents and everything familiar — Boaz uses language consciously echoing that of Genesis 12:1, "Go forth from your country, and from the land of your birth and from your father's house to the land that I will show you." But the Patriarch's leap into the unknown was at the call of God; Ruth cut herself loose from her moorings out of love for a human being created in the image of God. This, to Boaz, is so extraordinary that he has no words adequate to express his wonder. As a representative of the people whom Ruth has elected to join, he can only bless her in the name of the God she has chosen to worship, or as he puts it: "the Lord God of Israel, under Whose wings you have come to take refuge."[28] You deserve praise and reward beyond the capacity of mere mortals to give; only God can properly reward such courage and devotion.

Ruth's response is to say, in effect, that you have already rewarded me with your kind words. As a stranger, alone and vulnerable in a world I only imperfectly understand, your kindness has eased my anxiety and brought comfort to me in my harsh situation. Ruth has been referring to herself as Boaz's maid-servant,[29] a common phrase in polite conversation with one superior in age or status, or one who has conferred some benefit. In its context it simply means "I am deeply indebted to you"; and so Boaz has taken it — as mere politeness. But now Ruth switches gears. Of course, being rich, Boaz has real maid-servants in his household. Now, if we are correct in our rendering of the end of Ruth's remarks,[30] Ruth is making her second audacious move of the day, one that puts her former one into the shadow:

---

[27]The Hebrew term for unconditional and unearned love and devotion is *hesed*, a term that is repeated several times in the Book (1:8, 2:20, 3:10), and that highlights one of its leading themes. See Chapter 6, note 4.

[28]Note well this phrase. We will return to it in the next chapter.

[29]Because Hebrew is a gender-inflected language, there is no such thing as "a servant." Every servant is either a man-servant or a maid-servant. In our translation it is important to emphasize the gender because this will become significant later in the development of the story.

[30]See note 26 above.

"As for me, would that I may be as one of your maid-servants."

This can be taken as further flowery Oriental hyperbole. But it can also be taken as expressing the wish that Ruth become part of Boaz's household. In effect Ruth is dropping a hint: I am a young woman and I find you interesting. Does Boaz get the hint? It is on this note that the conversation closes. Permission granted, we can assume that Ruth retires to glean in the field.

A Growing Relationship?

Assuming that Boaz arrived at mid-morning to check on his holdings (considering his wealth he probably has several fields, not necessarily adjacent), a couple of hours must pass until the noonday lunch break. Mealtime finds Boaz still present, joining his workers in their repast.

> At mealtime Boaz said to her: "Come over here; partake of the meal[31] and dip your morsel in the relish."[32] So she sat beside the reapers, and he passed to her some roasted grain. She ate her fill and even had some left over.[33] When she rose to glean, Boaz gave orders to his young men, saying: "Let her glean even among the sheaves; do not humiliate her. Moreover, pull out some for her from the handfuls and leave them for her to glean. Do not rebuke her" (2:14–16).

Expanding on his permission to drink from the water jars that he provides for his workers, Boaz now calls her over and invites her to join the staff in lunch (gleaners would normally eat by themselves of whatever food they brought with them). "Feel free to dip your piece of bread in the relish provided for the workers," he tells her. The relish, wine vinegar (possibly laced with a bit of olive oil) was used the same way that liquid dips are used today, to soften the slightly stale bread pieces and to give them taste. Ruth accepts the invitation and seats herself next to the reapers. And if this were not enough, Boaz passes over to her some handfuls of roasted grain.[34] He is certainly showing interest in her.

And now the clincher: as Ruth returns to the field to glean Boaz reminds his workers that Ruth has permission to glean among the sheaves where the pickings are the best. Don't let me catch you making derogatory remarks to her or commenting in her presence about the special treatment she is getting. Furthermore, the reapers are instructed to actually pull out some of the stalks of grain from the handfuls that they have reaped and drop them for her to pick up!

Why is Boaz so dramatically bending the rules for Ruth? His interest in her seems to exceed normal kindness. Is he taken with her? Is he picking up on her hint that she is interested in him? Is something more than a platonic protective relationship in the process of forming?

> So she gleaned in the field till evening, and beat out what she had gleaned — it was about an ephah[35] of barley. Then she carried it into the city (2:17–18).

After reaping (gleaning is merely picking up the leftovers of the reapers), the next stage of harvesting is the process of separating the grain from the stalks, and the kernels from the husks surrounding them. The process is called threshing and winnowing. This is a semi-industrialized process that was usually carried out communally.[36] But this large-scale process was not for

---

[31]Literally, "eat of the bread." Bread, the "staff of life," is often used as a synonym for food.

[32]Literally, "vinegar" (see below).

[33]Literally, "she ate, she was satisfied, she had some left over."

[34]Hebrew *keli*: dried grain, pan roasted, keeps well and was a common food in ancient Israel. It was munched as is (if freshly prepared it might be roasted in a bit of olive oil to enhance its taste).

[35]Ephah: a dry measure roughly equivalent to a little over half a bushel, or a bit under 30 lbs. in weight.

[36]Threshing, the breaking up of the sheaves to free the kernels of grain, was accomplished by laying the sheaves on a large flat area and having oxen drag heavy wooden sledges over them. An alternative process was to drive oxen back and forth over the sheaves, the hoofs doing the crushing. Winnowing will be described in the next chapter.

small amounts. These would be placed on a flat stone and beaten with a stick until the grain stalks would be broken up. Then, by means of a sieve, the kernels would be separated from the husks that covered them and the remains of the stalks, collectively termed chaff. Beating out grain by hand and then sifting the results was an arduous process that must have lasted well into the evening.

The amount Ruth has amassed is startling — about half a bushel — attesting both to Boaz's generosity and Ruth's industry. R.L. Hubbard refers to the records of ancient Mari where the daily ration of a male worker rarely exceeded two lbs. per day, while women received half this amount. "This meant that Ruth collected the equivalent of at least half a month's wages [of a man] in one day."[37] Worry for where their next meal was coming from was no longer a factor for Ruth and Naomi.

Night must already have fallen as Ruth picks up the grain she has beaten out (probably in a basket she has brought for the purpose) and, carrying it on her head, trudges back into Bethlehem.

> Now when her mother-in-law saw what she had gleaned (and when she took out what remained from her filling meal[38] and gave it to her), her mother-in-law said to her: "Where did you glean today? Where did you work? Blessed be the one who took notice of you!" So she told her mother-in-law with whom she had worked, and said: "The name of the man with whom I worked is Boaz." Then Naomi said to her daughter-in-law: "Blessed be he of the Lord, Who did not abandon His kindness to the living and the dead!" Then Naomi said to her: "The man is a kinsman of ours, he numbers among our Redeemers!"[39] (2:19–20).

Naomi is stunned by the amount of grain Ruth brings home. And when Ruth pulls out the bundle of ready-to-eat food that comprises the leftovers of her lunch, Naomi's joy knows no bounds. Bounty such as this can only be explained by extraordinary circumstances; someone must have provided unusual opportunities for Ruth. She breaks out in a staccato series of questions, culminating in invoking a blessing upon the generosity of the person who made possible such a windfall. Ruth's response that it was Boaz who was responsible brings a further blessing. It is then that Ruth learns, obviously for the first time, that Boaz is a kinsman of both Naomi's late husband and of her own, and further, in accord with the customary practice in Israel, as a close relative he is bound by the rules of the Redeemer. And with this statement new possibilities begin to open before Naomi's eyes.

We remember Naomi's bitter plaint to Orpah and Ruth on the road out of Moab: how she saw her own life a dead end; how she pleaded with her daughters-in-law not to tie their fates to hers because she had nothing to offer them; how remaining with her would mean renouncing all possibility of marriage and family. Now suddenly Naomi realizes that perhaps she has been wrong. Under Israel's kinship rules relatives were obligated to act as Redeemers of the childless widows of near kin "to raise up the name of the dead upon his inheritance" (4:5), that is, to insure that no man die without heirs to continue his line.[40] This responsibility, which was absolutely obligating to immediate relatives, held with diminishing force as the degree of relationship receded. That Boaz was not immediate family is clear. He may have been a cousin to Elimelech, or even a more distant relation.[41] Naomi knew that neither she nor social pressure

---

[37]Hubbard, *Ruth*, p. 179.

[38]Literally, "from her being satisfied"; a reference to the conclusion of verse 14.

[39]See Chapter 1 for this term.

[40]See Chapter 1.

[41]RASHI, basing himself on the Midrash Rabbah, is of the opinion that Boaz's father and Elimelech were brothers, thus making the relationship between Elimelech and Boaz that of uncle and nephew — but all this is no more than conjecture.

could force him to act. And indeed his failure to come forward upon Naomi's return had demonstrated clearly that he felt no obligation to assume responsibility for the widows of his distant relatives. But here he was, demonstrating clearly his interest in Ruth, not so much as an in-law but as a woman. Possibly something might yet come of this interest. And as this possibility dawns on her, Naomi spontaneously bursts out in a prayer of thanksgiving: thanksgiving for the kindness and attention of Boaz (amplifying her earlier blessing of the then anonymous benefactor), and thanksgiving to her God Who, contrary to her former complaints, has abandoned neither the living (Naomi and Ruth) and what is due to them — future, family, progeny — nor the dead (Elimelech and Machlon) and what is due to them — remembrance, heirs.

With this realization that, despite all that has befallen her, a future is possible, Naomi undergoes a transformation. We suddenly begin to see a different Naomi. In the place of a person filled with bitterness and resignation we suddenly see emerging before our eyes a resolute and resourceful person, forward looking and filled with hope. Or perhaps we are simply seeing the real Naomi, restored to her former self after having been crushed and devastated by the calamities that have overtaken her. It is this different, or restored, Naomi that now explains her sudden paean of thanksgiving to the possibly startled Ruth by elucidating Boaz's relationship to the family, and its implications.

Ruth responds to the revelation by filling Naomi in on an aspect of the day's events that we know, but of which Naomi is not yet cognizant:

> "What is more," Ruth the Moabitess said, "He told me: 'Stick close to my young men until they have finished all my harvest.'" Then Naomi said to Ruth, her daughter-in-law: "It is best, my daughter, that you go out [to work] with his young women lest, in another field, you be molested" (2:21–22).

Ruth is paraphrasing Boaz's instructions but the essence is being conveyed: don't go elsewhere; here you are safe. Naomi, ever practical, refines the general into the specific: excellent, but stick with his women workers as well as to his fields. In other fields you may be molested, and even in Boaz's fields advances may be made if you fraternize with the men workers. With his women you are safe. Naomi is unaware that Boaz has given orders to his men not to touch Ruth, but over and above her concern for Ruth's safety, Naomi probably does not want to take the risk of a relationship developing between Ruth and one of the workers. She wants to keep Ruth unattached and permanently in the eye of Boaz. He is the ideal catch. After the barley is in, the wheat harvest begins. By the time that harvest is completed over two months will have passed. Hopefully propinquity will do its work and the relationship between Ruth and Boaz, begun so promisingly today, will ripen into love and marriage.

Ruth, ever dutiful (when instructions coincide with her own take on things), complies.

> So she stuck close to Boaz's young women, gleaning until the ending of the barley harvest and of the wheat harvest; and she lived with her mother-in-law (2:23).

CHAPTER 4

The Winning of Boaz

> It is a truth universally acknowledged, that a single man
> in possession of a good fortune, must be in want of a wife.
> — Jane Austen, *Pride and Prejudice*

Two months have passed, fruitful months in a material sense — if the productivity of Ruth's gleaning has been maintained at anything like that of the first day they now have a store that will last them over a year, and enough left over to trade for wine, oil, and other necessities. In narrow terms the harvest season has been an unqualified success. But in terms of the larger picture nothing has moved. After a promising start, the relationship between Ruth and Boaz has plateaued. The harvest season is over and matters stand as they stood at the beginning. Propinquity has not succeeded in moving things along. Something more will be needed.

It is important at this point to remind ourselves that Ruth is a very personable and desirable woman. As a widow she is free to choose whomever she wishes as a future mate, and we may assert with confidence that a goodly number of men are interested in her.[1] Why does she fix her sights on Boaz? That Boaz is rich is probably a subsidiary factor (Ruth is far from being an impractical romantic), but it is hardly the main reason. Let us return to that first meeting between Ruth and Boaz:

> Then Boaz said to Ruth: "Hear me well, my daughter! Do not go to glean in another field;
> indeed, do not leave this one. Stick close to my girls here.... I will command the young men not
> to molest you. And if you get thirsty, go to the vessels and drink...." Then she fell on her face
> and bowed down to the ground and said to him: "Why have I found favor in your eyes, that you
> should take notice of me, when I am a foreigner?" (2:8–10).

Ruth's reaction to Boaz's kindness is revealing. She is amazed at his generosity and con-

---

[1]In this context it is important to bear in mind how the dangers inherent in inbreeding affect marriage patterns in rural societies. While we have little to no explicit knowledge of marriage customs in Ancient Israel beyond those of incest restrictions (Leviticus 18, 20), the practices of Ethiopian Jews in the 19th and early 20th centuries can be instructive. The Ethiopian Jews lived as subsistence farmers in small villages, in an economy not dissimilar to that of 11th century BCE in Israel. More to the point, they had maintained continuity with the lifestyle of Ancient Israel and had continued to practice a modified form of biblical religion, including animal sacrifice. In this culture only persons removed from one another by at least *seven* degrees of blood relationship might marry! This virtually insured that one could only find a mate outside of one's own village. If similar practices maintained in rural biblical society we can understand that, all things being equal, Ruth — unrelated to anyone in Bethlehem — would be the focus of intense interest to any man looking to marry.

cern. He not only grants her presumptuous request, over and above what the law mandates,[2] but he takes her under his protection, insuring that she will not be molested while she gleans. And he is considerate as well, granting her permission to drink whenever she desires from the water jugs provided for his workers. This is not the treatment that she, a poor foreigner, had anticipated. What had she been expecting? Grudging permission or indifference at best, discrimination and hostile rebuff at worst. Instead she finds she is dealing with a person who treats her with kindness; and more, is concerned for her safety and well-being. Furthermore, as she is soon to learn, here is a person who appreciates her for her loyalty to her mother-in-law, and respects her for her decision to commit herself to the God of Israel and to His people (2:11–12).

We are not told what kind of person her late husband, Mahlon, was. Perhaps her surprised reaction to Boaz's kindness and respect hints at a less than ideal relationship. It may be that, by contrast, Boaz's maturity and consideration stand out all the more. Ruth avows:

> May I find favor in your sight, my lord, for you have comforted me, and because you have spoken to the heart of your maidservant" (2:13).

This is far more than mere politeness, more even than an expression of heartfelt gratitude for the solicitude shown to her. Ruth is here expressing her real admiration for the character and person of Boaz. Witness her subsequent hint:

> "And as for me, would that I may be as one of your maid-servants" (2:13).

Here Ruth is indicating that Boaz has made a hit with her.

What we are saying comes down to this: Ruth is not only an attractive and desirable woman but also a mature and experienced one. She has been married, and by this point in her life has a very clear idea of the kind of character she is looking for in a man. And in Boaz she has found it; hence the hint that she finds him interesting. Beyond this she cannot go. In that society it is up to the man to make the overt advances. A pushy woman is not only unacceptable but will drive men away. As it is, Ruth has been pushing the limits of the decently possible for one in her social position. It is now up to Boaz.

For his part Boaz exhibits real interest in Ruth. He is obviously attracted to her. Beyond his openhanded permission to glean among the sheaves, his offer of protection and his public remarks to Ruth, he invites her to lunch, he shares some of his food with her and, most blatant, he specifically instructs his workers to be inefficient and leave stalks of grain for her. Lacking indications to the contrary, we are free to assume that this pattern continues for the entire harvest season: that Ruth continues to take her meals with the workers and that Boaz continues to make his inspection trips, often taking his noontime meal with his staff. So why, after close to two months in which they meet several days a week for lunch, doesn't Boaz make a move?

Here we don't have to speculate; Boaz himself will tell us. As we will shortly learn from his own mouth, Boaz is shy. He is an older man who is acutely conscious of the age gap between himself and Ruth. He is sure that she will be attracted to men more her own age, and there is no lack of these in Bethlehem. She would never dream of linking herself, he assumes, to an old fogy like himself. It is the fear of a humiliating rebuff that makes him conceal his hand. So he adopts a paternal attitude, refers to her as "my daughter," protects and helps her but dares go no further. And here the matter rests.

In the face of this predicament Ruth is helpless. It takes Naomi, an older and more experienced person, to find a way of breaking the impasse. The issue will have to be forced. But how?

---

[2]See Chapter 3.

There are two issues that will have to be taken in consideration: first — whatever approach is used it cannot be crass, and it must take Boaz's social status into account. No man relishes having a woman back him into a corner and insist that he marry her. To do so publicly would be humiliating in the extreme. So, and this is the second point, the approach must be private. To openly force his hand would run the risk of Ruth being publicly rejected; a risk that she cannot afford to take.[3]

The answer to the first issue is obvious to Naomi. In place of seeming to usurp his male prerogatives, the appeal must be to his familial and clan duties and to his sense of social responsibility as a Redeemer. But as to arranging for a private interview — the second crucial problem — here lies the crux. Life in a village or a town in those days meant one was constantly in the public eye. It was like living in a fishbowl. Everyone knew everyone else's business; we have already noted how well the "town telegraph" worked. Ruth had not been in Bethlehem for more than two or three days before Boaz, without ever setting eyes on her, knew everything about her. In the normal run of things there was no place that Boaz and Ruth could meet without everyone being aware of it. How Naomi copes with this problem forms the starting point of the next episode in our tale.

Far from the Madding Crowd

Then Naomi, her mother-in-law, said to her: "My daughter, should I not secure a resting place[4] for you, that it will be well with you? And now, isn't Boaz (he with whose young women you have been), our kinsman? Behold, he is winnowing barley this very night at the threshing floor. So wash yourself, anoint yourself[5] and put on your [best] clothes[6]; then go down to the threshing floor. Do not make yourself known to the man until he has finished eating and drinking. But when he lies down, note the spot where he lies; then go and uncover his feet and lie down. He will tell you what to do." She [Ruth] said to her: "Everything that you tell me I will do" (3:1–5).

To meet Boaz privately can only be under cover of darkness, but with sunset he and all the adults of that era go to sleep. Ruth certainly cannot attempt to meet him in his home. No one lived alone in those days, and living conditions were crowded.[7] However Naomi realizes that the end of the harvest season provides a unique opportunity: the winnowing of the grain at the town threshing-floor. This was a flat area, ideally of exposed bedrock, otherwise of hard, stamped earth, where the grain would first be broken loose from the stalks (straw), and the kernels loosened from the husks surrounding them.[8] This threshing process produced a mix of grain and waste material, called chaff. The separation of the grain from the chaff, called winnowing, completed the harvesting process.

Winnowing was accomplished by repeatedly throwing the mixture into the air with a shovel

---

[3]A public rebuff by Boaz would probably scare off any other possible suitors for Ruth's hand.

[4]Hebrew *manoah*: we have met previously with this term (in a different grammatical form) in 1:9. The sense, there as well as here, is a home in which her daughter-in-law can find security and permanence.

[5]That is, with perfumed oil.

[6]The sense of the phrase is "get dressed up."

[7]There has been much speculation about Boaz's marital status. It is most unlikely that a man of his age would be a bachelor. It is much more likely that he was a widower (while the possibility exists that he was married — polygamy was practiced in those days — one does not get the sense from the story that Ruth was aiming to join Boaz's household as wife number two). In all events Boaz would be living with younger children (if any) of a previous marriage, servants and probably one or two relatives, making privacy at home an impossibility.

[8]See Chapter 3, note 36.

or fork. The chaff, being light, would be carried a short distance downwind, while the grain, being heavier, would fall directly back to the ground next to the winnower. This process required that the threshing floor be in an open area exposed to the west (in Israel the prevailing winds blow from west to east). Bethlehem was sited on a hilltop, while the threshing floor was located a short distance downhill on the western slope of the hill. Winnowing took place in the late afternoon and into the evening—this is the time of day that the prevailing winds blow. Having completed the winnowing the farmers would eat a festive meal (getting in the harvest was a cause for celebration) and would remain the night to guard the grain from thieves.[9] It was heaped up in individual piles around the perimeter of the field. And in the fact that Boaz would be spending the night in the open Naomi sees her opportunity. Here is the possibility for Ruth to maneuver a private meeting with Boaz.

It is in the light of this background that we must view Naomi's proposal to Ruth. After having made herself presentable (if her aim is to persuade a man to marry her she should take pains to put her best foot forward), she is to leave town under cover of night and go down to the threshing floor. She is not to show herself until all the eating and drinking is over, the fires die down and the men compose themselves for sleep, each next to his own pile of grain. Be very careful to note exactly where Boaz lies down, Naomi instructs Ruth; making a mistake in the dark with the wrong man will not only be embarrassing—it will be disastrous! Then, when everyone is asleep, go over to Boaz, uncover his feet (all the men will have covered themselves— the nights get quite cold) and lie down by him.[10] The idea is that when his feet, clad, if at all, only in sandals, get good and cold he will wake up of his own accord and find her there. And what then? Naomi tells Ruth that, having set the scene, she should let Boaz take charge.

It is a very dangerous course of action that Naomi is suggesting to Ruth. Knowing Boaz's character, Naomi is gambling that he is not the kind of person to take advantage of Ruth sexually. But even if Naomi is right about Boaz, Ruth's surprising presence lying next to him in the dark is susceptible of misinterpretation—that she is attempting to seduce him, or worse, set him up for blackmail. Should she stumble over someone in the dark she could be taken for a thief. The truth is that should anything go wrong—and in a touchy situation such as this there is much that might go wrong—Ruth could find herself fatally compromised. Ruth is not stupid; she fully realizes the risks, but these must be weighed against the prize to be gained. It has well been said:

> Faint heart never won fair lady!
> Nothing venture, nothing win—[11]

But the reverse is equally true: faint heart never won procrastinating gentleman. Ruth does not hesitate:

> She said to her: "Everything that you tell me, I will do." And she went down to the threshing floor and did everything that her mother-in-law commanded her. So Boaz ate and drank, and his

---

[9] On the morrow the grain would be carted to the individual homes for storage (in three-foot high pottery containers in a storage room on the ground floor of the house). The byproducts of threshing and winnowing would be utilized as follows: the stalks would be dried into straw and used to feed the livestock, while the chaff was used for fuel.

[10] There is little doubt that the author is leading the reader on, building up suspense. The phrase "lie down" (in Hebrew *lishkav*)—used in various forms by Naomi no less than three times, and later used in the text a further five, making a grand total of eight times—has sexual connotations even as it has in English. The tension builds up in the mind of the audience: will she or won't she? Will he or won't he? For the means by which the author deftly ends the suspense see note 27 below.

[11] Gilbert, *Iolanthe*, II.

heart was merry; then he went to lie down at the edge of the grain pile. Then she came softly, uncovered his feet and lay down. Now it happened, around midnight,[12] that the man shivered, groped about[13] [to recover his extremities], and behold, a woman was lying at his feet! He said: "Who are you?" And she said: "I am Ruth, your maid-servant; spread your wing[14] over your maid-servant, for you are a Redeemer" (3:5–9).

Ruth has promised to do exactly what her mother-in-law instructed her to do, and so she does, but with a difference. She steals down to the threshing floor, remaining in the deep shadows and observing the feasting of the men. When the party draws to a close Boaz is feeling good after having eaten and drunk his fill.[15] Ruth watches him make his way to the edge of his grain pile, lie down, cover himself with his robe and compose himself for sleep. When she judges him fast asleep she stealthily approaches him, carefully lifts aside the robe uncovering his feet, and then lies down, not beside him but at his feet. So far she has carried out Naomi's instructions to the letter.

The minutes stretch out, the temperature continues to drop, as it does in the Judean hills at night, and the increasingly uncomfortable condition of his feet begins to register upon the sleeping Boaz. He begins to shiver with cold, awakes to find his feet uncovered, and groping around to find the cover and replace it he gets a jolt: there is someone lying at his feet — and it is a woman! The text clearly registers his shock as he demands to know: "Who are you?"

At this point Naomi's instructions to Ruth are: "He will tell you what to do," that is, remain passive and let him take the initiative. But it is just here that Ruth departs from her orders. Instead of remaining passive she seizes control of the situation. Instead of letting Boaz tell her what to do, she tells him what he is to do.

And she said: "I am Ruth your maid-servant."

So far so good, she has identified herself and in polite form (though remember the hint she had dropped at their first meeting, "would that I may be as one of your maid-servants")[16]; now she turns this politeness into a new reality. She quickly continues:

Spread your "wing" over your maidservant, for you are a Redeemer" (3:9).

---

[12]Literally, "Now it came to pass, in the middle of the night." The term means the midway point between dusk and dawn.

[13]The Hebrew term *lapat* is a rare one, appearing but three times in the Bible. E.C. Campbell makes a strong case that the term relates to actions done with the hand: to reach or touch, hence, in this context, "to grope" (Campbell, *Ruth*, p. 122).

[14]Reading with the *Ketib* (the consonantal text) and all the ancient versions. The vowelation (*Qrei*) reads "wings" in the plural.

[15]While wine was an integral part of all feasting, and the phrase *his heart was merry* can imply drunkenness (as in 1 Samuel 25:36, Esther 1:10, etc.) in this context it has the meaning of "relaxed," "a bit high," "euphoric." No one could afford to get drunk on a night when they had to guard the grain. Equally to the point, a man in a drunken stupor or sufficiently befuddled as not to have his wits about him would have been no use in what Naomi was planning.

[16]See pp. 48–50. There is a subtle difference in the language Ruth uses. In her original meeting with Boaz (2:13) she referred to herself twice as his *shifhah*. Now she refers to herself (again twice) as his *amah* (3:9). The terms are synonymous — both mean maidservant. Yet the use of the term *amah* in a tomb inscription dating about 700 BCE to refer to a woman, obviously the wife of the royal steward with which she is buried, suggests the possibility that this term for a maidservant implied the eligibility for a marital relationship. The use of the same term in 1 Samuel 25:41, again within the context of an impending marriage, strengthens the possibility. Is Ruth's shift in terminology accidental, or is it part and parcel of the fact that she is proposing marriage to Boaz? *The New JPS Bible* highlights this possibility by translating *shifhah* (2:13) as "maidservant" while rendering *amah* (3:9) as "handmaid."

There is a lot going on in this seemingly simple remark. The robes worn by the wealthy and those of high status had richly embroidered hems that were scalloped, cut out in a sort of zigzag pattern. These V-shaped scallops were called "wings" because in shape they resembled the wings of birds. So while, on its most literal level, what Ruth is saying is "I am also cold, please spread the hem of your robe over me," actually Ruth's request means much more than that. To cover someone with one's robe meant in those days to take that person under one's protection, to assume responsibility for him or her. More — to spread one's garment, and specifically one's "wing" over a woman was to claim her in marriage.[17] So what Ruth is really saying to Boaz is: marry me! And needless to say, Boaz understands exactly what Ruth is telling him.

There is a yet further implication to Ruth's remark. Who can forget Boaz's beautiful blessing when he first met Ruth:

"may your reward be full from the Lord, the God of Israel, under Whose wings you have come to take refuge" (2:12).

Ruth has certainly not forgotten. She is now turning Boaz's blessing back on him. In effect she is reminding him that she has done her part, embracing the God of Israel, taking refuge under His wings. "Now it is your turn," she is telling him, "to take me under your wing. It is your responsibility to provide me refuge, *for you are a Redeemer*. Do your duty to your family and your clan; and incidentally also to me!"

Then he said; "May you be blessed by the Lord, my daughter; your latest kindness[18] is greater than the first, in that you have not gone after the young men, whether poor or rich" (3:10).

Boaz's response is a cry of relief and of joy. Far from feeling pressured into assuming an unwanted social responsibility, he is hearing what he has wanted to hear but feared that he never would. He breaks out in a fervent blessing that, despite their difference in age, she prefers him to those of her generation.

Yet even here Boaz preserves the proprieties. Ruth has couched her proposal of marriage in the form of a demand that he fulfill his family and clan obligations (she is being "pushy" not for herself— heaven forbid!— but simply in order to fulfill her responsibility to the family into which she has married, to produce an heir to carry on the family line). Boaz quickly adapts himself to Ruth's script.[19] He continues:

"And now, my daughter, do not fear. I will do to you everything that you say: for all the gate of my people[20] know that you are a woman of worth.[21] Now it is true that I am a Redeemer, however there is a Redeemer nearer than I.[22] Remain [here] this night. In the morning,[23] if he will redeem you, well and good. But if he is not willing to redeem you, then, as the Lord lives, I will redeem you. Lie down till morning" (3:11–13).

---

[17]This is clear in Deuteronomy 23:1 (Christian Bibles 22:30), 27:20 and especially Ezekiel 16:8. It is also attested by Arab custom, both ancient and modern.

[18]See Chapter 3, note 27, and Chapter 6, note 4.

[19]So adept is Boaz in covering his personal feelings in a cloak of loyalty to family that many commentators read this burst of personal relief to say that he is blessing Ruth for forgoing her personal happiness with one of her own age for the sake of producing an heir for the good of the family, despite the age of the kinsman who must father it.

[20]That is, everyone who goes in and out of the city gate; in other words "everybody."

[21]That is "a fine woman," "a virtuous woman"; Hebrew *eshet hayil*. Two thirds of a chapter of the Book of Proverbs (Proverbs 31:10–31) is devoted to the definition and praise of the ideal of the worthy, virtuous woman. See also Proverbs 12:4.

[22]That is, one who is a closer relation to the late Elimelech and Machlon than I am.

[23]Literally, "And it shall be, if in the morning."

Boaz moves quickly to allay any fears that Ruth may have. He assures her that despite her foreign background and her unconventional (to say the least) approach he holds her in high regard, as does everyone in Bethlehem. The term he uses, *a woman of worth*, is the highest compliment that can be paid to an Israelite woman, and echoes the description of Boaz as a "man of substance" (2:1)—in the Hebrew the similarity of the phrases is even more striking than in translation.[24] Boaz is telling Ruth that he considers her to be in his class. Moreover he recognizes his familial responsibilities and will accept them. In effect he accepts Ruth's proposal of marriage and is willing to marry her. But there is a problem. Ruth has made her approach to Boaz within the framework of clan responsibilities and Boaz has accepted on these terms. But if one accepts the framework then one must realize that these responsibilities fall upon the closest blood relative and Boaz is only second in line. There is a closer relative. Only if he voluntarily steps aside does the responsibility pass to Boaz.

His response to Ruth is exemplary: he will see to it that the right thing is done by her. She will get a husband to father an heir to Elimelech's line. If the closest relative will do his duty—wonderful. If not, he vows not to leave her hanging. Either way, Boaz tells Ruth, you will be taken care of. Tomorrow everything will be settled. You can lie down and rest easy.

But all of Boaz's subsequent actions belie this noble and disinterested proclamation. He wants Ruth for himself, and from this moment onward all his thoughts are devoted to removing the obstacle in their path. His first object must be to cover all traces of their midnight meeting. Besides the effect on Ruth's reputation, should it become known that he and she are interested in each other, a strong card would be placed in his rival's hand. This relative would be in a position to assert his rights to Ruth and demand compensation for relinquishing them. In effect he would be in a position to extort a serious sum from Boaz.

> So she lay at his feet till morning, and rose before one man could recognize another, for he said: "Let is not be known that the woman came to the threshing floor." Then he said: "Hold out the shawl you are wearing, hold it tight." So she held it and he measured out six [measures of] barley, and he placed [the bundle] on her. Then she went into the city[25] (3:14–15).

These verses require more attention than they ordinarily receive. If Boaz's primary desire is secrecy—"Let it not be known that the woman came to the threshing floor"—why does he keep her by him for half the night? Why not send her away at once? I think that there were several considerations. Boaz may have been concerned for her safety; who knows what thieves and other undesirables might be hanging around in the vicinity of the threshing floor hoping for a chance at some easy pickings? By first dawn these might be counted on to have dispersed. Then again, on the night of the harvest threshing there might be some townspeople about. A woman seen sneaking into town from the countryside in the middle of the night would occasion comment. Of course, the reason may simply be that, as a walled town accessible only by a gate, if the gates were closed at night Ruth could not have gotten back into town until dawn. Furthermore, was it absolutely necessary to give Ruth a gift of grain on the spot? Was this some sort of belated recognition of his long overlooked responsibility to Naomi (see verse 17, quoted below) or an engagement gift? Couldn't it have waited until later in the day when he had settled matters, not to mention avoiding turning Ruth into a beast of burden?[26] I think that the

---

[24]See Chapter 3, note 6.

[25]Reading with Syr. and numerous Hebrew manuscripts. MT reads "Then he went into the city."

[26]While the text does not tell us what measure of grain was used (this omission of the unit of measurement is common in Ancient Near Eastern texts; the context made the unit self-evident to the locals), the most reasonable assumption is that the *seah* (one third of an *ephah*—see Chapter 3, note 35) was meant. Six *seahs* would come to something close to sixty lbs.—manageable for a farm girl but hardly easy.

grain gift was as much to substantiate a cover story as anything else. Women routinely rose before dawn to begin the daily chores. A woman entering the city at dawn or just after with a heavy bundle on her head would occasion no comment. That's what women did at that time of day in that era.

Note also that the text insists that Ruth did not lie down beside Boaz but rather returned to her former position at his feet. Both Ruth and Boaz are very respectable people; they continue to observe the proprieties.[27]

> Now when she came to her mother-in-law, she [Naomi] said: "How do things stand with you, my daughter?"[28] And she told her everything the man had done for her. And she added[29]: "He gave me these six measures of barley, because he said to me[30]: 'You must not go back empty-handed to your mother-in-law.'" She [Naomi] said: "Sit still, my daughter, till you know how the matter will fall out. For the man will not rest, but will finish the matter today" (3:16–18).

Boaz's remark, as reported by Ruth to Naomi, is significant. The word *reikam*, which we have rendered as "empty-handed," is the same word used by Naomi in her bitter complaint to the women of Bethlehem:

> "the Almighty has dealt very bitterly with me! I went out full and the Lord brought me back *empty*" (1:21).

Her words, repeated around town and remembered by Boaz (was her loud-mouthed bitterness a reason for his having kept his distance?)[31] now prompt him to send what amounts to a belated apology via Ruth. This is what he should have done on that first day. Ruth has not only prompted Boaz to assume his responsibilities to her, but to his prospective mother-in-law as well.[32]

Naomi's counsel to Ruth echoes that of Boaz: he told her to rest easy, he will take care of things tomorrow (3:13). Now Naomi instructs Ruth to sit tight. She knows Boaz: when he takes matters in hand, things get done. One way or the other it will all be settled by nightfall.

---

[27]There has been speculation, even much fantasizing, on the part of some commentators that Ruth and Boaz consummated their "engagement" on the spot. Not only is there no hint of such a development, but also the text goes out of its way to deny any such "goings on." The author deftly pulls the plug on the suspense that has been building up (see note 10 above). When Boaz tells Ruth to *remain* (here) *this night* (3:13) he uses the verb *lalun* (literally "to lodge"), a term that unlike *lishkav* ("lie down") is totally devoid of sexual connotations. Then the text reinforces the propriety of their relationship by its insistence that "she lay *at his feet* till morning" (3:14).

[28]Literally, "Who are you, my daughter?" The translation renders the intent of the question.

[29]Literally, "said."

[30]Reading with the *Qeri* (the vowelated text).

[31]It is worth noting that nowhere in the story does the author depict Naomi and Boaz as meeting! In a small town like Bethlehem this could scarcely be coincidental. Were they purposely avoiding each other, or is this apparent non-contact an artifact of the author's extreme contraction of the narrative, narrowing the focus to the development of the Ruth-Boaz relationship?

[32]When Naomi complained about her "emptiness" she was referring not only to destitution, but also to loss of children and grandchildren; there was no one to carry on the family name. Rectifying this second "emptiness" is to be the burden of the next chapter.

CHAPTER 5

At Bethlehem's Gate

If you can look into the seeds of time,
And say which grain will grow and which will not...
— William Shakespeare, *Macbeth, I*

Boaz justifies his reputation; the sun is not high in the sky and he has already made his appearance in the city gate, the commercial and civic center of Bethlehem.[1]

> Now Boaz went up to the city gate and sat down there; and behold, the Redeemer of whom Boaz had spoken was passing by. So he [Boaz] said: "You, Mr. So-and-so, turn aside and sit down here!"[2] So he turned aside and sat down. Then he [Boaz] took ten men of the city's elders and said to them: "Sit down here." So they sat down (4:1–2).

Numerous city gates of the early Israelite period have been excavated. They all show that provisions had been made for seating, both within the gate complex and outside, in the immediate vicinity of the plaza, either by building benches into the tower walls, or by providing stone benches right next to them. Boaz, arriving in the early morning direct from the threshing floor, seats himself on one of these benches. No sooner is he seated than he observes his relative, the Redeemer he had mentioned to Ruth, passing by (probably leaving the city to go to his field). Hailing him, Boaz peremptorily demands of him that he seat himself. Note his curtness. Boaz does not deem a "please" at all necessary. It is not so much a request as a command, reflecting perhaps a significant difference in social status.[3] Without a word the man seats himself.[4] Boaz then selects from the onlookers and passers-by ten of the elders of the city (a quorum?) and bids them take their places. Boaz is convening a court. Once they are seated the business can commence. Boaz has not only determined that whatever is to take place between him and the Redeemer, who has priority over him, will be fully public, but has also arranged that a court will witness whatever conclusions the two reach, and will formally ratify them. Nothing will later be deniable.

---

[1]The gate to a walled city was a strongly fortified complex flanked by towers, which served as the sole entry and exit point for a town such as Bethlehem. Unlike the town layout of Greek cities, Ancient Near East towns did not contain an *agora*. Instead, civic affairs were conducted in the gate complex and the adjacent plaza. It was here that courts were convened to adjudicate criminal and civil cases, to ratify contracts and settlements, etc.

[2]Literally, "Turn aside and sit down here, So-and-so." Boaz's relative, the Redeemer, obviously had a name and Boaz would address him by name in a public setting. The question of why the author deliberately suppresses his name and substitutes the anonymous designation *ploni almoni* (Mr. So-and-so) will be discussed later in the chapter.

[3]But then again Boaz was far more courteous in greeting his own workers (2:4). Perhaps something more than social distance underlay the brusque form of his speech.

61

Having set the scene, Boaz proceeds directly to business.

> Then he said to the Redeemer: "The portion of the field that belonged to our brother, Elimelech, was sold by Naomi, she who has returned from the land of Moab. Now I thought[5] that I will lay it open to you,[6] saying: 'Buy it in the presence of those sitting here, and in the presence of the elders of my people.' If you will redeem it, redeem it; but if you will not redeem it, tell me, that I may know; for there is no one else to redeem it but you, and I come after you." And he said: "I will redeem it" (4:3–4).

Wait a minute, what is going on? Boaz promised to settle the matter of Ruth, yet here he is raising an altogether different issue to the strangely unnamed Redeemer — that of the landed property sold by Elimelech prior to his departure for Moab over twelve years ago.[7] Against all custom, this land has been alienated from the wider family, the clan, for an unconscionable amount of time. Naomi's return to Bethlehem in a condition of destitution, Boaz implies, should remind people of their responsibilities. Now all this is true, but what has this got to do with Ruth?

We have discussed in Chapter 1 the fact that entailed estates could not be permanently alienated from their owners; that in effect all sales were no more than open-ended leases giving the purchaser the use of the land. These "purchases" could be revoked at any time on the part of the original owner by the act of Redemption — the repurchase of the land. Should the owner prove unable to redeem the land, the responsibility then devolved upon close relatives. At all events, it was deemed imperative that the land be returned to the possession of the family.[8] Elimelech being dead, it is up to his kin; his closest blood relative being the unnamed Mr. So-and-so.

Boaz is now publicly putting him on the spot: "Remember that parcel of land that Elimelech sold years ago?[9] This matter has been drawn out too long. This year's harvest is over and next year's planting is due. This is the time to end this anomalous situation. Let's get it back into the family. You are Elimelech's closest living relative; you should buy it back. If you are willing — do it. If not, then tell me, for I am next in line and will have to take up the responsibility. But one way or the other we can't leave this matter hanging."[10]

The answer Boaz receives is short and to the point: "I will redeem it."

> Then Boaz said: "Now on the day you acquire the property from Naomi's hand you[11] [must] also acquire Ruth,[12] the Moabitess, the wife of the deceased, to raise up the name of the dead upon his

---

[4]Vul., on the other hand, has the relative replying something like: "What do you want of me?"

[5]Literally, "I said."

[6]Literally, "unstop your ears," that is "reveal."

[7]The fact that Boaz refers to Elimelech as "our brother" does not mean that he, Elimelech and the unnamed *Redeemer* were all three sons of the same father. The term "brother" is often used in the Bible to refer to a kinsman. It is the fact that they both are related to the late Elimelech that Boaz is stressing, and therefore they bear the responsibilities that devolve upon blood relatives.

[8]See Chapter 1: "The Three Faces of the Redeemer."

[9]Why Boaz refers to Naomi as having made the sale will be discussed later. Suffice it here to say that if the land belonged to Elimelech, as Boaz states, only he had the legal right to sell it.

[10]The question of exactly who holds title at this time to the land under discussion, and under what conditions, is a tangled one beset with numerous uncertainties. It is, however, a side issue that does not affect our understanding either of the Book's plot or of its deeper meaning. The background on land ownership in biblical times, and on the responsibility to redeem family land, issues crucial to understanding the story line of the Book, have been dealt with in Chapter 1. Those interested in the side issue of what happened to Elimelech's property can turn to Appendix I: From Whom Did Boaz Buy the Field?

[11]Reading with Qeri. The consonantal text (Ketib) reads "I acquire."

[12]Reading with Syr., LXX, and Vul. MT reads "from the hand of Naomi and from Ruth."

inheritance." The Redeemer replied[13]: "I cannot redeem it for myself, lest I impair my own inheritance; you take my right of Redemption upon yourself for I cannot redeem [it]" (4:5–6).

"Wonderful," Boaz says, "all credit to you for your good intention. But remember, if you are going to take on the responsibility of the Redemption, if you are going to be the Redeemer for the family, you have a second responsibility — that of Ruth, the widow of Mahlon, Elimelech's son. When you redeem the land you also have to redeem Ruth, that is, marry her." And here Boaz not only drives the knife home but twists it as well: "You have to marry Ruth for the express purpose of producing an heir to Machlon,[14] so that Elimelech's family line can continue to own the family estate." That is the clear meaning of the phrase "to raise up the name of the dead upon his inheritance." And with these words the trap that Boaz has so ingeniously engineered closes in on his relative.

Let us understand the dead end into which Boaz has maneuvered Mr. So-and-so. The relative obviously has a family — family-less bachelors were virtually non-existent in Ancient Israel. And with a family goes the responsibility to provide for their future. The proposition that Boaz first puts to his relative is simple: buy back Elimelech's field. Mr. So-and-so apparently has the cash to swing the deal. He may be laying out almost all his life's savings but he will be getting a valuable field in return. Being Elimelech's closest living relative, he is Elimelech's heir. The field will be his in perpetuity. Instead of his children inheriting his money they will inherit the field that will now be his. Neither he nor they will be the losers. Understanding this perfectly, he has no hesitation in agreeing to the proposal: "I will redeem it."

Once committed, Boaz now throws him a fast curve. "One moment; if you take upon yourself the role of the family Redeemer you must go all the way. There is another piece of unfinished business." Up to now Boaz has been harping on Naomi.[15] Ruth has been conveniently forgotten. Now Boaz reminds all present that the issue is not Elimelech and Naomi, but their deceased sons, Machlon and Chilion. Machlon has left a childless widow, young and probably capable of bearing a son. And the son will be Machlon's heir, the legal owner of the field. This puts a very different complexion on the matter. Mr. So-and-so is now being put into a position where he will have to put out his money to buy a field, and also to father a son that will inherit that field. He will be left with neither money nor field to pass on to his children.[16] No wonder he speaks of "impairing his own inheritance." Boaz, having maneuvered him into this impossible situation, is leaving him no choice: he retracts his acceptance and passes on his Redeemer's rights to Boaz who is next in line, which is exactly what Boaz has been aiming for.[17]

[13]Literally "said."

[14]The child of Ruth and the Redeemer would be the legal heir of Machlon, and thus the inheritor of the family property. See discussion in Chapter 1.

[15]If Mr. So-and-so had even given a thought to the issue of his responsibility to raise an heir to Elimelech, the focus on Naomi would have caused him to dismiss it from his mind. Naomi is an old woman, well past childbearing age. No union with her could produce an heir, so marriage was out of the question.

[16]It is obvious that no piddling sum is involved if spending it will largely wipe out the inheritance of Mr. So-and-so's sons. As the price of a field was determined by how many harvests remained to be reaped before the Jubilee Year, which would cause the property to revert to its original owner (see Chapter 1, especially note 22), the price would decline the closer one got to the Jubilee. The significant outlay required to redeem the field indicates that the Jubilee was still far in the future.

[17]Why doesn't the same bind apply to Boaz? The simplest answer is that Boaz is rich. He can easily afford the price of the land and has plenty left over to provide handsomely for any children he may have. But further, his fulfilling a family duty to the deceased Machlon is strictly pro forma. His real purpose is to marry Ruth; he will consider her children as his own (and legally adopt them), joining Elimelech's line to his own. We will see the results of this approach when we get to the end of the Book.

Now all that remains is to effect the legal transfer of Redeemer rights and obligations from Mr. So-and-so to Boaz.

> [Now in former times in Israel this was the way to ratify all matters of Redemption or exchange[18]: a man would remove his shoe[19] and hand it to the other. This was the practice of attestation in Israel.] So the Redeemer said to Boaz: "Buy it yourself," and he removed his shoe[20] (4:7–8).

At this point in the narrative the author feels the necessity to intrude an editorial comment. Back in the pre-monarchial era, before the age when legal matters were routinely ratified by means of signing and witnessing a legal document,[21] the method that began to become normative from the latter part of the Davidic regime, it was customary for the participants to close a transaction by performing a symbolic act in the presence of witnesses. For example, in ancient Nuzi it was customary to validate a transfer of land by the previous owner removing his foot from the property in question and placing the foot of the new owner on it. To make matters clear to readers a century or more removed from the events, the author tells us that in the age of the Judges the practice in Israel was for the party transferring property or rights to take off his shoe and hand it to the receiving party in the presence of witnesses.[22]

After this note of explanation the author resumes the narrative: the Redeemer takes off his shoe and hands it to Boaz with the words "Buy it yourself." The man with the right of first refusal has refused.[23]

> Then Boaz said to the elders and to all the people: "You are witnesses this day that I have acquired from Naomi everything that belonged to Elimelech and everything that belonged to Chilion and to Mahlon. And moreover, I have acquired Ruth the Moabitess, wife of Mahlon, as my wife, to raise up the name of the dead upon his inheritance, that the name of the dead not be cut off from among his brethren, and from the gate of his place[24]; you are witnesses this day." And all the people who were in the gate, and the elders, said: "We are witnesses! May the Lord grant that the woman that is coming to your house be like Rachel and like Leah, the two of

[18]Literally, "concerning Redemption and concerning exchange, to ratify anything."

[19]The term "shoe" means any foot covering: Ancient Near Eastern pictures show sandals, low boots and even shoes with upturned pointed toes.

[20]LXX adds "and gave [it] to him."

[21]Several centuries later, in the only other example we have of Redemption of land in the Bible, the Redemption will be ratified by the witnessing of a formal written contract (in two copies). See Jeremiah 32.

[22]Many scholars have contended that this aside, in which the author feels the need to insert an explanation of how things were done "in former times," implies the passage of many centuries in which the custom in question has died out and been forgotten. This argument, however, is seriously flawed. E.F. Campbell has pointed out that the phrase "in former times" is not an uncommon one in the Bible, and often refers to the passage of no more than a generation, sometimes even less (Campbell, *Ruth*, p. 148). M. Weinfeld summarizes, and then effectively rebuts the scholars' contention:

> It seems that the author of the book lived in a time when business transactions like these were already subject to written obligations (cf., e.g., Jeremiah 32:11ff.) and therefore he found it necessary to explain to his generation that in those days the "taking off the sandal," and not the written document, validated the transaction. However, this change in the judicial-legislative reality does not necessarily imply a very big gap in time between the event and its description. The establishment of the monarchy itself caused a great turning point in the economic-social life and even a few decades would be enough to create this transition in the judicial sphere (Weinfeld, "The Book of Ruth," p. 521).

[23]And now perhaps we can explain the anomaly that in a book abounding in names (92 names in 81 verses, that is, an average of more than one name per verse), one of the key players, Mr. So-and-so, is conspicuously not named. "Why did the text deliberately refer to him as the 'anonymous' one? He who did not wish to 'raise up' the 'name' of the dead did not deserve to have his *name* remembered" (Porten, "The Scroll of Ruth," p. 44).

[24]That is, the gate of his town, Bethlehem; thus the assembly of the citizens of the town. Note the parallel expression in 3:11.

whom built the House of Israel. May you prosper in Ephrata and be renowned in Bethlehem. And may your house become like the House of Perez, whom Tamar bore to Judah, from the seed which the Lord shall give to you from this young woman" (4:9–12).

What Boaz has acquired is the *right* to be the Redeemer, and it is this transfer of rights of Redemption, that the court witnesses and ratifies. So far no redeeming has taken place. No money has changed hands. Ruth has not been married. In fact neither Ruth nor the current owner of the land, whomever he or she may be, are present. Boaz, now having the rights and responsibilities of Redeemer transferred to him, simply pledges to fulfill his responsibilities, and the court and the onlookers take him at his word.

With regard to Ruth, we will shortly be informed that he does marry her. While we are not told so (the issue of the land being tangential to the main thrust of the story, no more than a ploy used by Boaz to attain his objective — Ruth), we can safely assume that he also follows through by repurchasing the portion of the field that had belonged to Elimelech.

The congratulatory pronouncement made by the elders and the onlookers is instructive. Like the author, they ignore the issue of the land and focus on the real issue: Ruth. Their expectations are lavish: she is compared to Rachel and Leah, the matriarchs who gave birth to the progenitors of nine of the tribes of Israel. They also liken her to Tamar, mother of Perez, the father of some of the most illustrious families in Judah, the lines of Elimelech and Boaz among others.[25] There is a link between these illustrious women: none of them was a native Israelite. From pagan backgrounds, they all came to the people and the faith of Israel through marriage. It is no accident that the people propose these women as the ideal prototypes for Ruth. What they are implying is that Ruth's foreign background will be no hindrance to her achieving status and honor in Israel. It is not where you came from, but what you make of yourself that is the determining factor in how you are remembered. If Boaz's statement, "For all the gate of my people know that you are a woman of worth" (3:11), is more than an expression of his personal opinion, the reputation that Ruth has earned by her behavior during the roughly two months of her sojourn in Bethlehem has laid the foundation of the high hopes for her future. These hopes will not be disappointed.

Fulfillment

So Boaz took Ruth, and she became his wife. And he came in to her, and the Lord gave her conception and she bore a son. Then the women said to Naomi: "Blessed be the Lord Who has not left you without a Redeemer this day; may his name be famous in Israel! He shall be to you a restorer of life, and a nourisher of your old age. For your daughter-in-law who loves you, who is better to you than seven sons, has born him." So Naomi took the child and held him to her bosom, and she became his foster-mother (4:13–16).[26]

The obstacles removed to the resolution of the crisis in the lives of Ruth and Naomi, the author now rushes to wrap up the loose ends and arrive at the dramatic conclusion of the tale. Once again Boaz proves as good as his word. In quick order we are told that Boaz marries Ruth, and that she becomes pregnant and bears a son.[27]

---

[25]There is a further implication to the mention of Tamar in the context of Ruth. Perez was the result of a *Redemption* union with Judah. And just as Ruth has "not gone after the young men, whether rich or poor" (3:10) but has focused her efforts to secure her future security and happiness on a path that simultaneously will secure the preservation of the family line of Elimelech and Machlon, so was Tamar notable in her daring efforts to insure the preservation of the family line of Judah and his son Er. See Chapter 7.

[26]Literally "nurse" (in the sense of care-taker, not that she nursed him).

[27]The significance of the phrase "the Lord gave her conception" will be discussed in Chapter 6.

The women of Bethlehem, serving as a chorus to highlight the significance of the events, once again make their appearance.[28] As they greeted with shock and dismay Naomi's disastrous return to Bethlehem, so now they underline her fulfillment as they voice their delight on the birth of Ruth's child. In her grandson Naomi now has an immediate male kinsman who will act as her Redeemer, not only in a legal sense but in the larger scheme of things: he has redeemed her life from meaninglessness; his birth has rejuvenated her, and he will be there to care for her and insure her well-being in old age. She will no longer be alone. So Naomi signals her new lease on life by formally assuming the role of foster-mother to the child.

> And the neighborhood women gave him a name, saying: "A son is born to Naomi." And they named him Obed[29] (4:17a).

Highlighting the theme that, with the birth of a grandson, the line of Elimelech continues (remember, legally the child is the son and heir of Mahlon), Naomi not only assumes the role of foster-mother but the women proclaim him Elimelech's heir. And then, in a strange departure from normal practice, they bestow upon him the name Obed.[30] Conventionally, throughout the Bible, it is the parents who name a newborn child; most commonly it is the privilege of the mother, more rarely the task devolves onto the father. There are only two exceptions to this rule: in the case of Tamar, when it is the midwife who names the newborn child Perez,[31] and in our present case when it falls to the women of the neighborhood to bestow the name. These are also the only cases of Redemption Marriage recorded in the Bible. Perhaps in cases such as these, due to the unique status of the child, the community through its representatives preempts the prerogatives of the biological parents.

And now comes the big surprise, saved by the author to the very end of the tale. Who is Obed? What will be his role in the larger scheme of things? He will prove to be none other than the grandfather of David.

> And they named him Obed; he is the father of Jesse, the father of David! (4:17).

With these words the tight focus of the Book dissolves, the horizon widens, and we first realize that what has seemed up to now a private story of two women and their struggle to overcome harsh personal circumstances, a tale of character and personal fulfillment, is in truth a saga pregnant with destiny. Here Naomi and Ruth, all unknown to them, have been planting the seeds that, three generations hence, will sprout in the life of David, psalmist and king, and from him the destiny of his descendants. In the fate of Naomi and Ruth, and the fulfillment of their lives, is bound up the future of Israel and the spiritual future of mankind.

With this shocking dénouement the Book concludes. To this the author adds an appendix.[32] Balancing the introduction to the Book in which the antecedents to our narrow tale are

---

[28]This chorus of women that opens and closes the "Bethlehem" part of the story is more than simply a literary device but rather, like "the elders," an existing social institution pressed into service by the author to pass judgment on the outcome of events. The chorus of "elders" gives us the men's point of view; the "neighborhood women" the woman's viewpoint. Carol Meyers convincingly argues that the women of every village and town formed closely knit informal networks that dominated many aspects of life in Ancient Israel and were responsible for giving the clan much of its cohesiveness (Meyers, "Women of the Neighborhood," esp. pp. 116–124.)

[29]Literally, "and they called his name Obed."

[30]The name means "he who serves," and is probably a contraction of Obadiah: "the servant of the Lord."

[31]Genesis 38:29–30. Later in this book we will analyze in detail the story of Judah and Tamar. See Chapter 7.

[32]Against the views of perhaps the majority of scholars who hold that the Genealogy is not original to Ruth but was artificially tacked onto the Book at a late date, Moshe Weinfeld argues strongly, and in my opinion conclusively, that "there is no justification for the view that the genealogy does not form an integral part of the book and that it is a post–Exilic addition to the book" (Weinfeld, "The Book of Ruth," p. 519).

enumerated — Elimelech and his sons — and in which our protagonists, Naomi and Ruth are introduced, the author now puts them into the larger picture with the genealogy of the House of David.[33] Beginning with Tamar's son, Perez, the family line is brought, through Boaz,[34] to its climactic conclusion, David.

> Now these are the generations of Perez[35]: Perez was the father of Hezron[36]; and Hezron was the father of Ram, and Ram was the father of Amminadab; and Amminadab was the father of Salmon[37]; and Salmon was the father of Boaz, and Boaz was the father of Obed; and Obed was the father of Jesse, and Jesse was the father of David (4:18–22).

[33]K.A. Kitchen, in his analysis of biblical genealogies, points out that "it is clear that the Davidic line is much abbreviated before Boaz." The genealogy contains eleven generations between Perez and David (or, if we include Judah, the father of Perez, twelve generations), and this to cover a *minimum* of 730 years! This means that between Perez and Boaz the list has been telescoped by at least twelve generations. This abbreviation may have been due to data being lost in transmission; on the other hand it may have been due to a wish to keep a tight focus and prevent boredom caused by an overlong list of names. This was normal: beginnings and the endings of long genealogical lists were recorded exactly while the middle was tightened up. Kitchen quotes parallels from both Mesopotamia and Egypt to show that this was common practice in the Ancient Near East. "Thus, on all sides, the Hebrew usages were normal, in their world" (Kitchen, *On the Reliability of the Old Testament*, pp. 357–358. See also pp. 307–310).

[34]Note that the genealogy traces the line of David back through Boaz, and not through Machlon. Boaz is more than the biological father; he is also the adoptive father of Obed. Adoption was a well-attested practice in the Ancient Near East, and was practiced in Israel.

[35]In the sense of the descendants of Perez, his genealogical line.

[36]Literally, "Perez begot Hezron," that is, "caused him to be born."

[37]MT reads here *Salmah*, a variant form of the name.

CHAPTER 6

What Means This Tale?

Verily You are a God that hides Yourself,
O God of Israel, the Savior!
— Isaiah 45:15

A charming little story with beautifully delineated characters, a dramatic plot grounded in the complexities of an ancient legal system, and a happy ending; is that all there is to the Book of Ruth? That many people take it as such — Louise P. Smith begins her introduction to the Book by pointing out that "The old rhetorics were fond of citing the book of Ruth as a perfect example of simple narrative,"[1] G.A. Cooke refers to it as "a guileless piece of literature,"[2] while no less a literary icon than Johann Wolfgang von Goethe considered it the loveliest little epic and idyllic whole which has come down to us[3] — this should not deter us from wondering why, if so, the Book was ever included in the Bible. It is important that we not be blinded by the brilliance of the writer's literary technique, nor distracted by all the social and legal nuances of the narrative. It is far too easy to get sidetracked and lose focus on what is really important: namely, the central message of the book.

While it is true that many of the Books of the Bible are "high literature," the Bible is no mere literary anthology come down to us from ancient times. The Books that make up what we now know as the Bible were chosen not so much for stylistic success as for content: to convey messages regarding the purpose of life, the nature of humanity's relationship with God, and what our relationships with each other should be. In a word, the Books were chosen for their religious content. This being so, it becomes imperative in summing up this little Book to get behind the surface of the admittedly charming and beautifully written tale in order to grasp its inner meaning and purpose.

The Moral Lessons of Ruth

On the simplest level, this is a story of two women whose lives went disastrously wrong. It relates how, instead of being broken by the blows that befell them, they rallied and were able to turn their lives around. It is thus a chronicle of character: of how the human spirit is able to rise above the force of circumstance and make a new life out of the ruins of an old one. On this

[1]Smith, "The Book of Ruth," p. 829.
[2]Cooke, *Ruth*, p. xiii.
[3]Quoted by Slotki, "Ruth: Introduction," p. 36.

level, the Book is about courage, determination, optimism, and refusing to be defeated — character traits that enable one to turn defeat into victory, and to use the social circumstances in which one finds oneself, whatever they may be, as tools to better one's life. As such, these two women, Naomi and Ruth, are presented as examples on which one can model oneself.

This is also a book about caring. One of the key terms in the Book is *hesed*. This is a term extraordinarily difficult to translate. It refers to the manifestation of the qualities of goodness, kindness, and loyalty, above and beyond the call of duty. It is this attribute that, more than any other, typifies both Naomi and Ruth.[4]

Ruth cared for her late husband, Mahlon. Ruth cares for Naomi; she won't cut her losses and make a new life for herself, but rather insists on standing by her destitute mother-in-law. Naomi, for her part, cares for Ruth. She doesn't want to drag her down with her but counsels her to go back and live her own life. It is Ruth's insistence that forces her to accept her caring presence. She then acts to end the suspended animation of widowhood to which Ruth has confined herself, and arranges for her marriage. The Book is about how loving concern, kindness, and loyalty can bring about rejuvenation and redemption.

The Book is also about human choice, about our power to cross accepted boundaries, adopt new ways and to transform our lives. Ruth does more than cross a border and settle in a new land. Out of her love and concern for her mother-in-law Ruth adopts a strange people and their destiny as her own, and commits herself to a new faith and a new God. In a conscious act of will and commitment, she cuts her ties to her pagan past and becomes one of the covenanted people of God: one of the Children of Israel. What we are being told is that we hold our destinies — spiritual as well as physical — in our hands. We are not the playthings of fate.

The Book of Ruth as we have presented it thus far is a work about human life under stress that extols the virtues of courage in the face of adversity, loving care for others and our ability to break with our pasts and mold our futures; a humanistic gem whose purpose is to edify and instruct us in the conduct of our lives. And this is true as far as it goes. But the very humanistic stance that we have to this point been describing should give us pause, for if it is all that the Book has to say, Ruth would stand out in the Bible as an anomaly. And indeed so it is. Among the early Books of the Bible — that is, the Books whose narratives relate to happenings in the first centuries of the Biblical Era — Ruth can be categorized as an essentially secular work.

But is secular an appropriate description? How can a Book in which, as we have seen, God is mentioned on the average of once every four sentences be, by any stretch of the imagination, thought of as secular? But this is exactly the point: God is *mentioned*, He is on everyone's lips in this little work, but He is nowhere *present*. In the entire narrative God never *speaks* and He never *acts*. It is only human beings who speak and act.[5] This is a phenomenon so unusual in the early biblical texts that it needs to be investigated.

---

[4]*Hesed* is, first and foremost, a way that God manifests Himself to mankind. His care for humanity shows itself through His *hesed*, His loving kindness, giving people far more than they deserve. But human beings can manifest *hesed* through acts of unconditional kindness, love and loyalty to others far in excess of the normal, or what the other deserves based on his or her own behavior. In so doing they are reflecting God's grace. The Rabbinic sages, basing themselves on the principle of *Imitatio Dei*, made of this a central injunction: "As God is gracious and kind, so shall you be gracious and kind."

[5]Only twice in the narrative can the author be thought of as attributing an event to the direct intervention of God, and in both cases the comments are ambiguous in that they can be equally read as no more than clichés, conventional phrases typical of the period. They are: "for she [Naomi] had heard in the Land of Moab that the Lord had remembered His people and given them food" (1:6) and "the Lord gave her [Ruth] conception and she bore a son" (4:13). We will return to these two oblique remarks later in this analysis. For the present it is enough to realize that by the use of these phrases the author has not committed us to viewing God as an active participant in the story.

The Missing God

As we have already pointed out in the Introduction, the narrative Books of the Bible present a unified picture of the history of the world: it is the story of God's creation of the universe and of humanity, and of His ongoing relationship with His creatures. In other words it is His story. It is God Who acts, Who speaks, Who initiates and determines what takes place.[6] This is the dominant theme that creates a unity out of the thirty-nine diverse Books that make up the Hebrew Bible.

It is against this background that we must evaluate the Book of Ruth. Set in the age of the Judges, in the midst of this mighty epic, Ruth stands out starkly. In Ruth God *does not* set the agenda, He *does not* tell people what to do; God is silent. He does not once appear on stage. Elimelech, his sons, Naomi, Ruth, and Boaz all do what they do and act as they act on the basis of their own characters and motivations. Why, in the midst of a plethora of biblical narratives in which God is the central figure, do we find a Book in which He is so conspicuously absent?

But although God is absent from center stage, in the final words of the story we suddenly realize that the tale is much more than a "happy-ending" playlet featuring Naomi, Ruth and Boaz. The perspective shifts in the last few verses, and we grasp for the first time that what we have been reading is an account of the origins of David and his dynasty, and thus an episode in the epic saga of Israel's destiny. All unknown to them, and while thinking themselves the main actors in a family theatrical, Ruth, Naomi, and Boaz have been playing bit-parts in a vast drama that began centuries before their day, and that will continue into distant ages yet to come. And while God has not been on stage in this particular scene, He is the Director of the entire epic, and every part of the action in this mini-plot has been stage-managed by Him.

That this is indeed the intended understanding of the Book of Ruth is hinted at several times in the course of the narrative. We have already remarked on two clichés that seem to have been dropped nonchalantly by the author. It is time we examine them more closely, for they are the two instances in which the author departs, however ambiguously and provisionally, from the resolutely secular and humanistic stance maintained until the very end of the Book. In each case it is important that we bear in mind that there was no compelling reason for the author to use the particular phrasing that she does; the author could just as well have refrained from mentioning God while conveying the same surface meaning.

The first of these appears near the beginning of the Book, in the reason given for Naomi's decision to return home:

> for she [Naomi] had heard in the Land of Moab that the Lord had remembered His people and given them food (1:6).[7]

This refers back to the first verse of the Book of Ruth:

> Now it came to pass, in the days when the Judges ruled, that there was a famine in the land (1:1).

As we have already noted, famine was usually the result of drought — the lack of sufficient rain to adequately water the crops. Drought and the famine were, in the biblical world, con-

---

[6]Our focus is on the narrative portions of the Bible, but it would be well to note that those parts of the Bible written in poetry (i.e., most of the Books of the Prophets, the Psalms, etc.) reflect the same point of view.

[7]This could just as easily been phrased "for she had heard in the Land of Moab that the famine in the Land of Judah had ended" without loss of meaning.

sidered to be divine visitations.[8] Thus the very opening of the Book, in its setting the conditions within which the plot commences, would have unmistakably implied to readers of the Biblical Era that it is God Who has set the stage for what is to come.[9] The seemingly throwaway phrase, five verses later, "that the Lord had remembered His people and given them food" is simply a reminder, reinforcing the initial suggestion that the overall framework within which the human tale unfolds has been set by God. While God may not have made an appearance on stage — the author has not told us that it was God who told Elimelech to go to Moab, or that it was He Who was responsible for his death and the deaths of his two sons, or what God's attitude was to the decision of Mahlon and Chilion to marry pagan women — despite His silence and His non-appearance He is very much present behind the scenes.

Having set the scene, as it were, at the Book's opening, the author returns with an even broader hint near the close of Ruth, preparing us for the dramatic surprise ending. The author informs us

And he [Boaz] came in to her, and the Lord gave her [Ruth] conception and she bore a son[10] (4:13).

The phrasing is conventional: it was common in biblical narrative to ascribe conception or its lack to the will of God. The phrase deserves notice only because it is so out of keeping with the style and general tenor of the Book. That is why I do not think its use here is simply conventional but rather purposive. We must keep in mind what we learn from the surprise ending of the Book: that in the larger picture the entire purpose of the Naomi-Ruth-Boaz story is to produce Obed, the grandfather of David. Without Obed there will be no David. And the birth of Obed is no guaranteed event. Ruth was married for ten years and never became pregnant. Boaz is an older man; possibly old enough to be her father. The outcome does not seem particularly promising. What may be hinted here is that in the normal course of events she might have remained childless; it needed the direct intervention of God to jump-start her system so that Obed could be conceived and born.

There is a pattern emerging here. The first hint that God, by creating a famine, is the real initiator of the chain of events that plays out in the story of Naomi and Ruth (1:1), is underlined shortly thereafter by the comment that it is God Who has ended the famine by giving His people food (1:6). This pattern is now repeated. Once again the intimation that only through God's direct intervention is Ruth able to conceive (4:13), is immediately reinforced by the chorus of the women of Bethlehem who ascribe the happy outcome of events to God:

---

[8]One of the more explicit statements of this unquestioned belief of the Biblical Era can be found in the following:

Take heed lest your heart be deceived, and you turn aside and serve other gods and worship them; and the anger of the Lord be kindled against you, and He shut up the heavens and there be no rain, and the earth shall yield no fruit, and you shall speedily perish from off the good earth which the Lord is giving you (Deuteronomy 11:16–17).

[9]Indeed the very opening statement that places the Book chronologically "in the days when the Judges ruled" firmly fixes the setting of the plot in the midst of the well-known meta-history of mainstream biblical narrative, where God dominates the action and determines both events and outcomes. These nuances would not have been lost on the audience of the Biblical Age.

[10]Once again there was no need to *insist* that God was directly involved in her becoming pregnant. The matter could have been stated in a more neutral fashion, such as the report of the birth of Moses: "Now there went a man of the house of Levi, and took [to wife] a daughter of Levi. And the woman conceived and bore a son" (Exodus 2:1–2).

Then the women said to Naomi: "Blessed be the Lord Who has not left you without a Redeemer this day; may his name be famous in Israel" (4:14).[11]

The women's chorus here seems to be performing the same function that it has in a Greek drama: to comment on the action and to reveal its significance. As such it is expressing the view of the author that God is the true cause of everything that has happened. This, in turn, becomes the prologue to the surprise ending of the Book:

And the neighborhood women gave him a name, saying: "A son is born to Naomi." They named him Obed; he is the father of Jesse, the father of David! (4:17).

The Dramatist and His Purpose stand revealed at last.

The picture that emerges from all this is of a world in which God is not overtly present but rather covertly present. He does not have a "speaking role" in the drama but rather hides behind the scenes, directing the action from off stage, pulling the strings as it were and directly intervening, if at all, only when it is absolutely unavoidable. He is not the God Who is so familiar to us in most biblical narrative: the God Who Acts. He is the Hidden God.

The Hidden God

For us who live in the early years of the twenty-first century, Ruth is a Book that is easy to appreciate. Once we get past the social customs and legal practices of an ancient society we find much that is familiar. Unlike the Patriarch Abraham or the Prophet Moses, figures remote from us, who live in the constant and terrifying presence of God, called by Him to tasks of fearsome scope, the personages who people the Book of Ruth seem startlingly commonplace. With little effort we can grasp the plot, understand what is motivating the main characters and empathize with their concerns. We take to Naomi, Ruth and Boaz because their approach to life is essentially humanistic, and thus thoroughly comprehensible.

But was not the Biblical Age an age of faith? In a sense it was. Most people believed in God; that is, they accepted the existence of God and His wondrous works in the same way as they (and we) take for granted that each morning the sun will rise in the East. It was for them a fact of life.[12] More than 95% of the Israelites of those days being farmers, they participated in the yearly ceremony of bringing the first fruits of the harvest to the local shrine. There, after presenting their offerings to the presiding priest, each farmer was obligated to recite the following declaration:

"A wandering Aramean was my father,[13] and he went down into Egypt and sojourned there, few in number; and he became there a nation, great, mighty, and populous. And the Egyptians dealt ill with us, and afflicted us, and laid upon us hard bondage. And we cried unto the Lord, the God of our fathers, and the Lord heard our voice, and saw our affliction, and our toil, and our oppression. And the Lord brought us forth out of Egypt with a mighty hand, and with an outstretched arm, and with great terror, with signs and wonders. And He has brought us into this place and

---

[11]R.L. Hubbard sees the theological significance of these words thus: "the women gave Yahweh total credit for anything that had happened. In so doing, they probably voiced the author's view that Yahweh alone had brought those events about" (Hubbard, *Ruth*, p. 270). On the use of the term "Yahweh" see Introduction, note. 15.

[12]This is not to say that there were not those who questioned, or even rejected the existence of God. The Psalmist obviously had real contemporaries in mind when he wrote: "The fool says in his heart, 'There is no God'" (Psalm 53:2, in Christian Bibles 53:1). But this was written more than a century after the time of Ruth, and in an urban and cosmopolitan environment. Even there they were a very small minority.

[13]The reference is to the Patriarch Jacob.

has given us this land, a land flowing with milk and honey. And now, behold, I have brought the first fruit of the land which You, O Lord, have given me" (Deuteronomy 26:5–10).

And there is little doubt that virtually everyone believed every word they said. In those ancient times God had struck the Egyptians down with great plagues and had split the sea so that the Israelites could escape the pursuing Egyptians. He had led His people through the wilderness with a pillar of cloud by day, and a pillar of fire by night. With their own eyes their ancestors had seen it. And at the last He had brought them to the Promised Land and had given it to His people. But that was then and now is now. God still ruled His universe, and no doubt would send charismatic leaders from time to time to save His people from their enemies, but for day to day living one had to rely on one's own hard work and good sense. The days of wonders and miracles were long over.

This is the world that the Book of Ruth portrays, and we can be fairly certain that it is an accurate portrayal of how life was really lived. Naomi and Boaz bless each other in the name of God, give thanks to God when things go well, pray to God and, though we are not told, undoubtedly offer sacrifices on given occasions — everyone did. But the Book does make it clear that they neither asked for miracles nor expected any. Naomi did not wait for God to tell her what to do. With the death of her sons there was nothing to hold her in Moab, so she decided to go home.[14] Ruth, despite her act of faith in joining the people of Israel and accepting the God of Israel as her own, expects no reward from Him.[15] She will have to earn their daily bread by the sweat of her brow. Naomi plans a campaign to get Ruth an appropriate husband and Ruth implements it. Boaz expects no miracles; a hard-headed businessman, he executes a very clever legal maneuver in order to clear a potentially dangerous obstacle out of his way so that he can marry Ruth. The happy ending to the book is solely due to the efforts of the persons involved. All this we can appreciate because this is a world not all that different from ours. The world of Naomi, Boaz and Ruth is as secular as our own. The God of the days of old, the God Who told people what to do, the God Whose acts were daily visible to all, has departed from the stage.

And yet, the author is hinting from the very first words of the narrative, that this is not really the case. God merely appears to us to have vanished. Actually His hidden Hand is everywhere present; directing, arranging, moving things along to their desired conclusion — a conclusion totally unsuspected by the actors on the stage. To use a different metaphor: the actors on stage think that they are improvising both the plot and their lines as they go along. Only long after the scene has ended, and the players long departed from the stage, more than a century later we, the audience, begin to realize that the players were actually playing the roles scripted for them by the Producer of a drama whose existence they never suspected, and Who was directing every turn of the plot. God's Hand, though hidden from them, was involved in every twist and turn of events. Only with the retrospective evaluation of the chorus of the Women of Bethlehem and the surprise ending do we realize where everything has been going and why. Only from the viewpoint of more than a century later does the Hidden God emerge into the light of day.

---

[14]Though we are not told, it seems reasonable to assume that she timed her journey to arrive at the beginning of the harvest season. She knew hard times awaited her and that she could expect no manna from heaven.

[15]It is also important to note that Ruth did not convert as a result of some vision from God or some mystic experience. It was her attachment to her mother-in-law, her love and high regard for her that led her to take the drastic step of adopting Naomi's people and her God as her own.

[16]When we use the term *secular* in this context we mean a world that seems to the onlooker to be the very opposite of eternal, sacred, and spiritual, but rather temporal, worldly, and profane (*Webster's New International Dictionary of the English Language, Second Edition, Unabridged*).

The Defining Points of View

What can account for this unusual presentation of events, so out of tune with the normal run of biblical narrative? It seems to me that the author is attempting to grapple with a critical problem: in a world created by God and ruled by Him, why can't we see Him? Why is it that people do not perceive His Directing Hand in the day-to-day events of their lives, why do they live their lives as though He is, at best, remote and disinterested, or as though He does not exist? In a word, we talk about God, we pray to Him, but when we need Him He is nowhere to be found and so we have little choice but to place our reliance upon ourselves. In spite of our hopes and our dreams, and regardless of any faith that we can muster, the world we actually live in seems to our eyes irredeemably secular.[16] This, I believe, is what the Book is really about, the plot serving to illustrate the problem.

Here I think the author is propounding a startling thesis. The big surprise of the Book, the revelation that puts everything that has gone before into perspective, is written from the vantage point of a time when everyone knew who David was and why his life was so important. This means, at the earliest, the last years of his reign; more probably the first decades of the reign of his son Solomon. In other words, more than a century had to elapse from the Days of Ruth and Boaz before anyone could begin to see the larger picture, and begin to grasp the significance of the events that make up the plot of the Book of Ruth. What the author is doing is adding a new element to the analysis of why God seems to be absent from our lives: the time factor.

Albert Einstein, in his 1905 paper in which he presented his special theory of relativity, proposed that the location of the observer, his point of view, is critical to our understanding of events in the physical universe.[17] What the author seems to be proposing is something similar: where the observer is placed on the time continuum determines his or her understanding of the events observed. In this "Einsteinian" approach the significance of any series of events is determined by how close the observer is to them. Seen close up they appear in one light. Seen from the distance of a century or two they appear in an altogether different light; their significance changes radically.

This thesis is hardly novel. In a special sense it is virtually a cliché: we speak of not being able to see the forest for the trees. When one is in a forest, or right next to one, all one can see is trees. Only as one distances oneself by several dozen miles can one make out the contours of the forest as a whole. It is the same when one views a painting in a museum. Looked at from across the room one sees a harmonious whole, a vase of sunflowers on a table. Seen up close, holding one's eye three inches from the canvas, all one can see is the brushstrokes, and all one can appreciate from this point of view is the technique the artist used in applying the paint to the surface. That the same is true of one's viewpoint from a temporal point of view is also commonly appreciated.

What is novel is the author's application of this "Einsteinian" thesis to the realm of the religious. What the author is implying is that the religious point of view is synonymous with the long-term point of view. Seen close up our lives seem compounded by chance, random events. (What order and meaning we see are the patterns that our accomplishments give to them.) We are too close to things to be able to see the bigger picture. Only with the perspective of centuries do other patterns begin to emerge giving a view that we never suspected. To return to

---

[17]Another way of putting this is: "Facts seem not to have an independent objective existence, but rather are mediated in every case through an observer and are stated and known only relative to that observer" (Mills, *Space, Time, and Quanta*, p. 4).

the case in hand: from the vantage point of Naomi, Ruth, and Boaz they so managed their lives that they were able to achieve a secure and fulfilling outcome to their respective needs. Boaz found a wonderful woman to be his wife. Ruth married a fine and prosperous man, and was able to make a home and raise a family in a strange land. Naomi achieved a comfortable old age among her people, the fulfillment of a grandchild to take the place of her lost sons, and the satisfaction of knowing that the family name would not die with her — something very important to her. How could they tell that because of what they did and what they underwent, some day the tribes of Israel would be united into a centralized kingdom, that the pagan stronghold of Jebus would become the capital of this new kingdom and empire, the holy city of Jerusalem, that the psalms would be written, and that one of their descendants, Solomon, would build there a Temple to God? Only with the hindsight of centuries could this pattern become plain.

What the author seems to be saying is that the Hand of God can only be seen in the perspective of a long-term point of view. Only when one has distanced oneself by at least a century, often much more, does the Plan and Purpose of God begin to emerge from the seemingly random welter of events. In the short term God cannot be seen. And as human beings are by their very natures short-term creatures, our life-spans never long enough to enable us to see the larger pattern and purpose, we are condemned to live lives in which God seems to be absent from our world.

To summarize: the most significant message our author is trying to convey is that because of our short life-spans we are irrevocably condemned to live secular lives, lives in which we can never clearly perceive the Hand of God, lives in which we think that we are the only actors and that it is our motives and our abilities that accomplish whatever is achieved in this world of ours. It is only in retrospect, from an angle that can encompass scores of generations at a glance that God emerges into view. It all depends upon from which point on the time continuum we observe events. The secular is the outcome of the short-term view. Only from the viewpoint of centuries can we attain the religious perspective.

This suggestion that the here and now, the short term, is irredeemably secular while the long-term is the realm of the religious requires a total rethinking of the way we have traditionally viewed religion. To merit our consideration, much less our assent, this radical revision of our accepted ways of looking at things would require more than the underlying message of one lone Book. To be taken seriously a view such as this would need wide biblical support. So our question must be: is our author a lone voice in the biblical world, or is this thesis part of a more general trend, the starting point of an emerging consensus? My contention is that the thesis propounded in the Book of Ruth is not unique. It will be our aim to trace this theme elsewhere in the Bible to determine its implications for the religious life.

We now turn in our search to the story of a woman who the Book of Ruth claims as one of Ruth's spiritual prototypes; and who also figures as one of the forebears of David: Tamar.

CHAPTER 7

Tamar

With firmness in the right, as God gives us to see the right.
— Abraham Lincoln, Second
Inaugural Address, 4 March 1865

En ma fin git mon commencement.
(In my end is my beginning.)
— Mary, Queen of Scots, motto embroidered
with her mother's emblem

To reach our new subject we have to rewind the tape or, if you will, turn back the pages of the Bible almost to its beginning — Genesis Chapter 38. We are also simultaneously turning back the clock half a millennium to the last days of the Patriarchal Age.[1] The era in which we now find ourselves is very different from that with which we have just been scraping an acquaintance — the world of Ruth and Naomi. Towns recede into tents and farming to animal husbandry. The People of Israel, numerous and settled in their land, dwindle to no more than an extended family of "transhumant" herders of sheep and cattle,[2] an insignificant presence in a land not theirs.

Our tale concerns itself with one member of this extended family — Judah, fourth son of Jacob, the last of the Patriarchs.

> Now it came to pass at that time that Judah went down from his brothers and pitched his
> tent near a certain Adullamite[3] whose name was Hirah. And Judah saw there the daughter
> of a certain Canaanite whose name was Shua, and he took her [to wife], and went in to her;
> she conceived and bore a son, and she called his name Er. She conceived again and bore a

---

[1] Genesis 38 is imbedded in the grand saga of Joseph and his brothers that concludes with the last of the Patriarchs, Jacob, relocating with his family from the Promised Land to Egypt. This act brings the Patriarchal Age to a close. The Egyptologist K.A. Kitchen, dates the entry of the Israelites into Egypt around 1690/1680 BCE (Kitchen, *On the Reliability of the Old Testament*, p. 359; for the detailed analysis of the evidence on which this dating is based see pp. 318–60).

[2] The term "transhumant" refers to the type of herders of cattle and sheep that move their livestock, on a seasonal basis, up from the plains into the mountains in the spring, and then back down again to the plains in the fall.

[3] A man native to Adullam, a Canaanite walled city in the lowlands about thirteen miles southwest of Bethlehem and twelve miles northwest of Hebron.

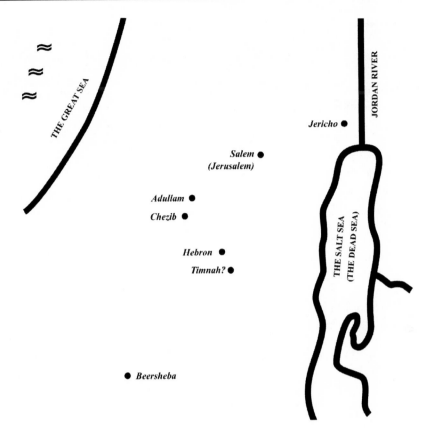

Map 2. Southern Canaan in the Late Patriarchal Age (approximately 1700 BCE).

son, and she called his name Onan. Yet again she bore a son, and she called his name Shelah; she[4] was in Chezib[5] when she bore him (Gen. 38:1–5).

This chapter, Genesis 38, is in many ways very like the Book of Ruth. Like Ruth it is a self-contained unit not directly dependent on what precedes it nor connected to what follows it.[6] It stands alone, and like Ruth it has a prologue, a central portion, and a concluding epilogue.[7] We have just read the prologue, which sets the scene for this mini-epic.

As in Ruth we are presented with the names of most of the protagonists involved in the tale (though, strangely, Judah's wife is not named — she will remain merely "Shua's daughter").

---

[4]Reading with LXX, MT reads "he."

[5]Probably identical with the town of Achzib, another lowland town, southwest of Adullam, mentioned in Joshua 15:44 and Micah 1:14.

[6]Though this chapter can be understood in its own terms (and indeed for the purposes of this book so it will be treated), Robert Alter has definitively demonstrated that both linguistically and conceptually it forms an integral part of the larger epic of "Joseph and his Brothers" (Alter, "A Literary Approach to the Bible," pp. 73–76). In a sense it acts in the same way that the chapter entitled "The Grand Inquisitor" functions in *The Brothers Karamazov*: the chapter forms a self-contained unit that can be understood in its own terms, yet also serves as one of the keys that unlocks the meaning of the novel.

[7]It seems likely, due to the large number of similarities in theme and organization that one of these two served as the inspiration and model for the other. In the section "Tamar and Ruth" below we will try to come to some conclusions in this matter.

As in Ruth we are told when the events took place.[8] And finally, just as Elimelech's move from Bethlehem to Moab precipitates the chain of events that constitute the Book of Ruth, it is Judah's relocation from the central highlands to the plains near Adullam that triggers the action in our chapter.[9]

According to Genesis 37:14 the family at that time was located in the vicinity of Hebron, one of the highest points of the region. Breaking with the past practice of pasturing the family herds collectively, Judah removes his sheep and makes the seasonal migration to the plains alone (note the words "went down").[10] Why he makes this move we are not told, but the suspicion arises that, after years of being immersed in an atmosphere of seething jealousy which culminated in the traumatic betrayal and disposal of their brother, Judah feels the need to break clean, start afresh and make a new life for himself. He makes new friends among the locals (we will learn that Hirah is not just a neighbor but becomes Judah's bosom companion), finds a girl, marries and settles down to raise a family. By the time his third son is born he has relocated his family to Chezib. Judah has taken up permanent residence in the plains.

The terseness of the account — "he saw," "he took," "he went in" followed by the staccato three-time repetition of the phrase "she bore a son" — emphasizes the feverish rapidity with which the events unfold: meeting, marriage, consummation; another year, another son. And now, as if in reaction to this frenetic pace, the story dries up. More than a dozen years will flow by until our tale resumes. Judah is now in his late thirties.

The Bartered Bride

Now Judah took a wife for Er, his first born, and her name was Tamar (38:6).

Now a middle-aged father of teenage sons, Judah takes responsibility for their future. His oldest is now of marriageable age. So Judah, the responsible parent, finds an appropriate bride for his oldest son, Er. Though we are not specifically told, she, like his wife, is undoubtedly of Canaanite stock.

---

[8]"Now it came to pass around that time that Judah went down from his brothers" is more than a bridging phrase meant to provide a smooth transition from the previous chapter (Genesis 37), which told how Joseph's brothers, including Judah, sold him into Egypt. It raises in our minds the suspicion that the very act of selling their brother has triggered the next step in the disintegration of the family: Judah's distancing himself from the circle of father and siblings. It further implies that the events in our chapter take place during the twenty-two years during which Joseph is working his way up from household slave to viceroy of Egypt, before the events that will once again unite the family.

[9]For centuries commentators on this chapter have stressed the impossibility of packing all its happenings into the tight time frame of 22 years. Some would go so far as to say that even forty years might be too little. But what has been obvious to medieval and modern scholars should have been equally obvious to the author (unless we assume that he never made it past second grade arithmetic). We will attempt to indirectly address the issue of the timing of the sequence of events in our treatment of the text. For a more detailed analysis of the chronological problems posed by the relationship between this chapter and the larger Joseph saga of which it is a part, see Appendix II: Can Judah and Tamar Be Fitted into the Joseph Narrative?

[10]Hebron, 19 miles south of Jerusalem, is over 3,000 feet above sea level while Adullam is about 1,000 feet. So on the simplest level the phrase "went down" reflects a descent of about 2,000 feet from the heights of Hebron to the plains of Adullam. But on a deeper level the verb *yarad* (to go down) reminds us of the wild grief of the aged Jacob who refuses to be consoled for the (supposed) death of his son Joseph. The previous chapter concluded with his wail: "I will go down [*ayred*] mourning to my son in the Pit" (37:35). But of course Joseph is not dead. The following chapter will begin with the words: "Now Joseph was taken down [*hurad*] to Egypt" (39:1). These three versions of the same verb, much more obvious in the Hebrew than in translation, is one expression of the ongoing and deeply ironic way the text treats the discrepancies between the reality of our actions, the way we perceive them and their unsuspected outcomes.

There is something interesting going on here. Judah's great-grandfather, Abraham, was insistent that his son not marry a Canaanite girl, and took great pains to ensure the proper choice of a bride for his son from among his own people.[11] Isaac, in his turn, was equally insistent that his son, Jacob, not take a Canaanite bride, and sent him abroad specifically to choose a wife for himself from among his own kin.[12] Jacob, on the other hand, does not seem to have been particularly concerned as to whom his children marry, or to have made any efforts to ensure appropriate marriages for them. (Indeed, Jacob seems to have exercised hardly any control over his children). We have already seen that Judah left home, married whom he willed, and whom he willed was a Canaanite woman. However, with regard to his son, the freedom of choice that he seized for himself will most decidedly not be permitted Er. *He* makes the choice for him; and considering his own marriage to a Canaanite woman he hardly has any scruples in the matter with regard to his son. What will become of God's Promise to Judah's progeny seems to be of little concern. More on this issue later.

> And Er, Judah's first born, was evil in the sight of the Lord, and the Lord slew him. Then Judah said to Onan: "Go in to your brother's wife, and perform the duty of a brother-in-law to her, and raise up seed to your brother" (38:7–8).

Things don't work out very well. How much time elapses between the marriage and Er's untimely death we are not told, but it does not seem to have been very much.[13] All that is relevant is that he leaves behind a young and childless widow (given the customs of the period Tamar was probably no more than fourteen years of age).

What comes next is familiar to us: we have already been introduced to Levirate Marriage.[14] It is vital that Er have heirs; his family line must not be allowed to die out. In Ruth, Boaz speaks of the need "to raise up the name of the dead upon his inheritance" (Ruth 4:5, 10). Here Judah uses a comparable expression: "raise up seed to your brother."[15] Onan, a year or so younger than Er, should be around sixteen at this point, possibly only fifteen. He may be a bit young for marriage by the standards of the time, but not overly so; he is certainly capable of "doing his duty by his brother." So Judah gives Onan his marching orders and Tamar moves in with him (or is it the other way around?). Note that Judah does not refer to Tamar by name, only as "your brother's wife." More on this, too, later.

> Now Onan knew that the seed would not be his, so whenever he went in to his brother's wife he spilled it [his semen] upon the ground, so as not to give seed to his brother. Now what he did was evil in the sight of the Lord, and He slew him also (38:9–10).

[11]"Swear by the Lord, the God of the heavens and the God of the earth, that you will not take a wife for my son from the daughters of the Canaanites among whom I dwell, but will go to the land of my birth and get a wife for my son Isaac" (Genesis 24:3–4).

[12]"He commanded him [Jacob] saying: "You shall not take a wife from among the daughters of Canaan. Arise, go to Paddan-aram, to the house of Bethuel, your mother's father, and there take a wife from among the daughters of Laban, your mother's brother" (Genesis 28:1–2).

[13]Umberto Cassuto feels that "in view of the phrasing of the text ... in the opinion of the author of our chapter Er died immediately after his marriage, in the very same year, and that Onan married his sister-in-law Tamar also in that year" (Cassuto, "The Story of Tamar and Judah," pp. 39–40). We are also not told in what way he was evil (it is irrelevant to the story). There may have been nothing at all. Inasmuch as in those days it was assumed that any sudden or untimely death must be God's doing, since God killed him He must have had good reasons for doing so. In other words, this may be no more than a conventional cliché.

[14]See the section "The Three Faces of the Redeemer" in Chapter 1, and especially note 28.

[15]The difference may be due to the fact that in later times, when the Israelites were settled farmers, entailed estates ("his inheritance") were a vital dimension of *Redemption*. Here, where neither Jacob nor any of his family owned land, only sheep and cattle, this issue was moot. Only keeping the family line alive and, of course, avenging murder, were the duties of the *Redeemer*.

Er's childless death has been a windfall for Onan. As one of two surviving sons, he can now look forward to inheriting fully half of Judah's estate. But should he father a son by Tamar, that son would become Er's heir, and Onan's share of the estate will revert to a mere third.[16] This Onan will do his utmost to prevent. We do not know if, at this early period, brothers had the right to refuse their duty to "raise up seed to [dead] brothers."[17] If Onan had no right of refusal, he will prove guilty of betraying his brother and his duty to him. If he had the right to refuse, he will be in addition guilty of hypocrisy — pretending to carry out his duty but secretly sabotaging it.

The means he employs is that whenever he beds Tamar he withdraws before reaching climax, "wasting" or "spilling" his seed upon the ground.[18] This gives Onan the best of both worlds: he has full and frequent sexual use of Tamar but also prevents her from producing an heir to her late husband. Again we are not told how long this continues but apparently in short order Onan follows his brother into the grave.

Judah now has a problem. This girl (whom, to his chagrin, he himself had chosen) has now buried two of his sons. Law and custom require him to provide her with his last remaining son, Shelah, to do what Onan had refused to do — provide an heir to Er. But what if this girl is a hex, a husband-burier? She may hasten his youngest son out of this world just as she dispatched his brothers. This Judah determines to prevent. He cannot simply refuse to give Shelah to her; both the law and public opinion will not permit open defiance of clear duty. So Judah takes the road of his late son: hypocritical pretense at compliance and secret sabotage.

> Then Judah said to Tamar his daughter-in-law: "Remain in widowhood in your father's house until Shelah, my son, grows up"; for he thought[19]: "He too might die like his brothers." So Tamar went and lived in her father's house [38:11].

Judah's excuse is that Shelah is too young to marry.[20] "Go home and wait, he tells Tamar. Don't call me; I'll call you when he is ready."[21]

Judah's treatment of Tamar is not only unjust but it is brutal. Instead of providing sympathy and support to his young daughter-in-law (who is undoubtedly traumatized by the rapid successive deaths of two husbands), Judah packs her off and washes his hands of her. Given the customs of the time Tamar has no choice but to comply.

---

[16]When we speak of Judah's estate we refer to his movable property, and especially the herds.

[17]They had this right at a later period, albeit at the price of public humiliation (see Deuteronomy 25:7–10). There is much that we don't know about law and its development in Israel and the Ancient Near East: "the simple fact [is] that the ancients mainly used law ... without chattering their heads off about it all the time" (Kitchen, *On The Reliability of the Old Testament*, p. 496).

[18]This practice, called coitus interruptus, was a primitive form of birth control.

[19]Literally, "for he said [to himself]." This is one of the few instances in the Bible where we are explicitly informed as to a person's motives, rather than leaving us to guess at them. All ambiguity has been banished. We are not being permitted to give Judah the benefit of the doubt, but are being forced to condemn the hurtful and unjust nature of his actions.

[20]Shelah may be only fourteen at this junction; he may even be younger than Tamar. As such Judah's claim is credible.

[21]Understandably, Judah seeks to preserve his own son, his youngest and last. Not without cause, he very likely fears a curse on his sons through Tamar, and he attempts to escape it. But we notice that in doing so he is willing to sacrifice not only the rightful claims of his daughter-in-law, whom he further humiliates by keeping her, a twice-married woman, confined to her father's house. He is also willing to ignore the duties that are owed to another son. To save one son, Shelah, he is willing to allow Er to disappear without a trace.... More generally, he is willing to neglect future generations in favor of the present one: he neglects the claims of lineage and future community needs for the sake of the love he feels for his youngest son" (Kass, *The Beginning of Wisdom*, p. 529).

Tamar is now in an unenviable position. She is a widow but not free to remarry. Under the rules of Levirate Marriage she is "betrothed" to Shelah and may marry only him.[22] Yet Judah has no intention of ever allowing the union to take place. Judah is leaving her with no options and with no future. He is even refusing to provide support, turning her out of her home and unloading her on her probably less than enthusiastic parents.[23] Judah's exercise in "responsible parenting" leaves much to be desired.

The Hooker at the Crossroads

Out of sight, out of mind. How long Tamar remains warehoused in her parents' home we are not told.[24] In the meantime Shelah grows up and nothing happens. A further question: how much time passes before Tamar realizes that she has "been had"? Again we are not told, but as a year or so passes and Shelah reaches the age when Onan had been given to her, and then another year and he has reached the age of Er when he married, the truth of the matter begins to sink in. Judah, of course, appreciates that Tamar will eventually realize that she has been hung out and left to dry, but expects that, after a period of complaints, she will resign herself to her fate. After all, given the status of women in the Canaanite world, what can she do? He has not counted on Tamar.

But then again why should he? It is quite clear that he does not know her. It is significant that not once does he refer to her by name. To him she is always a daughter-in-law, a wife of one of his sons, an appendage tacked on to the family. The arrangements for her marriage to his oldest son, Er, were made with her parents. It is questionable if the immature twelve to fourteen-year-old girl was even asked as to her opinion of her prospective bridegroom, or of the family into which she was destined to enter. Girls did what they were told. To Judah Tamar has always been an object, not a person. And so, never having known her, and having removed her from his presence during the years in which she was metamorphosing from girl into woman, Judah is completely unprepared for what awaits him.

In the meantime Judah has other things to occupy his mind. Even though he has shepherds to manage his flocks the business needs constant oversight. And then once again death strikes in the immediate family circle.

In the course of time[25] Shua's daughter, the wife of Judah, died; and when Judah was comforted[26] he went up to Timnah[27] to his sheepshearers, he and his friend Hirah the Adullamite. When Tamar was told: "Behold, your father-in-law is going up to Timnah to shear his sheep," she took off her widow's garments, covered herself with a veil, and perfuming herself [28] seated herself

---

[22]Shelah, of course, is under no such restriction. Given that polygamy was accepted practice in the Ancient Near East, despite his legal tie to Tamar, Shelah could marry any other woman of his choice.

[23]For some reason or other most commentators seem to be blind to Judah's repudiation of financial responsibility for his bereaved daughter-in-law.

[24]See note 25 below.

[25]Literally, "Now the days multiplied"; a vague and indeterminate expression that can mean anything from a year or two to as much as twenty years (1 Samuel 7:2).

[26]That is, when the period of mourning was over.

[27]This is not the Timnah in Philistia made famous by Samson, but the location in the highlands, southeast of Hebron, mentioned in Joshua 15:57.

[28]Adopting the rendering of M.J. Dahood, who bases himself on Ugaritic and Arabic cognates (Dahood, "Northwest Semitic Notes on Genesis," p. 80).

invitingly at Enayim, which is by the road to Timnah,[29] for she saw that Shelah had grown up but she had not been given to him as wife (38:12–14).

His wife's death and the incumbent period of mourning take Judah out of circulation for a while, but with the end of the mourning period business calls. Judah departs his home in the plains for the highlands where his sheep are being pastured. It is sheep-shearing time, a laborious and labor-intensive undertaking of several days' duration, which demands the involvement and oversight of the owner. The preparations for leaving take a little while, and Tamar learns of her father-in-law's imminent departure. The news stirs her into desperate activity.

Desperate is hardly the word for it. Tamar, as we shall see, is taking her life into her hands. For Tamar proposes to become, if only for a day, a prostitute; and if she is caught in the act, as a married woman, the penalty is death.[30] That this is no momentary impulse is evident. Advance planning and preparation are necessary to carry it off, not least being the ready availability of clothing appropriate to her "profession." It must have taken time to secretly accumulate the necessary garments (and cosmetics?) and to prepare a discreet retreat where she can switch costumes unobserved. Everything about Tamar's actions speaks of long and careful planning.

What impels Tamar to risk her life in so problematic a way? We have just been told: "for she saw that Shelah had grown up but she had not been given to him as wife." She understands fully what is being done to her, and she will not allow herself to be discarded like a worn-out sandal if there is anything she can do to prevent it. Her options are terribly limited: there is no one to whom she can appeal; there is no one to whom she can turn for help. Only through her own action can she alter her situation, and then only at appalling risk. She will fulfill her obligation to her late husband, Er, and bear him an heir. She will not permit his family line to die out if she can help it.

From the Book of Ruth we have become familiar with the workings of Redemption. When the nearest relative is unavailable then the obligation passes to the next in line. Er's brother, Shelah, being denied her, the next relative in line is none other than her late husband's father, Judah himself. So Tamar single-mindedly sets out to get herself pregnant by Judah.

She has planned carefully. Judah, of course, will never cooperate. In fact he is the very cause of the present impasse. He will have to be tricked and seduced, something impossible to do in his home territory where she would likely be recognized. Only off his home ground, in unfamiliar circumstances, can such a plan have any chance of success. She must get to him when away from his home. His departure to oversee the shearing of his sheep is the chance she has been waiting for.

There is another factor working in Tamar's favor. The death of Judah's wife (with possibly a preceding illness) and the mourning period that followed have enforced a period of sexual abstinence on him. He is now especially vulnerable to sexual advances.

Tamar acts! Stealing out of her parent's home to her secret retreat, she removes the widow's weeds that have been her garb these last bitter years, and dresses in clothing such as a common prostitute would wear. Then, repairing to the approaches of the town of Enayim, she takes up her position by the crossroads where Judah must pass on his way to Timnah, and assumes the attitude of a roadside prostitute soliciting customers. In due course Judah and his friend Hirah make their appearance.

When Judah saw her he thought she was a prostitute, for she had covered her face. So he went

[29]Understanding the phrase "bepetah enayim" to be a double entendre (*enayim* meaning both a place name, "Enayim," and "eyes"). Thus the phrase can mean both the spot where she waited for Judah, the "opening" or entrance to Enayim, and also the attitude of open sexual invitation that she adopted, as an "eye-opener" (Robinson, "*bepetah enayim*," p. 569).

[30]Technically, as "betrothed" to Shelah, Tamar's condition is that of a married woman; sexual relations with any but Shelah would fall into the category of adultery, which was a capital offense.

over to her at the roadside and said: "Here, please let me come in to you," for he did not know that she was his daughter-in-law (38:15–16).

No sooner does Judah see her than he gets right down to business (his prolonged abstinence must have made matters very urgent for Judah). No time for preliminary banter: "Look here, I want you!" But despite the urgency Judah remains the gentleman; he does not forget to add "please." The text stresses that he does not recognize her — her face was covered by her veil.[31] But I am not sure that he would have recognized her even without the veil; Tamar is now a grown woman, and with her face appropriately made up for the part (the use of cosmetics was a highly developed art in the Canaanite world) it is doubtful that she looked anything like the nubile girl that is all Judah could have remembered. At any rate, the text insists that he had no idea whom he was addressing. So on to business: the woman being willing, all that remains is to agree on price.

She replied[32]: "What will you give me that you may come into me?" (38:16).

No delicacy here. She feeds his blunt language right back to him, offering to let him propose the price. This creates a problem for Judah. He was not expecting to proposition a prostitute. This is a spur of the moment initiative prompted by what to him seems a chance encounter. He has no cash on him (no one normally carried cash — lumps of silver — it was mainly a barter economy). He has no alternative but to ask for credit. He is on his way to his flocks for the annual spring sheep shearing. He will send someone from there with a baby goat for her.[33]

And he said: "I will send you a kid from the flock." And she said: "[Only] if you give me[34] a pledge until you send it." And he said: "What pledge shall I give you?" And she said: "Your signet, your cord and the staff that is in your hand." So he gave them to her and went into her, and she conceived by him. Then she rose and went away; she took off her veil and put on her widow's garments (38:17–19).

The offer of a kid some time in the future leaves her cold; she does not accept promises in return for her services. She is willing, however, to offer secured credit: if he will leave with her an item of value as a deposit, to be held against the delivery of the kid, she will give him credit. Upon his asking what she will accept as a pledge she demands his signet, his cord and his staff.[35] These were all highly personal items, unique to the individual and of use only to him. But equally to the point, the owner would be seriously inconvenienced without them. Judah would want to get them back, and thus they guaranteed a speedy delivery of the promised kid. Robert Alter has compared them, in modern terms, to a demand that one leave all of one's major credit cards with a prostitute as pledge for cash payment.[36] It is a mark of the urgency felt by Judah that he surrenders them without argument.

[31]From everything we know, women were normally *unveiled* in those days. Tamar veils herself specifically so as not to be recognized.

[32]Literally, "she said."

[33]Judah's flocks, as was common then, consisted of goats as well as sheep. A kid was probably an overpayment but Judah was in no mood to bargain. Besides, he is asking for immediate services on credit.

[34]Reading with LXX and Syr.; MT omits "me."

[35]The signet, probably a cylinder seal, was a small tubular object made of metal or semiprecious stone and engraved on its outside surface with a unique design so that when rolled over soft clay it would leave an impression that was recognized as the owner's signature in all matters legal. It was usually worn around the neck by means of a cord passed through its hollow interior. The cord itself might have also been distinctive, woven in an unusual pattern of colored threads. The staff was probably carved with an original identifying design and may have been embossed with the name of the owner as well. Taken together these items not only identified the bearer but also proclaimed his status. Only a person of status would have such objects. Only a person of substance would be willing to temporarily part with them, certain of being able to immediately redeem them. Despite overpaying, a kid was small change for Judah.

[36]Alter, "A Literary Approach to the Bible," p. 76.

The terms mutually agreed, the transaction is consummated. Judah seduced, and with proof of her customer's identity in her hand, Tamar now packs up, removes her disguise, and reappears as the doleful widow dutifully residing with her parents. Though she cannot yet be sure, her encounter has indeed succeeded: she is pregnant.

Payment Deferred

Morning finds Judah at Timnah, fully involved with the shearing of the sheep, yet increasingly uneasy over having surrendered his signet and staff. The sooner he recovers them the better. So despite the pressure of the work on hand, Judah relieves his friend Hirah of his tasks and sends him with a kid to redeem his pledge. Once again no need for delicacy — having been present, Hirah knows exactly what went on and where to find the "woman of easy virtue."

> Now Judah sent a kid by the hand of his friend the Adullamite to take [back] the pledge from the woman, but he could not find her. So he asked the locals[37]: "Where is the courtesan,[38] she that was by the roadside at Enayim?" And they said: "There has been no courtesan here" (38:20–21).

She isn't there! At first this is not particularly worrisome. She must live somewhere in the vicinity and, as a "professional," will be well known. But inquiries meet a stone wall. The locals insist that there isn't, and never has been, a "courtesan" who frequented the entrance to the town. Perplexed, Hirah returns to Timnah to report.

> So he returned to Judah and said: "I could not find her; also the locals said: 'There has been no courtesan here.'" Then Judah said: "Let her keep it [the pledge] lest we be put to shame. I have sent this kid but you could not find her" (38:22–23).

Judah's reaction is interesting. Valuable as the articles are to him, he is ready to forgo them. Pursuing the matter will only result in publicizing the episode, and branding him as a person who patronizes common street prostitutes. This will hardly do wonders for his reputation. Indeed, he fears that he may become the laughing stock of the region — which is what the Hebrew term we have rendered as "put to shame" embodies. "Let it go," Judah counsels, "further inquiries will only result in my becoming the butt of dirty jokes. My conscience is clear. I promised to send payment and I did. It is only her fault if she was not there to receive it." So Judah writes off his signet, cord, and staff, hoping that by maintaining a low profile scandal will be averted. And there, for three months, the matter rests.

But Tamar is pregnant, and it is only a matter of time before the fact becomes evident.

> About three months later it was told to Judah: "Your daughter-in-law, Tamar has played the harlot; what is more, she is with child by harlotry!" And Judah said; "Bring her out and let her be burned!" (38:24).

[37]Literally, "the men of the place" (LXX and Syr.), MT reads "the men of her place."

[38]The Hebrew term *kadeshah* (literally, "holy woman") usually referred in biblical times to a woman who, as a devotee of one of the pagan fertility cults that flourished in the Ancient Near East, would offer herself to partakers of these religious rites. This term is often rendered as "cult prostitute." Jeffrey Tigay and Victor Hamilton point out, however, that in all the Ancient Near East there have been found no examples of "outreach"— that is, "cult prostitutes" ever operating outside temples and religious shrines, and certainly not at roadsides. Taken in conjunction with the fact that the term *kadeshah* is only used in conversation between Hirah and the locals, pagans all, and in Hirah's report to Judah in which he quotes the townspeople, whereas the narrator refers to her as a common professional, a "hooker," or as "the woman," after quoting numerous studies Tigay and Hamilton conclude that, out of deference to the sensibilities of the locals, Hirah used a more "refined" term when in conversation with them rather than employ crude language. I have therefore chosen to render the term by the equally *genteel*, semi-respectable (and archaic) designation of "courtesan" (from the Italian *courtigiane* or "female courtiers") (Tigay, *JPSTC Deuteronomy*, p. 387, note 65; Hamilton, *The Book of Genesis*, pp. 454–55).

It seems that legally, despite living in her parents' home Tamar is still under the jurisdiction of the father of her late husband. Judah's relations with his daughter-in-law have been cavalier in the extreme. He has refused her Shelah, he has avoided the expense of supporting her; indeed, since he sent her packing he has had (so far as he knows) nothing to do with her. But where *his honor* is concerned (note the phrase *"your daughter-in-law"*), the matter assumes a very different hue. Without even giving her a hearing he brutally orders her taken out to the city gate and burned.[39] Leaving matters to the very last moment, Tamar sends[40] a message to Judah along with the signet, cord, and staff she has been holding against this very eventuality.

> When she was brought forth she sent [word] to her father-in-law: "I am pregnant by the man to whom these belong. Do you recognize to whom these belong — the signet, and cord, and the staff?" And Judah recognized [them] and he said: "She is more in the right than I, inasmuch[41] as I did not give her to Shelah, my son." And he did not lie with her again[42] (38:25–26).

Judah has finally gotten his pledge back, but the price he now finds he must pay for his fling is far higher, and more bitter, than ever he anticipated. Not only has he to live with the ongoing embarrassment of his patronizing roadside prostitutes becoming common knowledge, but also he is now forced to publicly face his formidable failures of responsibility as a head of family.

Up to now Judah has not been presented to us in a very flattering light. It was he who initiated the sale of his brother into slavery.[43] It is he who then continues the process of breaking up the family by pulling his sheep out of the common herds, moving away and establishing residence in the lowlands among the Canaanites. It is he who first breaks the Abrahamic taboo against marrying Canaanite women, and his treatment of his Canaanite daughter-in-law has

[39]Under biblical law (see Leviticus 20:10, Deuteronomy 22:21) the penalty for adultery (which is the offense under consideration) is stoning to death. Was Judah proceeding under Canaanite law, ordering her to be burnt alive, or was he sending her to be stoned to death, and then her corpse to be burnt?

[40]Note the word "send." This has been a key term in this chapter. Judah promised to *send* the "woman" a kid from the flock; Tamar demands a pledge till he will *send* it. Judah *sends* the kid by the hand of Hirah, and when the "woman" can't be found he clears his conscience with the declaration that he fulfilled his obligation and *sent* the kid. Everything is third-hand, by indirection. But responsibility and reality can be kept at arm's length only so long. Now, come payoff time, Tamar *sends* to Judah the items that publicly proclaim both his responsibility and his disgrace.

[41]Implied is the clause: (she did this thing) "inasmuch as."

[42]Literally, "And he knew her again no more." As in English, the Hebrew term "to know" has several meanings. Here the context clearly requires the sense of sexual intercourse, which is why we have rendered the phrase as "and he did not lie with her again." But there are several ways this idea can be rendered in Hebrew, and since the author chooses to use the verb "to know" several scholars are of the opinion that beyond the surface meaning the author is hinting to the reader several additional thoughts: "The statement ... may have more than a legal, historical referent. Throughout most of the narrative Judah has not really known Tamar. She is a brother's wife (v. 8), a daughter-in-law (v. 11), a widow (v. 11), a prostitute (v. 15), and a woman (v. 20). Most conspicuously he did not 'know' Tamar as Tamar when he thought he was consorting with a prostitute" (Hamilton, *The Book of Genesis*, p. 451). Esther M. Menn suggests: "Although this phrase refers primarily to the fact that Judah never again had sexual relations with his daughter-in-law, the wording seems specially appropriate given that the reader of the narrative too knows too little about Tamar following her reprieve" (Menn, *Judah and Tamar*, p. 33). But 'knowing' aside, from a practical point of view why does Judah abstain from further relations with Tamar? Esther Menn does not think that moral squeamishness adequately explains Judah's restraint. She continues: "The narrator's final note concerning Judah, that 'He never knew her again' (Gen. 38:26), conveys more than a concern with the morality of the patriarch. It also expresses Judah's continuing wariness of the woman he suspects in his son's deaths and his resolve to distance himself from the dangers of her embrace" (Menn, *Judah and Tamar*, p. 47).

[43]Joseph. The text is not clear whether his motive was to save Joseph's life — slavery being the lesser of the evils to brutal murder — or cupidity, the desire to turn a dirty dollar: "What profit is there in killing our brother.... Come, let us sell him to the Ishmaelites.' ... So they sold Joseph to the Ishmaelites for twenty pieces of silver" (Genesis 37:26–27).

been callous in the extreme. What seems to underlie all this reprehensible behavior is an unwillingness to accept responsibility. Here, for the first time, Judah breaks the pattern. Instead of getting defensive, or angry at being publicly put on the spot, he proves big enough to admit that he is in the wrong and it is Tamar who is in the right. In fact, as Leon Kass acutely notes, Judah is the first person in the entire Bible to publicly admit his *own* unrighteousness. He also implies that his callous self-preoccupation is far worse than harlotry.[44]

It was he who had refused Tamar his third son, Shelah; worse, he had selfishly denied to his dead eldest son an heir. Unconventional though her actions were, Tamar had done the right thing. Having been denied the proper surrogate for her dead husband she had simply skipped to the next in the priority list. Denied the brother she had gone on to the father — Judah — and tricked him into "raising up seed" to her late husband. This admission does more than vindicate Tamar; it also marks the beginning of the process of maturation and assumption of responsibility that is to end with Judah becoming the moral leader of his brothers. Ultimately it is to lead Jacob to bestow upon Judah, from among all his sons, the blessing of Father Abraham: the promise that "kings shall come forth from you" (Genesis 17:6). It is Tamar who jump-starts Judah's rehabilitation.

The Fruits of Fortitude

Tamar's courage vindicated, her motives and actions approved by all, the narrative hastens to its consummation.

> Now when the time came for her to give birth, behold there were twins in her womb. And while she was in labor [one of them] thrust forth his hand, and the midwife took it and tied on his hand a scarlet thread, saying: "This came out first." But as he drew back his hand behold his brother came out. And she exclaimed[45]: "What a breach you have made for yourself!" Therefore his name was called Perez.[46] And afterwards his brother, upon whose hand was the scarlet thread, emerged; his name was called Zerah (38:27–30).

Perez is a name familiar to us. The Book of Ruth concludes with these words: "Now these are the generations of Perez: Perez was the father of Hezron ... and Salmon was the father of Boaz, and Boaz was the father of Obed; and Obed was the father of Jesse, and Jesse was the father of David" (Ruth 4:18–22). So to put things into the larger picture, what we have been reading in Genesis 38 is really the story behind the story of Ruth. And now we finally can understand the blessing that the elders and the people in the gate bestow upon Boaz: "May your house become like the house of Perez, whom Tamar bore to Judah" (Ruth 4:12). For not only was Tamar's legacy to the future her son, founder of the most illustrious clan of the tribe of Judah and ultimately her distant descendant King David, but also her remarkable story which, more than half a millennium later, still resonated, and which we have just read.

So how can we sum up Tamar? She was a woman of courage and determination (when she acted so decisively, she was no longer a young girl but seventeen or eighteen years of age, a mature woman in those days). She was a person who had a clear understanding of what was right and the will to see that the right be done come what may. She would be defeated neither by natural calamities nor the injustices of others. All this yes, but far more — an immature Canaanite

---

[44]Kass, *The Beginning of Wisdom*, p. 536.

[45]Literally, "said."

[46]Perez means "breach."

girl co-opted by marriage into a strange and God-possessed family, she eventually came to take its dark destiny far more seriously than did the members of the family itself. And if they proved too self-preoccupied to take responsibility for the future of the Promise, then she would shoulder the burdens that were rightfully theirs and do what had to be done that the family have a future. And in so doing she not only preserved the future physical existence of the seed of Judah, but by her example lit an answering fire of responsibility in the heart of her wayward father-in-law. Tamar's triumph was as much the making of the character of Judah as it was mothering the line that would bring forth kings; and ultimately the Messiah.

Tamar and Ruth

It has been long evident that there are strong connections between Genesis 38 and the Book of Ruth. We have already mentioned similarities of structure: they both are self-contained literary units possessing an Introduction which sets the scene and introduces most of the figures who will act out the drama; a Main Body in which the action occurs; and an Epilogue which not only brings closure to the events related but, by shifting the perspective and fitting these events into a larger scheme of things, gives them a significance previously unexpected.[47]

Beyond the similarity of structure there are many points of connection between these two narratives. Their hero is in both cases a woman, and one who is an outsider who became connected to the Israelite community through marriage. In both cases this central figure has been treated cruelly by life, but despite isolation in a world designed for men these women, through their own daring efforts, succeed in rebuilding their lives, turning unpromising beginnings into brilliantly successful conclusions. And of course the most obvious connections of all: both tales are uniquely enmeshed in a network of law and custom pertaining to the primitive social institution of Redemption and Levirate Marriage[48]; and the Book of Ruth specifically mentions the earlier victim-heroine, Tamar, and holds her up as a role model for Ruth to emulate.

Since the events depicted in Genesis 38 occurred some five centuries before those portrayed in the Book of Ruth, and the author of Ruth displays a familiarity with the story of Tamar, it is commonly taken for granted that Genesis 38 was written first, and that many of the similarities in structure and thrust of the two stories are due to the Book of Ruth having been modeled on the tale of Tamar. But this order of precedence is far from certain. The Book of Ruth shows no knowledge of Genesis 38, only of the general outlines of the story of Judah and Tamar. Inasmuch as the risqué tale of the progenitress of the premier clan of the tribe of Judah must have been part of the traditional folklore of the Judean clans for centuries before being cast into the literary form we know today as Genesis 38, the mention of Tamar at the end of Ruth is no guarantee that Genesis 38 was written first.

It could easily have been the other way around. In another page or so we will be discussing the question of when Genesis 38 was written. It will there become evident that both Ruth and Genesis 38 were products of the same period of intense literary creativity. It is certainly within the realm of possibility that it was Ruth that was written first, and provided the model for the way the story of Tamar was structured. Indeed, the hypothesis that Ruth was written first would explain several anomalies connected with Genesis 38. We have noted that the story of Judah

---

[47]See pp. 77–78.

[48]While Levirate Marriage is defined in one of the law codes in the Bible (Deuteronomy 25:5–10) and there are hints now and then to some aspects of the customs of *Redemption*, these are the only two narratives in the Bible where they form the foundation of the social context and determine the forms of the actions taken by the central protagonists.

and Tamar seems an intrusion into the story of Joseph, breaking the smooth flow of the narrative.[49] Could it be that the appearance of the Book of Ruth proved the inspiration that led the author of the Joseph Saga to insert the "Tale of Tamar" into the epic, thus providing the story behind the story of the birth of the Davidic dynasty. This would also explain another rather surprising aspect of the way Tamar's story is told: unlike Ruth, which highlights the "moral of the story" by emphasizing David as the surprise outcome of the drama of Ruth, Naomi and Boaz, Genesis 38 doesn't spell out the "moral" but leaves the reader to put the pieces together and recognize the significance of Perez's birth. Could the author assume that the average reader, especially those not from the tribe of Judah, would immediately connect the dots? But if Genesis 38 was written after Ruth, whose concluding genealogy specifically makes the point that Perez was the distant ancestor of David, the significance of Tamar's giving birth to Perez would be missed by no one. It would seem to me that the possibility of Ruth having preceded "The Tale of Tamar" is a real one. Ruth may very well have been both the inspiration and the model for Genesis 38. We will bear this possibility in mind in the later stages of our analysis.

Going beyond all the obvious resemblances in structure and general format, I would contend that underlying them is a far more significant resemblance in theme and purpose. Even as Ruth, Genesis 38 is essentially a secular story. Following the deaths of Tamar's first two husbands God plays no part in the drama, nor do any of the actors take Him into account. No one invites His intervention and no one expects it. It is only through the actions of the human actors that outcomes are determined. And it is possible to treat the laconic comments of the narrator that God put Er and Onan to death as no more than pious clichés. Indeed, to turn matters on their heads, it is possible to treat these two proffered comments the same way we treated two equally unnecessary comments in Ruth: as hints that the story is not necessarily as secular as it seems.

The world of Judah and Tamar may seem to be a world without God; a world in which what happens to a person is the result of chance, the actions of others and of one's own endeavors. People choose where they will live, who will be their friends, and whom they will marry. They are the ones who decide who will marry whom, and when. If some of your children die unexpectedly — in a world before antibiotics this was hardly an uncommon phenomenon — well, these things happen and one picks up and goes on from there. Life is not always fair, nor do you necessarily have to be fair in coping with the problems life serves up. You do the best you can. And if you have been victimized by those more powerful than yourself, you either accept your fate and learn to live with it, or you "take arms against a sea of troubles" and by your own efforts and daring attempt to gain the upper hand.

It is against this kind of attitude that the narrator is reacting, and by implying that the deaths of Er and Onan were not simply chance but purposive, is suggesting that matters may not be as simple as they seem. Tamar, through her own efforts, triumphs both over her situation and over the man who would have ruined her life. As the proud mother of two of Judah's sons[50] she will hold an honored place in the family, and her standing in society is now secure. From her point of view her life has succeeded. It is only in the Epilogue that later generations will grasp the true significance of these — let us admit it — rather parochial events.[51]

[49]Genesis 37 tells how Joseph's brothers turn on him and sell him into slavery. Genesis 38 breaks off the story of Joseph, which only continues in Genesis 39 with his travails in Egypt. See note 6 above, and also Appendix II: Can Judah and Tamar Be Fitted into the Joseph Narrative?, especially note 1.

[50]In the account of the descent of Jacob and his family to Egypt, Perez and Zerah are listed as Judah's sons, and not as the sons of Er (Genesis 46:12). It would seem that Judah has accepted them as substitutes for his dead sons.

[51]"Although an explicit divine perspective is lacking in *Genesis 38* ... the reader virtually assumes this perspec-

When was this chapter written? As we have already indicated, Genesis 38 is part of a larger literary unit, the saga of Joseph and his Brothers. This literary masterpiece, while based on stories dating from those early times, and passed down in oral form from generation to generation, is held to have been put into the written form we know sometime in the period of the United Kingdom, in the days of David and Solomon.[52] In other words, the "Tale of Tamar" was probably written at approximately the same time as the Book of Ruth. What this means is that, at the time it was written, the Epilogue to the "Tale of Tamar" had exactly the same impact as the Epilogue to Ruth. There was no need to spell out the connection with a genealogy as was done in Ruth; while there were many who might not have known exactly who Boaz was, quite a few people knew who Perez was: the illustrious founder of the clan from which King David had sprung. And if we are correct in our suggestion that Ruth was already in circulation, then the point was clear to everyone.

So once again we find a secular, parochial family tale centering on the character and initiative of a marginal woman — a tale that had been preserved on its own merits over the years — reframed by means of an Epilogue into a story of much vaster significance. Only more than six hundred years after the events could anyone begin to realize that by her actions Tamar was laying the foundations of the Davidic Kingdom yet to come. And again, by clear implication, it is the Hidden God, working behind the scenes and through unwitting human agents, Who is choreographing events to expedite His purposes. And once again we face the same disproportion between the human perspective and the divine. A tale that in human terms resolves itself within a decade or two can only be perceived as part of a divine drama after a lapse of six hundred years.[53]

Thus it is possible to view the "Tale of Tamar" as conveying the same theological message as Ruth, and to see each of these two tales about the origins of David and the Davidic monarchy as complementary stories whose messages reinforce each other.

But is it legitimate to generalize from just two cases, narratives that are manifestly interrelated and focused on the origins of the Davidic dynasty? We will need further examples — narratives even more unambiguously secular in nature and revealing divine concerns other than David — before we can pronounce definitely on the merits of our proposed thesis: that the Bible recognizes that the world often appears to its inhabitants as secular, that God seems absent and that the reason we are unable to perceive His workings is a fundamental discrepancy in time scales. God's purposes function over so vast a time that human beings, with their short life spans, rarely achieve the perspective necessary to grasp the larger long-term picture.

We therefore shift our investigation from the beginning of the Biblical Age to its very end, to one of the most unusual Books in the Bible — the Book of Esther.

---

tive due to his or her knowledge of the important consequences of the narrative" (Menn, "Judah and Tamar," pp. 47–48). If indeed Ruth was already in circulation when Genesis 38 appeared, the original audience would have had this knowledge.

[52]In the so-called "Solomonic Enlightenment" (see Chapter 1, note 35). For the dating of the Joseph Epic to this period, see for example Rendsberg, "Biblical Literature as Politics." Among those scholars who accept the Documentary Hypothesis (see Glossary), quite a few consider the "Tale of Tamar" to be part of the Pentateuchal source to which is assigned the letter "J." Currently it is widely held that the "J" source was composed during the "Solomonic Enlightenment." See also Appendix V: But Could She Read? for a discussion of views on the authorship of "J."

[53]According to the Joseph narrative, these events took place immediately prior to the descent of Jacob and his family into Egypt (see Appendix II for the chronology of the events). If we stay with Kitchen's dating of the arrival of the Israelites into Egypt at 1690–1680 BCE, then six hundred years will bring us to approximately the midpoint of David's reign, the earliest point where people would begin to appreciate his historical significance.

PART II

STRANGERS IN A STRANGE LAND

ESTHER, A TRAGI-COMEDY IN THREE ACTS

In winter when the fields are white,
I sing this song for your delight—

In spring, when woods are getting green,
I'll try and tell you what I mean.

In summer, when the days are long,
Perhaps you'll understand the song:

In autumn, when the leaves are brown,
Take pen and ink, and write it down.

—Lewis Carroll, *Through
the Looking Glass*

CHAPTER 8

Understanding Esther:
An Introduction

"Sir, what is poetry?"
"Why, Sir, it is much easier to say what it is not. We
all *know* what light is; but it is not easy to *tell* what it is."
— Samuel Johnson, Boswell's *Life of Johnson*

To reach Esther from the world of Tamar we have had to fast-forward more than a millennium. In almost thirteen hundred years much has happened and many changes have taken
place. The family of Jacob has become a people and has settled in its Promised Land — this is
the setting for the Book of Ruth. A monarchy has risen and the independent tribes have been
coalesced into a Unified State under King Saul and his successor, the brilliant David, descendant of Tamar and Ruth. This spectacular accomplishment, however, does not long survive:
upon the death of David's son, Solomon, the Unified State breaks in two. These two successor
kingdoms, Israel and Judah, also prove to be short-lived in historical terms. Israel, the larger
and more prosperous of the two, meets its doom first: after a mere two hundred years (928–721
BCE) it is annihilated by the Assyrians.[1] Its smaller sister state, Judea, manages a bit better, but
only a bit, surviving a further one hundred thirty-five years. Then it too is demolished, the survivors carried off captive into exile by the Babylonians (586 BCE).[2]

The larger world of the Ancient Near East has also undergone cataclysmic change during
this same thousand-year period. The two great empires of Tamar's time, Egypt and Babylonia,
have been transformed beyond recognition. Once the dominant civilizations that formed the
two poles of the Ancient Near East, we find them now no more than moderately sized administrative units in a vast empire ruled by peoples who were not even visible on the distant horizon a thousand years previously. The Persian Empire, which dominates the world of 483
BCE — the year our tale of Esther opens — is to be the setting of our story.

And lastly, the geographic locale has shifted. The Land of Israel, the site of all the action
to date, has vanished from the horizon. Though a tiny part of the vast Persian Empire, the Land
and Jerusalem play no part in our narrative; indeed are not even mentioned except in passing

---

[1]Assyrians: see Glossary. Much of the population that survived the disaster was deported to areas east of the
Tigris River never to return, becoming the fabled "Ten Lost Tribes."

[2]See Glossary.

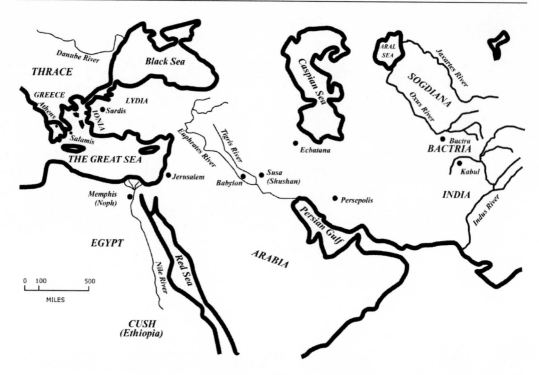

Map 3. The Achaemenian Empire when the Book of Esther opens (483 BCE).

as a vague historic memory. A people who were once at home in their own land we now find as a scattered minority, strangers in a world not their own. Let us examine this new world and how it came into being.

The Persian Setting

The Persians had their beginnings as a small mountain people that, around 650 BCE, migrated to Parsa (the modern Fars in southwest Iran). This region included a district called Anshan that became a small kingdom under the rule of a warrior by the name of Cyrus (later known as Cyrus I), the founder of the Achaemenian dynasty.[3] Persian history really begins with his grandson, also named Cyrus, and differentiated from his grandfather by being known as Cyrus II or more commonly Cyrus the Great. Succeeding to his grandfather's tiny kingdom in 559 BCE, in the remarkable space of twenty years he revolted against his overlords, the Medes,[4] defeated them, persuaded them to join him and conquered the two remaining great empires of those days: the Babylonian Empire and the Lydian Empire.[5] His son, Cambyses II, went on to conquer Egypt, "Ethiopia" (the upper Nile, i.e., Sudan) and Cyrenaica (Eastern Libya), while the last of the great Persian kings, Darius I, added "India" (the Indus Valley, basically modern Pakistan), Bactria (Afghanistan) and Sogdiana (the area of Central Asia now known as Uzbekistan,

[3]The dynasty was named after Cyrus's grandfather, Achaemenes. The empire his descendants founded and ruled remained for its entire existence a family affair, and thus is also known as the "Achaemenian Empire."

[4]The Medes and the Persians were two related peoples, both speaking Aryan languages. The Medes were by far the greater of the two, having carved out a vast empire at this time. See *Medes* in Glossary.

[5]See *Babylonians* and *Lydia* in Glossary.

as far as the Sea of Aral) to the conquests inherited from his predecessors. It is this enormous land mass, comprising an area roughly equivalent to the continental United States, with its crazy quilt of peoples, that comprises the Persian Empire and serves as the backdrop against which the Book of Esther plays itself out.

Before we can enter into a discussion of the historicity of what is being related in the Book of Esther we first must understand exactly what we are being told, and how this was understood by those for whom the Book was written — that is the Jews of the Achaemenian (Persian) Empire living at a remove of two to three generations at the most from the events portrayed.[6] The Book opens with the specific statement:

> Now it came to pass in the days of Ahasuerus — that is, the Ahasuerus who reigned over one hundred and twenty-seven provinces[7] from India to Ethiopia — in those days, when King Ahasuerus sat on his throne in the Acropolis[8] of Shushan, in the third year of his reign (1:1–3).

The King Ahasuerus that is being presented to us is the Persian monarch known to the Greeks as Xerxes; specifically Xerxes I.[9] He reigned from 486 to 465 BCE, so the third year of his reign, when our tale begins, would be 483 BCE.[10]

To understand this introduction the way the original audience of this Book did, let us proceed by means of an example. Supposing we were to open a book hot off the press and find on the opening page the following:

> During Roosevelt's presidency — that is, the Roosevelt who was president of forty-eight states — in the Capital of Washington in the ninth year of his Presidency, there occurred....

---

[6]See When Was Esther Written? in this chapter.

[7]Modern scholars, while commenting on the author's detailed knowledge of Persian government, administration, social customs and even palace layout, never cease to point out this "mistake": that, as reported by Herodotus, the Persian Empire only had twenty satrapies. (Actually this reflects the situation at the death of Cyrus the Great; changes made by Darius toward the end of his reign increased their number to 29). This, if true, would be a "mistake" so gross as to lead us to wonder how a knowledgeable author could ever make it, and not once but over and over again. What the critics fail to notice is that the author is not speaking of satrapies (he knows all about them since he refers to Satraps, the officials who ran satrapies) but of provinces and their governors, another matter entirely. The empire was organized in compact governmental units, often on a linguistic, ethnic or historic basis, called provinces. These were grouped for financial and military purposes into larger encompassing administrative structures called satrapies. For example, Judah (or *Yehud*, as it was then called) was defined as a "province." It possessed its own governor, appointed directly by the Persian king. It was part of the fifth satrapy, known as *Eber-nahara* (Beyond the River), which also included Samaria, Phoenicia, Syria and Cyprus. Why the author prefers to define Ahasuerus as ruling 127 provinces rather than 20 (or 29) satrapies is not clear. Perhaps he felt that "127 provinces" sounded so much grander.

[8]Literally, "fortress." Shushan (Susa), the administrative capital of the empire, was divided into a fortified government center containing the palace and other government buildings (hence "Acropolis," the Greek term for the fortified "Upper City" from which the "Lower City" was governed), and the much vaster, civilian part of the city where most of the people lived. "The citadel fortress was a rectangular platform 72 feet above the ground level of the city. It was surrounded by a huge wall two and a half miles long" (Breneman, *Ezra, Nehemiah, Esther*, p. 304).

[9]The Greeks found most Persian names unpronounceable. For example, Darius, Xerxes' father, possessed the Persian name that can only roughly be approximated in the Latin alphabet by *Darayavaush*. Can one really blame the Greeks for shortening this down to "Darius"? At least they could pronounce it. In our case the Hebrew *Achashverosh* (Ahasuerus is its English rendition) is actually much closer to the king's Persian name (something like *'khshaya'rsha*) than is the Greek "Xerxes." As the Greeks ultimately defeated the Persians, and it is the victors who write the histories, it is the Greek version of the name that has come down to us. So as Xerxes he will remain to us when we do not use the Ahasuerus of the text.

[10]Despite the fact that both LXX and Syr. render Ahasuerus as "Artaxerxes," "since the nineteenth century it has been clear from both linguistic and archeological evidence ... that *achashverosh* is Xerxes I" (Moore, *AB Esther*, p. 3).

Even if we were not certain whether we were reading a work of history or a historical novel we would immediately be able to identify the date and the setting into which we were being introduced (and if we were not fully conversant with the history of the United States of sixty to seventy years ago we could quickly refresh our knowledge from any one of dozens of easily available books). The Roosevelt is obviously Franklin Delano Roosevelt; when the other Roosevelt, Teddy, was president, the United States consisted of only forty-six states.[11] The ninth year of FDR's stewardship would thus be 1941. He would be at the beginning of his third term of office. We would therefore know that the United States was just beginning to come out of the Great Depression; that the Second World War had been raging for over a year; that Nazi Germany now dominated all of Western Europe and that England was on the ropes. We further would know that the United States was still neutral, having almost a year of neutrality ahead of her before she would be drawn into the war by the Japanese attack on Pearl Harbor. In much the same way the original readers of Esther would have approached the opening of the Book.

Everyone knew about Ahasuerus (Xerxes), the fourth king of the Achaemenian Empire.[12] He had served as Viceroy of Babylon for twelve years during the reign of his father, Darius I, before ascending the throne. Darius had been a very energetic monarch. Having murdered his way to the throne, a not uncommon occurrence among the Persians, he had extended the Empire's borders in both East and West.[13] But large numbers of Greek city states under his rule in Ionia (present-day western Turkey) were restless. Looking across the Aegean Sea to their independent brothers in Greece, they yearned to regain their own independence. In 499 BCE, with the support of Athens and Eretria, they rose in rebellion against Darius, a revolt that lasted six years. From this experience Darius concluded that as long as Greece remained independent there was no way in which the western provinces of the Persian Empire could be kept secure. Greece would have to go.

In 490 BCE Darius struck. Eretria was destroyed and its survivors sold into slavery, but the amphibious assault aimed at Athens was defeated at Marathon. Darius was not a person to be disheartened by setbacks, but troubles in Egypt diverted him from immediate attention to the Greek problem. Then he died (486 BCE), leaving this unfinished business to his son and heir, Ahasuerus (Xerxes). Picking up where his father left off, Ahasuerus threw himself into the vast preparations for an overwhelming invasion of Greece.[14] Darius had detailed about 25,000 men for the Marathon assault; he would mobilize at least ten times that number.[15] In 480 BCE (the sixth year of his reign) this juggernaut crossed from Asia into Europe, and rolling down from the north into Greece, smashed through the bottleneck of Thermopylae (the defending Spartans fighting to the last man). In September of that year Athens was burned to the ground.

The basic problem facing the Persians was how to feed this huge army. Only by sea could this

[11]There was another Xerxes — Xerxes II (423 BCE) — but only Xerxes I ruled an empire of 127 provinces.

[12]Actually if we want to be accurate he was the fifth. At the end of the reign of the second great king of the empire, Cambyses II, the throne was seized by someone claiming to be Bardiya (Herodotus calls him "Smerdis"), son of Cyrus the Great and brother of Cambyses (he wasn't; Cambyses had killed his brother years before). He didn't last long, being murdered by a distant relative, Darius, who ruled as Darius I, the last of the great Persian Empire builders.

[13]Besides rounding out Cyrus's western conquests, he had crossed into Europe and had conquered Thrace and Macedonia (essentially the region south and west of the Black Sea and south of the Danube River).

[14]The "Greek problem" had to be put off for the first two years of Xerxes' reign as he was occupied "pacifying" Egypt and putting down a revolt in Bactria. It was only in his third year (483 BCE) that he was able to repair to Susa, consolidate his regime and begin mobilizing his armies for the Greek adventure. It is at this point that we find him as the Book of Esther commences.

[15]The Greek historian, Herodotus, claims that the invasion army, including its sea arm, numbered over five million men and women, but modern historians scale these numbers down to a quarter of a million at most; probably the figure of 200,000 might be closer to the truth — even this was no paltry number!

mammoth horde be kept supplied, so the whole campaign really hung on the question of who would control the sea. This was decided at the naval battle of Salamis. Sitting on a throne placed on the slopes of Mount Aegaleos, overlooking the bay of Salamis, Xerxes watched helplessly as the Greek fleet (mostly Athenian) decisively defeated the Persian fleet. Their supply lines cut, the Persian Army had no choice but to retreat north into Thrace. The following summer, at Plataea, the much-reduced Persian army was defeated by the Greeks. These defeats broke Xerxes[16] and ended Persian attempts to conquer Greece. The tide had turned. From now on Persia would be on the defensive.

All this background was known to the original audience for whom the Book of Esther was written; if not all the details then certainly the overall outline of the mobilization from every province of the Empire, the vast army led personally by the king into Greece and the terrible defeats that sent the Persian forces reeling back into Asia, never to emerge again. So the author, by informing us that the story starts in the third year of the reign of King Ahasuerus, is telling us that the gargantuan banquet with which the tale commences takes place in years following the failure of the first Persian attempt to conquer Greece and during the preparations for the second great invasion that is to prove the turning point in the history of the Persian Empire. It is against this background that we must judge the authenticity of Esther.

Persia as Portrayed

To start with, the author seems to be quite knowledgeable about Persian society, the layout of the palace, the structure of Imperial administration and the workings of the court. The operative term is *seems*. It is important to bear in mind that our knowledge of Persia of the Achaemenian period leaves much to be desired. Both Empire and society were pretty well destroyed by the Greeks.[17] And much of what we do know comes from hostile sources: the very Greeks who fought against, and ultimately destroyed the Persians. Our most comprehensive, and often our only source for the age of Xerxes I, the Greek epic historian Herodotus, has been shown wrong so often that we must be very careful about accepting uncritically anything that he says.[18] Thus when there seem to be contradictions between what our author reports and what

---

[16]The failure of the Greek expedition seems to have produced paralysis in the Persian court. The king became increasingly involved in harem intrigues, and fell under the influence of courtiers and eunuchs. His remaining energies were devoted to completing the building projects in Persepolis begun by his father. In 465 he was murdered by his uncle, Artabanus, who raised Artaxerxes I to the throne.

[17]An outstanding example of the blatant vandalism that accompanied the dismembering of the Persian Empire was the destruction of the Royal Palace of Persepolis, the one great accomplishment of the reign of our Ahasuerus, and considered one of the greatest architectural masterpieces of the ancient world. It was burnt to the ground by Alexander the Great and his generals as the grand climax to a drunken orgy.

[18]Herodotus of Halicarnassus was a marvelous writer, an acute observer, widely traveled for his day and remarkably free from bias. Yet he lacked command of the languages of the Persian Empire and rarely had access to what we would regard as primary sources. As such he was at the mercy of his guides, and often accepted uncritically the most blatant misinformation. For example he reports naively that the hieroglyphic inscriptions he saw on the Great Pyramid when he visited Egypt are an account of the sums of money spent on the onions and leeks consumed by the workmen who built the pyramid! This was probably the story his guide told him when called upon to satisfy this tourist's curiosity. Herodotus, when we can check up on him, proves highly erratic. He gets some things right, others wildly wrong. When in Babylon, he saw the great buildings of a king whose name is still familiar to us today: King Nebuchadnezzar. Herodotus got the date when the buildings were constructed approximately right, but gets the sex of the ruler wrong: he turns Nebuchadnezzar into a woman, calling him Queen Nitocris. He even makes mistakes in basic geography. He informs us that the Pass of Thermopylae, site of one of the most famous battles in history (and less than 80 miles from Athens where he lived for an extended period) is oriented north-south. It actually runs east-west. Despite writing extensively about the critical battle, he apparently never took the trouble to visit the site. In short, one has to be very careful about accepting anything Herodotus says unless there is independent corroborative evidence.

we think we know about Ancient Persia it is the better part of wisdom not to leap to the conclusion that it is our author who is unreliable.

This said, it is also important to bear in mind that our author is not an historian in the modern sense of the term, presenting us with an objective and balanced report of certain events, nor does he pretend to be. Our author has an agenda and makes no attempt to conceal it. He is unabashedly critical of the Persian world in which he finds himself and ruthlessly attacks it. The weapons that he employs are satire and ridicule. Our King Ahasuerus is pictured as a pompous fool. The Persian government and court are portrayed as a farce, and life in them as a black comedy. Needless to say, satire involves exaggeration, bias, and partisanship. This having been said, we must nonetheless remember that humor, in order to be effective (and Esther is a very funny book) must start from a solid base of fact. Only if a book's audience can recognize themselves and the world that they know amid the absurd juxtapositions will they find them funny. I think that it will not be amiss if we adopt, as a working hypothesis, that behind the farce and the ridicule lies a substratum of hard fact, known to both author and audience. In other words, I think we can accept the main characters in the story (Ahasuerus, Mordecai, Haman, and of course Esther) as historical figures, and the minor supporting figures as well. And I also think that we can accept the main events that are presented as historical.[19]

But this is but part of the picture. When one is called to testify in court one is compelled to swear to tell "the truth, the whole truth, and nothing but the truth." Making allowances for the exaggerations and the skewed point of view demanded by the author's satirical and humorous style, we have been told "the truth," but not "the whole truth." When we begin to think about what we have *not* been told, when we consider the deep silences that envelop entire aspects of the tale, we begin to realize that what is being presented to us is a very partial picture, a half truth that amounts to an untruth. Or to be more pointed, since the omissions are conscious and by design — large and vital parts of the Book are simply false.

What is it that is so vital that has been omitted or censured from our text? The answer in one word is: religion. It has often been noted that Esther is the one Book of the Bible in which God is never mentioned — not once! It is more than God being erased from the narrative; we have already seen this in Ruth and in the tale of Tamar. But in those tales, God, though absent, is on everyone's lips. Here, no one mentions God, no one invokes Him. His very name has been struck from the record. And this is pure falsification, historically speaking. Both Ezra and Nehemiah were contemporaries of Esther, roughly speaking.[20] We have what amounts to their autobiographies, and the Books of Ezra and Nehemiah reveal them to be intensely religious individuals living in a religious society. Everything we know of the period indicates that the Jews organized and lived their lives as a *religious* minority and not as an ethnic minority. Their central institution was the Synagogue.

What is more, the Persian world is equally being falsified. The Persian ruling elite was also an intensely religious one. Their burning faith in their Zoroastrian religion was one of the key elements that produced the élan that raised this small people to be rulers of most of the known world. From his own proclamations we know that Darius I was a devout Zoroastrian. The same is true of Ahasuerus (Xerxes I), who spent the best energies of the second

---

[19]This is the position reached by Robert Gordis when, after a lengthy analysis of the supposedly "unhistoric mistakes" made by the author, he concludes: "We therefore believe that the book is to be regarded as a basically historical account of an anti–Semitic attempt at genocide which was foiled during the reign of Xerxes. The book may be described as typological, because it is concerned with a phenomenon destined to remain a constant in Jewish experience for millennia" (Gordis, "Religion, Wisdom and History in the Book of Esther," p. 388).

[20]Both Ezra and Nehemiah were active during the reign of Xerxes' successor, Artaxerxes I (464–424 BCE).

part of his reign raising up Persepolis to be a magnificent cathedral city, a paean to the great god Ahura Mazda. Yet both the god and all the religious pomp and ritual that surrounded Persian royal life are conspicuous by their absence. This too is historical falsification.

There is a further area of silence that should be noted. This was a period when great and stirring events were taking place in the Jewish world. A little over fifty years prior to the opening of our tale Cyrus the Great, having conquered Babylon, issued a Proclamation that freed the exiled Jews, permitting them to return to Jerusalem and to rebuild it and their ancient Temple. At the time of Esther these soul-stirring projects were in progress. During the reign of Darius a beginning was made to the rebuilding of the Temple in Jerusalem.[21] It was to Xerxes that those opposed to the rebuilding of the Temple appealed.[22] Both Ezra and Nehemiah were high officials of the Persian government; they followed the events taking place in Jerusalem closely and were so concerned with the way things were going that, at great damage to their careers, they managed to arrange leaves of absence to enable them to go to Jerusalem in order to set things right.[23] With these facts in mind, the studied silence of Esther to the rebuilding of Jerusalem and the Temple, issues that were in the air and undoubtedly of major concern to the Jewish community of Persia, seems strange indeed.

We may then tentatively conclude that the picture presented in the Book of Esther is essentially true as far as it is presented, always allowing for the distortions of the author's humor and satiric approach.[24] But the impression given of a totally secular society, Jewish and non–Jewish alike, by the conscious omission of all mention of religion is patently unhistorical. In like manner the absence in our tale of the yearning for Zion, the Jew's ancient homeland, the rebuilding of the holy city of Jerusalem and of God's holy Temple is also unhistorical. Because they do not fit into the author's agenda, they are omitted. The author does not *tell an untruth*, but by conscious omission the picture that emerges is essentially unhistorical.

The Jewish Problem

The Book of Esther is unique on many levels. Not only is it the only narrative Book in the Bible in which God is not mentioned,[25] but it is also the first work in the world to address the phenomenon of anti–Semitism; what some people politely refer to as "the Jewish Problem." This "first" is due to the phenomenon itself being of recent vintage. It would seem that the emergence of anti–Semitism was a direct outgrowth of the Babylonian Exile (586–538 BCE): the uprooting of the Israelites from their homeland and their dispersal as a small minority in the wider pagan world.

Prior to the Exile the People of Israel had lived encapsulated within its own land. Contact with the "Gentiles" had been sporadic and minimal. In Ruth we have seen a few examples of this: a solitary family goes to live in Moab, a solitary individual comes to settle in Bethlehem. For almost eight hundred years the primary interactions between Israel and her neighbors had been through

[21]Haggai 2:1–10, Zechariah 7:1, 8:9.

[22]Ezra 4:6.

[23]In Nehemiah 1:1 the author reveals that he was a high official in Susa during the reign of Artaxerxes I.

[24]"Is the story essentially true? It could be. Apart from a few improbable details ... the story is believable enough" (Moore, "Archaeology and the Book of Esther," p. 68).

[25]It is debatable whether Canticles 8:6 is a reference to God or not. Either way Canticles (The Song of Songs) is an overtly secular work but, being written in poetry, falls outside the purview of this book.

diplomacy, through war and through trade; and due to the pre-commercial peasant economics of those days even trade had been restricted both in extent and influence. Only with the destruction of the states of Israel and Judah, and the forced dispersal of survivors, did the pagan world get its first widespread exposure to Jews.[26] The Book of Esther takes place a century after this seismic upheaval.

With the passage of a hundred years, the pagan world has begun to become acquainted with these Jews and is not very happy with what it is finding out. The Jews do not fit into the common pattern: their customs and their norms are different, they are clannish and hold themselves apart, and they resist easy assimilation into the larger world. In a word they are different, and this difference begins to provoke a reaction to their presence. To use a simile, it is almost as if the Jews are perceived as an alien entity within the pagan body politic, and the result is an "immune reaction." If we can picture anti–Semitism as a sort of immune reaction of the Gentile world to a perceived alien intrusion, then we will better begin to understand the next stage of the story; the body politic rejecting the alien presence and attempting to expel or destroy it.

The type of anti–Semitism encountered in the Book of Esther is the simple or primary form of the disease: a rejection of the Jew not because of what he does or believes, but simply for what he is — different; an alien. This is why we can attempt to illuminate the issue by the use of a biological simile. In Esther we have the first description and exploration of the phenomenon, and historically all other versions of anti–Semitism appear much later. Its emergence must have administered a terrible shock to the Jews of those times, and raised agonizing questions as to the cause of the rising tide of hatred, as well as to what could be done about it. These questions define one of the central thrusts of the author's agenda.

The Book of Esther is thus not only the first description and explanation of this early type of anti–Semitism, but in many ways it is the definitive exposition. It is portrayed as a total rejection of the Jew, unbridgeable by economic cooperation, neighborly relations or assimilation. The Jew, as Jew, is "other" and thus must be rejected, expelled or annihilated. This racial matrix becomes the foundation upon which all later, "secondary" forms of anti–Semitism will be based. For the racial anti–Semite there is but one "solution." There is no way that the Jew can cease to be a Jew, and so long as the Jew exists "the Jewish Problem" will continue to inflame society. Therefore the only solution to the "Jewish Problem" is of necessity a "Final Solution." It is this that Haman proposes and attempts to implement. It is to this that nineteenth century racial anti–Semitism will revert, to find its purest form in Nazi ideology and practice. In this sense Esther is a very modern book.

When Was Esther Written?

Obviously Esther had to be written after the events portrayed in it; that is sometime after the twelfth year of King Ahasuerus (Esther 3:7) — but how long after? The essential data for determining when the Book was written is the evidence in its linguistic structures and in the content of the Book itself. With regard to the language of Esther, the discovery of the Dead Sea Scrolls at Qumran about half a century ago has placed a horde of second century BCE literature at our disposal. As David Noel Freedman states: "Esther's Hebrew has practically nothing in common with it; that alone would rule out a second century date for Esther, and make a

---

[26]The term "Jew" first appears at this time (see Chapter 10). It began as a national designation: exiles from the State of Judah. It came to mean ex–Israelites who were widely dispersed, and living as minorities among other peoples, yet maintaining a common identity.

third century date unlikely."[27] The complete lack of Greek words in Esther, along with the multiplicity of Persian loan words and names, underlines this evaluation and points clearly to a time in the Persian era.

But the Persian Era, even that segment remaining after the reign of Xerxes, amounts to a period of over one hundred forty years, approximately the same amount of time that has passed from the end of the American Civil War to the present. Can we linguistically narrow down the possible time of composition yet further? The Hebrew of Esther is most like that of the Book of Chronicles. Freedman places the composition of Chronicles shortly after the completion of the Second Temple around the year 515 BCE.[28] If Freedman is right, then Esther must have been written somewhere during the first half of the fifth century to account for the similarity of style, or at the most no more than fifty years after the last events related in the Book of Esther (that is, roughly between 470 and 420 BCE). Given the sense of retrospective that pervades the Book, perhaps sometime during the reign of Xerxes' successor, Artaxerxes I (465–424 BCE) might be ventured as the age in which Esther was written.

Another line of reasoning is that of Albert Friedberg and Vincent DeCaen who analyze biblical styles of dating. During the First Commonwealth era, while the Israelites dwelt in their own land, months were designated by number alone, or by number and the Canaanite name: for example, "In the fourth year of Solomon's reign over Israel, in the month of Ziv, which is the second month, that he began to build the house of the Lord" (1 Kings 6:1). With the Babylonian Exile the Jews began using the Babylonian names for the months, coupling them with the old numbering system for clarity: for example, "On the twenty-fourth day of the eleventh month, which is the month of Shebat, in the second year of Darius,[29] the word of the Lord came to Zechariah" (Zechariah 1:7). With the passage of time the Jews became fully accustomed to the use of the Babylonian month names and ceased to designate the months by numbers: for example, "Now it came to pass in the month of Nisan, in the twentieth year of Artaxerxes the king" (Nehemiah 2:1).[30]

What characterizes the dates cited in Esther is that they always mention the Babylonian month name coupled with the old numbering system, just as is done in the Book of Zechariah. This would seem to indicate a closer proximity to the age of Zechariah than that of Nehemiah. Friedberg and DeCaen conclude: "Thus we arrive at a date somewhere in the late fifth century: crucially, two centuries earlier than the consensus third-century dating."[31]

Yet another way of trying to fix the date of the Book's composition is to follow Yehezkel Kaufmann's analysis of the *type* of anti–Semitism Esther describes.[32] It is neither the Christian nor the Hellenistic model. That the anti–Semitism of Haman bears no resemblance to the form it took under Christianity is obvious. Christian anti–Semitism centers on the charge of deicide: the charge that the Jews, in rejecting and killing Jesus, are thus an accursed people. No hint of this charge can be found in Esther.

---

[27]As quoted in Moore, *Esther*, p. lvii. A century ago the idea was common that the Book was a product of the Greek era, sometime in the first century BCE. The basis of this was the widespread belief that the plot of the Book of Esther (Haman's attempt to exterminate the Jews) was a "disguised description" of the Antiochan Persecutions of 168–165 BCE. This position has very few supporters today.

[28]Freedman, "The Chronicler's Purpose," p. 442.

[29]That is, 520 BCE.

[30]That is, 444 BCE. Of course the Book of Nehemiah was written well after this date; possibly around 425 BCE if Nehemiah himself wrote it.

[31]Friedberg, "Dating the Composition of the Book of Esther," p. 428.

[32]Kaufmann, *Toldot Ha'emunah Hayisraelit*, Vol. VIII, pp. 439–51.

Moving back into pre–Christian times we find ourselves in the Hellenistic Age. This period — inaugurated by Alexander the Great's conquest of the Persian Empire (334–323 BCE) and the subsequent superimposition of a diluted and barbarized version of classical Greek culture upon its subject populations — very quickly manifested a widespread and virulent form of anti–Semitism. We know of this from many sources. Probably the most complete picture of Hellenistic-Roman anti–Semitism emerges from the work of Flavius Josephus, *Contra Apion*.[33] This book, a systematic rebuttal of the canards of one Apion, the most widely known and vicious anti–Semite of that era, of necessity contains a complete summary of the contentions of contemporary anti–Semitism. The charge of Hellenistic anti–Semitism was that the Jews despise the religions of the nations; that they want to destroy all the images of the gods; that they therefore separate themselves from all non–Jews and hate anyone who is not Jewish. Once again none of these accusations, the staples of Hellenistic anti–Semitism, find any echoes in Esther. Thus all lines of evidence — linguistic, month-citation and content — converge to reject not only the Hellenistic age but also the late Persian era. We are squarely in the middle Persian period.

Though the Ancient World knew examples of peoples holding negative attitudes to other religions — the Egyptians and the Zoroastrians are prime examples — Haman does not charge the Jews with this attitude. The Book of Esther reflects a widespread and deeply felt antipathy toward the Jews and their perceived "otherness," their self-isolation and their alien customs. But the feeling is not yet focused on a cause other than the Jews as Jews; in other words, racism. More than two centuries must elapse before the masses will begin to understand the source of their antipathy: that Jewish "otherness" and self-isolation are due to their religion. By that time we are well into the Hellenistic Age.[34]

Since the antipathy is racial rather than religious, we can be quite secure in pronouncing the Book a product of the Persian Age, fairly close in time to the events portrayed and thus a reasonably accurate reflection of them.

The Place of Esther in the Bible

The Hebrew Book of Esther is a remarkably good read: it is funny, has a good plot, is fast paced, full of suspense, and with enough tension and twists of plot to keep the reader turning the pages (with periodic pauses for laughter) all the way.[35] Yet despite its many virtues Esther did not have easy sledding when it came to getting canonized, that is, admitted into the Bible. And even when it was canonized, it was not universally accepted. Some Jewish groups during the Second Temple period refused to accept the Book as canonical.[36] For centuries, though

---

[33]*Against Apion* (or *On the Antiquity of the Jews*, its original title) is a work in two parts: the first part contains extracts from a large number of anti–Semitic works no longer extant, and sets out to refute their contentions. The second part focuses on the inner value of Judaism and its ethical superiority to Hellenism. Both parts are written with great literary skill and persuasiveness. For Josephus see Glossary.

[34]It was the upper class that caught on first. At the end of the fifth century BCE the Egyptian priests instigated a pogrom against the Jews of Elephantine, specifically targeting the Jewish sanctuary for destruction. In Persia it took time until the total Jewish rejection of "the gods" penetrated the consciousness of the population at large. Before it did the Persian Age was over and the Hellenistic Age was in full swing.

[35]We are referring to MT, the Esther as it appears in the Hebrew Bible, the basis of virtually all English translations. The Greek versions, though also very good reads, are another matter entirely: they will be discussed in Appendix III: It's Greek to Me.

[36]According to Josephus, Judaism in the first century CE was divided into three main religious groupings — Saducees, Pharisees, and Essenes (as well as numerous minor ones). The Essenes apparently refused to accept Esther. It is the only biblical Book of which no remains have been found at Qumran. It appears likely that several minor sects, loosely aligned in practice and theology with the Essenes, also did not accept Esther as part of their Bible.

accepted by Western Churches, many of the Eastern Churches held it at arm's length. And despite the eventual acceptance of Esther as canonical by mainstream Judaism and Christianity there have been, all through the ages, circles which have been uneasy, to say the least, in the presence of Esther.[37] What can explain this hesitancy on the one hand, and the eventual acceptance of Esther as Holy Writ on the other?

It would seem that the major impediment to the acceptance of Esther was the very element that makes it so interesting to us: its extreme secularism. It seemed scandalous that while Ahasuerus, a mere king of flesh and blood, and a Gentile at that, is mentioned no less than one hundred ninety times in the Book, yet God receives no mention at all. There is not even an allusion to the Torah,[38] the foundation scriptures of Judaism. Circumcision receives no mention, nor do prayer, the Temple or sacrifice.[39] The only "religious practice" highlighted in the Book is fasting, a practice not unique to the Jewish religion. Pagans fasted as well. To add to the scandal, the heroine, Esther, marries a non–Jew, conceals her Jewish identity and, as was recognized by Jewish commentators from the beginning, could hardly have observed the Jewish religious requirements of Sabbath observance and dietary laws in her pagan court environment.[40]

That Esther was nonetheless canonized, despite its "religious shortcomings," testifies to the keen insight of the early rabbis that there was something more here than merely a "good read." The part of the Bible to which Esther was assigned, the Ketubim or Writings,[41] is composed of Books defined as written under divine inspiration. In other words, by canonizing Esther they were officially recognizing the Book as a religious work, despite its apparent "deficiencies." One of the main purposes of our study of Esther is to identify the inner meaning of the Book which led the early rabbis to canonize it.[42]

When was Esther canonized? Up until quite recently it was conventional to speak of the Council of Jamnia (or more correctly Yavneh) of 90 CE as the time and place where the canon was finalized. This is no longer the consensus view. "It is now agreed that canonization was a gradual process that occurred over many years, and not a one time act by a group of rabbis."[43] Or as C.A. Moore comments: "'Jamnia in A. D. 90' is ... a convenient phrase or symbol to mark the closing of the Jewish canonization process rather than a definitive date."[44] In other words, Esther did not have to wait until 90 CE to receive an official "Seal of Approval" and be admitted into

---

[37]One of the classic examples of this in more recent times is the much quoted remark of Martin Luther: "I am so hostile to this book [2 Maccabees] and to Esther that I could wish they did not exist at all" (Luther, *Table Talk*, p. 13). He cited "Judaizing" and "pagan impropriety" as his reasons, but there may have been others as well.

[38]See Glossary. For a discussion of the way the Hebrew Bible is organized, and how this organization differs from that of Christian Bibles, see the last pages of Chapter 1.

[39]Following the decree of Cyrus the Temple had been rebuilt. Jews of this period living in the Diaspora routinely prayed facing toward the Holy Temple in Jerusalem.

[40]LXX goes out of its way to "cover up" for Esther, and for Mordecai as well. Both in the major Additions to the text and in various minor changes, it insists that Mordecai instructed Esther to maintain her observance of all Jewish laws and customs while in the palace, and that she did so. For a discussion of the Greek versions of Esther (of which LXX is one) see Appendix III: It's Greek to Me.

[41]See note 38 above.

[42]There is no question that a parallel motive was that Esther provided the raison d'être for the, by that time, established and popular observance of the Festival of Purim, and indeed authorized it. (A discussion of Purim is deferred until Chapter 19, when we will be better prepared to understand the issues involved.) But this was hardly the determining factor. Hanukkah was to become as deeply entrenched a religious holiday as Purim, yet this did not lead to the canonization of either 1 Macabees or 2 Macabees.

[43]Berlin, *Esther*, p. xliii.

[44]Moore, *Esther*, p. xxi.

the Bible. It was doubtless accepted as Sacred Scripture long before. The question is: how long before? Without getting involved in the scholarly debate on the matter, it would seem that the acceptance of Esther into the Bible had to have taken place well before the appearance of the Greek versions of the Book. The purpose of the Greek versions was to make available to non-- Hebrew-speaking Jews the Books of the Bible in a form they could read. It would appear that the Septuagint (LXX) of Esther can be dated to 114 BCE.[45] This would mean that from about the middle of the second century BCE Esther was already an accepted part of the Bible.[46]

This was to prove decisive to Christianity's stance. By the time of the birth of Christianity, the canonical status of Esther was entrenched in normative or mainstream Judaism. Despite all hesitations and reservations about Esther's secularity, the fact that it was an established part of the Jewish Bible ultimately insured that the Book was enshrined in the Christian Bible as well.[47]

Having reached this point, we should have sufficient background to enable us to plunge directly into the Book of Esther itself.

[45]This is based on the colophon (appendix) to the LXX that dates the translation to "the fourth year of the reign of Ptolemy and Cleopatra." It would appear that the reference is to Ptolemy VII.

[46]It is only fair to mention that this position is rejected by Harry Orlinsky who, basing himself on the work of Solomon Zeitlin (Zeitlin, "Study of Canonization," pp. 132–134), argues strongly (but to my mind unconvincingly) that "there was no formal canonization of the Book by the rabbis" and that it was "public pressure" that somehow got Esther into the Bible in the latter half of the 2nd century CE (Orlinsky, "The Canonization of the Hebrew Bible," pp. 272–275). It is one thing to say that canonization was a gradual process to which the rabbis at the end gave definitive status, and quite another to claim that there never was a formal canonization and that somehow "public pressure" took the place of the rabbis. It furthermore does nothing to explain why the Jews of Alexandria produced (and accepted as canonical) a Greek translation of a non-canonical Book.

[47]The only issue that remained was in what form. This matter will be dealt with as part of the discussion of the problem of the Greek versions in Appendix III: It's Greek to Me.

Act I: The Women in His Life

> Business was his aversion; pleasure was his business.
> — Maria Edgeworth, *The Contrast*

CHAPTER 9

Party Time in Old Persia, or Lessons on How to Run an Empire

> A very merry, dancing, drinking,
> Laughing, quaffing, and unthinking time.
> — John Dryden, *Secular Masque, I*

> What times! What manners!
> — Marcus Tillius Cicero, *In Catilinam*

The Big Bash

This is a tale bathed in more than oriental splendor (to use Kipling's pointed phrase). It is a tale of Eastern kings and queens, crafty courtiers, scheming eunuchs and grand viziers. It begins, quite appropriately, with a party. But not just any old party; this is a party to end all parties, one befitting a king who rules the greatest empire humanity has ever known. And lest we assume that all this is a fairytale, an unbounded flight of the imagination designed to intrigue, titillate and amuse, the author does not begin with a time-honored phrase such as: "Once upon a time there was a king who threw a party." No, our author opens by naming names and specifying dates. If what is related will amaze, amuse and scandalize that is not because it is fantastical. The form the narrative will take will be one of exposé. If reputations will be ruined, so be it.

Now it came to pass in the days of Ahasuerus — that is, the Ahasuerus who reigned over one hundred and twenty-seven provinces from India to Ethiopia — in those days, when King Ahasuerus sat on his throne in the Acropolis[1] of Shushan,[2] in the third year of his reign he threw a party for all his officials and courtiers; [the chief officers of] the army of Persia and Media,[3] the nobles and the

---

[1]See Chapter 8, note 8.

[2]The Achaemenian Empire had several capitals, each with its own specialized focus: Persepolis, Ecbatana, Babylon and Susa (the Shushan of the Bible). Susa, the ancient capital of Elam, was located 200 miles east of Babylon. Because of its central position, it served as the administrative center of the Empire and was the hub of the communications system that held the vast Empire together.

[3]The key to the creation of the Achaemenian Empire was the victory of Cyrus II (the Great) over the Medes and the capture of their capital, Ecbatana, in 550 BCE. His success in welding the Median and Persian people together into one unified force under his command made possible the conquests that established the Empire.

governors of the provinces who were present. For many days — even a hundred and eighty days!— he showed off the vast wealth of his kingdom and the glorious splendor of his majesty (1:1–4).

In Chapter 8 we have tried to show how these opening words would have worked for the original audience for whom the Book of Esther was written: the Jewish population of Susa and other imperial centers. Both they and we know that we are in the period leading up to the invasion of Greece. The author has chosen to open our tale with this setting. The great war council Herodotus reports to have been called in 483 BCE, and the bombastic and arrogant speeches Xerxes is reported to have made in order to whip up the enthusiasm and mobilize the cooperation of the elite of his empire for his venture, fit well with the extravaganza pictured here.[4] But in our story not a word of war, not a mention of the looming catastrophe is to be heard. Only the oblique hint of the date — the third year of the reign of King Ahasuerus (483 BCE) — obtrudes to color the pompous and vainglorious scene. The author concentrates our attention solely on the ostentation, the conspicuous consumption, the illustrious guest list, the interminable duration of the proceedings.

A word on partying in ancient Persia: the Hebrew term used here and elsewhere in the Book, *mishteh*, is usually rendered in English as "banquet" or "feast." But *mishteh* here really means a social occasion given over to drinking, a drinking bout. Indeed we hear of no eating at any of the various parties that punctuate the Book, only heavy and continuous drinking. The closest parallel we have in our world is the cocktail party. But a cocktail party only lasts for a couple of hours, and everyone remains standing. In Persia the guests lay on couches and the drinking could go on for days. (The 180 days, even if the imperial elite came and went in relays,[5] may be a bit of an exaggeration, but then the aim of the author is satire and he regularly employs exaggeration as a way of making his point.)

Having at long last finished with his showing off to his officials and to the military brass, the king now continues his vulgar display with a week-long open house for the inhabitants of the capital.

> Now at the end of these days, the king threw a seven-day party for all the people who were present in the Acropolis of Shushan, the great and the small alike, in the court of the garden of the king's pavilion[6] (1:5).

To handle the crowds the royal banquet hall will not suffice, so the king throws open the court abutting on the royal gardens. And now the author, in the best tradition of a syndicated gossip columnist, begins to show us around this vast area.[7]

> [There were hangings of] white cotton and blue, caught up by purple cords of fine linen on silver rods and marble columns; there were couches of gold and silver on a pavement of porphyry, marble, mother-of-pearl and colored stone. The drinks were served in golden goblets, all sorts of goblets, and limitless royal wine — as befits a king. And the rule for drinking was: There are no limits; for the king had given orders to all his stewards to do just what everyone wanted. Now Vashti the queen also gave a [parallel] party for the women in King Ahasuerus' royal palace (1:6–9).

---

[4]Herodotus, *Histories*, Book VII, 8.

[5]Above and beyond the organization of the pending invasion of Greece, inviting all his generals, governors, etc. from the furthest reaches of the empire would serve the purpose of consolidating his regime: Ahasuerus needed to get to know the key officials of his far flung government face to face, and to impress himself upon them as their new ruler.

[6]"An open structure, probably a colonnaded open hall" (Oppenheim, "On Royal Gardens in Mesopotamia," p. 332).

[7]How uncharacteristic this is of biblical literature will become evident by comparison with Ruth and Genesis 38. "Need to know" is the overriding rule; action and speech are everything, while description of surroundings virtually non-existent. See "Conventions and Context" in the Introduction.

And here we learn something else: the carouse in the open court outside the gardens is a stag party. All the beautiful and *costly* decorations — marble pillars, inlaid stone floors, gold and silver couches, colored curtains hung from silver rods tied with purple cords — are no more than a stage setting for a mob of high life and low life busy drinking themselves into a stupor. Persian palace drinking was usually a very formal and ritualized affair. When the king drank, everyone was required to drink. When he abstained so did they. Yet for this week all the rules are suspended. Everyone can drink when he wants and as much as he wants. And out of goblets of *gold*! Each goblet a *work of art*! How the plaza must have looked after two or three days defies imagination. At the far end of the court, possibly on a raised platform, surrounded by his counselors, his courtiers and his cronies lies the king.

Meanwhile, inside the palace, out of sight but probably not out of hearing, Queen Vashti and the ladies are having their own drinking party (yes, the term *mishteh* is used for the queen's party as well) — hopefully more moderate and more decorous than the debauch in the gardens. Welcome to high life in Old Persia.

"She Won't Come!": The Social Order Is Threatened

> On the seventh day, when the king's heart was merry with wine, he commanded Mehuman, Bizzetha, Harbona, Bigtha, and Abagtha, Zethar and Careas, the seven eunuchs who served King Ahasuerus, to bring Vashti the queen before the king wearing the royal crown, to show the peoples and the princes her beauty, for she was very beautiful.[8] But Queen Vashti refused to come at the king's command [as conveyed] by the eunuchs! The king was furious, and his anger burned in him (1:10–12).

The party is at long last winding down. After six days the gorgeous inlayed pavement is littered with articles of clothing, scattered utensils, and those guests who have drunk themselves into a stupor; couches are filthy; the guests still conscious are sullen and morose. As is often the case with overlong parties the end is turning into an anti-climax.

The king is not in the best of shape but he is still there. We are told that "the king's heart was merry with wine," which means that he was very drunk but was still short of passing out. He is acutely aware that things are turning sour; the party is fizzling out. It is imperative that something be done to put some life back into it, to end the party with a bang. In his besoused state, in a flash of inebriated genius he knows just the thing: bring on the girls. And not just any girls; show the boys the king's own stunning beauty: the World-Famous Queen Vashti.

But Ahasuerus is, after all, a king. And a king, no matter how smashed, still must act with propriety. So he loudly orders up an official delegation, made up of the seven (count them, seven!) royal eunuchs to fetch the queen. Their names are actually recorded![9] We can picture the royal secretary, probably very much worse for wear, frantically scribbling an official protocol of the royal command. So off go the seven royal eunuchs, attempting to retain as much dignity as possible under the circumstances, with the king calling after them to make sure the queen is wearing her crown when she shows. That certainly woke them up! The courtyard is electric with anticipation.

---

[8]Literally, "for she was fair to look upon."

[9]Of course the command had to be conveyed by eunuchs: no one else was permitted into the women's quarters (the harem). But seven? Wouldn't one do?

What exactly does the king intend? There are serious differences of opinion, mainly between the ancient commentators and the modern ones. Many of the ancients took the command to wear the royal crown to mean that that is all Vashti is to wear: what is intended is a strip show with the queen exhibiting herself naked before the drunken crowd, the crown serving as ornamentation. Most modern commentators, more scholarly — or perhaps just more prudish — than the ancients, insist that no king, no matter how drunk, could ever intend to show his wife naked in public.[10] But it is irrelevant to get involved in an argument as to what exactly the potted king is intending because his expectations, whatever they are, are thwarted. Vashti rebuffs the delegation with a flat "no." She refuses to come!

The king's embarrassment is enormous. Our author does not consider the statement "the king was furious" sufficient to the occasion, but supplements it with the phrase "and his anger burned in him." In other words, Ahasuerus goes into one of his fits of wild and irrational fury. He is famous for them.[11] When the fit is upon him no one knows what to expect. One can easily imagine the eunuchs, their job done, quickly making themselves scarce. The members of the Advisory Council have no such option; they are among the honored invitees on the dais. They have no choice but to remain.

> Then the king turned to the experts who knew the precedents[12] (for this was the practice of the king in the presence of all who were versed in law and procedure; his closest advisors being Charshena, Shethat, Admatha, Tarshish, Meres, Marsena and Memucan, the seven princes of Persia and Media who had access to the royal presence and who ranked first in the kingdom[13]): "According to the law, what should be done with Queen Vashti, since she has not obeyed the command of King Ahasuerus, [as conveyed to her] by the eunuchs?" (1:13–15).

The shock of being turned down has sobered Ahasuerus a bit, but not much. Mainly it has had the effect of turning him from a boisterous and convivial drunk into a self-conscious and pompous drunk. Furious he remains. He now turns to his advisors — a long aside informs us who they are, what their rank is, their especial area of expertise and that they are among the few with direct access to the king[14] — and demands to be advised. What are we to do with this Queen who dares to disobey the express command of King Ahasuerus? (note the pompous use of the third person) — conveyed by an official delegation of eunuchs, no less! Make sure, he continues, that the advice you give me is one hundred percent legal. And this from the man who has just broken all precedent by his (probably illegal) command that his legal wife display herself at a stag party![15] Ahasuerus is the worst kind of drunk: an unpredictable one.

---

[10]Interestingly, there were stories current in the ancient world of kings doing just that. Herodotus (*Histories*, Book I, 8–13) relates an episode in which the Lydian king, Candaules, arranged for a peep show to exhibit his beautiful wife while she was undressing. Unlike the Vashti affair, she was not forewarned and only later learned what had happened. She was not amused!

[11]One example among many: while on the march with his army to the invasion of Greece, Xerxes and his troops were lavishly entertained at Celaenae by one Pythius, the richest man in the Empire. Later at Sardis, unwisely banking on the king's gratitude for his extravagant gesture, he asked a favor of the king: that his eldest son, who was serving in the army, be transferred from active duty and allowed to stay at home with his father. In fury at what he regarded the insolent demand of a "slave," Xerxes had the son cut in two, one half placed at each side of the gate of Sardis through which the army then marched on its way to Greece.

[12]Literally, "said to the wise men who knew the times"; that is, his advisors and legal experts.

[13]Literally, "who saw the king's face and sat first in the kingdom."

[14]Remember this point; it will become important later.

[15]While Persian law and custom permitted concubines at a drinking party, a stag party would most certainly be off limits to a *legal wife*.

The Saving of the Social Order

The members of the Royal Advisory Council — princes of Persia and Media, men of the first rank, and so on — are probably wishing they had drunk considerably less. If they don't handle this furious and unpredictable king just right, not only their jobs but also their very necks may be forfeit. It is Memucan, one of the king's councilors, who sizes up the situation and steps into the breach.

In what follows, ridiculous though it may sound, we have an extremely astute presentation by a councilor who has kept a clear head, and who has a penetrating understanding of his capricious master and what it will take to handle him. The king is in one of his pompous, self-important moods: his *dignity* has been *affronted*. He sent a *delegation* of royal eunuchs to fetch the queen — and even then she turned him down! But he doesn't turn to a friend or crony for a suggestion as to how to handle his difficult wife, he turns to the *Royal Council,* who hold in the hollow of their hands the very running of the Empire. It is not a husband who has been slapped down; it is *King Ahasuerus*! This is a *National Crisis*! So Memucan shrewdly plays to the skewered royal ego, transmuting a ridiculous domestic spat into a threat to the social order.

> Then Memucan spoke before the king and the princes: "It is not only the king that Queen Vashti has wronged, but also all the princes and all the peoples that are in all the provinces of King Ahasuerus! For when the queen's deed becomes known to all the women, it will cause them to despise their husbands, for they will say: 'King Ahasuerus commanded that Queen Vashti be brought before him, and she would not come!' This very day the ladies[16] of Persia and Media who have heard of the queen's behavior will rebel[17] against all the king's princes; there will be no end of contempt and anger!" (1:16–18).

In other words, this act of Vashti will spark a feminist rebellion that will destroy the social order!

> "[Therefore], if it please the king, let a royal decree go out from him, and let it be written in the laws of Persia and Media so that it may not be revoked,[18] that Vashti[19] no more come into the presence of King Ahasuerus. And as to her royal state — let the king confer it upon someone more worthy than she. Then, when the king's decree, which he has proclaimed, is heard throughout his kingdom, vast as it is, all women will treat their husbands with respect,[20] great and small alike" (1:19–20).

The counsel of Memucan consists of two parts: one deals with the immediate issue of slapping down the "rebellious" Vashti, the other with the preventing of a feminist revolution and preserving social stability. The first, of course, is merely the means of accomplishing the second; the king must not appear petty. Vashti wouldn't come to the king when called; she will not now be allowed to come to the king even when she *wants* to come. What this means is that

---

[16]That is, the wives of the princes present at the king's extravaganza.

[17]Reading *tamreyna*, to rebel (fem.); MT reads "they will say" (but what will they say?) The word lacks a direct object. All attempts to keep the text as is involve the insertion of an implied direct object, which not only makes unwarranted assumptions but tortures the text. The cure is worse than the disease.

[18]One of the assumptions that lies behind the Book is that Royal Decrees, once recorded in writing, become as immutable and irrevocable as the laws of Persia and Media. In fact, the traditional tribal law of the Persians and the Medes was unalterable, but whether royal decrees could be written into the law and thus become unalterable is another question. Our current state of knowledge makes it difficult to determine if indeed this was the case. Perhaps this is just part of the omnipresent exaggeration, one of the main vehicles of the sarcasm that pervades the Book. We will go further into this matter in Chapter 17.

[19]Note that Vashti's title of queen is here omitted — probably intentionally: Queen Vashti has become plain Vashti. She is in the process of becoming a non-person.

[20]Literally, "will give honor to their husbands."

she is being permanently confined to quarters, a kind of house arrest. No woman, once married to the king, could leave the women's quarters of the palace unless to attend upon the king, and by his leave.[21] This decision will turn the harem into a life-long prison for Vashti. What is more, she is to be stripped of her royal status. She will no longer be able to lord it over the other women in the harem; her days at the head of the pecking order among the women will be over.

And here Memucan inserts a clause whose purpose is to provide himself with a personal insurance policy. The danger of initiating the queen's demotion lies in the risk of the king later changing his mind. If Vashti is ever reinstated, Memucan's future is bleak indeed; once back as queen, Vashti will make certain of that. So Memucan proposes that the king make a royal proclamation of her banishment, and that it furthermore be recorded among the permanent laws of Persia and Media.

Having covered himself, Memucan rushes on to the "big picture," before the king can grasp all the implications of the proposal. This awful example of the king's justice, when proclaimed throughout the Empire — from India to Ethiopia — will stop the incipient feminist uprising in its tracks. No woman will dare rebel against her *lawful lord and master*; from the top to the bottom of the social order all wives will hereafter show *respect* to their husbands. The king's example will underwrite the status of every husband, and social stability will prevail.

Now this is the kind of advice a king like Ahasuerus likes to hear: simple, precise, and infinitely boosting to the bruised royal ego. Not a moment must be lost in putting it into effect.

> This advice[22] pleased the king and the princes, and the king did as Memucan advised.[23] So he sent dispatches to all the king's provinces, to every province in its own script, and to every people in its own language,[24] to the effect that every man should be master in his own house, and speak the language of his own people[25] (1:21–22).

Chaos and social disorder have been averted, the king's dignity has been preserved, and everyone can go home with the serene sense that all is right with the world. This is the way to run an empire, especially the mightiest empire on earth.

---

[21]We shall see what risks were involved should a woman take the initiative and try to force herself upon the king's presence.

[22]Literally, "The word."

[23]Literally, "according to the word of Memucan."

[24]The empire being polyglot, different languages and scripts prevailed in different provinces. Usually royal decrees were issued in Aramaic, the lingua franca of the Empire. But for this supremely important decree it is imperative that every husband and wife understand what is demanded of them, so even the most out of the way language of the most obscure portion of the population must be used so that no one will fail to understand who is to be boss in every single home.

[25]"When a marriage took place between people of different ethnic backgrounds, the mother's language would normally prevail in the home and tend to become the language of the children. Nehemiah explicitly complains that when some Jews married foreign wives, their children spoke the language of their mothers (*Nehemiah* 13: 23–24). Ahasuerus' edict was designed to make the father's language dominant in the home" (Gordis, "Studies in the Esther Narrative," p. 53).

CHAPTER 10

The Substitute

There are certainly not so many men of large fortune
in the world as there are pretty women to deserve them.
— Jane Austen, *Mansfield Park*

By this time the humor of what we have been reading has begun to impress itself upon us. The vast gatherings of intoxicated Persians, the pompous parades of eunuchs, the proposed girlie-show featuring the queen as the star stripper, the ludicrous Royal Decree mandating the unchallengeable supremacy of every fool of a husband in his hovel, and, far from least, the besotted fool sitting on the throne — all form one hilarious tableau. The whole vast empire — from India to Ethiopia — stands revealed to us as nothing more than a stage setting for a farce.

There are some scholars who contend that this is exactly what the Book of Esther is: no more than a comedy written to entertain a bored and jaded leisure class. But if this were so we would be hard pressed to explain what such a book is doing in the Bible. Starting with the assumption that those persons who were responsible for canonizing the Bible[1] were serious human beings, one could expect their choices to be anything but frivolous. This line of reasoning would lead us to suspect that, far from the undoubted humor being an end in itself, it serves as a means to serious ends: the humor is the sugar coating on a pill that contains the messages and purposes of the Book of Esther. We will learn that it is a bitter pill indeed, making understandable the need for sugar-coating to enable the reader to swallow it. For the present it is sufficient to note that the humor takes the form of a biting sarcasm, and what we have been reading is a devastating attack upon the Achaemenian Empire: upon its waste, its lechery, its debauchery and its fool of a ruler.[2] The attack is comprehensive because the rot is structural: this is not the fault of one man or a group of men; the society itself is in decline, and encour-

---

[1]That is, selecting the books that would be defined as sacred writings. See Chapter 8.

[2]To understand the relevance of the satire to its period we have to realize that Xerxes' reign marked a turning point in social morals. Both Herodotus (*Histories*, Book I:80) and Xenophon (*Cyropaedia* I, 2:8) inform us that until the reign of Xerxes (Ahasuerus) the Persians were abstemious in food and drink, eating only one meal per day and drinking nothing but water. From the time of Xerxes "one meal a day" was interpreted by the court and the upper classes to mean a meal stretching from noon to well after dark, and drunkenness became the common vice of every class. The Persian code of virtue that had built the empire has given way to the hedonistic indulgence that would bring it down. On one level, then, this Book is a vicious assault, using satire and sarcasm as its main tools, upon the "signs of the times."

ages the stupidity and corruption that ensure its ultimate collapse. In Persian political terms this is a very subversive work; there is no more potent weapon than satire to undermine a social order. What we have been seeing is the government of the vast and imposing empire turned into a laughing-stock, its ruling elite portrayed as a pack of pompous drunken fools and self-serving sybarites. Worse is to come.

The Morning After

The trouble with the partying life lies in those cold and bleak times between the parties, when one has to pick up the pieces and face the consequences of one's extravagant behavior. After the extended debauch that had been occupying Ahasuerus, sobering up must have been a painful process.

> Some time later,[3] when King Ahasuerus' anger had subsided, he remembered Vashti and what she had done, and what had been decreed against her (2:1).

After the hangover has passed, second thoughts start to rise. He begins to remember how beautiful Vashti was, how proud he had been of her. Now that he has cooled down a bit he begins to wonder if, after all, what she did was all that terrible. Did she really deserve the punishment she received? Note the language used: he remembered what *she* had done. The author does not continue that he remembered what *he* had done to her, but rather what *had been done* to her. *He* was not responsible; it was *others* who had given advice, *others* who had prepared the decree; he had just signed the paper thrust before him at a time when he was not at his best. One can see where this is likely to lead. The king is interested in changing his mind, and finding that he has been maneuvered into a position where he cannot reinstate Vashti, the next step is likely to be that it is his advisors who will bear the brunt of his frustration.[4]

We are not the only ones able to gauge which way the wind is blowing; those in close attendance on the king can read the signs. At all costs Ahasuerus must not be allowed to brood on Vashti. His thoughts must be diverted elsewhere.

> Then the king's youths[5] who attended him said: "Let there be sought for the king beautiful young virgins; let the king appoint officials in all the provinces of his kingdom that they may gather all the beautiful young virgins to the Acropolis of Shushan, to the harem, under the supervision of Hegai[6] the King's Eunuch, Keeper of the Women, and let them receive their beauty treatment.[7] And let the maiden who most pleases the king rule in place of Vashti." The thing pleased the king, and he did so (2:2–4).

Drunk or sober, the king seems to go for extravagant, gigantic proposals with embedded concern for picayune administrative detail. Last time it was a Royal Decree determining how every husband in the empire, from Asiatic Greek to Hindu peasant, was to order his domestic affairs. Now it is to be a Miss Persia contest, run in each of the one hundred twenty-seven

---

[3]Literally, "After these events," an expression denoting the passage of an indefinite period of time.

[4]The fact that the councilor who gave the advice, Memucan, never resurfaces in the Book has led some early commentators to conclude that Ahasuerus did indeed settle the score with him.

[5]As most Persian kings, Ahasuerus was bisexual. As such, it was common for kings to be personally attended by adolescent boys who, of necessity, became adept in manipulating their master.

[6]Here the Hebrew reads *Hege*; a contracted form of *Hegai* which we find in 2:8 and 2:15. We have preferred to use the fuller form of the name here for the sake of consistency; there are enough strange Persian names to confuse us without augmenting the problem with different versions of the same name. Herodotus (*Histories*, Book IX: 33) refers to a eunuch of Xerxes by the name of '*egias*, who may be the same person.

[7]Literally, "their massage." More on Persian beauty treatments further on.

provinces of the empire, with the winners (*and* the runners-up?) sent to the capital for the final run-offs. The contestants are to be the pick of the beautiful young virgins of the empire. At the final judging of the regional winners at Susa, the sole judge will be none other than Ahasuerus himself; he will get to try out each of the contestants and the winner will get to be a queen.[8] This is exactly the kind of proposal that will seize Ahasuerus's imagination. The king gives his approval and the orders go out. The empire prepares for the contest to end all contests. And while the king is busy "judging," when will he find either time or inclination to think of Vashti? With this king, damage control is a non-stop problem.

Enter the Jew

Up to now the entire focus has been upon the troubles the king of Persia has been having with his wife Vashti. Not counting a few counselors and eunuchs, who are thrown in as a supporting cast, the king and his wife are the central figures of a satire on the Persian Empire and the way it is governed. But at this point, unexpectedly, two new characters walk onto the stage, and the entire focus shifts. In retrospect we will realize that the new actors are really the heroes of the drama, and that all that has gone on before is mere prologue; in the unfolding plot even King Ahasuerus has no greater role than that of straight man.

Unlike everyone who has been on stage until now, our newcomers are not Persians, the people who created the empire and who dominate it. We have already had our attention drawn to the fact that this vast empire encompasses hundreds of separate ethnic and linguistic groups. It is a structure teeming with minorities. It is from one of the smallest of these minorities, numerically speaking, that the new protagonists are drawn. They are Jews.

Who are the Jews and what are they doing in Susa? From the Bible we know much about their antecedents, the Children of Israel, or for short, the Israelites. Exiled to Babylon following the destruction of their Kingdom of Judah and its capital, Jerusalem, they came to be known to their neighbors (and to themselves) as "Jews"—persons who had come from the land

---

[8]It has been objected by literalists that this scenario is impossible. Herodotus claims that Achaemenian kings could marry only women from the seven chief noble families of Persia, so Ahasuerus couldn't have chosen a queen in this "democratic" manner. This "constitutional limitation," however, is highly questionable. Xerxes' own mother, Atossa, was not from one of the approved families. We further tend to assume that Persian kings were monogamous. They weren't. "Several of the Persian kings had more than one wife; for Darius I, we hear of six ... polygamy was probably the norm," says Amelie Kuhrt. Furthermore, she points out that Persian kings took non–Persian women as concubines; Artaxerxes I, son of Xerxes I, had a Babylonian concubine who bore the son who succeeded his father as Darius II (Kuhrt, *The Ancient Near East*, pp. 683, 687, 696–97). But even if Herodotus was right, this still overlooks the central fact that the Book is a satire, and exaggeration its main tool. We know that Persian kings had harems of dazzling beauties numbering in the hundreds (Plutarch, among others, charges Alexander the Great with copying Persian customs, and claims he gathered a harem of 360 beauties). Ahasuerus could very well have used some such means to restock his harem and choose a favorite bedmate. It is important to note that while the Book says that the king crowned Esther, it never says that he *married* her. Further, Werner Dommershausen has convincingly argued that while the Book refers repeatedly to "The King" and to "King Ahasuerus" it *never* refers to Esther as "The Queen" or to "Queen Esther," but only to "Esther the queen" (as opposed to Vashti who is twice referred to as "Queen Vashti"—1:12, 15 — and once as "The Queen"—1:17), emphasizing that while Ahasuerus *was* king, Esther was merely *one* of his many *wives* (Dommershausen, *Die Estherrolle*, p. 140). The purpose of a noble wife, that is, a queen, is *to produce legitimate heirs to the throne*. The purpose of these women is to be bedmates for the king. It is significant that Esther never has children (at least the Book records none). This is no accident. Any children fathered by Ahasuerus on Esther might be illegitimate (or perhaps not, note the case of Darius II above), but either way would be in a position to contest the succession (Persian history contains many such episodes). Precautions would have been taken to insure that no *unwanted* children would ensue from Ahasuerus' nighttime revels. See note 34 below.

of Judah.[9] By the time they were liberated by Cyrus the Great a half-century later, only about 42,360 took advantage of the opportunity to return to their ancient homeland.[10] Most Jews were sufficiently integrated in their new surroundings to stay put. In the half-century that has passed between the Proclamation of Cyrus freeing the exiles and the opening of our story, we find that the Jews have spread throughout the Persian Empire. There is a Jewish community in Susa, and probably in every major center of the vast regions ruled by the Achaemenian dynasty.

Their very names tell us much about these newcomers to our drama. Mordecai and Esther are not traditional Israelite names. They do not appear in the Bible prior to the Babylonian Exile, and for good reason. They are the names of two Babylonian deities: Marduk and Ishtar (Astarte)! This bespeaks a level of assimilation to their pagan surroundings that is well advanced.[11] We will find other symptoms of this assimilation as we proceed.

> Now a certain Jew was in the Acropolis of Shushan, and his name was Mordecai, son of Jair, son of Shimie, the son of Kish, a Benjamite. He had been exiled from Jerusalem with the captives that were exiled with Jeconiah, king of Judah, whom Nebuchadnezzar, King of Babylon, had carried away. Now he was foster father to Hadassah (that is Esther), his uncle's daughter, for she had neither father nor mother. The maiden had a gorgeous figure and was beautiful[12]; now with the death of her father and mother Mordecai took her as his daughter (2:5–7).

Jeconiah, otherwise known as Jehoiachin, was the last king of Judah.[13] Following a failed revolt against the Babylonians he was deported to Babylon in 597 BCE, along with most of the nobility, the top officials of the kingdom and the most capable of the craftsmen. It is to this earlier deportation that Mordecai traces his exile. This means that it must have been Shimie, Mordecai's grandfather, who had been exiled with his king 114 years before the opening of our story (or perhaps it was his great-grandfather).[14] The family has acclimatized, first to Babylonia, then to Persian society, and has worked its way up the social and economic

---

[9]In our present state of knowledge, the first appearance of the term "Jew," also in the sense of nationality — a person of or from the Kingdom of Judah — is in an extra-biblical source. In the *Annals of Sennacherib*, in his account of his campaign of 701 BCE in Western Asia, the great Assyrian warlord describes the provocations of King "Hezekiah the Jew" that led to the unsuccessful siege of Jerusalem.

[10]Ezra 2:64, Nehemiah 7:66.

[11]A Jew bearing the name Mordecai is not unique to our book. We find the name born by one of the leaders of the Jews who left Babylon to return to Judah and Jerusalem following the Decree of Cyrus, almost half a century before the opening of our tale. Several others among the leaders also had Babylonian names. One had a Persian name (Ezra 2:2, Nehemiah 7:7). It is significant that our heroes bear the names of Babylonian, and not Persian, deities. In the century that has followed their exile it would seem that the Jews have accommodated themselves well to their Babylonian environment, but are still relatively new to the vastly different Persian one. On the other hand one must not make too much of Jews having Babylonian names. It in no way implies that they had adopted Babylonian idolatry. The fact that Christians have adopted the Roman name for their Sabbath, Sunday, does not imply that they worship the sun any more than American Jews with names such as John, Paul, Mary and Mark can thereby be identified as practicing Christians.

[12]Literally, "of beautiful form and fair to look upon." The first term, *yefat toar*, refers to the figure; the second, *tovat mareh*, refers to the face.

[13]See 2 Kings 24:6–17. His uncle, Zedekiah, whom the Babylonians placed on the throne to be their puppet, was not king but Regent in the absence of his nephew, Jeconiah, the legitimate king.

[14]The person exiled in 597 BCE could not have been Mordecai. Not only would he have been at least 114 years old (assuming that he was an infant at the time of the exile), but it has been calculated that if such were the case, Esther could be no younger than sixty. The text obviously refers to one of his forebears. The other alternative, that the author did not know how to count, is not very credible. The Persians kept excellent records, and had inherited Babylonian archives as well. An error of five or six years is possible; an error of seventy to eighty years does not bear consideration.

ladder. So we find Mordecai in Susa, probably a senior-level official of the Persian government.[15]

We are also informed that Mordecai is of noble descent, a member of the House of Kish.[16] For a brief and glorious moment more than five hundred years before, the most illustrious member of that House, Saul, had ruled all Israel as its first king. The passage of the years has not dimmed the memory of that ancient glory; Mordecai's lineage is emphasized and he is undoubtedly proud that royal blood flows in his veins. In his own eyes, as well as in those of his fellow Jews, he is an important person; any memorable accomplishments of his own will only add to his inherited luster.[17]

And now we come to his foster daughter, Esther. Although they are first cousins (Mordecai's father and Esther's father being brothers), by the logic of the tale at least a generation must separate them in age; Esther is probably no older than fifteen, possibly even younger.[18] We are further informed that, besides the name by which she is known to the Persian public, Esther also has the "Jewish name" of Hadassah.[19] It seems that the widespread practice among Jews living in the Diaspora, of having both a vernacular and a Hebrew name, was already common practice in Persian period.[20] In all probability Mordecai also had a Hebrew or Jewish name, but if so we are not informed. Despite the fact that Esther has a Hebrew name, and that the Book that bears her name was written by a Jew for Jews, her vernacular name of Esther is used throughout. As Esther she was known, and as Esther she has remained. As an orphan, her older cousin has taken her under his wing. Though adoption was both known and practiced in the biblical world we are not told that Mordecai adopted her. He acted as her guardian and mentor. Lastly, we are informed that Esther is stunningly beautiful. It has been said that a woman's appearance is her destiny; this is certainly true in the case of Esther. But let us not make the mistake that more than one Bible commentator has made: that Esther was a pretty face manipulated by Mordecai. That there was more to Esther than mere surface beauty we will shortly learn.

Now when the king's edict was proclaimed, and when many maidens were gathered to the Acropolis of Shushan into the custody of Hegai, Esther was taken to the king's palace,[21] to the custody

[15]We have a record of one *Marduka* (the good Babylonian name of which *Mordecai* is the Hebraized version), who was an accountant and one of a commission of inspection dispatched from Susa during either the last years of Darius, or the early years of the reign of Xerxes. This person may not have been our Mordecai, though Arthur Ungnad is probably right when he says, "it is improbable that there were two Mardukas as high officials in Susa" at the same time (Ungnad, "Keilinschriftliche," p. 244). The reason for assuming that Mordecai was an employee of the Persian government will be discussed in the next chapter.

[16]"Names of the form *X-ben-Y* are sometimes met in which Y is a distinguished remote ancestor.... This is a reminder that *ben* 'son,' referred not only to a real son but also to a descendant.... It follows from this that chronological calculations cannot be safely based on a man's name by taking it as a complete genealogy, unless the relationships are established by other evidence" (Anderson, "Israelite Kinship Terminology," pp. 31, 34).

[17]As a Benjamite (that is, belonging to the tribe of Benjamin) Mordecai should not have been involved in the Babylonian Exile. Benjamin, strictly speaking, was part of the Northern Kingdom of Israel, and thus should have been involved in the earlier Assyrian disaster of 721 BCE that produced the "Ten Lost Tribes." However, in the period before 721 the kingdom of Judah had succeeded in annexing Benjamin, thus saving the Benjamites from the Assyrian deluge. That is how Mordecai's ancestors came to be in Jerusalem when the Babylonians deported the nobility along with King Jeconiah.

[18]The specification that contestants to the beauty contest be *young virgins* was no doubt strictly adhered to.

[19]While hardly a name with religious connotations, as are so many in the Bible, Hadassah is a typical Hebrew women's name of the biblical period. It means "myrtle," a species of aromatic bush.

[20]In the Babylonian Exile the prophet Daniel had two names (his vernacular or Babylonian name was Belteshazzar), as did his three companions (Daniel 1:7); for that matter so did Joseph in Egypt some thousand years earlier (Genesis 41:45).

[21]Literally, "the king's house."

of Hegai, Keeper of the Women. The maiden pleased him and gained his favor,[22] so that he promptly started her on her beauty regimen and her rations, and provided her with the seven maidens that were her due from the king's palace, and transferred her and her maidens to the best [place] in the Women's Quarters.[23] Now Esther revealed neither her people nor her kindred, for Mordecai had ordered her not to reveal it. And every day Mordecai would take a walk in front of the court of the Women's Quarters, to find out how Esther was doing, and what was [likely] to become of her (2:8–11).

Did Esther volunteer to be a contestant? Was it Mordecai who pushed her forward? Or was she known as the neighborhood beauty and simply drafted? We are not told.[24] All we know is that Esther finds herself in the Women's Quarters of the Palace, in the care of Hegai, the king's eunuch. His job is to sort out the girls, keep order and prepare them for their being "judged" by the king. He is in charge of a large dormitory, an extensive beauty salon and, though not specifically stated, obviously a training program in manners and deportment. Once the girl enters the royal bedroom his responsibilities end; she will not return to his jurisdiction and he probably will never see her again.

The most interesting aspect of these few verses is the fact that Esther conceals the fact that she is Jewish. Mordecai specifically instructs her to "pass" as a Gentile, obviously not a Persian (she didn't even have a Persian name) but as a Babylonian. Despite the fact that there must have been other Babylonian girls among the contestants, she is sufficiently assimilated, and sufficiently in control of herself, to pull it off.

Why? The only reason that comes to mind is that Mordecai feels that if it is known that Esther is Jewish it will harm her chances. This in turn hints at a pervasive undercurrent of anti–Semitism in palace circles, or perhaps in Shushan in general. Most authorities find this difficult to believe, pointing to the generally tolerant policies of the empire, and stressing that we have no extra-biblical evidence of any anti–Jewish prejudice in Persia. Yet neither of these arguments is persuasive. Imperial policy may indeed have been tolerant — it had to be if the polyglot empire was to hold together — yet this would neither be the first time nor the last that official government policy, formulated to advance vital state interests, ran counter to the personal feelings of many members of that very government, not to mention the commonality of the realm.

The lack of external evidence of anti–Semitism is also not persuasive. We know so little about the Persian Empire that it is dangerous even to generalize from evidence in hand; to attempt to draw conclusions from evidence we *don't* have — from lack of evidence — is to embark on very perilous waters. Carey Moore rightly points out that Egyptian sources give us not a hint of the pervasive hostility to Jews at Elephantine that existed in this period (and we know far more about Egypt than we do about Persia). Had it not been for the chance find of the Elephantine Papyri, we would assume that the Jews of Elephantine lived in an environment free of anti–Semitism.[25]

---

[22]Hebrew *hesed*. When used of human beings *hesed* refers to a free and uncoerced *action* performed by a person who is in a position superior to the other, and which fills a need that the person in need cannot meet. Human *hesed* is always performed within an existing relationship. See also Chapter 3, note 27 and Chapter 6, note 4.

[23]Literally, "the House of Women."

[24]The tendency today is to see Esther and the other contestants as status-mad girls who would marry any man, no matter how repulsive, in order to obtain high position. (Later we will have more to say about the bad press that Esther has received over the years.) But this canard is out of place. True, Ahasuerus was a drunk and a fool, but so are not a few Hollywood actors. Xerxes was extremely good-looking; indeed he was considered the handsomest man in his empire (Maspero, *The Passing of Empires*, p. 715). Just as many men are willing to overlook serious faults in a beautiful woman, so are many women willing to put up with much for a ravishingly handsome husband.

[25]Moore, *AB Esther*, p. lii. For further information on *Elephantine* see Glossary.

Getting a bit ahead of ourselves, when we think about it we realize that our arch-villain, Haman (who is yet to be introduced), did have to come from somewhere. He didn't fall from Mars. For his demagogic denunciations to find the resonance that they did, argues, at the very least, for a preexistent tendency among many to look upon Jews with suspicion. By being told that both Mordecai and Esther feel it wise to conceal her Jewish identity we have been put on notice. This is our first hint of things to come.

To take matters a step further, Esther's success in concealing her origins argues for years of experience in keeping a low profile, of evidencing no behavior that differs in the slightest from the social norm; in other words, of passing as a Gentile.[26] In the crowded environment of the harem one lives in a fishbowl. There is not a moment of privacy, and the girls with whom she is constantly in contact are her fierce competitors for the prize of prizes. Harems are, by their natures, hotbeds of jealousy and intrigue. The least slip or inconsistency will instantly be noted. That Esther is able to keep up the masquerade for years is proof of the truth of Moore's observation: "Unlike some beautiful women, she did not rely exclusively on her good looks."[27]

Self-control and an iron determination we can now postulate. To this add ambition: whether or not Esther is in the "contest" of her own volition, it is doubtful if she could succeed were she not highly motivated. To these factors, we must add yet a further ingredient to the complex personality that is Esther: her charm. She has a way of winning the hearts of all about her. In the entire Book we do not hear of her making a single enemy.[28] No sooner does she arrive at the Women's Quarters than she catches the eye of Hegai, and wins him over completely. He shortly moves her to the top of the priority list, assigns her daily food rations, puts her into the beauty-treatment pipeline, assigns her the seven servant girls (probably the pick of the crop) that were her due as a potential royal favorite-in-training, and gives her some of the nicest living accommodations available.

This preferment is not just due to charm. Let us look at the matter from the perspective of Hegai. In the first place we must realize that in order to rise to his present high responsibility Hegai must be a very talented individual. He must be an accomplished manager of women and an expert smoother of ruffled feathers. Given the climate of the Persian court he must have a flair for intrigue. And above all, he must be a superlative judge of character. In Esther he senses a winner: if he can make friends with her, promote her and steer her to victory, he can gain a powerful source of influence. His evaluation goes deeper than just surface beauty; in Esther he glimpses the intelligence and good sense that can make of her a valuable ally. Needless to say, Esther grasps Hegai's intentions perfectly. Her job is to win, and then to promote Hegai. His job is to help her to win, and then to be her spokesman in the closed world of the eunuch brotherhood, and her agent in the dangerous world of palace intrigue. Two highly intelligent and competent personalities have recognized in each other a kindred soul. An alliance of interests has been formed.

[26]Over the years Jewish commentators have been puzzled and distressed by Esther, a Jewish hero by all accounts, "passing." In so doing, as they rightly recognized, she would have had to break many of the sancta of Judaism. To start with she married a Gentile; she must have routinely eaten forbidden (non-kosher) food; she couldn't have observed the Sabbath and religious Holidays, and so on. Furthermore (though the Book never mentions a word of it), in a devout court — Xerxes was a pious Zoroastrian — as royal consort Esther could not have avoided participating in the worship of Ahura Mazda, their great deity. None of this seems to have caused her any crisis of conscience. Whatever degree of formal Jewish observance that she had maintained in her parents' home and in that of her foster father, it was left behind when she entered the palace as the price of pursuing her destiny. Whether she even felt any regrets we are not told.

[27]Moore, *AB Esther*, p. 27.

[28]Esther did not make Haman her enemy; *she* became his and she destroyed him. For his part, he was as charmed by Esther as everyone else, and so was totally unprepared for the blow when it fell. He thought that they were "friends," and went about boasting about how highly she regarded him.

The Picking of Miss Persia

How does one run a beauty contest? As this is a first time for the Persian Empire we are given a synopsis of the ground rules. We begin with the required beauty regimen: it seems that unpleasant odors are absolute disqualifiers.[29] Deodorants not yet having been invented, perfuming prospective bedmates with acceptable scents is the alternative. But the external application of perfume to mask the natural body odors is deemed insufficient: after a few hours the perfume wears off. The preferred treatment thus is a prolonged procedure in which the perfumes are absorbed by the skin and become, for an extended period, the dominant odor of that person.[30] Myrrh, the base odor, was an extremely expensive perfume. This is then topped off with assorted spices, perhaps to provide individual accents. Along with this latter phase go cosmetics, nails, hairdo, and so on. With a straight face we are told that the process lasted an entire year — probably more than a bit of an exaggeration, in line with the satirical cast of everything that has gone before.[31] The picture of one hundred twenty seven girls, the winners of the initial Provincial Contests (or perhaps two hundred fifty-four if we add in the runners-up)[32] spending an entire year making themselves smell sweet enough to grace the bed of the king for a one night stand has its humorous aspects.

> Now when the turn of each girl came to go into King Ahasuerus at the conclusion of the women's mandatory twelve month [regimen] — for this is the way the beauty treatment went: six months of oil of myrrh and six months of [assorted] perfumes[33] and women's

[29]There is a legend among the Persians, persisting to our time, that Alexander the Great was half Persian: the result of a union between a Persian king and a Greek concubine. After one night the king threw her out and sent her back to Greece because she had bad breath. While the story of a Persian king fathering Alexander is unhistorical, the idea that no Persian king would tolerate a woman with bad breath is probably based on a widely known truth.

[30]One method is repeated massage with perfumed oils that are absorbed by the skin. Another is cosmetic fumigation. W.F. Albright, starting from the discovery of what he defines as "cosmetic burners" from the Persian period, quotes a description of the process from Sir S.W. Baker's 1886 book *The Nile Tributaries of Abyssinia*:

> The women have a peculiar method of scenting their bodies and clothes.... In the floor of the tent or hut ... a small hole is excavated sufficiently large to hold ... a fire of charcoal ... into which the woman about-to-be-scented throws a handful of various drugs. She then takes off the cloth or tope which forms her dress, and crouches naked over the fumes while she arranges her robe to fall as a mantle from her neck to the ground like a tent.... None of the precious fumes can escape, all being kept under the robe, exactly as if she wore a crinoline with an incense burner.... She now begins to perspire freely in the hut or tent and ... the volatile oil from the burning perfumes is immediately absorbed [by her skin]. By the time that the fire has expired the scenting process is completed and both her person and the robe are redolent of incense with which they are so thoroughly impregnated that I have frequently smelt a party of women a full one hundred yards distant.

Albright concludes by citing our passage, Esther 2:12, and remarking: "The commentators have been understandingly very chary about speculating on just what this may have meant actually, but it now seems obvious that the periods of conditioning were accompanied by the extensive use of fumigation, which would have both hygienic and therapeutic value" (Albright, "The Lachish Cosmetic Burner," pp. 28–29, 31).

[31]Even if exaggerated, B.W. Jones hits the nail on the head when he refers to this description as "'conspicuous consumption' in the extreme" (Jones, "Two Misconceptions about the Book of Esther," p. 175). It is also hard to believe that Ahasuerus would have been willing to wait an entire year before he could start "judging" the contestants unless, of course, all this was going on while he was away at the wars.

[32]I owe the idea of adding the runners-up to Maurice Samuel (Samuel, "*Certain People of the Book*, p. 12), though even he admits that having to "try out" 256 women must have been very "trying" for Ahasuerus. But this is as nothing compared with the fantasies of L.B. Paton, who comes up with the extravagant calculation of 1,460 girls (one girl every night for four years!). He then, correctly, rejects these calculations as absurd (Paton, *ICC Esther*, pp. 172–73).

[33]Literally, "spices."

cosmetics[34]—when the girl would come to the king she would be given anything she asked for to take with her from the harem to the palace. In the evening she would go and in the morning she returned again[35] to the harem, to the custody of Shaashgaz, the King's Eunuch, Keeper of the Concubines. She would never again come to the king unless he especially desired her, and she was summoned by name (2:12–14).

Each *sweet-smelling* girl (to our way of thinking probably sickeningly sweet-smelling) was allowed to doll herself up any way she wanted when her turn came. No costume, however exotic, no device to stimulate and enhance, was denied. No girl could say later, while pining in Shaashgaz' harem of the concubines, waiting in vain for an invitation for a repeat performance, that she had not gotten a fair chance.

And it is precisely here that we have our first demonstration of Esther's intelligence and good sense: brains trump beauty. All the contestants are stunning beauties; that is why they are there. To win one must stand out from the field. All the girls are racking their brains to find some way to impress on the king that they are different from the others. Esther doesn't bother. No one knows better than Hegai the likes and dislikes of the king. If he didn't he would never have lasted in the job. So Esther puts herself totally in his hands; her job will be to implement his advice. This is the whole point to their alliance. And it works.

> Now when it came the turn of Esther, daughter of Abihail, the uncle of Mordecai (who had taken her as his daughter) to come to the king, she asked for nothing but what Hegai, the King's Eunuch, Keeper of the Women, told her. (Now Esther charmed everyone who saw her.) So Esther was taken to King Ahasuerus, to his royal apartment, in the tenth month (which is the month of Tebeth), in the seventh year of his reign. And the king loved Esther more than all the [other] women, and she won his grace and favor more than all the [other] maidens. So he placed the royal crown on her head, and made her his queen in place of Vashti. Then the king threw a huge party[36] for all his officials and courtiers, a party [in honor] of Esther, and proclaimed[37] a remission of taxes to the provinces, and gave gifts with royal munificence (2:15–18).

Esther has pulled it off!

At this point we have to go back a bit. The author thinks it is sufficiently important to break the suspense for a moment to tell us the date when Esther so entranced the king, and we should take note. We have already learned the significance of the date of Ahasuerus's "Big Bash" with which the Book opens (483 BCE): the eve of the invasion of Greece. We are now given a second date, the tenth month of the seventh year of the reign of Ahasuerus (December 479 BCE). No one in those days would have missed the significance: this was the year following the disastrous Battle of Salamis and less than four months after the even more calamitous defeat of

---

[34]The term, which we have rendered as *beauty treatment* and *cosmetics*, has at its base meaning "scraping," "rubbing," and "cleansing." This leads Joseph Prouser to suggest another possible purpose for the prolonged preparation for the king's bed, one that does not contradict but supplements what has been said up to now: a lengthy contraceptive protocol. Relying upon the works of John M. Riddle ("Ever since Eve ... Birth Control in the Ancient World" and *Contraception and Abortion from the Ancient World to the Renaissance*), he points out that myrrh was once widely used as both a contraceptive and an abortifacient agent, and lists numerous spices often used with myrrh for these purposes. He further suggests a possible reason for so extended a treatment: "Perhaps, too, a conservative, gradual process would allow a cumulative pharmacological impact, while avoiding the toxic effects risked by higher dosages" (Prousner, "'As is the Practice of Women,'" p. 55).

[35]Reading *shenit*, the final *taw* denoting the feminine having dropped due to scribal abbreviation, a not uncommon phenomenon (Gordis, "Studies in the Esther Narrative," p. 54).

[36]*Mishteh*: a drinking party.

[37]Literally, "made."

Plataea,[38] which doomed the Persian attempt to conquer Greece. The high tide of Persian expansion has come, and now the ebb tide is setting in. Persia is on its way down.

So to put our story into the larger perspective, in 483 BCE Ahasuerus throws a monster party, and in its aftermath dumps Vashti. He then mobilizes the greatest army the world has ever seen, invades Greece, and is decisively defeated. The year 479 BCE finds him back in Susa "judging" the Miss Persia beauty contest organized in his absence. And having chosen his new favorite he once again throws a "Super-Party," complete with lavish gifts and tax breaks. Things have come full circle. We started with a party; we end with a party. This is a king who is better at giving parties than at winning wars.

---

[38]Salamis (480 BCE) was the naval battle that lost Persia control of the seas. But Persia was primarily a land power. At Plataea (August 479), about twenty-five miles NW of Salamis, the Persian *army* was broken. It never recovered from the shock of this defeat.

Act II: The War Against the Jews

> It is not my business to do justice. It is my business to annihilate
> and exterminate — that's all. — Hermann Göring

CHAPTER 11

Prologue: The Night of the Assassins

> Plots, true or false, are necessary things,
> To raise up commonwealths and ruin kings.
> — John Dryden, *Absalom and Achitophel*

In passing from Act I to Act II we leave the world of the harem and enter the world of men, abandoning "feminine frivolity" for high politics and deadly intrigue. But before so doing we need to return to a brief note which we passed over in silence. In our fascinated attention to Esther in her contest with the one hundred twenty-six other ravishing beauties (or is it two hundred fifty three?), we have lost sight of her foster-father Mordecai. What has he been doing since he bid Esther good-bye with the advice that she keep her identity under deep cover? Perhaps we should pay closer attention to the notice we skipped over:

Every day Mordecai would take a walk in front of the court of the harem to find out how Esther was doing, and what was [likely] to become of her (2:11).

Beyond telling us that Mordecai cared deeply for his foster-daughter, and was concerned about her career prospects, at first glance the verse imparts little. Beyond the exercise, what good would his daily walks do? The harem was a sealed compound; it was death for a man to enter, and no woman could leave. But this did not mean that there could be no communication. There was one class, neither man nor woman, which could and did enter and leave: the eunuchs. Through them contact could be established. What is being hinted here is that Mordecai has inside sources of information. Strangely, Mordecai the Jew, the quintessential outsider, is really an insider. He has found a way of penetrating the closed brotherhood of eunuchs, and has established a secure line of communication with Esther. Right now he is getting a daily update on the status and progress of his young cousin.

On what basis would a eunuch be willing to be used in this manner? Of course there is always money. Bribery was endemic in the Persian Empire. But perhaps it is something more: mutual interest — one hand washes the other — some sort of alliance such as Esther has forged inside the harem. But what has a Jew to offer a eunuch?

Perhaps we have been approaching the problem from the wrong angle.

Now Mordecai had his seat in the King's Gate [2:19].[1]

---

[1]Reading with LXX; MT reads: "And when the virgins were gathered a second time, now Mordecai…" LXX omits the first phrase, and indeed, as MT stands, no one seems to understand what it means. Not only does LXX elaborate and amplify the text we possess (MT), it also deletes (see Appendix III: It's Greek to Me).

From Ruth, Chapter 4, we are aware that in the Ancient Near East the gate complex at the entrance to a city served as a civic and administrative center. The informal scene we encountered in Ruth became formalized and much enlarged with the institution of centralized government. In Imperial Susa, administrative hub of a vast empire, the King's Gate has expanded to a gargantuan complex of administrative offices, auxiliary structures, storerooms, and so on.[2] Herodotus and Xenophon tell us that one hundred twenty officials were stationed at the gate to the royal palace.[3] So the phrase "Now Mordecai had his seat in the King's gate" simply means that this is the place where he has his office. In other words Mordecai is a senior member of the Persian civil service.[4]

Now we can better understand Mordecai's insider sources of information and his contacts with the eunuchs. As a senior member of the civil service (only upper level officials would have their offices at the prestigious King's Gate), his contacts with palace personnel must be extensive. Whatever branch of the government he serves, he has much to trade in the way of influence and information for the cooperation of one or more of the harem eunuchs. We can now picture him, perhaps on his daily walk to his office, strolling by the outer court of the harem complex, stopping to chat for a few moments with one of them. Then, having gotten his daily update on Esther (and probably all sorts of tidbits of harem gossip), and maybe passing on a message of encouragement in return, he strolls on to his office and the daily routine.[5]

Now that we have a better idea of who Mordecai is, we are prepared for the prologue to Act II.

> Esther had not told anyone who her kindred and her people were, even as Mordecai had instructed her. Now Esther obeyed Mordecai, just as she had done while she was being brought up by him. At that time, while Mordecai was sitting in the King's Gate, Bigthan and Teresh, two of the King's Eunuchs, who were among the Guards of the Threshold,[6] became angry with King Ahasuerus and plotted to assassinate him.[7] The matter became known to Mordecai, who told it to Esther the queen, and Esther informed the king in Mordecai's name. When the matter was investigated and found [to be true], both of them were hanged on the gallows, and it was recorded in the king's daily diary[8] (2:20–23).

This incident serves to introduce us to the realities of high politics in Persia. It takes place sometime after Esther has won the Miss Persia contest. She is now firmly ensconced as the king's

---

[1] (cont.) Inasmuch as the phrase in MT is not understandable we have decided to follow LXX and delete this phrase. With the rest of the verse we follow MT (LXX reads "Now Mordecai served in the King's Court," a mistake in translation). Literally MT reads: "Now Mordecai sat."

[2] The King's Gate may refer either to the gateway accessing the Acropolis of Susa and its palace complex, or to the gate of the palace complex proper (the archeological picture of Susa is not as clear as we would like). It is not the main gate to the civilian outer city.

[3] Herodotus, *Histories*, Book III:120; Xenophon, *Cyropaedia* VIII:1, 6.

[4] Adele Berlin goes further and postulates that he was a member of the Persian secret police, known as "The Eyes and The Ears of the King" (Berlin, *JPSBC Esther*, p. 31), but I think this assumption is unwarranted. The secret police had direct channels to the king. Mordecai passes his information through Esther. Not only would he not have needed to, had he been part of the secret police, but he probably would have been severely reprimanded, if not punished, for not going through channels.

[5] Lest we find it strange that Mordecai is serving in a senior post in the Imperial Administration, it is important to stress that the Service employed large numbers of non–Persians at this period: Even though Persia was at war with Greece, there were Greeks at all levels of the Imperial government, right up to official advisors to the king.

[6] The special unit guarding the entrance to the king's personal living quarters.

[7] More literally, "to lay hands on him."

[8] Literally, "The Book of Daily Things Before the King"; that is, an ongoing account of occurrences concerning the king.

favorite. All this while, like a good girl, she has been keeping her Jewish identity a dark secret (just as Mordecai had instructed her to do). In the course of his duties Mordecai gets wind of a plot by two of the king's personal bodyguards to assassinate him. What their grudge against him was, or whether this was part of a larger plot, we are not told; this information is irrelevant to our tale.[9] Mordecai, using the secure line of communication he has established, passes on the information to Esther, a person who is in daily contact with the king (in these early days the king's ardor seems not to have cooled). Esther passes on the warning to Ahasuerus, citing Mordecai as the source. The result is an immediate investigation by the security police; Persian kings were justifiably paranoid on the issue of assassination. The report proving true, the two traitors are strung up, and an entry summarizing the case is entered into the king's daily diary, which seems to have been something between a day-by-day record of the king's main activities and secret service reports concerning the king's security.

This brief episode stands in stark contrast to everything that has gone before. From a world of extravagant drunken partying, beauty contests and pompous posturing we are shown another, parallel world of government offices, bureaucratic networking, security services, assassination plots and public executions. It is like a trip to another planet. We recognize this world: it is the world of big government and the struggle for power, one uncomfortably similar to the world we inhabit. It is these two worlds — the glamorous world of beautiful women and spectacular parties alternating with a grim world of faceless bureaucrats, ruthless politicians, murderous plots and endless intrigues — that form the context of our drama. And both are ancient Persia, two sides of the same coin.

The stage is now set, the parameters of the play defined and the main characters introduced; but not quite. One more personage remains to be ushered in. Once presented, the curtain can rise on the real business of the Book of Esther.

---

[9]Actually it is not all that uncommon for heads of state to be murdered by their bodyguards, in consequence of having deeply offended their guardians' sensibilities. For example, the president of India, Indira Gandhi, was assassinated on October 31, 1984, by her Sikh bodyguards, whom she had infuriated by ordering the Indian army to attack the Golden Temple, the holiest shrine of the Sikh religion. But in Ancient Persia, far more frequent was the assassination of rulers as part of a putsch to seize power. The father of Ahasuerus, Darius I, came to the throne by murdering his predecessor, Bardiya. Xerxes himself was destined to meet his end in his bedroom at the hand of Artabanus, his vizier or chief executive officer, who in turn was murdered by Artaxerxes I who seized the throne. In theory a king chose his successor from among his sons. In practice most successions were by assassination. Injured feeling ran a poor second to ruthless politics as a motive for assassination in Persia.

CHAPTER 12

The Man Who Would Not Bow

I sent a message to the fish:
I told them, "This is what I wish."

The little fishes of the sea,
They sent an answer back to me.

The little fishes' answer was
"We cannot do it Sir, because —"

— Lewis Carroll, *Through
the Looking Glass*

The New Broom

> After these things[1] King Ahasuerus promoted Haman, the son of Hammedatha the Agagite, advancing him and setting his seat above all his fellow officials (3:1).

Who is this Haman, from where does he come, and what can explain his sudden appearance at the pinnacle of Persian officialdom? This is no normal promotion. Our author has been careful to give us lists of the names of the top officials of the empire; his name is not to be found among them. Haman has been leapfrogged over the entire policy-making echelon of government to a commanding position, second only to the king.

Among all of the four key players in our drama we are told the least about him. Ahasuerus, of course, needed no introduction. After being identified, everyone knew who he was, and how he came to be where he was.[2] Both Mordecai and Esther are explained in detail: where they came from, how they got to Babylon (and by inference from there to Shushan), what their status is (of royal extraction), and how it came about that Mordecai is serving as guardian to his young cousin Esther. We are even told Esther's Hebrew name (which she never uses in the Book). Of Haman we are told next to nothing; we will have to work hard to get some idea of whom we are dealing with.

We are given his father's name, which is no help as we never have heard of Hammedatha. We are informed that he is an Agagite — more on this later, when we shall find this snippet highly

---

[1]That is, sometime during the five year period between the seventh and the twelfth years of the reign of Ahasuerus (i.e., 479–474 BCE). See also Chapter 10, note 3.

[2]The son of Darius I, he had been designated as heir apparent; as governor of Babylon, for twelve years he had kept that unruly province more or less in its place, and upon his father's death he had, most uncharacteristically, succeeded him on the throne (i.e., he didn't have to murder his way to the top like his father).

124

revealing. We will learn that he is immensely, indeed obscenely, rich. And we have been told that he has been catapulted onto the very top of the governmental hierarchy: "[Ahasuerus] advancing him and setting his seat above all his fellow officials."

A word about Persian government. The empire was headed by the king[3] whose power, at least theoretically, was absolute; he could kill with a word, without trial or without even giving a reason. In practice, however, his power was limited by the nobility, specifically by the seven noble families as represented by the Royal Advisory Council of Seven. This council was consulted in all matters of vital interest by the early kings from Cyrus the Great to Darius I, Ahasuerus' father. We found Ahasuerus consulting this council on the issue of Vashti's disobedience, as it was, at least to him, a matter of "vital interest."

The Book of Esther refers to precedents that directed the kingdom (1:13). The only precedents that were binding were earlier royal decrees. William Durant calls attention to the boast of Persia that its laws never changed, and that a royal promise or decree was irrevocable.[4] This combination of royal will, irrevocable law and precedent, and Royal Advisory Council created a system of checks and balances that were a precondition to the meteoric rise of the Persian Empire. We are now to witness the first of the steps that will lead to a dismantling of this winning system.

With the advent of Haman the system is breached. Haman has his seat set "above all his fellow officials," that is, above the Royal Advisory Council. Indeed, we do not hear of this council being consulted again. In effect a new position has been created, one "second only to the king." The implications of this are two-fold: the king no longer hears advice from multiple sources that represent disparate constituencies within the nobility. He now leans on one person who, as his appointee, is totally dependent upon him. The check of a semi-independent nobility is now a thing of the past. The "second only to the king" will be, of necessity, a yes-man. Indeed, we do not hear of Haman undertaking even the most petty of actions without getting prior authorization from the king.

The second implication of this new position is that Ahasuerus is delegating his authority to a kind of chief executive officer (CEO).[5] Up to now the kings ruled directly. Now, for the first time, we will have a king who reigns but does not rule. The day-to-day running of the empire will be in someone else's hands, leaving the king free to spend most of his time doing what he does best: that is, having a good time. This new position does not as yet have a name; we will refer to it by the name by which it came later to be known — the vizier.[6] It is inevitable that the vizier will have an agenda. To what degree it will be the king's, and to what extent his own, will become one of the central issues of Persian government.[7]

Why does the king make so drastic a change in the way the realm will be run? Perhaps the answer is hinted at in the first words of this critical section: "After these things King Ahasuerus

---

[3]The title of the king was *Khshathra* which means "warrior," and which indicates the military origin and character of the Persian monarchy. The modern title of Shah derives from this ancient term.

[4]This point will become important later. See also Chapter 9, note 18. The full quotation from Durant and a discussion of the issue will be found in Chapter 17.

[5]We use the term *CEO* (Chief Executive Officer), common now in corporate America, because it most closely approximates the purpose and the responsibilities of this new office. For the meaning of the term *vizier*, by which the office later came to be known, see the next note.

[6]From *wazir*, a bearer of burdens, a porter. The job of the vizier was to bear the burdens of rule, leaving the king free.

[7]It is a matter of history that when the interests of the king and the vizier diverged, one of the two had to go. Often it was the vizier, but not infrequently it was the king. Ahasuerus will be assassinated by one of his later viziers (not Haman) in 465 BCE.

promoted Haman." What things? The events immediately preceding the announcement of Haman's promotion in the Book are Mordecai's uncovering of an assassination plot against the king, the investigation that verified the existence of the conspiracy and the execution of at least two of the conspirators. Could the juxtaposition of these two sets of occurrences imply cause and effect? Did the discovery of the plot trigger a deep-seated paranoiac reaction on the part of the king? Not only did the plot develop undetected by the king's security apparatus — it took an outsider, Mordecai, to uncover it — but perhaps Bigthan and Teresh, among the most trusted of his personal bodyguards, were but the tip of the iceberg. Who among the nobility might have been behind it? Perhaps the king came to the conclusion that what he needed was a new broom, someone from outside the palace establishment, and without an independent power base, a strong man answerable only to him, to take charge of things and keep an eye on the potentially dangerous nobles.[8]

It is certain that Haman was not part of the establishment. Yet he must have had some sort of track record to bring him to the king's attention. Had he been a governor of one of the one hundred twenty-seven provinces? Or, perhaps a satrap,[9] one who had done exceptionally well in that position; "well" usually meaning, in Persian terms, that he had been successful in "pacifying" a rebellious population while taxing them mercilessly. It might be the successful bleeding of the provinces entrusted to him that led to Haman's fabulous wealth.[10]

Having introduced Haman as an outsider and a nouveau riche brought in to initiate a new order of things as Ahasuerus's CEO, all that remains is to see what he makes of his new position.

The New Order

Haman faces serious problems. Any outsider inserted into a hierarchical bureaucratic structure is unwelcome. If that person has been brought in to shake up the system, and has been promoted over the heads of the establishment, one can expect savage resentment. The instinctive reaction will be to close ranks against the intruder. Lip service and formal politeness will only partially conceal systemic sabotage. The Persian bureaucracy was no different from any other. They may even be cold-shouldering Haman, studiously avoiding him and acting as though he doesn't exist. If he doesn't assert his authority quickly he will be finished.

Haman undoubtedly employs several strategies, but the one means of which we are told is to force his subordinates to render him public deference, which apparently they were not doing. Turning to the king, he extracts a royal order to the effect that every government official must kneel and bow to him. Inasmuch as Persians routinely bowed down to superiors,[11] the fact that

[8]Perhaps another factor in the decision was the mess Ahasuerus had made of the Greek war; he would henceforth make policy but someone else would be empowered to implement it, thus creating a convenient scapegoat for things that go wrong.

[9]Provinces were organized into larger units called Satrapies (Darius I had left his son twenty-nine of them — see Chapter 8, note 7), each ruled by a "satrap."

[10]Each satrapy was expected to forward a fixed amount of money and goods to the central government on an annual basis. For example, India sent 4,680 talents of silver a year, Egypt 700, Assyria and Babylonia 1,000, and so on. Everything over this that the governor or satrap succeeded in squeezing out of the public went into his own pocket. (For *talents* see Glossary.)

[11]Herodotus tells us: "When they meet each other in the streets, you may know if the persons meeting are of equal rank by the following token.... Where the difference of rank is great, the inferior prostrates himself upon the ground" (Heodotus, *Histories*, Book I:134).

the king has to decree that Haman's subordinates bow to him argues for a serious degree of resistance to his authority.

> Now all the king's officials[12] who were at the King's Gate would kneel and bow down to Haman, for so the king had commanded concerning him. But Mordecai would neither kneel nor bow. Then the king's officials who were at the King's Gate said to Mordecai: "Why do you disobey the king's command?" Now when they had spoken to him[13] day after day, and he would not listen to them, they told Haman in order to see whether Mordecai's behavior would prevail[14] (for he had told them that he was a Jew). When Haman saw that Mordecai did not kneel nor bow to him he was filled with fury (3:2–5).

It is at this point that occurs the event that triggers the entire tale. Mordecai takes a stand; despite the fact that all the other officials stationed at the King's Gate cave in, Mordecai steadfastly refuses to kneel and bow.

Why? Strangely enough, though this is the pivotal act in the Book, we are given no explanation as to what motivates Mordecai to a line of conduct that amounts to open rebellion against his superior (as vizier Haman is Mordecai's boss), and also violates a direct order of the king. Yet this strange and self-destructive behavior, so untypical of the model bureaucrat that Mordecai seems to be, cries out for explanation. And it is precisely here that we face total disagreement among commentators and scholars. No one seems to be able to come up with an answer that is generally satisfying.

One of the few hints the Book gives us is that Mordecai's stand seems somehow to stem from the fact that he is Jewish. That at least appears to be the import of the parenthetical phrase, ("for he had told them that he was a Jew"); that is, that when his fellow bureaucrats try to convince him to go along with the inevitable, or at least to get some explanation for his bull-headed obstinacy, his answer to them seems to have tied his refusal to the fact that he is a Jew.[15] Certain it is that when his co-workers bring his obstinate refusal to the attention of Haman, the fact of his Jewishness forms a vital part of the report.[16]

Our problem troubled the ancients no less than the modern scholars. When the Book of Esther was translated into Greek, the translators inserted several additions in an attempt to clarify this, as well as other obscure points in the Book.[17] So they wrote a prayer and put it into Mordecai's mouth in which he explains his behavior to God:

> "You know all things; You know, Lord, that it was not because of insolence or arrogance or vanity that I did this, that I did not bow down before arrogant Haman; for I would have been quite willing to have kissed the soles of his feet for Israel's sake. But I did it in order that I might not put the glory of a man above the glory of God" (LXX Addition C:5–7, Alpha Text 5:14–15, trans. C.A. Moore).[18]

[12]Literally, "servants."

[13]Reading with the Qeri (the vowelized text).

[14]Literally, "to see whether Mordecai's thing [action] would stand."

[15]Was this fact known to his fellow officials previously, or is this the first time Mordecai reveals himself as a Jew?

[16]Here, at least, we are told what motivates Mordecai's fellow officials: Mordecai has taken a public stand against the newcomer. By bringing it to the official attention of Haman they are provoking a showdown. If Mordecai can force Haman to back down the establishment will have won. This is the meaning of the remark: "they told Haman in order to see whether Mordecai's behavior would prevail" (3:4).

[17]They also were deeply troubled by the lack of religion in the Book and attempted to remedy this deficiency. See note 18 below.

[18]There are two Greek versions of the Book of Esther: The Septuagint (LXX) and the "Alpha" (or "A-text"), which contain seven additional sections not appearing in the Hebrew Masoretic Text (MT). See Appendix III: It's Greek to Me: The Greek Versions of Esther.

In other words, as a matter of religious principle Mordecai will bow to no man, only to God.[19] But this reason, which the Greek translators try to read into the text, does not really hold water. Mordecai, once he succeeds Haman as vizier (8:2, 10:3), must have bowed to the king.[20] The Book portrays Esther doing so without any hint of condemnation (8:3).[21] The issue is thus not a refusal to bow to *a* human being on religious grounds, but rather the refusal to bow to *a specific* human being: Haman.

Modern commentators have proposed various motives for Mordecai's refusal to bow to Haman: that it was a political protest against the restructuring of Persian government,[22] a refusal to "lose face,"[23] an expression of Jewish national spirit and pride,[24] a historic ethnic enmity to a descendant of the Amalekites[25]—none by themselves overly persuasive. But the last two bring us to the second hint we have in the text.

We return to Haman's introduction:

> After these things, King Ahasuerus promoted Haman, the son of Hammedatha the Agagite (3:1).

Both Haman and Hammedatha are names of Iranian (or possibly Elamite) origin. "The Agagite" sounds like an ethnic designation but it is not such, not, at least in a Persian context. It seems to mean here a descendant of one Agag, who lived about 550 years previously and had been king of a people known as the Amalekites. The Bible tells us that, after centuries of enmity the Amalekites were defeated in battle by King Saul, and that Agag was executed for war crimes by the prophet Samuel (1 Samuel 15). This calls to mind our Book's introduction of Mordecai:

> Now a certain Jew was in the Acropolis of Shushan, and his name was Mordecai, son of Jair, son of Shimie, the son of Kish, a Benjamite (2:5).

As we have already noted, this makes Mordecai one of the family of King Saul. Any Jew in the Persian era would at once have recognized in Mordecai and Haman the descendants of those ancient enemies King Saul and King Agag, and on that basis understood, even expected, the ancient enmity to be revived.

It is this that prompts Moore to say: "Mordecai simply would not bow down to a descendant of Agag of the Amalekites, that cursed people who had opposed the Israelites"[26] and Berlin to opine: "we have a Jew refusing on Jewish ethnic grounds to bow before Haman.... The more definitive Jewish reason is supplied by the ancient ethnic enmity between the Israelites and the Amalekites."[27] But is it really credible to suppose an "ethnic" or "national" grudge to have continued 550 years, and still retain sufficient force to motivate Mordecai's extreme, and, at the least, job threatening stance? It would seem, at least to me, that something more immediate and more

---

[19]This interpretation was picked up and expanded upon by the rabbis of the following generations.

[20]Herodotus insists that in the presence of the king one had to prostrate oneself, and gives two examples from the reign of Xerxes (Herodotus, *Histories*, Book VII:136 and VIII:118).

[21]This is simply the continuation of generally acceptable Jewish practice: the Bible records numerous examples of persons bowing to human beings and they are never regarded as doing any wrong thereby. (See Genesis 23:7, 33:3, 43:28; Exodus 18:7; 1 Samuel 24:9; 2 Samuel 14:4; 1 Kings 1:16; etc.)

[22]Hazony, *The Dawn*, pp. 48ff. Hazony's political analysis is astute, and forms the basis of much of the political discussion in this book. In fairness it should be noted that, in Hazony's analysis, Mordecai's political opposition to the restructuring of the government is made on an ethical basis.

[23]Elias Bickerman proposes: "For Mordecai to pay this respect to Haman would be to 'lose face' and acknowledge the new rank of his rival" (Bickerman, *Four Strange Books*, p. 180; see also pp. 220–21).

[24]Moore, *AB Esther*, pp. 36–37 (endorsing the opinion of A.B. Ehrlich).

[25]Berlin, *JPSBC Esther*, p. 35; Jobes, *Esther*, pp. 119–120.

[26]Moore, *AB Esther*, p. 37.

[27]Berlin, *JPSBC Esther*, p. 35.

vital than an ancient grudge must lie behind Mordecai's decision to violate the king's command; which leaves us back where we started.

Perhaps what has brought us to this impasse is that we have been approaching the text from a modern perspective, in isolation from its literary context. Biblical authors wrote within a literary tradition, and it is to this tradition that we must be sensitive if we want to see where our author is leading. We return to the account of Mordecai's stand:

> Then the king's officials who were at the King's Gate said to Mordecai: "Why do you disobey the king's command?" Now when they had spoken to him day after day, and he would not listen to them... (3:3–4).

To anyone who is intimately familiar with the Bible, this last half-verse calls to mind an almost identical formulation found in Genesis, drawn from the story of Joseph in Egypt. This is not the first time, nor is it the last, that the Book of Esther consciously echoes the Joseph saga.[28]

The context is as follows: Joseph, having been sold as a slave into Egypt, finds himself serving as a majordomo on the estate of one Potiphar, where he has to contend with the advances of his master's wife who is trying to seduce him. The tale continues:

> Now when she had spoken to Joseph day after day, and he would not listen to her (Genesis 39:10).

The virtually word for word echo of this verse in our text calls attention to the larger parallel: Joseph also was involved in a situation that led him to take a dangerous stand: despite being a slave totally at the mercy of the whims of his masters he opts to resist her advances on the grounds:

> "Behold, my master ... has given me authority over[29] everything in his house ... and has not withheld anything from me except you, because you are his wife. How then can I do this great wickedness, and sin against God?" [Genesis 39:8–9].

Besides the obvious attractions of allowing himself to be seduced, Joseph is aware that there is little danger involved. He admits as much: his master is not aware of what is going on in the house and trusts him implicitly.[30] Indeed all the danger lies in refusing.[31] Yet refuse he does, on strictly moral grounds: he will not commit adultery because to do so is not only a betrayal of the husband who trusts him, but because it is a sin against God. This was not simply an Israelite view. The Ancient Near East was united in the conviction that adultery was not simply a civil offense but a sin against God (or "the gods," as the case may be). It was "the great sin." And so in order not to commit "this great wickedness and sin against God" Joseph was willing to risk imprisonment, even death. All this is being called to mind by the author of Esther in using the language of Genesis to phrase the comment:

> Now when they had spoken to him day by day, and he would not listen to them (3:4).

What the parallel language is implying is that the cases of Mordecai and Joseph are parallel, that they both involve a lone individual taking a very dangerous stand. The further implication

---

[28]The dependence of Esther on the Joseph narrative in Genesis was first noted by Ludwig Rosenthal over a century ago. More recent commentators often mention the influence of Genesis in passing but rarely draw any conclusions from the fact. (See Chapter 14, note 3.) The larger implications of this dependence will be elaborated in Chapter 21.

[29]Literally, "placed in my hand."

[30]"Behold, my master, having me, doesn't concern himself with anything in the house, having put everything that he has into my hand" (Genesis 39:8).

[31]The consequences of persisting in his refusal to go to bed with his master's wife lead her, in a fit of fury at his rejection of her, to accuse him of attempted rape. He is thrown into prison. An Egyptian prison was no place a sane individual would want to spend even a day.

is that just as Joseph's stand was motivated by an overriding *moral and religious principle*, so too is the stand of Mordecai. The question is, what principle?[32]

To answer this question we should return to the Agagite hint but in far greater depth, for the struggle between Israel and the Amalekites did not begin with Agag and Saul but it reaches centuries further back. We will have to go back to its beginnings to understand it as the people of the Biblical Era understood it.

He Did Not Fear God

Who or what is Amalek?

Besides a reference in the Book of Genesis, which places them in the area of Kadesh in the early Patriarchal Age,[33] the Amalekites first appear in history at the early stages of the Israelite exodus from Egypt. Entering the Sinai desert, the Israelites were viciously attacked by the Amalekites. The event was traumatic; it was deemed a miracle that the Amalekites were driven off and that they failed to exterminate the Israelites.[34] This moment in history seared itself into the national consciousness. We are informed that, immediately after the encounter, God instructed Moses:

> "Write this for a memorial in a scroll, and read it aloud to Joshua, for I will utterly blot out the memory of Amalek from under the heavens." So Moses built an altar, and named it Adonai-nisi.[35] And he said: "[The name means] 'Hand upon the throne of the Lord: The Lord will wage war with Amalek from generation to generation'"[36] (Exodus 17:14–16).

As if this were not enough, in Deuteronomy this intention and oath are codified as an injunction:

> Remember what Amalek did to you on the way as you came out of Egypt. How he fell on you on the road, when you were faint and weary, cutting down all the stragglers in your rear; he did not fear[37] God! Therefore, when the Lord your God has given you rest from all your enemies around you, in the land that the Lord your God is giving you as an inheritance, to possess it, you shall blot out the memory of Amalek from under the heavens. You shall not forget! (Deuteronomy 25:17–19).

What can explain this undying hatred, this tenacious grudge? The terrible experience of grinding slavery in Egypt did not produce such a reaction. Quite the contrary, that experience engendered an understanding of the plight of the downtrodden, and resulted in ethical exhortations to lend him a helping hand.[38] Other battles in the wilderness period, and the experi-

---

[32]In this sense the instinct of the Greek translators of the Bible was correct: they sought the reason for Mordecai's stand in the realm of moral and/or religious principles, as did the rabbis of later generations. They were looking in the right place; their problem was that they picked the wrong moral principle.

[33]Kadesh-barnea is an oasis on the edge of the Sinai desert. This account relates to the period of Abraham, possibly the 18th century BCE. Analysis of the place names in this narrative lead some to date it to the 20th century BCE. At any rate it seems that they had been in the region for centuries.

[34]According to Exodus 17:8–13, only the act of Moses managing to hold aloft his staff, "the rod of God," for the entire day insured the divine aid that allowed the Israelites to barely beat off the assault.

[35]That is, "The Lord is my banner."

[36]That is, eternally.

[37]The Hebrew term, *Yirah*, has the meanings of *awe* and *reverence* as well as the meaning of fear. All are implied here.

[38]For example: "You shall not oppress a stranger; you know the heart of a stranger, for you were strangers in the land of Egypt (Exodus 23:9). See also Exodus 22:20; Leviticus 19:33, 25:35–38; Deuteronomy 10:17–19, 15:12–15, 24:17–22.

ence of bitter servitude and horrifying massacre afterwards never led to undying hatred. What was so special about the encounter with Amalek that made it unique?

I would suggest that the key lies in the phrase; "he did not fear God!" The concept of "the fear of God" is an unusual one.[39] It always refers to common decency, as manifested in one's relationship with those weaker than oneself, that is, the minimum of morality. An example from the Book of Exodus is especially relevant to our case. Pharaoh, king of Egypt, plans a genocidal "final solution" to his "Jewish problem." He will murder all Jewish male infants. His first idea is to utilize, for this purpose, midwives who, in the process of assisting Israelite women in labor, will kill at birth all male children. For what probably is a trial run of this procedure, he chooses two midwives. But the plan doesn't work.

> Now the midwives feared God, and did not do as the king of Egypt told them; they let the boys live (Exodus 1:17).

It was their common decency, their "fear of God," that would not allow them to be instrumental in the murder of infants. The idea, therefore, is that there are things that no person should ever do if he possesses even the minimum of human decency.[40]

The parallel with Amalek is instructive. In opposition to the midwives, the Amalekites are stigmatized as totally lacking in this elemental decency. The phrase is used in conjunction with a description of their attack upon the Israelite column. Instead of assaulting the main body, where they could either destroy a perceived threat or at least expect to find loot, they spend their energies cutting down the stragglers: the weak, the sick, the aged, the cripples, solitary children — all those who had not the strength to keep up with the column. This was simply the killing of defenseless human beings for the sake of killing.

I am reminded of the episode in Shakespeare's play, *Henry V*, in which a party of French knights attacks the deserted English camp during the battle of Agincourt. The attack makes no military sense. It will in no way affect the outcome of the battle. All English soldiers are away fighting. The only occupants of the camp are non-combatants, young boys. These the knights wantonly massacre. King Henry's reaction, when he sees the carnage, is sobering: "I was not angry since I came to France until this instant."[41] It is the senseless slaughter of the defenseless that drives him to fury. I think that the reaction of Moses and the Israelites was similar.

As the generations passed, this bitter memory probably would have faded had not the Amalekites, by their incessant atrocities, kept it burning. Raids into Israelite territory, with their attendant massacres, were constant. Again and again they allied themselves with Israel's enemies, often providing these enemies their margin of victory.[42] Eventually the term *Amalek* came to be indelibly associated with genocidal intentions,[43] with mass murder, with savage massacre and horrifying brutality.

---

[39]As opposed to "the fear of the Lord" (the God of Israel), the term "the fear of God" (or "the awe of God") is more general. It is usually used, especially in early biblical literature, with reference to non–Jews who, after all, do not recognize the Lord, God of Israel, but do acknowledge a divine realm that holds man to account.

[40]A less extreme example of minimal common decency mandated by the Bible in this context is Leviticus 19:14 ("You shall not curse a deaf person, nor put a stumbling block before one who is blind; but you shall fear your God"). Some others are Leviticus 19:32 (showing respect for the elderly) and 25:36 (not taking interest on a loan made to a poor person). See also Leviticus 25:17, 25:43, and so on.

[41]Shakespeare, *Henry V*, Act IV, scene 7.

[42]As allies of the kingdom of Moab they conquered and helped to hold down part of Israel for 18 years (Judges 3:12–14). Allied with the Midianites and the "People of the East," they carried out devastating yearly raids upon central Israel (Judges 6:1–6).

[43]Psalm 83:1–8 lists Amalek as one of the peoples who plan to exterminate the Children of Israel:
They have said: "Come, let us cut them off from being a nation;
That the name of Israel may no more be remembered" (83:5).

With the passage of time the Amalekite menace was reduced to manageable proportions. Saul broke them as a serious military power (1 Samuel 15). With their subsequent defeat by David they ceased to pose an existential threat to the Israelites. Remnants of the Amalekites persist as late as the end of the eighth century BCE and then they disappear from the historical record.[44] But the name lives on; the Israelites have never forgotten.

While it is certainly possible that isolated persons in the Persian period could trace their ancestry back half a millennium to illustrious Amalekite forbears, it seems more probable that the term "Agagite" is being used as a pejorative epithet when applied to Haman, a description of character, much as one might describe someone today as a "fascist" or a "Nazi." And just as nowadays calling a person a "Nazi" does not mean to suggest that, prior to 1945, the person in question was a card-carrying member of the German National Socialist Party; so calling Haman an "Agagite" may not have been referring to his ancestors, but rather to what he was.

As we have pointed out, Haman must have had a reputation. One does not get appointed number two in the empire, second only to the king, without a track record. We have theorized that he had been, prior to his startling promotion, a satrap or the governor of a province. We have also mentioned that one of the few things we know about Haman is that he is incredibly rich.[45] The way governors and satraps enriched themselves at the expense of those whom they governed are well known; yet to squeeze out such vast sums implies a level of bloody-minded ruthlessness that boggles the imagination. This line of reasoning seems to be confirmed by Haman's actions upon attaining the pinnacle of power. The one project that we know that the new vizier inaugurated is a program of genocide: the annihilation of every last Jew in the empire.

What I am suggesting, then, is that the term "Agagite" is a description of Haman's character. I am suggesting that Haman's reputation had preceded him to Shushan: a person with pockets bulging with the loot of his victims and clothes soaked with their blood; a person without a speck of human decency; a revolting monster who *did not fear God*. This was the new "CEO" of Persia, come to apply his well-tested methods to the entire empire.

And this is the person whom Mordecai will not serve. What I am proposing is that Mordecai's stand does indeed parallel that of Joseph. Joseph will not sin against God by committing adultery. Mordecai will not sin against God by becoming an accomplice to this "Agagite" who does not fear God. Others, more "realistic" than Mordecai, will find ways to explain to themselves the need to come to terms with the unspeakable, avert their eyes, follow orders and go along "with the inevitable." Mordecai cannot. As a Jew, come what may, Mordecai will not bow to Haman.[46]

---

[44]The last mention of Amalekites is in 1 Chronicles 4:41–43, which informs us that in the days of King Hezekiah (720–692 BCE) an expeditionary force from the tribe of Simon displaced Amalekite elements residing in the Akaba region among the Edomites (Meyers, *AB 1 Chronicles*, p. 31).

[45]When Haman will present to the king his plan for "a final solution to the Jewish Problem," to induce acceptance of his proposal he adds, as a sweetener, an offer of ten thousand talents of silver out of his own pocket! This sum amounts to almost two-thirds of the annual income of the Persian Empire! Even if, in line with the general tendency of the Book, this is a bit of an exaggeration, a clear picture of Haman's financial status emerges. The assertion of D. Daube (Daube, "The Last Chapter of Esther," p. 141), among others, that Haman was not intending to pay this astronomical sum out of his own pocket but rather from funds to be looted from the Jews really does not hold water. A key element of Haman's plan to exterminate the Jews by means of mob action rested on motivating the mob by inciting them to plunder the Jews (see Chapter 13, "Blueprint For Mass Murder: How?"). At the conclusion of the anticipated orgy of killing and looting little would have remained for the king's treasury (unless we suppose that Haman was naïve enough to believe that he could somehow "repossess" Jewish wealth plundered by the mob).

[46]We realize, of course, that this entire proposed scenario, while grounded in the text and in what we know of ancient Persia, is mainly speculation. But then so are all the other attempts to explain Mordecai's strange stand. The bottom line is that not having been told, we simply don't know Mordecai's motivation. All we can do is speculate as others before us have done.

CHAPTER 13

The War Commences

The Jew is to be eliminated and the state has no regard for the manner of his elimination.
> — Eric Mills, *Letter of 12 November 1935*[1]

The Jews are a race which must be wiped out. Whenever we catch one — he will be exterminated.
> — Hans Frank, governor-general of German-occupied
> Poland, speech to Nazi Party speakers, Cracow,
> 4 March 1944

Before Mordecai's co-workers so helpfully brought his defiance to Haman's august attention, was Haman unaware of it, or did he prefer not to notice and so avoid the trouble of having to deal with the issue? Either way, now that it has officially been brought to his attention he must pay heed. His reaction is utter fury.

When Haman saw that Mordecai did not kneel or bow to him he was filled with fury. Now he disdained[2] to lay hands on Mordecai alone. So seeing that they had told him who Mordecai's people were, Haman sought to wipe out all the Jews, the people of Mordecai, throughout the whole kingdom of Ahasuerus (3:5–6).

The extent of Haman's reaction is breathtaking. He will take action not just against Mordecai alone, not just against the Jews of Susa, but against *all* the Jews in the *entire* Persian Empire. Inasmuch as the Persian Empire at that time encompassed all the Jews in the world, Haman has resolved upon a "final solution to the Jewish Problem."[3] But is it indeed an overreaction, or is it the spark that ignited the tinder of a pre-existing anti–Semitic hatred? Or perhaps it is not even this, but merely an excuse for implementing a preexistent plan of extermination. Was

---

[1]Eric Mills was a high-ranking British civil servant. This quote from a letter to his superiors is a follow up to his official report to London on a meeting with members of the German Economic Ministry in Berlin, whose purpose was to sound out the Nazi authorities as to their intentions with regard to the Jews. The letter, as well as the report, is cited in Gilbert, *The Holocaust*, p. 49.

[2]Literally, "Now it seemed contemptible in his eyes."

[3]The phrase "final solution," coined by the Nazis (one of its first uses was by Hermann Göring on 20 May 1941), was used as an innocuous sounding designation for their program of genocide of the Jews, and has become a synonym for "the extermination of the Jews."

Haman waiting to reach a rank in the government from which he would be able to put it into effect? Not being told, we can only speculate, but it is difficult to credit a personal insult as the sole cause of a genocidal plot against an entire people.

Did Mordecai realize what effect his action would have? It is hard to believe that he did. Unless there is much of which we are unaware, this is the first systematic attempt in recorded history to exterminate all the Jews.[4] Being that there was no precedent, the Jews, Mordecai included, have been caught unprepared. It is one thing to risk one's job, even one's life, for principled reasons (or for personal ones for that matter). It is another thing entirely to knowingly provoke the massacre of one's people. Mordecai was undoubtedly as astounded as anyone by what followed.

Blueprint for Mass Murder: How?

Haman has made his strategic decision to kill all the Jews. There now remain only tactical issues to be considered: how to carry out this audacious plan, when to put it into practice and getting the necessary permission from the king. These now become Haman's focus, and ours.

The scope and audacity of Haman's intent is on so large a scale that it is virtually impossible for people to grasp what a plan such as this would entail in real terms. In much the same way, outside of trained architects, few people can look at a set of blueprints and get any concrete idea of what the projected building will look like when the plans are executed. That is why models and drawings are made: to concretize for people the implications of the abstract plans. For us, genocide is little more than a vague word. Saying that Haman was planning mass murder conjures up no pictures in our minds, and evokes few emotions. We too need a model to make sense of Haman's blueprint.

Unfortunately we have such a model. Within the recent past Haman's plan to murder all the Jews was put into practice. While the Nazi "Final Solution to the Jewish Problem" differed from Haman's plan in detail and methodology, it yet remained close enough in aim and scope to give us a practical picture of what Haman intended.[5] As such we will, from time to time, refer to the Holocaust (as well as several other "murderous episodes" in our unhappy and inhuman era) to clarify the theory and practice of genocide, then and now.

Haman's first problem is one of pure scale. Having determined to wipe out all the Jews ... throughout the whole kingdom of Ahasuerus (3:6) he is confronting a landmass covering parts of two continents. In the century since their exile from their ancient homeland the Jews have spread widely. We know that they are in Susa, in Babylon, in Nippur, in Egypt, and now back in Jerusalem. They are almost certainly in Ecbatana and Persepolis, the summer and religious capitals respectively of the Achaemenian dynasty. They probably are in India and Ethiopia as well, not to mention Kabul and Bactria and probably in Central Asia (Sogdiana). Pursuing the

---

[4]The only possible precedent, the attempt of an Egyptian ruler to murder all male Israelite infants about 800 years before, while well known to the Jews of Persia (it was recorded in Exodus 1:15–22) was so far in the misty past and under such different conditions that it would not have been deemed relevant in any practical way to their "modern situation." And besides, it had not been successful; spottily implemented, the program had simply petered out.

[5]In the more than two thousand years that elapsed between the Persia of Haman and the Germany of Hitler much progress had been made in the realms of technology and administration. Needless to say the Germans, an advanced people, were quick to adapt the overall plan to the improved means of implementation, thus updating and modernizing the original Persian blueprint.

lure of opportunity, the Jews have followed in the footsteps of the conquering Persian armies where they have not preceded them (as in Egypt).[6] How is one to locate them all, much less implement their murder? The Persian state machinery is simply not up to the job.

Haman's solution is ingenious. Since the state can't do it, he will keep the state out of the picture. The state may not be able to locate every last Jew, but the Jews' neighbors know who and where they are. Haman will rely on the local populations, the dwellers of every city and every province in the empire. If he can incite them into mob action they will do the job of locating and killing the Jews. And Haman feels certain that he can motivate them. The only action that will be required of the authorities, the forces of law and order, will be to stand aside and not prevent the carnage and massacre. In a word, Haman proposes to orchestrate and unleash an empire-wide pogrom.[7]

There are implications to this line of thinking. Haman is not a stupid or incompetent person; he would not have risen so high if he were. If he feels that he can successfully promote a pogrom, this means that in the century since the dispersal of the Jews, a deep-seated and virulent anti–Semitism has taken root in large parts of the population, and to the furthest reaches of the empire. Not only can Haman rely (he is convinced) on sufficiently large groups of people to rise and massacre the Jews if given the chance, but also that a climate of opinion has been created which will guarantee that, among the larger reaches of the majority population that will not actively participate in the attack on the Jews, no one will so much as lift a finger to help or defend them. To add to this base of simmering hatred and exclusion, and to widen the appeal, Haman adds the lure of loot. This in turn implies that there is something there to loot. From penniless refugees, in the space of a century the Jews have become a prosperous people. Here Haman taps into the latent envy a successful minority inevitably excites in their less industrious and less prosperous neighbors. Thus Haman proposes: "to wipe out, to slaughter and to destroy all the Jews, young and old, children [as well as] women in one day ... and to plunder their possessions (3:13). Combining hatred of the Jew with envy, and bloodlust with plunder, Haman is certain he has a winning combination.

Blueprint for Mass Murder: When?

The methodology settled, the issue now becomes: when? To insure success, timing is everything. Haman envisions a "surgical strike"; a coordinated, empire-wide purge "in one day" (3:13). But it must be the right day.

We are all familiar with the concept of lucky days and unlucky days. In the Western World, although some hotels do omit a thirteenth floor, most people regard with skepticism the labeling of Friday the Thirteenth as an unlucky day. Most businesses are not run, nor government policy set, on the basis of propitious or unpropitious days.

But many non–Western societies are built on very different premises. In South East Asia, for example, business virtually comes to a halt on days calculated as "unlucky." Astrologers serve as official government consultants and their advice is routinely taken when setting state policy. And there are certain seasons when no one will contract an engagement, get married or make a business deal; any such marriage or business deal, they believe, is certain to lead to disastrous

---

[6]Haman intimates as much in his request to the King when he identifies his target as scattered among "all the provinces of your kingdom" (3:8). This does not imply any great population density in most of the provinces — a few families here, a few there — with most of the Jews to be found in less than half a dozen urban centers and their vicinities.

[7]Pogrom: a Russian term (in Russian the word means "devastation") and a typically Russian institution. It means a state-organized massacre of helpless people (originally of Jews in Russia).

outcomes. Conversely, business deals made or marriages contracted on propitious days have the likelihood of success marvelously enhanced. Ancient Persia was also such a society.

It is important, therefore, to realize that Haman, when he called in experts to consult the auguries, was not indulging in a personal idiosyncrasy. He was behaving in accord with the accepted norms of his society; indeed, had he acted in any other way his competence would have been called into question. We cannot appreciate how the plot of Esther works itself to its resolution without understanding how acceptable was Haman's behavior to the Persia of his day, and how unquestionable is the appropriateness of the day chosen by these means for the massacre to come. Everyone, Jew and non–Jew alike, would have agreed that if there was to be a pogrom, the best day for it would be the date chosen by Haman's diviners.[8]

With this in mind we can now understand Haman's next move. He chooses the month of Nisan[9] to call in the experts and determine "the day." As the first month of the calendar year, Nisan is the Babylonian New Year; according to Babylonian mythology this is the season when the gods gather in conference to debate and determine the fate of humanity for the year to come.

> In the first month, that is the month of Nisan, in the twelfth year of King Ahasuerus, the "pur" [the lot] was cast[10] in the presence of Haman, day-by-day and month by month, until the lot fell on the thirteenth day of[11] the twelfth month, that is the month of Adar [3:7].

The method chosen is divination by means of casting a lot or tablet, called Pur,[12] by a skilled practitioner called a diviner, to the accompaniment of specific ritual and magical incantations. The lot is cast, very much as one throws a die (singular of dice), to achieve a "yes" or "no" answer. The casting takes place in the presence of Haman and is probably completed in one sitting. The methodology seems to be that the diviner goes systematically through the calendar, naming each day and each month, with a cast for each, until he determines the date of the thirteenth of the month of Adar[13] as the ideal setting for the massacre. The date is doubly propitious: not only

---

[8]In those days, in China, these matters were more fully systematized. In a tomb in Shuihudi, dating from 217 BCE, there was discovered the body of a magistrate who was buried along with his law library (possibly it was felt that he would need his reference works if he was to continue to practice law in the spirit world). Included among the reference works were two *Ri shu* (Books of Days), sorts of almanacs of propitious and unpropitious days for particular activities. They were to be consulted by the magistrate to decide the most suitable moment to conduct a trial or, based on the crime committed, what was the best day on which to conduct an interrogation of the suspect.

[9]Nisan is a Hebraized form of *Nisannu*, the name of the first month of the year in the Babylonian calendar. When in Babylon, the Jews adopted the Babylonian names of the months and use them to this day. The name of this month among Hebrew speaking peoples of Western Asia, found in the Bible and used by the Israelites prior to the Babylonian Exile, was *Abib*. As the Hebrew name indicates (*Abib* = Spring), Nisan roughly coincides with the month of April in the Gregorian calendar. See also Chapter 8.

[10]Literally "he [the astrologer, the diviner] cast the Pur." Incidentally, it is interesting that Haman chooses this old-fashioned form of divination rather than the new "science" of astrology to find his "lucky day." After more than a thousand years of painstaking endeavor the Babylonian astrologers (we today rate them as astronomers) had succeeded, several centuries before the time of our tale, in determining arithmetically the movements of the sun, the moon and the five visible planets. They were now able to determine the exact position of each on any given date in the past or future. Since 717 BCE they had been routinely (and accurately) predicting solar eclipses. Babylonian astrology had already by our date spread to India, and was soon to inundate China and Japan. This was "cutting edge science," yet Haman remains with the tried and true. It would seem that he was, by disposition, a conservative.

[11]Reading with LXX; MT omits "until the lot fell on the thirteenth day of." We read with AT (Alpha-Text) "thirteenth" in harmony with the rest of the Book (3:13, 8:12 and 9:1) instead of LXX that reads "fourteenth."

[12]*Pur* is the Babylonian term for lot (as the author hastens to explain, defining the foreign word with its Hebrew equivalent). It derives from the Akkadian *puru* of the same meaning.

[13]From the Babylonian *Addaru*, the last month of the calendar.

is thirteen a "lucky number," but being eleven months off one can make one's preparations in a leisurely manner, as opposed to working under pressure to meet a near deadline which might lead to a botched job. Haman now has his target date. All that remains is to get permission.[14]

Blueprint for Mass Murder: The OK

Why does Haman suppose that he can persuade Ahasuerus to permit the genocidal slaughter of an entire people? Would not such a request be expected to elicit a reaction of shock or disgust? Could it be that Ahasuerus is an anti–Semite, and that Haman knows it and banks on the backing of an ideological ally? But no, this cannot be the case, for Haman is very careful, when he makes his request, *not* to mention that the Jews are his target. He speaks only of an anonymous people who need to be destroyed due to certain loosely defined faults that make it inexpedient to allow them to continue to exist. Haman may be an anti–Semite, but he knows better than to play this card to the king.

Haman does not expect to get a shocked refusal. The Persians have no scruples about massacre. Herodotus accuses the Medes, co-rulers with the Persians of the Achaemenian Empire, of having carried out a frightful massacre of "the greater part of" the Scythians, and later he reports an extermination of Magi by Darius I, father of Ahasuerus.[15] But these were external or non-productive elements of society. The danger to Haman lies in the possibility that Ahasuerus will not be willing to sacrifice a people integral to the economy of the Persian Empire, and one of the more productive ones at that. It is to this issue that Haman primarily addresses himself in his presentation:

> Then Haman said to King Ahasuerus: "There is a certain people scattered, and [yet] separate, among the people throughout all the provinces of your kingdom; and their laws are different from those of every [other] people, neither do they obey the king's laws. Therefore it is not worthwhile for the king to tolerate them. If it please the king, let it be decreed[16] that they are to be destroyed, and I will pay ten thousand talents of silver to the relevant officials[17] for deposit to the king's treasury" (3:8–9).

In other words, Haman will turn over to the king a sum of money that will cover any possible loss to the state revenues resulting from the massacre.

> Then the king took his [signet] ring off his hand and gave it to Haman, son of Hammedatha the Agagite, the enemy of the Jews. And the king said to Haman: "Well, it's your money[18]; and as to the people, do with them what you want"[19] (3:10–11).

---

[14]Berlin is of the opinion that the author of Esther didn't believe in the efficacy of divination (Berlin, *JPSBC Esther*, p. 38). I can find no evidence in Esther to support this view. On the contrary, in harmony with the beliefs of that era I think that the author accepted that the date chosen by lot was the ideal day for the massacre, and expected his readers to feel the same. This point will become important later (see Chapter 19).

[15]Herodotus, *Histories*, Book I, p. 106; III, p. 79.

[16]Literally, "let it be written."

[17]Literally, "into the hands of those who have charge of the king's business."

[18]Taking the short Hebrew phrase to be an idiom meaning roughly, "The money belongs to you," the implication being that you have the right to dispose of it any way you want, and if you feel like giving it to me, well O.K. Following Carey Moore we have rendered it with the equally short English idiom: "Well, it's your money" (Moore, *AB Esther*, p. 40). Literally the Hebrew reads, "The money is given to you." For the reason behind this rendition see further on.

[19]Literally, "and the people, to do to it as is good in your eyes."

The first thing that strikes us is the shocking nonchalance with which an entire people are consigned to annihilation. There is no discussion, no consultation, no debate. The king does not enquire as to who this people is, what exactly they have done, how long this has been going on or what are the likely consequences of their destruction. There is no request for a second opinion or a discussion in the Imperial Advisory Council. Indeed, the entire matter seems to have been settled in an informal chat between the king and Haman. The most serious of matters is handled in the most unserious of ways: without a second thought the king takes off his royal signet ring (with which documents are stamped with the royal emblem — the equivalent of the king's signature — making them official) and hands it to Haman with the offhand remark: "Do with [it] whatever you wish." One is reminded of the scene in Shakespeare's play *Julius Caesar*, in which Marc Anthony, Octavius and Lepidus are discussing a list of their political enemies and by means of comradely tradeoffs decide whom they shall murder: for example, "you can kill my brother if you let me kill your sister's son." Marc Anthony nonchalantly agrees to his nephew's murder by languidly making a mark on the list next to his name and remarking: "Look, with a spot I damn him."[20]

It is an understatement to say such men hold life cheap. By giving Haman his signet ring the king is giving him the authority to frame the destruction of this "certain people" in any way it pleases him. The king doesn't even want to know when or how. All is left in the hands of Haman.

But not quite. There remains the issue of the money. Most scholars, following the way LXX renders the phrase "the money is given to you" (3:11) as "Keep the money," assume that good-hearted Ahasuerus is just too generous a soul to accept money from one of his dear officials. I agree with Moore that this misreads both the situation and Ahasuerus's character. In the next chapter (4:7) Mordecai explicitly states that the money (he knows the exact amount) is to be paid into the king's treasury, while Esther's remark, in 7:4, that "we have been sold" suggests that the money has already been handed over. We have already drawn attention to the immense sum involved; Ahasuerus was much more likely to accept than reject such a windfall.[21] How often are kings so flush with money that they can blithely pass up offers such as this? So as we see it, the Jews are now in Haman's hands, while the money will shortly be in the king's.

Lastly, we should pay close attention to Haman's charges against this "certain people." They are to become the prototype of the charges that will be leveled against the Jews for centuries to come. These amount to four: (1) This is a people that is "scattered ... among the peoples throughout all the provinces of your kingdom"— that is, they lack territorial integrity but are everywhere a minority. The national tragedy of the Jews, their loss of their own land and the disbursement of their remnants to the four winds has been turned into an accusation. (2) Though *scattered*, and everywhere a minority, they nonetheless remain *separate*, they do not assimilate into the majority. Against all logic and precedent they remain a distinct entity. This leads to (3) No matter where they are, they maintain a distinct life style that sets them apart from everyone else: "their laws" (by which Haman means not only binding rules and regulations but also customs and practices) "are different from those of every [other] people." So far, though the spin is distinctly negative, the report is factually accurate. With the last charge (4), and the point of the entire recitation, Haman departs from fact and enters the realm

---

[20]Shakespeare, Julius Caesar, IV:1.

[21]See Chapter 12, note 43. While it is true that Herodotus (Herodotus, *Histories*, Book VII, 27–29) records Xerxes turning down an even bigger sum, those were the euphoric days when he was poised to conquer Greece. In the gloomy days following the disastrous defeat, and with building expenses at Persepolis draining the treasury, Ahasuerus just might be in a more parsimonious frame of mind.

of malicious fantasy: "neither do they obey the king's laws," that is, they are a subversive element.

This is exceedingly clever: the empire is a potpourri of peoples, each with its own language, customs, and laws. In this the Jews are the same as everyone else, differing only in that they are not concentrated in one place but are a minority everywhere. As a minority they should assimilate; they don't. So what Haman does is to lump all the other peoples together, disregarding their radical differences (could there be anything more disparate than Egyptians, Greeks, Babylonians and Hindus?), insisting that the Jews differ from the norm, and that somehow the difference makes them subversive.[22] Therefore, their existence should not be tolerated: "Therefore it is not worthwhile for the king to tolerate them."

Future anti–Semitism will build on this foundation and add to it; but these four elements will remain, unaltered and central, down to the present day. In its first literary appearance anti–Semitism strides onto the stage full-blown.

The Plan Goes Public

Having secured the king's approval Haman wastes no time in setting the machinery into motion.

On the first month, on the thirteenth day, the King's stenographers were summoned, and [the decree] was written exactly as Haman dictated[23]: [it was addressed] to the king's satraps, and to the governors of every province, and to the officials of every people — every province in its own script and every people in its own language — in the name of King Ahasuerus was it written, and it was sealed with the king's seal. Dispatches were sent by couriers[24] to all the king's provinces: to wipe out, to slaughter and to destroy[25] all the Jews, young and old, [their] children and wives,[26] in one day, [namely] upon the thirteenth of the twelfth month, that is the month Adar, and to plunder their possessions. The contents of the decree are to be publicly proclaimed in every province to all the peoples, that they be ready for that day (3:12–14).

Haman works fast. Less than two weeks have passed since, at the advice of his diviners, he has finalized the date for the projected massacre and the dispatches are already going out.

[22]Logically this makes no sense, yet Haman's instincts are correct. There is a difference between the Jews and the other peoples, pagans all, that is unbridgeable. But that the difference lies in the religion of the Jews is not yet recognized; the strangeness, however, is nonetheless felt.

[23]Literally, "ordered."

[24]Literally, "runners"; but in 8:10, 14 the "runners" are described as being mounted. The term, a left-over from the times when dispatches were carried by foot, has now come to mean message bearers using the fastest means of transportation possible, always bearing in mind that in some terrains messengers on foot might still be the most efficient. Darius I had constructed a magnificent road system to connect the empire, which his successors constantly added to and improved. The imperial postal system, working mostly with mounted couriers in a system something like the famed 19th century Pony Express, was one of the marvels of the Ancient World. Considering that the Pony Express was able at times to cover the 1,838 miles from St. Joseph, MO, across the Rocky Mountains to Sacramento, CA, in ten days, we can be confident that dispatches from Susa could reach the most outlying provinces of the empire in well under a month.

[25]LXX omits the words "to slaughter and to destroy" as redundant, and some modern scholars likewise delete them. But this is simply Persian legalese. In much the same manner the participants of the Wannsee Conference (see note 29 below) repeatedly used the phrase "killing and eliminating and exterminating (*Toten und Eliminieren und Vernichten*)" when discussing their plans for the Jews. In 7:4 Esther, in quoting the decree, repeats all three words "to wipe out, to slaughter and to destroy."

[26]*Taf venashim* (children and wives): a common biblical idiom, invariably used in conjunction with some term that relates to, and defines, their men folk (in this case "the Jews, young and old").

The date the decree is officially proclaimed, the thirteenth of Nisan, is ironic. Does Haman know that this is the day before the Passover, the day the Jews celebrate the Exodus from Egypt? His latter day spiritual descendants, the Nazis, often scheduled *Aktionen*[27] against the Jews on the eve of Jewish holy days.[28] Or are we crediting Haman with a malice-based knowledge he didn't possess? If the latter, then the choice of date can only be termed providential. This is a point that we will consider at a later stage of our analysis. One thing, however, is certain: the Jews of Shushan did not have a very happy Passover Holiday.

> At the king's command the couriers went forth in haste, and the decree was proclaimed in the Acropolis of Shushan. The king and Haman sat down to drink, while the city of Shushan was flabbergasted (3:15).

One is reminded of the conclusion of the Wannsee Conference.[29] Once the main movers of the conference, SS-General Reinhard Heydrich, SS-Colonel Adolph Eichmann and SS-Lieutenant General Heinrich Müller, head of the Gestapo, had finalized and put into motion the extermination of the Jews they sat down to a convivial chat over glasses of brandy. In his later pre-trial interrogation in 1961 Eichmann recalled that they "sat very cozily near the stove ... we all sat together as comrades. Not to talk shop, but to rest after long hours of effort."[30] Having made public their plan to exterminate the Jews, with the sense of a tiresome task comfortably behind them, Haman and Ahasuerus sit down in the Acropolis to a well deserved round of drinks, while in contrast, in the city proper, the populace, hardly believing their ears, stare at each other dumbfounded.

---

[27]Plural of the German word *Aktion*, a drive, a military operation. This term was routinely used by the Nazis for quick roundups of Jews in a given area, either for immediate slaughter or for deportation to the death camps.

[28]Jewish holidays begin with sunset on the evening of the day before the holiday. Thus Passover begins with the sundown of the fourteenth of Nisan.

[29]Number 58 am GrossenWannsee is a villa overlooking the Grosse Wannsee, a lake outside Berlin. On January 20, 1942, a meeting was convened in this villa by Himmler's deputy, Reinhard Heydrich, of representatives of the main departments of the German government to coordinate which ministry would be responsible for which aspect of the liquidation of the Jews. It was at this meeting, known to history as the Wannsee Conference, that the operational plan for the extermination of the Jews of Europe and North Africa was finalized.

[30]As quoted in Gilbert, *The Holocaust*, p. 283.

Act III: Fighting for Their Lives

Yea, though I walk through the valley of the shadow of death, I will fear no evil, for Thou art with me; Thy rod and Thy staff, they comfort me.—Psalm 23:4

Comforter, where, where is your comforting?—Gerald M. Hopkins, "No Worse There Is None"

CHAPTER 14

In the Valley of the Shadow: Looking into the Abyss

You are frightened: do your hearts turn giddy?
Does the abyss here yawn for you?
— Friedrich Nietzsche, *Thus Spake Zarathustra*

The Decree has been made public; the power masters sit down, drinking to the success of their project, while the general public is dumbfounded by the news. And what about the Jews, the proclaimed targets of the coming massacre? Up to now we have been looking at the projected "Final Solution to the Jewish Problem" from the top down, that is from the perspective of Haman and of the State. It is now time to reverse matters and see things from the point of view of the prospective victims.

> Now Mordecai knew everything that had been done; and Mordecai tore his clothes and donned sackcloth and ashes,[1] and went out into the midst of the city and he cried out a great and bitter cry. He came as far as the King's Gate, for none might enter the King's Gate dressed in sackcloth. Now in every province, wherever the word of the king and his decree reached, there was great mourning among the Jews, and fasting, and crying and wailing, many of them lying in sackcloth and ashes (4:1–3).

Mordecai, we are told, not only knows what everyone else knows — the text of the decree — but, due to his insider sources of information, also the full story to which we are already privy: who initiated the decree issued in the king's name, and why. We find him, clad in sackcloth and with ashes on his head, overcome with grief (and perhaps guilt) wandering around the city like one demented, uttering heartrending cries and shrieks. And here, with a few deft words the author opens up to us the full horror that has invaded Mordecai's soul.

We have already noted that the author is writing his tale with the stories of the Patriarch Jacob

---

[1]Tearing one's clothes was (and still is among Jews) an expression of mourning, as in the case of the death of a near family member. Dressing in sackcloth (a coarse material used for baling agricultural produce) and putting ashes on one's head were also conventional ways of expressing grief and humiliation in biblical times (as in Genesis 37:29, 2 Kings 18:37, 2 Samuel 13:19). While this is the way a religious person would react in those days, so would a "non-religious" person. Persians had similar customs (note Herodotus, *Histories*, Book VIII, p. 99). Carey Moore is undoubtedly correct when he points out that rending one's clothes and donning sackcloth "need no more be interpreted as proof of deep religious faith than the presence of an officiating clergyman at an American funeral means that the deceased was a 'believer'" (Moore, *AB Esther*, p. 47). That was just the way things were done in those days.

and his sons, especially Joseph, in mind.[2] By copying the wording of an important event in the story of Joseph, we have seen him provide us with the key to the understanding of Mordecai's probable motivations. Now he repeats the stratagem, asking us to contemplate an episode that occurred in the days of Jacob's youth as a means to understand what Mordecai is feeling. We have been told that, as Mordecai wanders around the city, "he cried out a great and bitter cry" (4:1). The wording should remind us of an episode in Genesis[3]; let us examine it closely. The story is a familiar one: father Isaac, aged, ailing and blind tells his eldest son, Esau, to go, hunt a deer and prepare from its meat his favorite dish. Then, he continues, after he eats, he will bestow his blessing upon him, thus making him the head of the family. Esau leaves to carry out his father's wishes. In his absence his younger brother Jacob disguises himself, deceiving his father as to his identity, and, fraudulently, he receives the blessing meant for Esau. At long last Esau returns, prepares the venison to his father's taste, and brings it to him, expecting now to receive his blessing. Appalled at the deception that he now realizes was perpetrated upon him, old Isaac exclaims: "Who then is he that has taken venison and brought it to me, and I have eaten before you came, and I have blessed him? Indeed, he is blessed!" That is, the blessing, though obtained by fraud, is nonetheless irrevocable. "When Esau heard the words of his father, *he cried out with a great and bitter cry*" (Genesis 27:1–34).

Up until that moment Esau had lived in an orderly and secure world. He was the firstborn and the favorite son of his father in an age when these facts meant everything. They gave him status and pride of place, and secured his future. Yet, at the very moment when he was to receive the blessing that would confirm his status as head of the family and heir to his father, he learns that he has been defrauded of everything. In a moment his world has been overturned and all his certainties shattered. And in his terrible shock and anguish "he cried out with a great and bitter cry," giving voice to his unspeakable pain and despair with a terrible, inarticulate shriek. By using the identical wording, our author is illuminating for us the inner crisis of Mordecai in his extremity.

In this Mordecai is also serving as a representative of the Jews of his age. A hundred years have passed since that terrible day in 586 BCE when Jerusalem went up in flames and the few pitiful survivors were hauled off in chains to distant Babylon. That nightmare is but a faint and distant memory, half-remembered, stories passed down from grandfathers and great-grandfathers. From penniless prisoners in alien surroundings, in three or four generations their descendants have become settled citizens, with the best of them prosperous, established in the professions, and with rising careers in government. They feel themselves at home and secure in a world that they now call their own. And in one moment, with one decree, all their certainties are shattered: stability, security, prosperity, place in society — everything is stripped away. The Jews find themselves in a world that has no place for them, and will not even allow them their miserable lives. It is not merely the impending annihilation that is so shattering, but the sweeping away of all the certainties upon which their inner lives have been built. It is this that brings to the lips of Mordecai, the symbol of all the Jews of his day, the wordless shriek of bitter anguish. All this the author intimates by making Esau's cry the prototype of Mordecai's.[4]

---

[2]See Chapter 12.

[3]That Esther echoes Genesis, sometimes verbatim, has often been recognized. Moore calls attention to "Gen. xxvii 34; another parallel with the Joseph Cycle" but draws no conclusions from the fact (Moore, *AB Esther*, p. 47). Berlin also remarks that "Verbal and syntactic similarities appear at ... points in the story, even when the themes are unrelated," and lists several such. Strangely, she does not mention the present striking example (Berlin, *JPSBC Esther*, p. xxxvii).

[4]LXX, in its obsessive focus on leaving nothing to the imagination of the reader, puts words to Mordecai's "great and bitter cry": "An innocent people is condemned to death," thus robbing Mordecai (and by extension all the Jews) of his existential anguish, and turning his walk through the midst of the city into a kind of solo political protest march.

The Missing Rod and Staff

The Jews express their shock and anguish by the conventional acts of tearing their clothing, and many don sackcloth and lie on the ground, covering themselves with ashes. In a word, they go into mourning: they wail and they fast. One thing is conspicuous by its absence: we are not told that they pray. In the Bible the outer signs of mourning are always the accompaniment of prayer. When things go wrong, when crisis is upon you, you turn to God for assistance and for comfort. When the Israelites were oppressed in Egypt we are informed: "and they cried out, and their cry for help rose up to God" (Exodus 2:23). This became the paradigm: in trouble and crisis one turns to God.[5] Yet in the Book before us the Jews are not shown in prayer. Indeed the reaction of the Jews is so unconventional that its description cannot be anything but deliberate. We are being shown a Godless universe, cold and sterile, with neither hope nor comfort for a people abandoned by its neighbors to slaughter. This is the secular world we have been exploring, taken to its logical outer limits: only empty gestures, and acts without content, remain of what was once the biblical world of faith.

Mordecai is one of the more successful and acculturated of the Jews. He is at home in the Persian world (or so he thought), he is part of the Persian bureaucracy, and, significantly, it is he who counseled Esther to conceal her Jewish identity.[6] And strangely, he doesn't fast (or at least we are not told that he did). In place of prayers he utters wordless cries. Clad in sackcloth, ashes besmearing his face and hands, his steps lead him to the King's Gate, site of his office and entrance to the Acropolis, the seat of government. Clothed as he is, he can proceed no further.

The sight of the disheveled and distraught Mordecai occasions comment; the scandal spreads and reaches the ears of Esther's servants. Knowing of the connection they bring the news of this unusual behavior to the queen's attention.

> Now Esther's maids and her eunuchs came and told her [of Mordecai's appearance], and the queen was greatly disturbed.[7] She sent [proper] clothing to dress Mordecai so that he might remove his sackcloth, but he refused. Then Esther summoned Hathach, one of the eunuchs whom the king had appointed to serve her,[8] and ordered him to go to Mordecai to learn what this was, and why it was. Hathach went out to Mordecai in the city square that was before the King's Gate. Then Mordecai told him all that had happened to him, and the amount of money that Haman had promised to pay to the king's treasury for the destruction of the Jews. And he gave him a copy of the written decree that had been given out in Shushan for their annihilation, to show to Esther and to report to her, and to charge her to go to the king and to plead with him for her people (4:4–8).

Several interesting points emerge from this terse narrative. In the first place, Esther does not seem to know about the impending liquidation of her people. And this is very strange. Palaces are hotbeds of gossip; the speed with which the smallest tidbit of information becomes known in the furthest and most obscure corridors is proverbial. And to contend (as some do) that the harem was "sealed off" is naïve; the single most important unofficial "duty" of the eunuchs, the

---

[5]Many of the Psalms were specifically composed to provide inarticulate and normally tongue-tied persons with appropriate vehicles of expression by which they could turn to God in their distress and despair.

[6]Did he also conceal his own, only revealing it in the context of his refusal to bow to Haman, or was it known before? The text up to now is ambivalent on this matter. But see 6:10, where Mordecai is known to Ahasuerus as a Jew.

[7]To learn that Mordecai was wearing sackcloth (so LXX). The Hebrew term *hithalhal* (from the root which means "to writhe") is here used in a unique grammatical construction and seems to mean intense emotional anguish. It has also been rendered "distressed," "agitated" and "shocked."

[8]Literally, "whom he had caused to stand before her."

one upon which advancement and preferment most depended, was keeping the women of the harem up to date. Esther, with her carefully cultivated eunuch contacts, could be expected to be among the first to know anything, even before many of the top officials of the government. Yet here, despite the cumbersome creaking of the machinery necessary to grind out hundreds of copies of the decree, mobilize the couriers, give them their orders and send them on their way — a process that even under the most urgent prodding would have taken no less than several days — and which was impossible to keep secret even if anyone had wanted to do so, Esther seems oblivious to the knowledge possessed by every street urchin. Could this be an example of the massive indifference in upper circles to the fate of the Jews? Or is it a subject that, by common consent, no one mentions in conversation? We have no way of knowing, but it certainly gives us food for thought.[9]

The second point is that it does not seem that Mordecai has any immediate intention of enlisting Esther to intercede with the king. He makes no attempt to get in touch with her through his usual channels of communication. Indeed, by dressing as he does he has effectively cut himself off from his go-betweens; he cannot enter the Acropolis. Contact with Esther has been made all the more difficult. It is Esther who initiates communication by sending him clothing, yet Mordecai does not seize the opportunity to enlist Esther in the cause. It is only after this first meeting with Esther's eunuchs that it seems to dawn upon him that something should be done about the situation, and that perhaps Esther is the person properly placed to do so.[10] Mordecai is beginning to get a grip on himself.

> So Hathach told Esther [everything][11] Mordecai had said. Then Esther spoke to Hathach, and charged him [with this message] for Mordecai: "All the king's servants, and the people of the king's provinces know that there is one penalty[12] for any man or woman that approaches the king in the inner court without being summoned: that he be put to death. Only if the king extends to him the golden scepter may he live. As for me, I have not been summoned to the king these thirty days." And Hathach told Mordecai Esther's words[13] (4:9–12).

Esther's response to Mordecai's call to arms is simple: "You should know better than to ask. Everyone knows that to approach the king on one's own initiative is almost certain death, and I'm not exactly in favor at the present moment. He hasn't called for me in thirty days. Don't count on me."

There has been much discussion of this rule.[14] Was it a security measure, a safeguard against assassination? If so, was it absolutely necessary to include the king's wives in this general pro-

---

[9]Of course another possibility is that Esther knows and, fully aware of the dangers inherent in attempting to intervene, has prudently decided to disregard the matter and play dumb. After all, five years have passed since she became the king's consort (note 3:7); she is no longer spending her nights in the king's bed (as we shall shortly learn), and so no longer can count on being able to influence the king.

[10]Some scholars contend that Mordecai's donning of sackcloth and his wailing and screaming had the purpose of attracting the queen's attention. This is implausible: why should he use this bizarre and uncertain means of doing so, when he had rapid and secure lines of communication with her (as he proved in the matter of the assassination plot)?

[11]LXX and Vul. add "everything."

[12]Literally, "law."

[13]Reading with LXX and OL (the Old Latin translation of Esther); MT reads: "And they told."

[14]Herodotus claims that it was Deioces the Mede who instituted this rule, and that his Persian successors retained it (Herodotus, *Histories*, I:99, III:77, 84). The proper procedure was that one had to request an audience through one of the king's messenger-eunuchs, and then wait for a summons. Only the seven members of the Royal Advisory Council had the right to bypass this procedure and enter the king's presence unsummoned. (See Chapter 9, note 13.)

hibition, or was the rule also instituted to protect the king's privacy? In Maurice Samuel's charming study of the character of Ahasuerus, he has this to offer on the issue at hand:

> It appears that when the queen disobeyed the king [as in the case of Vashti] he could do no more, according to the law, than depose her, whereas if she approached him unasked for and unwanted, the penalty might be death. Disobedience in a queen was a civic offense, nagging could be treated as a capital crime. The royal prerogatives in Persia were not uniformly onerous.[15]

Esther has always known better than to be a nag, and considering the risks involved she is in no hurry suddenly to change her policy and become one.

Esther Bites the Bullet

This bucket of cold water, with which Esther douses Mordecai, does not dishearten him. On the contrary, it has the effect of strengthening his resolve. Mordecai now shifts from asking to aggressive demands and implied threats.

> Then Mordecai returned this answer to Esther: "Do not imagine that you, among all the Jews, will escape with your life [because you are in] the palace.[16] For if, at this time, you keep silent, relief and deliverance will come to the Jews from another quarter, while you and your father's house will perish. For who knows whether, for just such a time as this, you came to the throne"[17] (4:13–14).

This stinging rebuke that Mordecai flings in Esther's face is the first real hint that behind the human maneuvers and manipulations of a secular world may lie an unknowable pattern and purpose, separate and distinct from human designs. Does Mordecai realize what he is saying? The rebuke is Mordecai's: "Don't think you can save your skin by refusing to take responsibility for your people. You are uniquely positioned to help, but if you don't we will find some other way to save ourselves." But the way the rebuke is worded, with its hint that Providence has maneuvered Esther into her position in the palace for just this contingency, is the author's.

We are also being given a further hint. Let us return to the opening words of this chapter. We have recognized that the phrase "and he cried out a great and bitter cry" (4:1) was a direct quote from Genesis 27:34, and have spent considerable time analyzing the significance of the author's use of this passage. Two verses further on the author once again quotes Scripture:

> Now in every province, wherever the word of the king and his decree reached, there was great mourning among the Jews, and *fasting, and crying and wailing*, many of them lying in sackcloth and ashes (4:1–3).

The italicized phrase is a direct echo of Joel 2:12[18]:

---

[15]Samuel, *Certain People of the Book*, p. 14.

[16]Literally, "the king's house."

[17]Literally, "came to royalty."

[18]We know very little about the prophet Joel, and consequently there is no agreement as to when he lived and wrote. Scholars differ widely, some placing him in the pre-exilic age, some in the post-exilic era. James L. Crenshaw, one of the more persuasive of the latter, places Joel in Jerusalem in the period following the completion of the Second Temple (515 BCE), that is, the end of the sixth — beginning of the fifth centuries BCE (Crenshaw, *AB Joel*, pp. 23–24). Thus even if we accept Joel to be post-exilic, anywhere between 40 and 50 years separate the Book of Joel and our dating for the writing of Esther, more than enough time for Joel to have become widely disseminated among Diaspora Jewry and to have become known to the author of Esther.

"Yet even now," says the Lord, "turn back to Me with all your hearts; and with *fasting, and crying and wailing*.[19]

The prophet continues:

> Rend your hearts, and not your garments,
> And turn back to the Lord your God;
> For He is gracious and compassionate,
> Slow to anger and abounding in kindness,[20]
> And repents of evil.[21]
> *Who knows* whether He will not turn and repent,
> And leave a blessing behind Him? (Joel 2:13–14).

And suddenly we are brought back to Mordecai's rebuke:

> For *who knows* whether, for just such a time as this, you came to the throne (4:14).

By embedding in this description of the Jewish reaction to Haman's Decree of Annihilation and Mordecai's subsequent charge to Esther echoes from Joel, the author is leading us to read this episode in the light of the prophet's exhortation to Israel to repent. *For who knows*, perhaps God will find a way to avert the evil decree; perhaps Esther is the very tool God has prepared to save His people.

Mordecai has been presented to us as a totally secular Jew. Even in crisis he does not pray,[22] he does not fast. Having no religious faith he has nowhere to turn and can simply rend the air with cries of anguish. And when he pulls himself together he can see no recourse but to activate the human beings around him, especially his fellow Jews. It seems unlikely that Mordecai even considers the possibility that the God to Whom he doesn't pray, and Who he never even mentions, has arranged things in such a way that the path to salvation is ready to hand. So the words the author puts in his mouth make no mention of God and His guiding hand. In this the author is being true to his portrayal of Mordecai. Yet at the same time, in the way this episode has been presented, the perceptive reader can see in these same words a vision of a larger canvas beyond Mordecai's ken. We, the readers, have been put on notice: behind the façade of this secular world, greater forces are at work.

> Then Esther said in reply to Mordecai: "Go and gather[23] all the Jews that are in Shushan, and fast for me. Do not eat or drink for three days, neither night nor day. And I also, and my maids, will fast likewise.[24] And then will I go to the king, [even though] it is against the law; and if I perish, I perish!" (4:15–16).

---

[19]The individual words *tzom* (fasting), *behi* (crying), and *misped* (wailing) are common words in the Hebrew Bible, but only in Esther and in Joel do we find them combined in this distinctive manner. In biblical times, hearing this particular phrase would ring a bell in listener's ears, recalling the similar phrase from the words of the prophet Joel.

[20]*Hesed*, see Chapter 3, note 27.

[21]That is, refraining from imposing punishment.

[22]It is this terrible void in Mordecai's life that prompted the Hellenized Jews who translated Esther into Greek to compose a prayer for Mordecai and insert it after verse 17 of this chapter.

[23]Esther's use of the term *k'nos* (gather) suggests to Dommershausen a hint of religion: where were they to be gathered but in the *bet k'neset* (the House of Gathering, a traditional synonym for the Synagogue) (Dommershausen, *Den Estherrole*, p. 74)? While certainly possible, it would seem to me a rather roundabout and far-fetched way for the author to drop a hint. The wording of Mordecai's remonstrance to Esther (4:14) should be sufficient and is far more obvious.

[24]C.F. Keil points out that, in fact, the fast would have lasted from the afternoon of the first day until the morning of the third day, somewhere between forty and forty-five hours total (Keil, *Esther*, p. 355).

Esther has taken the plunge; she will do what she can regardless of risk. She also has no thought of God. She does not commend her life to His care. Nor does she ask her fellow Jews to pray for her. All she asks for is a demonstration of solidarity; she will fast and asks them to fast with her.[25] Then she will do what has to be done.

Were Esther and Mordecai really as irreligious as they are portrayed? In Chapter 8 I suggested that the bleak picture of a totally secular and Godless world is questionable historically. It is a literary artifact created by the author for his purposes. So the question of the "real Esther and Mordecai" is not at issue. We must deal with the Esther and Mordecai that the author has seen fit to draw for us. It is our task to make sense of them as they move through the Book of Esther, and to ponder the reasons for the author to so present them.

Returning to the tale, it is important to note that Esther's reply marks a major turning point in the Book. Up to now Mordecai has been the dominant member of the pair. No longer: with her decision Esther has taken charge. And having taken matters into her hands, she emerges as the dominant personality of the Book. From this moment onward, it is Esther who acts, initiates and dominates events. Everyone else — Haman, Ahasuerus, and even Mordecai — only react. We will now begin to understand why this Book is named The Book of Esther.

So Mordecai went his way,[26] and did everything that Esther had commanded him to do (4:17).[27]

While Mordecai gets to work organizing the Jewish community of Shushan, Esther begins her fast.

Now it came to pass on the third day that Esther put on her royal robes[28] and stood in the inner court of the palace, opposite the royal living quarters. And the king was sitting on his throne in the throne room, opposite the entrance to the palace. Now when the king saw Esther the queen standing in the court, she found favor in his eyes, and the king extended to Esther the golden scepter that was in his hand; then Esther approached and touched the tip of the scepter[29] (5:1–2).

The *Apadana* or Audience Hall of the palace of Susa was a huge room approximately 360 feet by 360 feet. The ceiling, over 40 feet high, was supported by six rows of six columns each,

---

[25]The passage from Joel, in whose light we have been led to read this section from Esther, continues as follows:
   Blow the horn in Zion;
   Sanctify a fast; call a solemn assembly!
   Gather the people,
   Sanctify the congregation;
   Assemble the elders, gather the children,
   Even nursing infants;
   Let the bridegroom come out of his room,
   And the bride her chamber...
   And say: "Spare Thy people, O Lord (Joel 2:15–17).

Karen Jobes, to whom I owe the insight of the relationship between Esther 4:1–15 and Joel 2:12–18, concludes as follows: "Whether Esther was mindful of Joel's prophecy or not, she in effect 'blows the trumpet in Zion,' commanding Mordecai to call a fast of all the Jews of Susa, to see if the Lord may relent from sending this calamity on her people. For the first time in this story Esther identifies herself with God's people and responds to the prophetic call to repentance by joining with the Jews of Susa in this fast" (Jobes, *Esther*, p. 137).

[26]Literally, "crossed over" (the Square? the river separating the Acropolis from the city of Susa proper?).

[27]LXX here inserts "The Prayer of Mordecai" and "The Prayer of Esther," two Hellenistic compositions designed to rescue the two heroes of the Book from the stigma of irreligiosity. They are to be found in Catholic Bibles, and in the Apocrypha of Protestant Bibles.

[28]Literally, "put on royalty," "robes" being understood. LXX inserts the missing word "robes."

[29]LXX expands this terse account into sixteen verses worthy of a melodramatic film of the silent era, featuring Lillian Gish in the star role. Esther is all fear and trepidation; the king on his throne, in his magnificent robes and jewels, looks terrifying; at the sight poor Esther faints dead away; at the sight of the unconscious beauty, Ahasuerus is overcome by pity, and so on. For those who like this kind of thing, it is all there in the Apocrypha as Addition D.

crowned by capitals ornamented with double bull-shaped *protomes* (foreparts). Each column weighed about 25 tons. Human beings were reduced to insignificance by these gargantuan surroundings. The throne was placed near the rear of the Hall, facing the entrance. Esther would have had to walk about one sixth of a mile from the entrance to reach the throne, down the central aisle between the huge columns — a progress designed to sap confidence even in those present by invitation. To Esther the slow walk down the Hall must have seemed endless.

> And the king said to her: "What do you want,[30] O Esther the queen, and what is your request? Even if it be half the kingdom and it shall be given to you!" (5:3).

Absence *does* make the heart grow fonder. Despite not having called for her for an entire month, Ahasuerus is not angry with his "neglected wife" for barging in on him unsummoned. Quite the contrary, he is glad to see her. But he is not stupid. He realizes perfectly well that Esther wouldn't have dressed up and walked in on him unless she wanted something. His grandiose offer of anything up to and including half the kingdom shouldn't be taken seriously. It was merely a stylized, formal phrase. Esther also is far from stupid. He is in a generous frame of mind, but not quite *that* generous. Now, perhaps, is the time to ask him to cancel the decree against the Jews. But Esther is far too clever to do the obvious.[31]

> Esther said: "If it please the king, let the king and Haman come to the party[32] that I have prepared for him today."[33] Then said the king: "Tell Haman to hurry[34] to do as Esther has said" (5:4–5a).

This is playing to Ahasuerus's weakness: here his beautiful Esther has come to rescue him from the dreary routine of governance, inviting him to do what he likes best, engage in a convivial session of boozing. And she has even thought of inviting his favorite drinking partner, his boon companion Haman. How wonderfully considerate; no wonder he hastens to accept.

Once again we quote from Maurice Samuel's study of Ahasuerus' character as he recreates the king's feeling of appreciation and pride toward Esther:

> He had reason to be proud. How wisely and with what masterly insight he had picked her out from among the hundreds of contestants with nothing more than a single night's acquaintanceship to go on! How different she was from Vashti! Not a hint of reproach for his long abstinence. It was of him alone that she was thinking. How adoring the woman was, how humble, how good-looking. And if he had only known, how hungry![35]

The mood having been set, the intimate little party of three is a resounding success. But Ahasuerus still suspects that he is being softened up. His wonderful Esther wants something.

---

[30]Literally, "What to you?" Perhaps a closer rendition in modern colloquial English might be "What gives?" But Hebrew is far too formal to permit such a rendering.

[31]Alternatively, Joshua Berman has suggested that, having nerved herself up to risking her life by coming in to see the king unannounced, Esther simply can't summon up the extra courage at this time to "come out of the closet" and reveal that she is a Jew. So in avoiding the issue and inviting Ahasuerus to a party she is playing for the time she needs to work up her courage (Berman, "Hadassah bat Abihail," p. 656).

[32]*Mishteh*: a drinking party.

[33]Note the tense. Esther has not only been fasting; she has been using her time to attend to the innumerable details involved in preparing an intimate little party that will run perfectly. Should she survive the unsummoned interview with the king, and should he accept her invitation everything will be ready to roll at a moment's notice.

[34]The sense of the Hebrew is: "Tell Haman to get a move on!" that is, to drop everything that he is doing and come at once. But this would be too colloquial a manner in which to render the text.

[35]Samuel, *Certain People of the Book,* p. 18.

So the king and Haman came to the party that Esther had made. At the wine party[36] the king said to Esther: "What is your wish and it shall be granted you, and what is your request, even if it be half of the kingdom it shall be given to you." Esther answered saying: "My wish and my request is: If I have found favor in the eyes of the king, and if it pleases the king to grant my wish and fulfill my request, then let the king and Haman come tomorrow[37] to the party that I will make for them, and tomorrow I will do as the king has said" (5:5b–8).

Esther is playing it coy. The suspense builds. Of course Ahasuerus realizes that she is stringing him along, but he is enjoying the process. This is so much more pleasant than presiding over endless discussions of government policy. He can actually look forward with anticipation to a "surprise party." So can Haman, who thinks that his part will be merely that of spectator.

---

[36]The term for party, *mishteh*, in the Persian text, means a party in which drinking is a major element. The addition of the word *wine* just emphasizes what will be the main preoccupation of the guests. Esther obviously did not match her guests cup for cup. Someone had to keep a clear head to orchestrate what was, as everyone but Haman realized, a preliminary to some request of the king.

[37]Reading with LXX; MT omits "tomorrow."

CHAPTER 15

Interlude: The Theater
of the Absurd

"What sort of people live about here?"

"In *that* direction," the Cat said, waving its right paw around,
"lives a Hatter: and in *that* direction," waving the other paw,
"lives a March Hare. Visit either you like: they're both mad."

"But I don't want to go among mad people," Alice remarked.

"Oh, you can't help that," said the Cat: "we're all mad here.
I'm mad. You're mad."

"How do you know I'm mad?" said Alice.

"You must be," said the Cat, "or you wouldn't have come here."

— Lewis Carroll, *Alice in Wonderland*

At this tense moment the curtain suddenly descends. It is intermission time; the headlong rush of the narrative is temporarily interrupted. Why? There seem to be several reasons. One may be the author's wish to intrude a pause for dramatic effect; making us wait to find out what happens next ratchets up the suspense by several notches. It is well to keep in mind that what we have before us is a drama. Another reason could also be dramatic: the need for comic relief. Just as Shakespeare intrudes comic interludes into his tragedies to provide a temporary release from the unfolding of the grim events, so our author may feel a parallel need.

But there seems to be a more fundamental reason, one that brings us back to the opening of the Book. At that time, surveying the outrageously extravagant drinking marathons, the bawdy entertainment program (fortunately aborted), the absurd imperial proclamations and so on, we suggested that the author is acutely unhappy with Persia and that he is relentlessly critical of it. In a word, there is a streak of irrationality that underlies Persian society and the author is drawing attention to it. This irrational streak is emphasized as the narrative unfolds: the "beauty contest" to choose a replacement for Vashti, the sudden change in the way in which the country is to be governed which is signaled by the appointment of Haman, the anti–Semitic phobia of this upstart and the ease with which he contrives to put into place a program of genocide. We have tried to explain each event as we have gone along in rational terms, but beyond all these explanations we see a fundamental irrationality.

This interlude finally brings this irrational streak into focus, for the break is not merely comic; it is insane. People work at cross-purposes, situations turn into their opposites, expectations are reversed and nothing makes any sense. We are in an *Alice in Wonderland* world. It seems entirely possible that the author is using this break to convey his conviction that Persia, perhaps the entire world, is insane. If this is indeed so — that what we perceive as a sane and orderly world is nothing more than the fruit of our efforts to impose ex cathedra some coherence upon an underlying chaotic irrationality — then this could explain the irruption of tragedy into a seemingly ordered and rational universe.

A further thought: as we have emphasized, the author has arbitrarily (and artificially) removed God and religion from his tale. Is the author also intimating that this is what a Godless universe is like — mad, where things turn into their opposites, and nothing seems to make sense? It might be well to keep these thoughts in mind as we plunge into a hilarious (and lunatic) interlude.

To recapitulate and put things into some sort of temporal perspective, Esther probably broke in on the king during his morning audience, which places the opening phase of her party about noon or maybe one o'clock in the afternoon.[1] It is getting toward evening when the drink-fest breaks up (but, as we learn, it is still daylight). How Esther has been feeling since her initial relief when the king spared her life we can only imagine: fear and horror at the impending massacre perhaps; loathing of Haman, anxiety over the prospects of her plan to avert the disaster and worry about what her fool of a husband will do when he learns that she is a Jew — all these are probable. But not a hint of any of this shows. Her clothing magnificent, her hairdo and makeup flawless, Esther is at her beautiful and charming best. The wine is superb, the service immaculate and the conversation flows effortlessly. Esther is a wonderful hostess; she can be witty when needed, but she knows how to listen, how to encourage her guests to talk. The party is everything that anyone could ask for, and a wonderful time is had by all. Now, according to plan (Esther's plan), there is to be a pause of about twenty hours. Tomorrow at noon the follow-up party will commence: the king will discover what the beautiful Esther is angling for, Haman will (hopefully) get his comeuppance and, if she can pull it off, the Jews will be saved. In the meantime we must be patient as everyone goes their way: the king and Esther most probably to bed, and Haman to his home.

The Fly in the Ointment

As he leaves the palace Haman is euphoric. The king trusts him. Esther likes him. More than the wine has gone to his head. His way home leads, as it must, through the King's Gate, and there whom does he run into but Mordecai, cleaned up and properly dressed, back on the job. And Mordecai turns his back on Haman: he neither rises nor stirs, he doesn't even acknowledge his presence; he keeps his eyes on his paperwork and pretends no one is there. From giddy heights Haman is plunged into fury; he can only with difficulty preserve appearances. His mood is ruined.

> Haman went out that day happy and in high spirits[2]; but when Haman saw Mordecai in the King's Gate,[3] [that he] neither rose nor even stirred on his account, then Haman was filled with

---

[1]Working backward, it would seem that it is still daylight, and the workday has not yet ended (we find Mordecai still on the job at the King's Gate) when Haman starts for home after Esther's party (5:9). Assuming that a Persian drinking party would hardly last less than four hours, this would place the start of the party at the latest in the early afternoon. While this temporal reconstruction is purely speculative, and not in any way essential to the understanding of the narrative, it does fit in well with the mid-day rest and "siesta" patterns that have prevailed in the Near East and surrounding regions for the last several thousand years.

[2]Literally, "good of heart."

[3]It is still light; office hours are not yet over and Mordecai is still on the job.

fury at Mordecai. Haman restrained himself and came to his house. He sent and summoned his cronies,[4] and Zeresh his wife. And Haman recounted to them the extent of his wealth, and the great number of his sons, and how the king had promoted him and raised him above the officials and servants of the king (5:9–11).

Arriving at his palatial dwelling (*house* is really too modest a term for the residence of one of his wealth and position), Haman's roiling emotions, mixed with the wine he had imbibed during the long afternoon, have created a mix that makes speech imperative. He must explain himself, and for this he needs an audience. He sends out the call: his wife for a start, then his coterie of friends, followers, and the inevitable crew of sycophants and hangers-on who gather about persons of high office. With these about him Haman holds forth: he tells them how wonderful he is, how rich, how many sons he has (ten — a large number of sons was a powerful status symbol in Persia), his promotion to vizier, the number-two in the kingdom, ranking higher even than the highest officials and aristocratic courtiers. And lastly, he has finally made the great social breakthrough!

We must never forget that Haman is a hated parvenu; he is not a member of the high Persian aristocracy, one of the "best families," but an outsider who has leap-frogged over all the others. If Mordecai can publicly snub him, what must the seven best families of Persia be doing? There are, without doubt, circles from which he is excluded, houses to which he is not invited. Haman must feel his outsider status keenly, and be correspondingly insecure. And now he has been invited by Esther, Miss Persia of five years ago and favorite bedfellow of the king, to an exclusive private party, with Ahasuerus the only other guest. And more, there is to be another such party tomorrow, with the same exclusive guest list.

> And Haman said: "Esther the queen made a party for the king, and invited[5] none except me! Also tomorrow I am invited along with the king. But all this is worth nothing to me every time I see the Jew Mordecai sitting in the King's Gate" (5:12–13).

How tragic! Poor Haman, he has everything anyone could desire and yet he cannot enjoy life. The sight of that cursed Jew ruins his day, turning the joy of all his achievements and accomplishments into ashes. But we must not despair. His wife and his cronies are quick to come to his rescue:

> Then his wife Zeresh and all his cronies advised[6] him: "Let them make [you] a gallows fifty cubits high, and in the morning speak to the king [for permission] that Mordecai be hanged on it. Then [you will be able to] enjoy the party with the king."[7] The advice[8] pleased Haman, and he had the gallows erected (5:14).

Now that's the way to make someone happy! Fifty cubits (seventy-five feet) may seem a bit excessive, but not if you want the dangling body clearly visible to all and sundry, far and wide.[9] Haman is won over by the absolute brilliance of the idea. Carpenters and joiners are quickly routed out of their homes. Half-eaten dinners grow cold on tables. Soon the sound of hammers is heard in the district. By dawn the gallows will be ready.

[4]Literally, "those who bore him love."

[5]Literally, "brought."

[6]Literally, "said to him."

[7]Literally, "come to the party with the king happy."

[8]Literally, "thing."

[9]The suggestion is not that the structure itself be seventy-five feet in height, but that it be erected on some eminence or building top so that, when hanged, the victim will be dangling at that height, displayed for all below to see.

In the Dead, Vast Middle of the Night

It is now late at night. The pleasant post-party interlude of the king with his favorite queen has concluded and Esther has returned to her quarters. The king composes himself for sleep, but slumber does not come. The text informs us that "sleep fled" from him, which seems to imply that he actively pursued it. Did they count sheep in those days? We have no way of knowing by what means the king tries to fall asleep, only that after an indeterminate period of futile effort he gives up. But Ahasuerus being Ahasuerus, he determines that if he isn't going to sleep, neither will his personal staff. They can spend the night entertaining him.

His staff awake, the king orders his secretary to read to him. And on what subject? Why obviously — himself!

> That night sleep deserted[10] the king, and he ordered that the Book of Records (the Daily Record) be brought, and they were read before the king. And it was found written that Mordecai had informed on Bigthana and Teresh, two of the king's eunuchs, who were among the Guards of the Threshold,[11] who had plotted to assassinate King Ahasuerus. The king said: "What honor and dignity[12] have been bestowed on Mordecai for this?" And the king's youths who attended him[13] said: "Nothing has been done for him" (6:1–3).

This nighttime reading is possibly not identical with "The Book of Daily Things before the King" referred to previously (2:23),[14] but rather a condensed version, with all the dull lists of appointments, staff-meetings and so forth left out. Thwarted assassination plots and accounts of the execution of the plotters make stimulating reading for an insomniac king. A question arises in the mind of Ahasuerus: how was Mordecai's sterling service to the crown rewarded? The question posed, the answer is dispiriting: he wasn't. Here Ahasuerus heads an empire with the most efficient bureaucracy humanity has ever known, and still the foul-ups are endless. Not only is it State Policy to reward informers, especially in so crucial a matter as this, but not doing so reflects poorly on the honor of the king. Worse, the fact that Mordecai wasn't rewarded is common knowledge, at least in the inner circles of the palace. His servants didn't have to do any research, check any records. They knew! It is the subject of gossip! What are they saying about him? That he is ungenerous, stingy, lacking in gratitude? Something must be done to correct the situation, and at once. He needs immediate advice.

> The king said: "Who is in the court?" (Now Haman had come to the outer court of the palace to speak to the king about hanging Mordecai on the gallows he had prepared for him.) So the king's youths said to him: "Behold, Haman is standing in the court." And the king said: "[Tell him to] enter" (6:4–5).

Upon asking as to who among his advisors is awake at this early hour he is told that Haman is currently to be found standing in the outer court. The servants are sent running to bring him into the king's presence.

Haman too has been unable to sleep, but here the cause is a frenzy of anticipation. Having made certain that the gallows will be ready on time, Haman hurries to the palace to be first on line when the king begins receiving officials. The wording used is instructive. Haman does not intend to *ask* the king for permission to hang Mordecai. He intends to *speak* to him; to inform him of what he will be doing, to run it by him, so to speak. He anticipates no difficulties;

[10]Literally, "fled."

[11]See Chapter 11, note 6 and also note 7.

[12]*Dignity:* in the sense of promotion.

[13]See Chapter 10, note 5. These are his personal servants and thus in continual attendance.

[14]See Chapter 11, note 8.

he is merely doing what any good subordinate does, keeping his superior informed as to what he is doing. He simply wants to get the formalities out of the way early, so that he can oversee the execution of this accursed Jew, perhaps take a nap (to compensate for his lack of sleep), and still have plenty of time to get himself ready for the party. Here it is not yet light, and he is being escorted into the presence of the king. It is the early bird that catches the worm.

But as urgent as are Haman's concerns, the king also has something on his mind, and before Haman can even open his mouth the king begins.

> So Haman came in and the king said to him: "What should be done to the man whom the king desires to honor?" And Haman said to himself[15]: "Whom would the king desire to honor more than me?" (6:6).

And here we begin a confusion of cross-purposes, each party engrossed in his own thoughts, each talking past the other and hearing only what he wants to hear. The king, preoccupied with his own problem, assumes that Haman is there with the sole purpose of being helpful. Haman's assumptions are perhaps a bit more involved. During his wait in the outer court he must have learned of the king's insomnia (these tidbits of information about the king's condition are the favorite fare of the palace gossips). It was indeed touching to reflect that what had kept the king sleepless was his worry as to how he could heap yet more honors on the head of his worthy vizier.[16] Haman's total self-absorption could permit him no other interpretation; his arrogance completes his undoing.

> So Haman said to the king: "The man whom the king desires to honor —" (6:7).

With this phrase, in which he is simply repeating the words of the king, Haman is stalling for time as he organizes his thoughts. Having determined what he will say, Haman launches forth:

> "— let there be brought royal apparel which the king [himself] has worn, and a horse upon which the king himself has ridden, one with a royal crown on its head, and let the apparel and the horse be given to one of the king's most noble officials, and let them robe the man whom the king desires to honor, and have him [mount and] lead him on the horse through the city square, proclaiming before him: 'Thus shall it be done to the man whom the king desires to honor!'" (6:7–9).

This is a remarkably arrogant request. Haman is presuming to appropriate to himself (for of course he thinks he is talking about himself) the public symbols of royalty; in effect to stand in for the king. When Adonijah, the older brother of Solomon, requested the hand of Abishag in marriage (Abishag the Shunammite had been the nurse of the late King David), Solomon's answer to his mother, through whom the request had been made, was:

> "Why do you ask for Adonijah Abishag the Shunammite? Ask for him [also] the kingdom! For he is my older brother...." Then King Solomon swore [an oath] by the Lord, saying: "The Lord do to me, and more also, if this word does not cost Adonijah his life!" (1 Kings 2:22–23).

Public appropriation of items closely associated with a king by a person close to the crown was perceived (and correctly so) as an indirect attempt to gain the throne. The ploy cost Adonijah his life. What probably saved Haman, the number two in the kingdom, from a similar fate was that, unbeknownst to himself, he was making this grandiloquent request not for himself but for another, and one with no possible claim to the crown. Even for Mordecai it would be a stretch.[17] Probably what

---

[15]Literally, "said in his heart."

[16]It is to M. Samuel that I owe this scenario (Samuel, *Certain People of the Book*, p. 22).

[17]It is told that when Artaxerxes II, a later successor of our king, agreed to one Teribazus wearing one of his robes, it was on the condition that he be proclaimed mad, the idea being that only a madman would presume to wear royal clothing that had been worn by a king (Plutarch, *Artaxerxes*, V).

swayed the king to approve in Mordecai's case was his sense of guilt at the long delay in recognizing Mordecai's service, leading to a willingness to go overboard to compensate. Besides, it was not Mordecai who made the request.

> Then the king said to Haman: "Hurry! Take the apparel and the horse, as you have said, and do so for Mordecai the Jew, who sits in the King's Gate. Omit nothing of all you have said!" (6:10).

What must Haman's feelings have been as he somehow got through the next couple of terrible hours we can only imagine.

> So Haman took the [royal] apparel and the horse, and robed Mordecai and led him [mounted] through the city square, proclaiming before him: "Thus shall it be done to the man whom the king desires to honor!" (6:11).

But let us take our speculations a step further: what must have been the maelstrom of conflicting thoughts that poured through the minds of the onlookers of this bewildering spectacle? By now everyone knows the contents of the decree, and probably word has gotten around as to the true author of its terms. Yet here is a prominent Jew, condemned to death with all his fellow–Jews, being publicly honored in the most extravagant of manners. And by none other than the arch anti–Semite and author of the upcoming pogrom, who bleats out at regular intervals his formula of praise as he leads the crowned horse[18] and its magnificently clad rider around and around the vast square before the King's Gate. To make things more confusing, both honoree and the vizier "honoring" him look as though they are sick to their stomachs. It is enough to makes one's head whirl.[19] One can only conclude that the world has gone mad, and that sanity is fled to distant shores.

Turnabout

We began this chapter with a question: what is the purpose of this interlude? We made several suggestions: a dramatic pause in the action to heighten the tension; a comic interlude to momentarily lighten an over-serious plot; an episode to focus our attention on the fundamental irrationality of life. The time has come to offer yet another suggestion, one not in conflict with the preceding hints but one that rather offers a further dimension to our understanding: this hilarious tale functions as a turning point, the pivot about which the Book turns. Up to this point the Book has chronicled the rising threat to the Jews: the precipitous leap to power of the arch anti–Semite, Haman, the fabrication of a genocidal plot to murder them all, its approval by the king and the mobilization of the state machinery necessary to promulgate the decree. The doom of the Jews seems inevitable as the empire readies for "J-Day."

Those scholars who focus on the way the author wrote Esther point out that the Book is structured so as to form a balanced literary unit. For example, the Book begins with two parties, will end with two parties, and has two parties in the middle. Moreover, the second half of the Book is in the way of being a mirror image of the first. The first two parties are thrown by the king and celebrate the glory, wealth and power of Persia. The Jews are so insignificant as to be invisible. The parties with which the Book ends are thrown by the Jews to celebrate their deliverance. The king, and even Persia have faded into the background. The first half of the

---

[18]It would seem that horses once used by the king wore special headdresses — "crowns"— to identify them.

[19]We may laugh at Haman's discomfiture, but we can be sure Mordecai was not enjoying himself. Considering that he and all of his fellow Jews were slated to die, he would not exactly feel in a laughing mood.

Book chronicles the rise of Haman and the threat of anti–Semitism while the second half records the fall of Haman, the defeat of the anti–Semites and the salvation and empowerment of the Jews, etc. This pattern plays itself out in continuous detail.

One of the central themes of the Book is the surprising reversals that life can take. Along with the theme of seeming irrationality, goes the author's conviction that nothing is sure; what seems most certain is, in reality, far from certain. The most surprising reversals can and do take place. Or, as Yogi Berra has been wont to put it: it's never over till its over.

It is time to take a closer look at the two mid-book parties in Esther. Unlike the celebrations that begin and end the Book, which are huge affairs encompassing masses of people, these two parties given by Esther are small and intimate. It is between Esther and her two guests that the large issues affecting tens of thousands of people will be decided. And between these two parties falls our ridiculous episode that turns everything around. Haman comes to the king expecting to finish off Mordecai; instead Mordecai is honored and Haman humiliated. This is the beginning of the end for Haman, and the start of the rise of Mordecai. And the two parties mirror this reversal. At the first Haman leaves happy and in high spirits; he will exit from the second to be conveyed to his execution.

What effects this reversal? It is certainly not the result of human intention. It is not the king; he did not will his attack of insomnia. No one planned to read to the king the account of Mordecai uncovering the plot to assassinate him. No one arranged for Haman to be there. The whole thing is a series of "coincidences." But the sum effect of these "coincidences" is to bring about a seismic shift. From now on everything will be different. As we shall see, Haman's wife and "wise men" immediately sense this shift. Soon everyone will. Once more, quietly and by indirection, our author is intimating that the whole world may seem to us irrational, even insane, yet behind the façade of human events unknown forces are moving. The literary structure of the Book and its balance is being used by the author as a symbol of an underlying purpose and pattern behind the clutter of seemingly chaotic events.

We return to the aftermath of what we have entitled "The Theater of the Absurd."

The Omen

The ghastly farce is over at long last, Mordecai goes back to the office from which he was so unexpectedly summoned, and Haman flees home to hide his face behind bolted doors and shuttered windows.

> Then Mordecai returned to the King's Gate, and Haman hastened home, in mourning and with covered head.[20] And Haman told Zeresh, his wife, and all his cronies everything that had happened to him. Then his wise men[21] and Zeresh his wife said to him: "If Mordecai, before whom you have begun to fall, is of Jewish stock,[22] you will not prevail against him, but will certainly fall before him" (6:12–13).

We have already spoken at length about the superstitious mindset of the Persians in general, and of Haman in particular. The shocking and unexpected turn of events must mean something, but what? We were not informed that his wise men were summoned last night. Then all was going well and they were not necessary (a fallacy common to humankind), but now that

---

[20]In the Ancient Near East, one of the signs of mourning was to cover one's head.

[21]His astrologers and diviners, those whom he consulted for omens and to get direction. See Chapter 13, especially note 10.

[22]Literally, "of the seed of the Jews."

things have taken a turn for the worse, counsel is needed. The news could not be more unwelcome: what has happened is an omen. Your luck has changed. Your star, formerly in the ascendant, is now in the decline relative to the rising star of the Jews. Since Mordecai is a Jew, in your personal conflict you will not succeed in besting him; it is he who will best you.

> While they were still speaking with him, the king's eunuchs arrived, hurrying to bring Haman to the party that Esther had made (6:14).

Time is up. The interlude is over, and the main issues resume their rush toward resolution. Without leaving him any time to digest the dire words of his wise men, the king's eunuchs escort Haman to the palace, hurrying to ensure that he will not commit the ultimate faux pas of being late. His heart in turmoil, the heavens dark with foreboding, Haman is conveyed to the party that is to determine his fate.

CHAPTER 16

Esther Triumphant

Victory is not a name strong enough for such a scene.
—Horatio Lord Nelson, 1798

Esther's wine party is being held in the royal pavilion. We remember this structure. The seven-day open-to-all-comers extravaganza with which our Book opened was held in the large paved area fronting it. Behind the pavilion are the royal gardens; a large, beautifully kept expanse of fruit trees, shrubs and flowers in natural profusion, intersected by paths and small, gurgling brooks. The building itself is a one-story structure, colonnaded and open on all sides; it is late April, and spring in Susa is very warm. The cool breezes and the sweet odors wafting in from the garden are equally welcome. It is an ideal place for an intimate party.[1]

Inside the pavilion three couches have been placed so as to facilitate the conversation of the revelers. Next to them are low tables on which wine cups share space with plates of hors d'oeuvres. The décor is opulent. In the background hover the servants: waiters to serve the guests and, of course, the eunuch bodyguards of the king. The guests arrive and arrange themselves upon their respective couches, the wine is poured, the first cup raised, the first tidbit nibbled. The king turns to Esther.

> So the king and Haman came to drink[2] with Esther the queen. And also at the wine party on the second day the king said to Esther: "What is your wish and it shall be granted you, and what is your request, even if it be half the kingdom it shall be given to you" (7:1–2).

This is the third time the king has asked. Esther puts him off no longer.

> And Esther the queen answered, saying: "If I have found favor in your eyes, O king, and if it pleases the king, let my life be given me at my wish and my people at my request. For we are sold, I and my people, to be wiped out, to be slaughtered and to be destroyed![3] Now if we had

[1]This description is to a large extent based on the representation of a pavilion fronting on a park-like garden with small watercourses, paths and many trees found on a stone relief from the palace of Asshurbanapal in Nineveh. We are fairly certain that Persian palace gardens of this period were strongly influenced by the garden culture of Assyria and Babylonia, if not actually copied from them. Archeological evidence for such pavilions comes from the park of the Persian king in Pasargadae (Oppenheim, "On Royal Gardens in Mesopotamia," p. 332–33).

[2]For some reason most translators seem loath to admit that the purpose of a *wine party* is to drink, and insist upon rendering *leshtot* as "to feast," "to banquet," and so on. Only Y. Hazony translates the word literally as *to drink* (Hazony, *The Dawn*, p. 157). See also Chapter 14, note 36.

[3]Literally, "to wipe out, to slaughter and to destroy." Esther is quoting the exact wording of the decree which is in the active tense, despite the context that demands the passive tense. The listener to the plea, the king, is expected to make the grammatical transformation mentally.

[merely] been sold to be slaves, male and female, I would have kept quiet, for our distress would not have justified troubling the king" (7:3–4).

Esther does not scream or yell. Her plea is a masterpiece of understatement. She is even apologetic: she is truly sorry to be troubling the king over such a minor matter as her impending murder, and incidentally also the massacre of her entire people. If it had only been a matter of herself and her people being sold into slavery she would never have dreamed of interrupting the king's drinking and so spoiling his mood. But since it is actually a matter of having her throat slit, or worse — and here she quotes the actual wording of the decree — she has been emboldened to bother the king to beg for her life.

Up until the moment that Esther quotes the decree Haman has no idea of what she is talking about. He has never suspected that Esther is Jewish. Only now does he begin to connect the dots. The king, for his part, is only able to grasp that someone is threatening harm to his beloved Esther.

> Then King Ahasuerus spoke [up] and said to Esther the queen: "Who is he, and where is he who dares to do so?"[4] And Esther said: "A foe and an enemy, this evil Haman!" And Haman was overcome with terror before the king and the queen[5] (7:5–6).

And with a dramatic gesture Esther directs the king's attention to the cowering Haman.

Ahasuerus is dumbfounded. What! Haman? The king needs a moment to clear his head, to adjust to this new shocking information, and to decide how to handle things.

> Then, in his fury, the king rose from the wine party [and rushed out] to the pavilion garden; while Haman remained to plead for his life from Esther the queen, for he saw that the king was determined to do him ill (7:7).

Haman makes no move to follow the king. One look at Ahasuerus' face is enough to tell Haman that he is no mood to listen. His only chance is Esther. If he can win her over, she may be able to get him off. So he throws himself on her mercy. And in this he makes a bad mistake, an error he never would have allowed himself to commit had he not been mad with terror. Rushing back from the garden as suddenly as he rushed out, the king's eyes are greeted by the sight of Esther cowering at the furthest corner of her couch, with Haman half on, half off the couch, desperately clutching at Esther's withdrawn feet. Ahasuerus puts the worst possible interpretation on what he sees.

> Returning from the pavilion garden to the wine party the king [found] Haman sprawled[6] on the couch upon which Esther was! And the king exclaimed[7]: "Will he actually assault the queen in my presence, in my own house!" The word went out of the king's mouth, and the face of Haman was covered[8] (7:8).

To even approach closely a consort of a Persian king was a capital crime, much less actually to touch her. Here Haman seems to be sexually assaulting Esther. The command is given and the king's bodyguards seize Haman. He is doomed. And at this point one of the ever-helpful servants judges it the appropriate moment to offer a "helpful suggestion."

> Then Harbona, one of the king's eunuchs, spoke up[9]: "May I call your [majesty's] attention also

[4]Literally, "who fills his heart to do so?"

[5]The Hebrew *nibat*, which we have rendered as "overcome with terror," also has the sense of "to be startled," "to be shocked." Both meanings are implied: Haman is both terrified and in a state of shock.

[6]Literally, "fallen."

[7]Literally, "said."

[8]"In Greek and Roman cultures criminal's faces were covered before being taken away to be executed. This may indicate the same practice, but we have no other evidence that it was customary in Persia" (Breneman, *Ezra, Nehemiah, Esther,* p. 350).

[9]Literally, "said."

[to the] gallows[10] that Haman has made for Mordecai, who saved the king's life[11]; it is standing at Haman's house, fifty cubits high." And the king said: "Hang him on it!" So they hung Haman on the gallows that he had prepared for Mordecai; and the king's fury abated (7:9–10).

The king's explosive fury may be over with Haman's execution, but the king is not yet through. He follows up the hanging with the confiscation of Haman's estate. By estate we mean not only his Susa residence, but also all other properties owned by him and all his liquid assets. All these he bestows upon his poor endangered and assaulted Esther.

On that very day the King Ahasuerus bestowed upon Esther the queen the estate[12] of Haman, the enemy of the Jews (8:1a).

Haman's demise has created a vacuum at the pinnacle of the Persian power structure. Riding the wave of the king's generosity, Esther proposes a suitable replacement: none other than that sterling official, that loyal servant of the State, that savior of the king's sacred life who only this morning was so prominently honored in the city square — Mordecai (who, incidentally, just happens to be her beloved cousin and guardian). In short order Mordecai has been routed out of his office and is being presented to the king.

So Mordecai came before the king, for Esther had told him [the king] what he was to her. And the king took off his [signet] ring that he had taken from Haman, and gave it to Mordecai (8:1b–2a).

Haman, of course, had, before his execution, been divested of his insignia of office, which included the signet ring[13]; this the king now hands to Mordecai, thereby appointing him the new *Vizier* of Persia. Haman's rout is now complete.

And Esther put Mordecai in charge of Haman's estate (8:2b).

As the recipient of Haman's estate, Esther is now an extremely wealthy woman. But she has no need of her vast resources as she lives in the palace harem at the king's expense. Nor has she either the opportunity or the knowledge that would permit her to administer her huge assets. For this she appoints Mordecai as her agent. As he will administer the kingdom in Ahasuerus's name, so will he administer Esther's holdings as her proxy. And so this full day, which began before dawn in the king's bedchamber, comes at long last to a close.

By all rights, at this point the Book should end.[14] The Book of Esther began with a drinking party and now concludes with one. At each party there occurs a critical incident: at the first Vashti is deposed, setting in motion the train of events that culminates in Haman's fall and execution, the occurrence that dominates the second party. This brings the epic struggle between Mordecai and Haman to its happy conclusion. Virtue is vindicated. As a result of Esther's brilliantly orchestrated intervention Good triumphs over Evil. And on this note the curtain should ring down.

But it doesn't.

[10]Literally, "Behold, also the gallows."

[11]Literally, "who spoke good concerning the king."

[12]Literally, "house." The term is used here as a collective noun to include all of Haman's holdings. Beyond his palatial mansion in Susa and his opulent "bank account," he possessed at a minimum a similar residence at Ecbatana, the summer abode of the Persian kings (and thus the de facto capital during these months) and at least one major country estate. His wealth and position would have demanded no less. As an executed criminal, all of Haman's holdings automatically revert to the crown (Herodotus, *Histories*, III:128–29).

[13]The possessor of this ring had the authority to seal (i.e., to sign in the king's name) royal documents and proclamations, making them official. See Chapter 13.

[14]And indeed C.C. Torrey tries to make a case (unsuccessfully, I think) that the "original *Book of Esther*" did conclude with Chapter 7 (Torrey, "The Older Book of Esther," pp. 14ff).

CHAPTER 17

Reversing the Engine

The evil that men do lives after them.
—William Shakespeare, *Julius Caesar,* III

If Esther were a fairy tale or a historical novel, as is claimed by so many modern scholars, the Book would have ended with the hanging of Haman and his replacement by Mordecai. But its primary aim is not entertainment or to provide a justification for a carnival.[1] Its essence is a profound meditation on the precarious condition of the Jew in the world, and a grave consideration of what it means to live in a Godless universe.

The question at hand is not the maneuvering of two Persian officials for primacy, but genocide. Haman may be dead, but the process that he put into motion is alive. The program of extermination no longer needs its initiator. Unless somehow derailed, in less than eleven months all the Jews of the Persian Empire will be massacred. It is to this issue that Esther now bends her efforts.[2]

The Petition

And Esther spoke yet again before the king, fell at his feet[3] and cried, and pleaded with him to cancel[4] the evil of Haman the Agagite, and his plot that he plotted against the Jews. And the king extended the golden scepter to Esther, and she stood up before the king. And she said: "If it

---

[1]More on this point in Chapter 20.

[2]It has been claimed that this eleven month delay between decree and pogrom is clear evidence that we are not dealing with an historical account but dramatic fiction, where the purpose of the time gap is to create suspense and artificially provide the necessary opportunity to foil the plot. L.B. Paton is typical of this school of thought when he remarks: "The massacres of St. Bartholomew would not have been a great success if the Huguenots had been informed a year ahead" (Paton, *ICC Esther*, p. 209). But the St. Bartholomew's Day Massacre is not a legitimate parallel. The Huguenots (Protestants) had gathered in Paris, a Catholic city, in 1572 to attend the wedding of their leader, King Henry of Navarre, to the sister of King Charles of France; an event heralded as a grand moment of reconciliation. Had they been warned they could have fled Paris to those areas of France (and Europe) that they controlled. Even after the massacre had slain most of their leadership they were able, in a series of military showdowns, to defeat the Catholic armies and advance to the gates of Paris. The Jews of Persia, on the other hand, had no homeland, no area that they controlled and no armies. More to the point, as the Persian Empire virtually encompassed "the known world," they had no place to run to. They were trapped, much as the Jews of Europe in the Hitler era. Haman felt, with good reason, that he had all the time in the world.

[3]Literally, "before his feet."

[4]Literally, "to put away."

pleases the king, and if I have found favor before him, and the matter seems proper to the king, and if I be pleasing in his eyes, let it be written to revoke the letters, the plot of Haman, son of Hammedatha the Agagite, that he wrote to destroy the Jews that are in all the provinces of the king; for how can I bear to see the evil that will overtake my people, and how will I be able to endure the sight of[5] the destruction of my kindred?" (8:3–6).

The first thing that strikes us about Esther's plea is its purely personal nature. There is no appeal to moral principles, to the intrinsic wrongness of genocide. Esther was too smart to pass up a good argument if she felt that it would be persuasive. Its omission can only mean that in Esther's estimate moral arguments would cut no ice with Ahasuerus. And she was probably right. The king who had felt no qualms about approving a program of genocide could hardly be expected to be moved by appeals to a higher duty — to hold life sacred. So Esther's appeal is: "Please spare me the pain of having to witness the murder of my kindred. Surely my wonderful and considerate king wouldn't want me to suffer." And the appeal works. This is something the king can understand.

A second aspect of Esther's plea that should attract our attention is the language she uses. She consistently speaks to the king in the third person. Only when referring to herself does she shift to the first person. Esther is very careful never to become too intimate when addressing Ahasuerus. When referring to herself she can be informal; when addressing the king she maintains distance, stressing the great gap in social status between them, emphasizing the king's dignity, ever enhancing his image in his own eyes. The king's *majesty* is so *exalted*; it is absolutely *wonderful* to her how he condescends to even *take notice* of her, much less *care* for her. Her manner, falling at his feet and inviting him to extend his scepter to her, initiates a replay of that dramatic moment when she came unbidden to the throne room. By calling to mind his magnanimous response she is laying the emotional groundwork for a similar positive response to her current request.[6] Esther's handling of Ahasuerus could be used as a textbook for intelligent women as to how to manage a difficult husband.

The problem Esther faces is threefold: in the first place Ahasuerus really does not care, one way or the other, about the Jews. They are a matter of total indifference to him, nor can he really be made to care. Secondly, he thinks he has already done enough for Esther: he has hung Haman, he has expropriated Haman's wealth and given it to Esther, and he has promoted her cousin Mordecai to Haman's place. What more can reasonably be expected of him? And lastly — there is no way he can repeal the decree. Once issued, a royal decree is irreversible.

Carte Blanche

Then King Ahasuerus said to Esther the queen and to Mordecai the Jew: "Behold, the house of Haman have I given to Esther, and him have they hung on the gallows because he intended to harm the Jews.[7] And as for you, write regarding the Jews anything you want[8] in the king's name, and seal it with the king's seal; but [remember] that an edict written in the king's name and sealed with the king's seal is irreversible" [8:7–8].

[5]The phrase rendered "how can I bear to see the evil that" and the one rendered "how will I be able to endure the sight of" are, in the Hebrew, identical and have only been rendered differently for English stylistic reasons.

[6]The very wording of Esther's plea plainly echoes the climax of Judah's plea before the Viceroy of Egypt (Genesis 44:34) that leads Joseph to break down and reveal himself to his brothers. The wording thus prepares us for Ahasuerus' magnanimous response. See Chapter 21 for the significance of the repeated echoes and references to the Joseph Saga.

[7]Literally, "put forth his hand against the Jews."

[8]Literally, "whatever is good in your eyes." The order is in the plural, addressed to both Esther and Mordecai.

In other words, I give you carte blanche; do whatever you like in my name. But may I remind you that anything written and sealed in the king's name is irreversible.

The Laws of the Medes and the Persians

This last point needs elaboration, especially as most modern scholars believe it to be unhistorical. Their claim is based on two arguments: first, that we have no extra-biblical evidence of such a legal structure and second, no country could function that way; the system would be too inflexible to work.[9] The answer to the first objection, of course, is to point out that a want of evidence proves nothing.[10] And keeping in mind how little we really know about Achaemenian Persia, missing information on any given point cannot disqualify what we are told from another source.[11]

The second objection, that no country could hobble itself with so absurd a restriction and still continue to function, reveals a woeful ignorance of the vagaries of human affairs. History is replete with examples of peoples, for reasons that seemed at the time worthy, hedging themselves in with restrictions that make life extremely difficult. The Polish-Lithuanian Empire, which achieved a dominant position in northern Europe in the 16th century, functioned from 1632 onward under the rather absurd rule that all laws required *unanimous consent* in order to be enacted. One negative vote in the *Sejm*, the Polish legislature, would veto the bill. One wonders how, under such a constitution, any laws could be passed and any such state function. Yet laws were passed, and Poland managed to survive under this so-called *liberum veto* for 139 years, until the crisis that led to its abolition.

What led the Poles to bind themselves into this straightjacket of a constitution was a burst of egalitarian zeal, and the desire to prevent majorities from riding roughshod over the rights of minorities. But what could have led the Persians to hobble themselves in an admittedly less draconian but still highly restrictive manner? To answer this requires us to view matters not from our perspective but rather from that of Persian society. Elias Bickerman explains:

> The idea that the royal word is unalterable comes from theology. Of Oriental gods it is said again and again that their decision is unalterable. A capricious and fickle omnipotence would be insufferable.... In this respect oriental kings imitated the gods. It means not that every utterance of the king was unchangeable but that "the statutes of Persia and Media" could not be changed. In expressing this idea, the authors of Daniel (6:9, 6:13) and of Esther (1:19) use the Persian loan-word *dat*. To become a statute, the order must be in writing and the writing ratified by inscription of the royal name by means of the royal seal ... the decree, to become irrevocable, must also be entered "into the statutes of Persia and Media."[12]

Taking matters further, Pierre Briant stresses the religious nature of the Persian monarchy:

[9]It is worth noting that these scholars are making the same "mistake" that they are complaining about — they are treating the need to change laws as a universal unchanging constant. But it is making just such assumptions (that this or that will never change) that lead founders of legal systems to institute laws that cannot be changed (Elijah Millgram, private communication).

[10]"On the basis of Herodotus' omission, many scholars denied the existence of Belshazzar [the last king of Babylon]; later archeological discoveries confirmed the historicity of *Daniel* 5" (Brenerman, *Ezra, Nehemiah, Esther*, p. 290).

[11]"No collections of Persian laws have survived and information on the legal system is scant. [The most that can be said is] the traditional, tribal law was unalterable, but the king could issue decrees" (Munn-Ranken, "Persian History: Law," p. 660).

[12]Bickerman, *Four Strange Books of the Bible*, pp. 192–93.

The entire imperial system was dominated by the king. While not regarded as a god himself, the Persian King was viewed as the earthly lieutenant of the great deities of the empire, the first among them being the god Ahura Mazda.[13]

Among the few modern scholars to take seriously the claim that Persian royal decrees were irrevocable is Will Durant. The official ideology, that Persian kings were the viceroys of the deity on earth, leads him to conclude:

> It was the proud boast of Persia that its laws never changed, and that a royal promise or decree was irrevocable. In his edicts and judgments the king was supposed to be inspired by the god Ahura Mazda himself; therefore the law of the realm was the Divine Will, and any infraction of it was an offense against the deity.[14]

The word of the god, promulgated by means of a decree by his lieutenant on earth was, of necessity, irrevocable.

The most important rebuttal of the notion of the fictitious nature of the irrevocability of Persian Royal Decrees lies in the fact that this Book was written for a Persian audience. Whether we accept Esther as factual or see it as a historical novel,[15] either way it had to be credible to its readers. *Gone with the Wind* is an unabashed work of fiction set in the period of the Civil War and its aftermath. Despite its being a work of fiction, its author could not have made Rhett Butler a captain in the Confederate air force; it is common knowledge that airplanes had not yet been invented at the time of the Civil War. The Book of Esther assumes that Royal Edicts cannot be revoked, and were this not the case the original audience of Esther would have known this and would have rejected Esther as ridiculous. Whether fact or fiction, the background had to be credible for the Book to be taken seriously by its readership.

All this having been said, I propose that we ourselves take seriously this basic assumption made by the Book: that Persia indeed labored under the rule that a Royal Decree issued in writing and sealed with the king's royal seal could not be repealed. But inevitably circumstances might arise that required abrogation, as in the current case. How would the government cope? There are many possible mechanisms for dealing with such a situation. In Esther we have a concrete case.

A Newtonian Resolution

Two months and ten days have elapsed since Haman dispatched his notorious edict. Did it take that long to figure out a way of circumventing the decree? Could it have been that the transition from Haman to Mordecai as head of the bureaucracy was far from smooth, and that it took some two months until power was firmly in his hands? Or were there other political factors unknown to us that were responsible for the gap between original edict and Mordecai's counter-edict? As usual our author dispenses with background and keeps things simple: we are given merely the date and the action taken. The rest is left to our imaginations.

> At that time, on the twenty-third day of the third month, which is the month of Sivan, the king's secretaries were summoned, and [an edict] was written concerning[16] the Jews, exactly as Mordecai

---

[13]Briant, "Persian Empire," p. 241.

[14]Durant, *Our Oriental Heritage*, p. 361. We have already paraphrased this statement in Chapter 12.

[15]This is the stance taken by most modern scholars who, while seeing the story of Esther as fiction, are forced to admit that the background mostly "proves out" as historical. See the discussion on the historicity of Esther in Chapter 8.

[16]Reading with Syr., MT reads "to."

dictated[17]: to the satraps, and the governors and the officers of the one hundred and twenty seven provinces, even from India to Ethiopia, to every province in its own script and to every people in its own language — and to the Jews in their script and language. He wrote in the name of King Ahasuerus and he sealed it with the king's seal, and sent dispatches by mounted couriers riding on swift steeds that were used in the royal service, bred from the royal stud[18] [to the effect that]... (8:9–10).

Yes, yes — and after all this long digression, what is the decree? The truth is that we are not quite sure. The fact of the matter is that the text of the decree as we have it in the Hebrew (MT) is very badly written. Unlike Haman's original edict, which is clarity itself, Mordecai's counter-decree is verbose,[19] syntactically confused, and subject to various interpretations. (This is not immediately evident in translation, for in order to make the decree readable and comprehensible the various renditions smooth over the rough spots, often rearranging the words and phrases in order to achieve an artificial clarity.) We will explore this problem, and try to understand why the decree of Mordecai is so badly written. If this matter does not interest you feel free to skip the next four paragraphs.

In line with our basic assumption that the story before us is historically based,[20] and that there indeed was a decree issued in the king's name by Mordecai, then we must take into account the fact that an Imperial Persian decree would be written in Persian. What we have then is a Hebrew translation from the Persian, probably a literal translation that would tend to follow the word order of the original.[21] This by itself could account for some of the awkwardness of style. But there is a more fundamental problem. Mordecai's decree is not a straight composition but rather a cut and paste job; it is patched together from pieces and phrases taken from Haman's decree, pieces which comprise more than half its total.[22] Most of what remains is connective tissue. In my translation I have attempted to make this clear by printing the borrowed phrases in italics, and as they are not even in the same order as they were in the original, but cut apart and rearranged, I have enclosed each fragment in quotation marks.

Lastly, Mordecai's literary style seems to be poor.[23] It was he who, besides being the author of the Persian original (8:9), may very well also have been the one who translated it into Hebrew. The problem may be no more than habituation to the bureaucratic jargon current in the

---

[17]Literally, "ordered."

[18]While the overall meaning of this verse (which is essentially nothing more than padding meant to extend the story and heighten suspense) is clear, it abounds in technical terms whose precise meanings are not fully understood. The reading here, while expressing the current consensus, is mainly conjectural.

[19]It is one and a half times as long as Haman's; 57 words in the Hebrew as opposed to a mere 37 words.

[20]Those scholars who hold that Esther is a work of fiction have the problem of accounting for the author's sudden lapse of style, an issue which none seem to have faced. The way the decree is worded is quite different from the fluid and clear writing that characterizes the rest of the Book.

[21]Indeed, we have been specifically told that the decree was translated into various languages, "and to the Jews in their script and language" (8:11). It is this Hebrew version of the decree that is the basis of our text, if not identical with it.

[22]Fully 33 out of the 57 words that comprise the Hebrew of Mordecai's decree are embedded in phrases that are lifted out of Haman's. It is Robert Gordis who has called attention to fact that Mordecai's decree contains quotes from the edict of Haman (Gordis, "Studies in the Esther Narrative," p. 52). But even he underestimates the extent of the problem.

[23]S. Talmon, despite trying to make the case that Esther is a classic "Wisdom" text that presents Mordecai as a prototype courtier (who must possess "proficiency in languages and a skilled tongue coupled with an agile mind and readiness to act," nonetheless is forced to admit that "Mordecai is not presented as a skillful speaker" (Talmon, "'Wisdom' in the Book of Esther," pp. 436–37). He does not seem to be a very proficient writer either.

Persian bureaucracy of which Mordecai was a part, or it may be a severe lack of literary ability.[24]

The bottom line is that the text before us rambles, is grammatically confusing (the relationship between the verbs, subjects and objects is unclear), the exact meaning of certain key terms are uncertain, and a fine miasma of ambiguity suffuses all. It is this that has led to a lack of unanimity as to the exact meaning of the decree and to the different ways in which it has been translated.

In my rendering of the Hebrew text I freely admit that I do not follow the lead of the majority of scholars but rather am part of a minority point of view. For those interested, an exposition of the different ways these difficult verses have been treated, the reasons why I have translated them the way I have, and the implications of the different positions, will be found in Appendix IV: Mordecai's Decree.

So what did Mordecai declare in the name of the king?

> The king has granted [permission] to the Jews in every city to assemble and to defend themselves[25]; *"to wipe out, to slaughter and to destroy"* any armed force of a people or a province that would attack them,[26] *"[their] children and wives," "and to plunder their possessions"—"in one day,"* in all the provinces of King Ahasuerus, *"[namely] upon the thirteenth of the twelfth month, that is the month of Adar." "The contents of the decree are to be publicly proclaimed in every province to all the people that"* the Jews *"be ready for that day"* to avenge themselves on their enemies (8:11–13).

Let us attempt to understand what is being said. Since Haman's decree cannot be repealed, it must somehow be neutralized by this new edict. What Mordecai does is give the Jews the right to organize for their self-defense — "to assemble" — and obviously to arm themselves (neither of which would be possible without the approval and active support of the authorities). Then they are encouraged "to defend themselves" against any and all who come to "attack them" with the intent to kill "them, *[their] children and wives, and to plunder their possessions.*" To the force of Haman's edict is now opposed a counter-force: that of Jewish self-defense.

All this is not merely conveyed to the Jews themselves but to the general public and, most crucially, to the constituted local authorities ("the satraps, and the governors and the officers of the one hundred and twenty-seven provinces"). Everyone is being put on notice that there has been a shift in policy. Where the government had previously stood behind the anti–Semitic mob, and indeed encouraged the killing and the plundering of the Jews the government has now moved its support to the intended victims. One can attack them only at one's own peril. Local officials (who by the very nature of things are intensely concerned with the question of on which side their bread is buttered) have been put on notice. We shall see the effects of this presently. This is not a restoration of law and order. It means simply that the Jews are not consigned to the role of sheep being led to slaughter. The state is now giving them a fighting chance to survive. This is far from ideal, but as a start it is enough.

---

[24]Both Haman and Mordecai dictated their decrees. When we compare Haman's decree with his recorded speeches (3:8–9, 5:12–13, 6:7–9) we find the styles congruent: simple, direct and unambiguous. With Mordecai the matter is less clear. In the first place we have less data. Strangely, of all the major characters he speaks least: we have only one speech from him in the entire Book (4:13–14). That this short speech is more convoluted and ambiguous than those of Haman seems clear, but the sample is too small to permit unambiguous conclusions as to Mordecai's style or lack of it.

[25]Literally, "to stand for their lives."

[26]"Attack them," that is, the Jews; the following phrases are almost without exception direct quotes from the prior decree authored by Haman.

So hurried on by the king's command[27] the couriers, mounted on swift steeds that were used in the royal service went forth; and the decree was proclaimed in the Acropolis of Shushan (8:14).

The Image Maker

We were not told what had been the public reaction to Haman's appointment. Perhaps there had been none: the new style of governance introduced by Ahasuerus, that of deputizing a vizier to manage the empire for him, would have taken some getting used to before public opinion could have begun to coalesce. If we are correct in assuming that there would have been resistance to Haman by elements of the entrenched bureaucracy, and if there is any truth in our speculations as to his ruthless and predatory reputation, we may be able to make some sense out of the public reaction to Mordecai's first public appearance.

We speak here not of the Acropolis, the government complex which houses the ruler and the government of the empire, but of the greater civilian city of Shushan. Once before we were informed of the mood of the city: upon the proclamation of Haman's decree we were told that "the city of Shushan was flabbergasted" (3:15). This time around, Mordecai's formal public appearance, apparently his first, generates a demonstration of approval and enthusiasm by the populace.

> And Mordecai went out from the presence of the king in royal garb of blue and white, and a great golden turban[28] and a cloak of linen and purple; and the city of Shushan shouted and was happy (8:15).

It would seem that Mordecai's formal "coming out" was on the same day that his decree was made public in Shushan, but one cannot conclude from this that the public was rejoicing because the Jews could now defend themselves. Nor is it likely that the general population was voicing its approval that a Jew would now be running things. It seems to me far more likely that Haman had been hated and feared, and that his downfall was unable to allay the dread that another of his predatory ilk would succeed him. With Mordecai's investiture the uncertainty is ended, and apparently on a positive note. To the extent that the celebratory demonstration was indeed spontaneous I would suggest that it was more in the nature of an expression of relief at Haman's fall than a demonstration of support for Mordecai.

But there is another possible interpretation of these events. Let us rethink them, using as our starting point the question: why does Mordecai take so long to make his grand public appearance? After all, it is now more than two months since the fall of Haman and Mordecai's elevation to position of vizier.

But wait a moment; *is* this Mordecai's first grand public appearance? Have we forgotten that bizarre spectacle of Mordecai, dressed in the king's robes and mounted on the king's crowned horse, being paraded around the great square fronting on the King's Gate by his archenemy, Haman? That, indeed, was the humorous highpoint in a Book that opened with wild parties, and which has continued (in tandem with ever-increasing tragedy) its madcap hilarious take on life in Old Persia. That mad moment of the condemned man in royal robes

[27]Literally, "word."

[28]"A headdress to be distinguished from the royal crown (*Keter*) of 1:11, 2:17, 6:18" (Moore, *AB Esther*, p. 81). Joyce Baldwin, while agreeing that our text insists that Mordecai was not wearing anything like the king's crown, finds the use of the word "turban" problematic. "In Esther 8:15 the word 'coronet' would maintain the distinction from the royal crown and keep the right image; the evidence for 'turban' is scanty" (Baldwin, *Esther*, pp. 98–99, note 2).

being lauded by his erstwhile executioner is the last gasp of humor in Esther. From now on we are in a world of ruthless power politics and bloodletting. By day's end one of the participants in that episode of black comedy is dead, his body on display to all who had previously cringed and prostrated themselves before him, while the other has had the burdens and responsibilities of government thrust upon him.

Mordecai could have followed up this charade of a debut with a proper public appearance reflecting his true ascent to power. Yet he held off. Why? Answering this question requires that we reexamine, from a different perspective, the genocidal crisis confronting the Jews.

We have seen that Haman's plan was not that of a massacre carried out by the arms of the State (the army, police, etc.) but rather of a pogrom: turning the mob loose on the Jews, Rwanda style. We argued that this presupposed the existence of a substratum of antipathy toward the Jews. In addition to a hard core of rabid anti–Semites in all the cities and provinces, which of necessity would be a rather small minority of the population, there must have existed a much larger reservoir of people who bore no love for the Jews and could be stirred to action against them under the right circumstances and with the right leadership. Creating these circumstances was the purpose of Haman's decree. Proclaiming well in advance a date on which it would be open season on the Jews, and on which the forces of law and order would not operate — and adding to this the prospect of an orgy of looting to which no penalties would be attached — created the conditions ripe for a pogrom. The authorities would not only refuse to protect the victims but would aid and abet the mob. The worst elements of society, egged on and led by the anti–Semitic activists, could rape, kill, and loot to their heart's content. Under such conditions decent citizens would do little more than avert their eyes and deplore the "tragic breakdown of law and order," while some would solemnly declare that by their clannishness, superior airs, pushiness and so forth the Jews had brought this upon themselves. Under these circumstances the individual Jewish family would find itself alone with the mob at the door. Mordecai confronts this impending scenario when he arrives at the corridors of power. And Haman's decree cannot be revoked.

His first move is to attempt to neutralize Haman's edict with a counter-decree, allowing (and more important, encouraging) the Jews to organize, arm and assemble for self-defense. But while this may avert a genocidal massacre it cannot prevent pitched battles between an embattled minority and a rapacious majority; such a battle cannot but lead to a massive loss of Jewish lives, countless Jewish homes pillaged and Synagogues burnt. More than mere self-defense is needed; an entire climate of opinion must be changed. Mordecai must somehow build an alliance of pro–Jewish forces sufficiently powerful for the anti–Semites to be abandoned by their following.

At this point we rely upon the astute analysis of Yoram Hazony:

> Herein lies the fundamental question which is the subject of politics: How can the individual, weak as he is, move the group of the many to act in accordance with his will?
>
> In politics, weakness does not attract the interest of strength.... But strength attracts strength, and power attracts power.... And thus to the fundamental question of all politics, there is only one possible answer: The weak, to the degree they can make themselves seem strong, can attract the support of the strong, thereby becoming strong in reality; and to the degree that they fail in this, they can expect no help from men.[29]

Mordecai's actions can only be explained by recognizing that he felt that he had extracted from the king all that could be gotten. He now relies only on himself and his understanding of the political options open to him, which are pretty much those of Hazony. It is in this light that we must view Mordecai's moves.

Let us recognize that his first act, his decree, is as much a piece of propaganda as an enabling

[29]Hazony, *The Dawn*, p. 189.

edict, if not more so.[30] In this proclamation Mordecai is letting everyone know that government policy has shifted, that the anti–Semites have lost their protector while the Jews have gained one in him. And he follows up the public proclamation of the edict in the capital by his first public appearance: a grand and ostentatious display of power.[31] Mordecai is doing his utmost to make an impression. This leads us to wonder whether the demonstrations were quite as spontaneous as we first imagined. The orchestration of "spontaneous demonstrations" of enthusiasm and support is not a twentieth century invention; the practice has been a standby of autocratic regimes going back thousands of years. This blatant display of power has several immediate purposes: to restore the confidence of the Jews so as to put heart into them for the coming confrontation, and to deflate the morale of the anti–Semites, to awaken in them fear of the consequences in defying the all-powerful Mordecai, thus deterring them from acting on the fatal day. How well Mordecai succeeds with this initial move we will now see.

The reaction of the Jewish community of Shushan is immediate, and probably completely spontaneous.

For the Jews there was light, and happiness, and joy and honor (8:16).

For a community that has been living in dread anticipation of slaughter for seventy days the relief of the new decree, immediately followed by an ostentatious public display of power by a Jew, must have seemed to them as if the heavens were opening. And as word of the decree spreads:

And in every province and in every city, wherever the king's command and edict reached, there was happiness and joy for the Jews, feasting and holiday (8:17a).

Note that something has been added in the provinces. In addition to the relief and joy, there is added a public display of "feasting and holiday." Hazony is of the opinion that these public displays were orchestrated by Mordecai as part of his program to project an image of confidence and strength, and thus create a new reality.[32] And he very well may be right.

And what of the non–Jews, especially those who had been looking forward in anticipation to the day when they would be allowed to massacre their Jewish neighbors and loot their property?

And many from among the peoples of the land professed to be Jews, for the fear of the Jews had fallen upon them (8:17b).

Mordecai's program is working. Sensing from which quarter the wind is now blowing, and out of fear of the consequences of being caught with the losing camp in the coming showdown, many non–Jews switch sides and publicly identify with the Jews. Does this mean that they converted to Judaism?[33] Some may have. Joining the ranks of the Jewish people began with the

---

[30]So, for that matter, was the edict of Haman. Its basic purpose was to empower the anti–Semitic elements of the empire by creating a sense of invincible strength, thus attracting a large enough following to create the critical mass necessary for genocide.

[31]Significantly, the text goes into far greater detail in describing Mordecai's appearance here than when he was being paraded by Haman in the king's clothes: on that occasion what were the colors of his robe? What was he wearing on his head? There we are not told, but here Mordecai's sartorial splendor is given in detail.

[32]*Ibid.*, p. 191.

[33]The Hebrew term *mityahadim* (literally "made themselves into Jews") appears here for the first time; there were no "Jews" prior to this era (see Chapter 10). It has been rendered as meaning anything from "they pretended to be Jews" to "they converted to Judaism." While in Modern Hebrew the term means "to convert to Judaism" it is far from certain that it had this meaning at that time. LXX clearly understands the term to mean religious conversion, reading: "And many of the Gentiles were circumcised and became Jews," but this simply may be reading the practice of the Hellenistic Age back into the Persian Period. On the other hand, religious conversion may have been intended, yet since all mention of religion and God have been strenuously excluded

Patriarchal age (the wives of all the Patriarchs were not Jews), and we have already gotten to know Tamar and, of course, Ruth from a later era. But, in this case, probably most were opportunists who did not do much more than profess, "we are with you," taking out an insurance policy for the firestorm to come. I doubt very much if any of the hard-core anti–Semites were to be found among them. Of the anti–Semites we will learn later.

What is clear from all this is that a fundamental shift in public mood is taking place. Now it is the enemies of the Jews who feel insecure and are on the defensive. Mordecai has generated a counter-reaction.

[33](cont.) from the Book, the author could not say that many persons feared the Lord and worshiped Him, and so thus invented a religiously neutral term to take its place. Recognizing the lack of clarity I have opted to use the phrase "professed to be Jews," thus leaving the question open.

CHAPTER 18

Judgment Day

And where the offense is let the great axe fall.
— William Shakespeare, *Hamlet*, IV

Fear is an instructor of great sagacity.
— Ralph Waldo Emerson, *Essays, First Series* (1841)

The Restricted Vision

Following Yoram Hazony, we have attempted to lay bare both the principles and the understanding of the world that underlie Mordecai's actions. They can only be described as cynical: power begets power while weakness is a sure recipe for victimhood. The way to survive and prosper in the world is to be strong. The way to become strong is to project to others an image of strength, and if you can do so convincingly then people will flock to you and you will be strong. If Hazony is correct in his conclusions that these are indeed the principles upon which Mordecai acts (and I think he is probably right) then two observations are in order.

First, does this mean that Mordecai has no ideals; that right and wrong, justice, mercy, pity and compassion have no place in his life? I believe the record shows that this is not so. If our understanding of the reasons for Mordecai's refusal to bow to Haman is right, then those reasons show him to be an idealist.[1] Seeing Haman for what he is, an amoral monster who has enriched and advanced himself by the unbridled exploitation of the peoples entrusted to his governorship, Mordecai is willing to endanger his career, even life itself, rather than serve such a tyrant. But, and here is the crucial point, for Mordecai, ideals are purely personal. Ideals are the way one should lead one's life; they are not the working order of the world. To his mind it seems there is no connection between the inner life of the person and the outer world. The world in which we find ourselves is a grim place of power and brute force, with no pity, compassion, justice or mercy. It is a world in which might is the only right and weakness the only wrong, where the only logic is the logic of power. To apply personal ideals to such a world is stupidity at best.

But the inner life plays by different rules. People can have ideals, and can live their lives

---

[1]See Chapter 12.

171

in accord with them. They know that when their private life and the outer world collide, they will have to make decisions and take the consequences. Mordecai may be willing to stake his life on his principles, but when he has public responsibilities he cannot in good conscience apply them to public policy. He will neither make appeals to public decency nor try to enlist the good will of governors and satraps. Having been placed in a position of power, he will play the power game by its own brutal rules; creating fear becomes his basic weapon.

The second observation relates to the question of why Mordecai, a more than decent person as the world goes, holds such a radically divided view of the world, where good is purely personal and the world outside an amoral system of forces? And in answering this question we begin to approach the core insight of our author. The most astounding aspect of the way the Book of Esther is crafted is the absence of God in the text.[2] Our author is showing us a world without God. It is a world not unlike that portrayed by the unhappy Jewish author Franz Kafka: an irrational world of absurdities, permeated with horror, where human beings are annihilated by large impersonal forces; a world in which people can only look into themselves for meaning and values, but whose destinies are at the mercy of unbridled, often fitful power. Only in a world created and ruled by God, our author seems to imply, can one look for reason and order, and expect moral values to hold sway. Remove God and this Kafkaesque world is what you have. So Mordecai, as an inhabitant of a world from which God is absent, accepts this reality, and while trying to preserve some spark of inner decency within himself will do what it takes in such a universe to save his people.

We shall return to this issue when we come to sum up the Book. Now we continue with an elaboration of Mordecai's rescue operation and its outcome.

Intimidation

Let us reconstruct Mordecai's political program and its outcomes from what we are told in the Book of Esther. We have discussed his decree and its implications, and his ostentatious public appearance upon the decree's proclamation in Shushan. Mordecai is projecting an image of irresistible power; let all take note and beware! We have also noted the reaction that takes place in the general populace: it is one of uncertainty and fear, leading many to publicly switch sides. Mordecai does not stop here. In the eight months remaining before the dread date he relentlessly pursues a three-pronged policy. We are given the outcomes; let us work back to what led to them.

The first priority of Mordecai is to prepare the Jews for the looming confrontation. They must be organized, concentrated in defensible sites and provided with adequate leadership. For this, local community organizations can provide a base. Then they must be armed and drilled in the use of arms. While we know that Jewish communities composed of professional soldiers existed,[3] there were hardly enough of such professionals to even begin to form a core of resistance. Most Jews in those days were either farmers or engaged in commercial activities. They would have to be introduced to the use of arms from scratch. And not least was the issue of morale: it was essential that the Jews be confident in their ability to meet their would-be killers on at least equal terms. Probably one of the purposes behind the "feasting and holiday" (8:17)

---

[2]We have already pointed out that this is entirely a construct of the author and entirely unhistorical; the Persian period was an intensely religious era. See Chapter 8.

[3]In the far western reaches of the empire, at Elephantine on the southern Egyptian border, we have extensive data about such a Jewish military colony. There may have been others.

in every community was to build morale, a sense of solidarity and a confidence in victory. So we read:

> The Jews assembled in their cities in all the provinces of King Ahasuerus to lay hands[4] on those who sought to do them ill. Not a man could stand against them, for the fear of them had fallen upon all the people (9:2).

The organization, training and morale building prove sufficient, especially as the confidence of the anti–Semites has been undermined.

Mordecai's second priority is to build support for the Jews in the provincial hierarchy, "the satraps, and the governors and the officers of the one hundred twenty-seven provinces" (8:9). The attitude and the actions of these men would be decisive on the local level. These officials can be divided into two categories. The first of these consists of those who are sympathetic to the plight of the Jews. To these can be added those who, while not caring much one way or the other, have been quick to jump onto the new bandwagon as soon as they got their first whiff of the shift in government policy. All these require little more of Mordecai than some encouragement, appreciation and hints of future favor. The more problematic category of officialdom is comprised of those who harbor various degrees of antipathy to the Jews and those who, for various reasons, have allied themselves with the anti–Semitic camp. These will have to be forced to realign themselves. The methods used are covert and overt intimidation. Mordecai has to convince these satraps, governors and officials that he is not to be trifled with, that their careers, even their lives are on the line, and that he has the power to make good his threats. And here again he proves successful.

> All the officials of the provinces, and the satraps, the governors, and all who conducted the king's business aided the Jews, for the fear of Mordecai had fallen upon them (9:3).

The third part of Mordecai's program has already been mentioned: the intimidation of the larger part of the population of the empire so that they will come to the conclusion that the risk involved in attacking the Jews is just not worth taking. By the decree, the public displays, the new assertive confidence displayed by the Jews and their increasingly open preparations for "the day," large parts of the population are cowed into abandoning any idea of attacking the Jews, and some are sufficiently terrorized as to openly side with them:

> And many from among the peoples of the land professed to be Jews, for the fear of the Jews had fallen upon them (8:17).

The key term is "fear." Three times the word is repeated,[5] driving home the terror Mordecai has succeeded in generating. This large scale intimidation will effectively deprive the hard-core anti–Semites of their following. At its end it is not the Jews who find themselves weak and alone but the anti–Semites.

High Noon

> Now on the thirteenth day of the twelfth month, that is the month of Adar, when the king's command and his edict were to have been executed — on the day when the enemies of the Jews hoped to gain mastery over them — the opposite occurred: the Jews gained mastery over their enemies. The Jews assembled in their cities in all the provinces of King Ahasuerus to lay

---

[4]Literally, "to send the hand against."

[5]8:17, 9:2, 9:3.

hands[6] on those who sought to do them ill. Not a man could stand against them, for the fear of them had fallen upon all the peoples. All the officials of the provinces, and the satraps, the governors and all who conducted the king's business aided the Jews, for the fear of Mordecai had fallen upon them. For Mordecai was great in the King's House, and his reputation[7] spread through all the provinces; for the man Mordecai grew ever more powerful. So the Jews smote all their enemies with the sword, killing and destroying; and they did with those who hated them just as they wished (9:1–5).

At first blush it seems surprising that with all the changes that have taken place in the previous eight months the anti–Semites don't take alarm, and call off their long-awaited attack on the Jews. But then perhaps once their hatred of the Jews has been set aflame, they are incapable of putting on the brakes. Impervious to reason and blind to the shift in public opinion they launch their attack, only to discover that with the loss of their following they have forfeited the critical mass necessary to carry the day. Instead of slaughtering the Jews, it is they who are cut down.

And in the Acropolis of Shushan the Jews killed and destroyed five hundred men. And they also killed: Parshandatha, and Dalphon, and Aspatha, and Poratha, and Adalia, and Aridatha, and Parmashta, and Arisai, and Aridau, and Vaizatha, the ten sons of Haman, enemy of the Jews; but they laid no hand on the plunder (9:6–10).

Are there no Jewish casualties? Obviously there are; no matter how one-sided the fighting there is no way that casualties can be limited to one side. But in line with the overall policy of intimidation only non–Jewish deaths are publicly reported. Jewish losses remain unmentioned.

When, at the conclusion of the fighting (that five hundred dead on the side of the attackers alone indicates a series of very bitter battles) the corpses are examined, the bodies of Haman's ten sons are found. Was it a desire to revenge the death of their father that led his sons to range themselves in the forefront of the fighting? The assumption that Haman's sons took leadership roles in the assaults on the Jewish community of Shushan is the most reasonable explanation for all ten of them dying on that day.

By the universal rules of combat in the ancient world the victors have the right to strip the bodies of the defeated. Yet surprisingly, against all custom, at the end of the day the Jews forego this ancient privilege:

but they laid no hand on the plunder (9:10).

Rubbing It In

That day the number of those killed in the Acropolis of Shushan[8] was brought before the king. And the king said to Esther the queen: "In the Acropolis of Shushan [alone] the Jews have killed and destroyed five hundred men, [including] the ten sons of Haman; what then [must they] have done in the rest of the king's provinces!" (9:11–12a).

The king is taking the whole affair very lightly; he seems to be keeping score as though it is a sporting event. But then he never took the matter of the Jews seriously. If this is what it takes to keep Esther happy, then so be it.[9] He continues:

[6]Literally, "to send the hand against."

[7]Literally, "his name."

[8]LXX reads "killed in Shushan," omitting "the Acropolis of," which is probable inasmuch as it seems doubtful that the king would have permitted fighting in the government center itself.

[9]This casual disregard for human life is typical of Achaemenian rulers. After Cyrus II, they usually won their wars by their willingness to absorb limitless casualties.

"Now what is your wish and it shall be granted to you, and what further do you request, and it shall be given to you." Then Esther said: "If it please the king, may tomorrow also be granted to the Jews who are in Shushan to do according to this day's edict; and have [the bodies of] Haman's ten sons hung on the gallows."[10] And the king commanded[11] that this be done; so a decree was issued in Shushan, and the [bodies of] Haman's ten sons were exposed [to public view][12] (9:12–14).

Most commentators on the Book of Esther profess to be absolutely horrified at Esther's answer. They can't find harsh enough words to express their disgust. How could a decent girl even make such a request? Paton pontificates: "for this horrible request no justification can be found."[13] Moore talks about "her reputation as a sophisticated Jael, i.e. a deceitful and bloodthirsty woman,"[14] Fuerst speaks of her "reputation for cold, ruthless vindictiveness,"[15] while Jobes talks about "a darker side to Esther's character" and states, "Both Christian and Jewish interpreters have found Esther's request morally troubling and *especially unbecoming to a woman.*"[16] There are two issues here, the first being the image of women implicit in these remarks. Paton, Moore, Fuerst and Jobes are betraying their assumption — shared with many others — that when men order wholesale slaughter it is perhaps deplorable but thoroughly understandable: it is natural and appropriate behavior. Whereas when women do likewise, it is unacceptable, unnatural and unladylike.

Perhaps it is time that we at long last put to rest some of the stereotypes that we have inherited. When Elizabeth I of England gave public and heartfelt thanks to God that thousands of Spanish soldiers, being transported for the invasion of England in the Great Armada, were drowned in a storm, no one pontificated that such rejoicing was unjustifiable, unbecoming, deceitful, and bloodthirsty. Elizabeth was perfectly aware of the horror of thousands of human beings dying terribly. But she was also acutely conscious of the fact that had they not drowned, these same human beings would be killing, raping, pillaging and burning a swathe of destruction across the English countryside. As a ruler Elizabeth could not allow her "finer feelings" (and she had them) get in the way of her responsibilities to safeguard the lives and the well-being of her people.[17]

When a human being, man or woman, occupies a position of power, he or she has certain responsibilities thrust upon them. There is no reason to assume that Esther was either a frivolous or a nasty person; quite the opposite. Only a deeply caring person would have risked her life to intercede for her threatened people. Furthermore, only a person who exhibits concern and empathy for all those about her could create the aura and the sympathy that marked her career and made her successful intercession possible. We have had reason to conclude that Esther was highly intelligent. This should lead us, instead of prejudging her by stereotypical standards,

[10]Or perhaps: "impaled on stakes." The Hebrew term used throughout the Book can mean either "gallows" or "stake." Both means of the public display of bodies were used by the Persians.

[11]Literally, "said."

[12]Literally, "hung up."

[13]Paton, *ICC Esther*, p. 287.

[14]Moore, *AB Esther*, p. 88.

[15]Fuerst, *The Books of Ruth, Esther, Ecclesiastes, The Song of Songs, Lamentations*, p. 84.

[16]Jobes, *Esther*, pp. 201, 200 (emphasis added).

[17]The philosopher, David Hume, in summing up the life of Queen Elizabeth I, reminds us that while we may normally tend to evaluate a woman in terms of a potential spouse or as a possible mistress, when a woman holds a position of responsibility (i.e., a ruler) one must apply an appropriate standard that is quite different (Hume, *The History of England*, Vol. IV, pp. 352–53).

to ask ourselves how she sees the situation, where she feels her responsibilities lie, and why she decides to do what she does.

Esther never saw Haman's program of genocide as a game. It was deadly serious, in the literal meaning of the term. And once she nerves herself to take the plunge and act, she conducts herself with determination and in a wholly focused manner. The situation being what it is, she can only influence events second hand, through the king. So her first job is to win him over and get him to cooperate. She does. Next on the priority list is to remove the key individual who put the program of genocide into operation: Haman. She does.[18] Next comes the matter of replacing him with someone sympathetic who can implement a new policy. The king can set policy; the government bureaucracy can either implement or sabotage it. She gets Mordecai appointed to the job.

Point four on Esther's agenda is to get the king to rescind Haman's decree, and here she runs into difficulty. He can't. However, we see how cleverly Esther and Mordecai finesse the situation,[19] creating an atmosphere that deprives the hard-core anti–Semites of much of their support, while organizing the Jews for self-defense. The results are spectacularly successful; genocide is averted and many of those who come to attack the Jews are killed. So why does Esther request that the bloodletting be prolonged?

We have already remarked on the one-sidedness of the casualty figures. We suggested that the figures are artificial, the Jewish body count being suppressed for propaganda purposes.[20] After all, what is important is not to kill, but rather to create a sense of Jewish invincibility so as to deter attacks. If this is so, then what Esther is asking includes the further spilling of *Jewish blood*. She must feel that sacrificing dozens, even many scores of Jewish lives will be essential to achieving her goal of a secure future for the Jews in the Persian Empire. What can be her reason?

Of course we can only speculate, but it seems to me that the essential element in her thinking is that the lesson of what happens to those who attack the Jews has not necessarily been fully learned. The lesson needs to be reinforced. Is it that anti–Semitism is more deeply entrenched in the capital than in the provinces, or does she feel that the example of Shushan will have empire wide effect and not require further action elsewhere? Whatever her reasoning, Esther decides to initiate a further round of bloodshed, but restricts it to the capital.

There is a further matter to consider. On the first day the Jews were reacting to attacks. Their posture has been entirely defensive. After getting such a bloody nose on the first day, could the Jew-haters be expected to attack again? I suspect that what Esther wants on the second day is a preemptive strike, possibly against key anti–Semites who have survived the mayhem of the first day.[21] Of course this will mean stretching the king's mandate. Esther has asked for a repeat

[18]There are commentators who fault Esther for not forgiving Haman and interceding for him when he was condemned to be executed. Paton, who considers Esther a work of fiction, suggests that the author could have made Esther "more attractive" by presenting her "as interceding for Haman even if the king did not grant her request" (Paton, *ICC Esther*, p. 264), while B.W. Anderson calls Esther "callous and indifferent as the once proud heathen asks for mercy ... she looks on in cold silence" (Anderson, *The Book of Esther*, p. 862). I suppose that had Hitler not committed suicide there would have been those who would have clamored for him to be "understood" and be spared the hangman's rope.

[19]There is no doubt, at least in my mind, that this is a joint endeavor. Mordecai is in no position to act independently. The mandate was given jointly to Esther and Mordecai (8:8), and it is Esther who has the influence, and therefore the power. I see Esther as at least an equal partner in the final decision on how to act, possibly reached after several sessions of brainstorming and consultation.

[20]Were the figures of casualties among the "enemies of the Jews" inflated for the same reasons? It seems likely; the figures certainly have been rounded out. At the very least they have been rounded upward.

[21]The Persians deployed a large and very efficient internal intelligence service: "The Eyes and Ears of the King" (see Chapter 11, note 4). They undoubtedly knew the identity and addresses of the anti–Semitic leadership of the planned pogrom. Esther and Mordecai had access to these lists.

of day one ("according to this day's edict," 9:13), that is, self-defense; and this is what has been granted and proclaimed. But after all, offense is the best defense, and perhaps she feels that the way the king is cooperating means that she can finish what she has started. At any rate, Esther may be calculating that the chance to deliver a paralyzing blow to what must be the top leadership remaining of the "enemies of the Jews" is worth the risk.

My own inclination is to trust Esther's evaluation of the situation. She is someone who takes her responsibilities seriously, and will do what the situation requires, no more, but also no less. In any case this second day, in tandem with the public display of the bodies of Haman's sons, seems to work: for at least a generation we do not hear of any significant attacks on Jews. What harassment that we know of is largely restricted to legal channels.[22]

> So the Jews of Shushan also assembled themselves on the fourteenth day of the month of Adar, and they killed three hundred men in Shushan, but laid no hand on plunder.
> Now the rest of the Jews that were in the king's provinces [also] assembled and defended themselves,[23] gaining rest from their enemies, killing of those who hated them seventy-five thousand on the thirteenth day of the month of Adar — but they laid no hand on plunder — and on the fourteenth day they rested — making it a day of partying[24] and rejoicing (9:15–17).

Three times the text repeats, almost like a mantra, that the Jews refrained from availing themselves of their legal and customary right to strip the slain. One calls to mind the precedent set by their ancestor Abraham when, after having successfully attacked the camp of King Chedorlaomer and his allies, and after rescuing his nephew Lot and the other inhabitants of Sodom who had been taken to be sold into slavery, he refuses to appropriate any plunder to himself, having done what he had to do in a situation not of his own making. When offered his rightful share of the booty by the grateful King of Sodom his answer is unequivocal:

> But Abram said to the King of Sodom: "I swear to the Lord, God Most High, Creator of heaven and earth: I will not take so much as a thread or a sandal strap of what is yours; you shall not say: 'It is I who made Abram rich'" (Genesis 14:22–23).

One does not use situations in which human lives are at stake to turn a profit.

On the day following the pitched battles the Jews celebrate, holding drinking parties like those of the Persians. It seems as though the Jews have also assimilated some of the less savory customs of the world which they now inhabit. Throughout the empire this is on the 14th of Adar, but in Shushan there is continued fighting. In the capital the celebrations are thus delayed until the 15th. This, the text explains (in what serves as a bridge to the concluding section of the Book), is the origin as to the varying customs of when the holiday of Purim will be celebrated.

> And the Jews that were in Shushan assembled themselves on the thirteenth and the fourteenth [of the month], and rested on the fifteenth, making it a day of partying and rejoicing. That is why the Jewish villagers dwelling in unwalled towns[25] make the fourteenth of the month of Adar a day of joy and partying, a holiday and [a day] of sending gifts one to another (9:18–19).

---

[22]Cf. Ezra 4:4–24.

[23]Literally, "stood for their lives."

[24]*Mishteh*, literally, "a day of drinking parties."

[25]There is no reason to read with the *Qeri* as do most commentators. The *Ketib*, as demonstrated by Gordis, is simply the plural of *paruz*, "villager," an inhabitant of an open settlement, as opposed to inhabitants of walled cities. But contra Gordis, we do not feel the need to delete "the redundancy" but leave the text as is (Gordis, "Studies in the Esther Narrative," pp. 56–57). See Glossary for *Qeri* and *Ketib*.

CHAPTER 19

Thou Shalt Not Forget!

"The horror of that moment," the King went on,
"I shall never, *never* forget!"

"You will, though," the Queen said, "if you don't
make a memorandum of it."

— Lewis Carroll, *Through the Looking Glass*

The crisis is over; the threatened genocide has been averted, the future of the Jews of Persia seems assured, and the anti–Semites have gotten a lesson that they will not soon forget. After the celebrations have died down, what remains but to say that they all lived happily ever after, and with this end the tale?[1]

But Mordecai and Esther see matters differently. Having been brought to the brink and having looked down into the abyss, they now realize in what a fool's paradise they had been living, and how unprepared they and the Jews in general had been for what had befallen them. Beyond having been forced into desperate, and ultimately successful action, Mordecai and Esther have received a sobering education. They now realize how precarious an existence is led by a scattered Jewish minority, and how virulent is the force of the hatred that drives the anti–Semite. How many there are! What a danger they pose! Only by the most fortuitous of circumstances have the Jews escaped annihilation. Next time, and Mordecai and Esther realize that sooner or later there *will be* a next time, if again caught unawares and unprepared the Jews may not be so lucky. The one thing that can prevent future catastrophe is a heightened awareness among Jews of the danger they face. It is imperative that the terrible lesson not be forgotten.

But people do forget. Without constant reminders any lesson will slip into oblivion with the passage of the years. This is true of individuals and of peoples alike. How can one avert this eventuality? Mordecai's first answer to the problem is to record the events, and to distribute the record as widely as possible throughout world Jewry. Without a written record the events themselves will be forgotten in a generation or two. Without wide distribution the record itself will not long survive the accidents of unfolding events. But even this, he realizes, will be far from

---

[1]Indeed, many scholars have been of the opinion that the Book of Esther originally ended with verse 9:19, while verses 9:20–10:3 are an appendix tacked on later by different hands (Paton, *ICC Esther*, pp. 57–60; Eissfeldt, *The Old Testament*, pp. 510–11). On the other hand Bruce W. Jones (Jones, "The So-called Appendix to the Book of Esther," pp. 36–43) argues strongly, and to my mind persuasively that, on the basis of a detailed analysis of the structure and the themes of Esther, the verses 9:20–10:3 *must* have been not only part of the original Book but indeed its summary, climax and coda. This view has become increasingly accepted in recent years; this chapter is based on these premises.

sufficient. How can the record be kept "in print," and more important, read from one generation to the next?

It is here that Mordecai's heritage as a Jew comes into play. Looking back over the frightening and stirring events of the month that is now drawing to a close—the fateful month of Adar—as a Jew he cannot help but also look forward to the coming month of Nisan when the Jews celebrate the Festival of Passover, remembering and reliving that epic moment when their ancestors were liberated from the slavery of Egypt.[2] Every year this event is commemorated, and the Jews have therefore never forgotten it. Perhaps this can be an answer to the present need. Just as that ancient formative event of liberation was embedded in the folk memory by means of an annual commemorative holiday, so the recent deliverance from impending genocide may be perpetuated in the consciousness of the people by a new festival.

In suggesting that the Passover Holiday serves Mordecai as a model for the creation of a new festival I do not intend to minimize the differences between the two. Passover, indeed all Jewish holidays up to that point, had been recorded in Holy Writ as ordained by God. How could Mordecai dare to usurp divine privilege and, on his own do what up to now only God had done?

But Mordecai and Esther have another precedent to guide them. In the traumatic period following the fall of the Kingdom of Judah and the destruction of Jerusalem, four days of fasting, mourning and supplication had been introduced. The prophet Zechariah refers to these days:

> The fast of the fourth month,[3] the fast of the fifth month,[4] the fast of the seventh month[5] and the fast of the tenth month[6] shall become [occasions] for joy and gladness, and for happy[7] festivals for the House of Judah; only love truth and peace (Zechariah 8:19).

These fasts were neither enjoined by God nor enshrined in Scripture. (Zechariah does not ordain these fasts. He simply refers to them as existing facts, and looks forward to the day when they will be abolished and turned into joyous festivals; when God will forgive His people and return them to their land.) If human beings could, on their own initiative, introduce days of fasting and lamentation to commemorate great national disasters, and have them accepted and observed by all Jews, then why can't human beings initiate a festival to commemorate a great national redemption? Indeed, this precedent will be alluded to in Esther's decree in which she enjoins all Jews to observe the new holiday.[8]

---

[2]In Chapter 13 we noted that the day Haman's decree of genocide was proclaimed to the public of Shushan was the eve of the Jewish Festival of Passover. Due to the policy of the author never to mention religion, the Passover Holy Day is never so much as hinted at. But by his citation of the calendar dates the juxtaposition is clear. Now the year is drawing to a close and the anniversary of the decree's proclamation is rapidly approaching, with its attendant memories of the bitter Passover that followed: the day on which, instead of celebrating the ancient liberation, "Mordecai tore his clothes and donned sackcloth and ashes, and went out into the midst of the city and he cried out a great and bitter cry" (4:1).

[3]The 9th of Tammuz, commemorating the date on which the walls of Jerusalem were breached and the Babylonians broke into the city (2 Kings 25:3–4). This fast is observed by present day Jews on the 17th of the month.

[4]The 9th of Av, commemorating the destruction of the Temple.

[5]The 3rd of Tishre, commemorating the anniversary of the assassination of Gedalia, son of Ahikam, the last governor of Judah (2 Kings 25:25). His death and the subsequent flight of the last survivors of the Babylonian conquest to Egypt mark the end of the Israelite community in the Holy Land until the return after the edict of Cyrus (see Chapter 8).

[6]The 10th of Tebeth, commemorating the start of the siege of Jerusalem (2 Kings 25:1).

[7]Literally, "good."

[8]See note 19 below.

So with the vital need to insure that future generations remember what had happened and be ever alert to the ongoing danger, Mordecai (and Esther) take it upon themselves to encourage the Jews to make an annual festival in celebration of their redemption.

> Now Mordecai wrote down these things, and he sent letters to all the Jews that were in all the provinces of King Ahasuerus, both near and far, enjoining them to celebrate the fourteenth day of the month of Adar, and the fifteenth day [as well] on an annual basis; as days on which the Jews had rest from their enemies, and as the month that had been changed for them from sorrow to joy, and from mourning into a holiday[9]— to make them days of partying, and of joy, and of sending gifts one to another [as well as] alms[10] to the poor. And the Jews undertook to do as they had begun, and as Mordecai had written to them [to do] (9:20–23).

Understanding that only a ritualized annual event will have the power to persist over countless generations, Mordecai uses his commanding government position to institute an annual holiday memorializing the traumatic events he wishes his people to remember. The form it is to take is modeled on the partying with which the Jews had celebrated their deliverance, the day after the street battles repulsing the attacks of the mobs. To this he adds a ritualized exchange of gifts and concern for the destitute fringes of the community, in order that they too fully participate in the general rejoicing.

In this annual celebration the risk to Jewish well-being and survival will be kept alive in Jewish awareness. This is to be the substance of the message of the day:

> For Haman, son of Hammedatha the Agagite, enemy of all the Jews, plotted[11] against the Jews to destroy them, and he cast a Pur (that is the lot) to crush and destroy them. But when she [Esther] came before the king he decreed in writing[12] that his [Haman's] evil plot which he had plotted against the Jews should recoil on his own head; so he and his sons were hanged on the gallows. Therefore these days are called "Purim," from [the word] "Pur" (9:24–26a).

Here it is well worth pausing to contemplate the implications of the name given to this new holiday. We remember the care with which Haman chose the "right day" for his planned massacre; how his astrologers and diviners cast lots until they chose the thirteenth of Adar as the ideal day for making "a big killing." And we commented then on the role superstition played in the Persian world.[13] Now we learn something else: that the Jews share this superstition. The text makes clear that the Jews accept that the choice of the thirteenth of Adar by lot-casting was a valid predictor of events — so much so that the very word "pur" becomes the basis of the name of the new festival. The diviners and astrologers were right in picking it as the ideal day for killing; the only surprise being that it is the anti–Semites that get

---

[9]Literally, "a good day" (a synonym for holiday).

[10]Literally, "presents."

[11]This word (Hebrew *hashav*), which we and most modern translations (RSV, NIV, NJPS, AB, etc.) render as "plotted," appears no less than three times in the space of two verses (9:24–25): twice in its verbal form, "plotted," and once as a noun, "plot." For reasons of style (a desire to avoid repeating the same word three times in a row) many translations substitute the synonym "devised" for "plotted" in verse 25. In so doing they obscure the purpose of the author, which is to focus our attention on this word. Repetition of a word or phrase is the main means of emphasis in biblical Hebrew; a three-fold repetition is the equivalent of writing these words in capitals, underlining them and then adding several exclamation points. Its aim would seem to be to recall to our minds the repetition of the same word (*hashav*) in Genesis 50:20. It is just one of the many oblique references to Genesis that our author makes to illuminate his narrative. Several we have already explored. This reference will be dealt with in Chapter 21.

[12]Literally, "said in a book."

[13]See Chapter 13.

killed, not the Jews.[14] So far the summary of the letter that Mordecai dispatches. Now to the results:

> Therefore, because of all that is written in this letter, and because of everything they had experienced[15] and what had happened to them, the Jews established and took upon themselves and upon their descendants and upon all those who joined them, that they would keep these two days as written, and at the proper time each year.[16] And that these days should be remembered and observed throughout every generation, by every family, in every province and in every city; and that these days of Purim should never cease from among the Jews, nor should their memory ever die from among their descendants (9:26b–28).

The gist of this passage is that the combination of what they had gone through along with the impact of Mordecai's letter was decisive. Its result was that the Jews took upon themselves, in perpetuity, the observance of the new holiday of Purim. Yet the very next verses deny this sweeping statement. There must have been resistance to this "newfangled innovation" in various quarters, for Esther feels it imperative to intervene. Mordecai's injunction "to celebrate the fourteenth day of the month of Adar" seems to have lacked the moral authority necessary to compel universal compliance. It is Esther, by throwing the full weight of her authority behind Mordecai in a second missive, who brings about the adoption of the holiday as binding.

> Then Esther the queen, the daughter of Abihail, and Mordecai the Jew, wrote with all authority to confirm this second letter of Purim. Letters were sent[17] to all the Jews, to [all] the hundred and twenty-seven provinces of the Kingdom of Ahasuerus: "Words of Peace and Truth:...."[18] These days of Purim are to be observed at their proper times as Mordecai the Jew and Esther the queen have enjoined, just as they have assumed for themselves and their descendants the obligation of the fasts with their lamentations.[19] So Esther's decree established these practices[20] of Purim; and it was recorded in the book[21] (9:29–32).

[14]The concept of an ambiguous oracle being misinterpreted was a staple of the ancient world. A classic example was that of Croesus, ruler of the Lydian Empire, who sent a question to the oracle of Delphi asking if he should go to war against the Persians. The answer he received was that if he went to war a great empire would be destroyed. Taking this as a sign that he should go ahead he commenced military operations against Cyrus the Great, only to be decisively defeated. Only too late did he and his contemporaries understand that the great empire destined to be destroyed was his own. In Shakespeare's *Macbeth* we see the same theme: the predictions of the witches are true; it is his misunderstanding of the predictions that brings disaster to Macbeth. In much the same way did the author of Esther interpret the events, as undoubtedly did the Jews of Persia: the choice of the 13th of Adar was correct; Haman's mistake was in misunderstanding what he was told; that is, *for whom* the day would prove lucky. In all these cases the fault lies in the listener: the recipient of the oracle hears what he wants to hear, and so dooms himself.

[15]Literally, "saw."

[16]Literally, "According to their time." The translation of these two and a half verses does not fully convey the appallingly poor style of the Hebrew original. It is officialese at its worst: government jargon rendered into Hebrew and almost unintelligible, as is most government jargon. (See also Chapter 17, note 22). The overall meaning, however, is clear.

[17]Literally, "he sent letters."

[18]This phrase, "Words of Peace and Truth," is best taken as a standard initial formula of greeting in an official letter of the period. Since the reader of the Book already knows the events, the probably lengthy letter is not quoted in full but rather summarized in verse 31 (Gordis, "Studies in the Esther Narrative," pp. 57–58).

[19]The rendering of the last phrase is in accordance with the opinion of H.L. Ginsberg (as quoted in Moore, *AB Esther*, p. 96) and adopted by the New JPS Bible. The Medieval Jewish commentator, Abraham Ibn Ezra, in his remarks on these verses (and on Zechariah 8:19) explains that just as the Jews had accepted the observance of four "fasts with their lamentations" to mourn the destruction of Jerusalem, and this without Scriptural authorization, so may they accept and observe a festival to celebrate their deliverance even though it is of human and not divine initiative. Esther's decree is thus citing this precedent as its justification. (See above, p. 179. See notes 3, 4, 5 and 6 above for an enumeration of the fasts referred to.)

[20]Literally, "things."

[21]A record of the events, and a compilation of the various decrees connected with them, which later served as one of the main sources for the author of Esther.

"With all authority" seems to mean that Esther (and Mordecai) are relying on the power of the Persian government to overawe the Jews and sweep aside any resistance to their "decree." Yet at the same time the text emphasizes their Jewishness. By stressing Esther's parentage (a "typically Jewish name") and the identity of Mordecai as "the Jew" both have fully come out of whatever closets they have been in to assume the leadership of Persian Jewry. The account ends by dropping the pretense that Mordecai and Esther are equal coauthors; the decree is labeled unambiguously as "Esther's decree." So the final word is that it is Esther who decisively establishes Purim in perpetuity.

Coming Out: From Playboy Foldout to Leading Lady

At this time it may be worth our while to cast a glance backward in order to fully appreciate the difficult road Esther has traveled, and the growth that has taken place in her over the past year or two. We began with Esther as she emerged from the rigors of the king's beauty contest. She was at this point the quintessential "playmate" of her lord and master, the chief playboy of Persia: sexy, alluring, charming, pleasing and compliant. Her own mind and her intelligence are as efficiently concealed as is her Jewish identity, not only to the king and the court but also to scores of commentators who have consistently underrated her, considering her as no more than a pretty doll manipulated by her cousin Mordecai.[22] And in this wonderfully successful role of a Gentile "playboy bunny" she is content to rest for five years.

The crisis that initiates the process of growth and change in Esther coincides with the onset of maturity: she is somewhere between the ages of eighteen and twenty-one.[23] With the publication of Haman's decree that alters her world she is still the compliant (and complacent) "playmate," apparently unaware of what has been going on. We have intimated that the picture presented is simply unacceptable, given the way palace rumor-mills work. If she doesn't know, it is because she doesn't want to know. It doesn't concern her. Concealing her Jewish identity, begun out of deference to Mordecai[24] and as a tactical measure to enhance her career possibilities, has by now become second nature. The Gentile-playmate façade has become her primary identity.

Esther's reactions to Mordecai at this juncture are instructive. Upon learning that he is wandering around the square before the King's Gate, disheveled, in disarray and screaming, her first thought is not to ask what is wrong but to clean him up. She sends out a change of clothes. We are told that she was "greatly disturbed" (4:4); since in the palace her connection with Mordecai is known,[25] what seems to be disturbing her is that his appearance and behavior will reflect badly upon her. Only when he refuses the change of garments does Esther send someone to find out what is troubling him. It is only then that Mordecai (after telling her the whole story of the

[22]But not by several top-ranking Eunuchs who appreciated her for what she was and worked closely with her. See Chapter 10.

[23]See Chapter 10.

[24]"Now Esther obeyed Mordecai, just as she had done while she was being brought up by him" (2:20).

[25]Mordecai had always been asking about her (2:11); when reporting to the king about the assassination plot she had cited Mordecai as her source (2:22). Communication between them via the eunuchs had probably continued over the years. The secret police undoubtedly had a dossier on her that contained the information that she had lived with Mordecai prior to coming to the palace. Certainly her maids and eunuchs knew enough about the connection to report Mordecai's bizarre behavior to her immediately. On the other hand it seems as though no one had as yet grasped that they are blood relatives.

plot against the Jews, and sending her a copy of the decree), tells the eunuch "to charge her to go to the king and to plead with him for her people"[26] (4:8).

"So Hathach [the eunuch] told Esther [everything] Mordecai had said. Then Esther spoke to Hathach" (4:9–10). This is the first time in the Book that Esther is given a speaking part and this "first" signals the beginning of a process of profound change. Esther's opening words in the Book are that she wants no part of Mordecai's plans. For the first time she refuses to do what he tells her to do. The sweet, compliant little girl has revealed that she has a mind of her own. True, her stance, which in effect is denying her identity, refusing to get involved — all a denial of responsibility — does not show her in a very favorable light. But we must not overlook that up to this point she has devoted her life to pleasing older men and complying with their wishes. This is the first time, as far as we know, that she has taken a stand and refused to do what she is told.

Mordecai's response is illuminating. He ignores her excuses, and addresses Esther's underlying reservations: her unwillingness to admit her true identity as a Jew, and to take responsibility for herself and for her people. Mordecai tells her: "Be a responsible human being. This is what you have been put here for." And this challenge works. Esther decides to assume her true role as a Jew with all the responsibility it entails. Another way of putting it is that Esther moves from a role of passivity to one of an actor and initiator. The transition is not easy.

A childhood of being a good little girl who "never speaks unless spoken to" has been followed by a year or more of preparing to be a good "playmate" and five years of living the role. This kind of background does not build a strong self-image, no matter how successful one may have been in those roles. As Joshua Berman has insightfully noted, despite her courageous decision to act, Esther has little confidence in her ability to change the course of events.[27] She will do her best, but expects to accomplish little beyond getting herself killed. "I will go to the king ... and if I perish, I perish!" (4:16) Esther's courage and stoicism are commendable, but when one compares her eventual accomplishments with her initial estimate of the situation one realizes how badly she underestimates herself. Esther is on a path of personal growth and maturation.

Her assertion of herself has begun a process. Despite her low estimate of her chances of success, she now begins to give Mordecai orders. She tells him:

> "Go and gather all the Jews that are in Shushan, and fast for me. Do not eat or drink for three days, neither night nor day" (4:15).

Having made her decision, Esther begins to take charge of the situation. And once started, she never stops. As she moves from success to success, and as her self-confidence consequently grows, she becomes the dominant person in the saga. From a girl who only reacted to others, she will transform herself into a woman to whom all others react. From the moment she accepts her destiny as a Jew, she becomes the pivot about which everything turns. All this does not happen at once, but by stages.

In her first (recorded) speech Esther, says *no* for the first time to a man old enough to be

---

[26]This is not a quote of Mordecai's words but a summary. Yet if this reflects what Mordecai said, in telling Hathach to tell Esther to go to the king and plead "for her people" he is letting the cat out of the bag. Was Mordecai, knowing Hathach, certain that he would keep his mouth shut, or was it that, under pressure of the crisis, Mordecai was throwing caution to the winds? Either way Esther's personal staff seems to have closed ranks and kept her secret: several days later neither Ahasuerus nor Haman have even a hint that Esther is Jewish.

[27]Berman, "Hadassah bat Abihail," p. 655.

her father, who has been dominating her (in a nice way) all her life. In her second speech she begins to give him orders, and surprise of surprises, he carries them out.[28] Things are changing, internally as well as externally, at a breakneck pace. But there is yet another element to this remarkable second speech: after ordering a community-wide three-day fast for the Jewish community,[29] Esther continues with the statement:

And I also, and my maids, will fast likewise (4:16).

Esther, in participating in a communal Jewish fast (even if secretly) is making her first overt act of identification with her people, the Jews. This is her first step in "coming out."[30]

We have already made the suggestion that the staged series of parties could have been, in part, a series of delaying actions, giving Esther some time to gather her resources for the next stage of self-assertion when she must reveal her true identity.[31] But even during the second party when Esther comes out of the closet and accuses Haman, she only comes partway out. She never says explicitly that she is a Jew. She only refers to "my people."

"For we are sold, I and my people, to be wiped out, to be slaughtered and to be destroyed" (7:4).

Haman, of course, knew at once to whom she was referring, but did Ahasuerus? Most probably not. Haman never asked permission to massacre the Jews, only "a certain people" (3:8), and it is highly unlikely that Ahasuerus ever troubled to check who was to be massacred. Why should he? Kings should be free for more important things.[32] So Esther's declaration and her Jewish identity simply do not make any connection in the king's head. What is important in Esther's internal development is that she has not yet nerved herself to use what Berman calls "the unspeakable 'J word.'"[33]

Of course the truth cannot long be kept from coming out. When Esther sells Mordecai to the king as the ideal replacement for the now deceased Haman, she takes the final step into the open.

So Mordecai came before the king, for Esther had told him [the king] what he was to her (8:1).

The king knew that Mordecai was a Jew,[34] so Esther, in revealing that he was her cousin (and foster-father) was simultaneously revealing that she too was a Jew. Esther now is completely "out of the closet."

---

[28]Of course, as a royal consort and favorite, for the last five years she has been giving orders, but only to women (her maids) and to her servants (eunuchs), never to men. And especially, never to dominant men.

[29]Ostensibly for her success (all fasts in the Ancient Near East were seen as supplications to the deities and were accompanied by prayer) but of course the author cannot permit himself to say this openly.

[30]Berman points out that, in enlisting her maids to fast with her, Esther must have told them why she was fasting, and therefore who she really was. In this Esther is beginning a staged process of "coming out of the closet" as well as enlisting a support group to bolster her in her old/new identity (Berman, "Hadassah bat Abihail," pp. 655–56).

[31]See Chapter 14, note 31.

[32]Had the king known that it was the Jews who were slated for destruction, it is most unlikely that he would have initiated and carried out the honoring of Mordecai in the way he did. He knew Mordecai was a Jew (he calls him "Mordecai the Jew" [6:10]); yet he has Haman, the arch anti–Semite, preside over the honors.

[33]Berman, "Hadassah bat Abihail," p. 665.

[34]Was the fact that Mordecai was a Jew known previously to Ahasuerus, or did he first learn of it from the secret service report read to him to help pass that sleepless night? By the time Ahasuerus gives Esther and Mordecai carte blanche to circumvent Haman's decree he has convinced himself that he hanged Haman not because he tried to "assault the queen in my presence, in my own house" (7:8) but "because he intended to harm the Jews" (8:7). Ahasuerus may not be growing (he remains an adolescent all his life) but under Esther's tutelage some of his ideas are being reshaped.

By the time our Book ends, Esther's development into a person whose self-confidence is equal to her abilities is complete. All pretenses to a partnership with Mordecai have been outgrown. She now stands openly as the leader of the empire-wide Jewish community, and thus she has the final word.

So Esther's decree established these practices of Purim; and it was recorded in the book (9:32).

Purim

With Esther and Mordecai insisting on compliance, probably coupled with annual follow up (and possibly pressure applied to uncooperative communities) the festival of Purim began to take hold. It was given an immense boost with the "publication" of the Book of Esther. Here was the message of the holiday presented with style; humorous, captivating and dramatic, with something in it for every taste. The public reading of the Book in the synagogue was to become the central ritual of the holiday.[35]

Despite the inherent seriousness of the message of Purim — that the Jews are a scattered and vulnerable minority — the Jews have always preferred to look upon the holiday as an annual reaffirmation of God's promise to His people to watch over them. Disregarding the obvious secularity of the Book, the Jews have always read it as a religious text with the Presence of God hovering over every verse. So the celebratory mood of the festival from its initial moments — "days of partying, and of joy" — remained predominant and indeed invaded even the reading of Esther in the Synagogue: cheering Mordecai and booing Haman.[36] The exchange of gifts mandated by Mordecai has also persisted (the Hebrew term rendered as "gifts" literally means "portions" and is normally used for food; thus Jews to this day exchange food delicacies), as has making donations to the poor. One further mark of the holiday's Persian origins has persisted: that of drinking. Strangely for a people whose powerful religious and social controls on drinking alcohol has reduced drunkenness to the status of a fringe phenomenon, the Jews have made drinking to excess a prominent aspect of the festival. This may be a holdover from the Persian past and its endless drinking parties, but it also may reveal an unconscious desire to drown in drink the "sea of sorrows" that is the focus of the holiday: the never-ending waves of hatred, the persecutions, the assaults and the massacres that have been the lot of the Jews from generation to generation.

There is little question that despite the partying, the humor, and the merrymaking that characterizes Purim, the stark reality that lies behind the sugarcoating is not lost on Jews. The aim of Esther and Mordecai has been achieved. The lesson has not been forgotten. After the Torah ("The Five Books of Moses"), the Book of Esther is the Book that stands out in its public reading in the Synagogue, and its tale is among the best known to Jews of all the portions of Scripture.[37] As long as anti–Semitism persists as an ongoing reality neither the Festival of Purim nor the Book of Esther are in any danger of losing their prominence.

[35]In accordance with 9:17–19 most Jews celebrate the holiday on the 14th of Adar, while Jews dwelling in cities with walls, such as Jerusalem, (or cities that once had walls), celebrate what is called "Shushan Purim"—that is, the holiday as it was celebrated in the walled city of Shushan — on the 15th of Adar.

[36]Certain passages relating to Mordecai, beginning with "Now a certain Jew was in the Acropolis of Shushan, and his name was Mordecai" (2:5) are joyously recited aloud by the entire congregation, breaking into the formal reading by the Reader, while every mention of Haman is booed and drowned out by noisemakers.

[37]The Nazis, well understanding the significance of Purim in maintaining the morale of the Jews, forbade its celebration as well as the reading of the Book of Esther. Yet despite the ban, the absence of copies of the Book and the frightful penalties threatened for violating the ban, on every Purim there usually could be found in each concentration camp someone who could recite the Book of Esther by heart (Gordis, *Megillat Esther*, p. 13).

Postscript:
(CHAPTER 10:1–3)

> Plus ça change, plus c'est la même chose.
> (The more things change,
> the more they stay the same.)
> — French Aphorism

The three verses that yet remain to the Book, despite being accorded the dignity of being designated as an entire chapter in MT, have not usually been given the attention they deserve. They are often treated as an anti-climax, and something of an embarrassment. At best they are looked upon as a sort of coda, a tying up of loose ends. But I think this misreads the ironic purpose of the author. This ending returns us to the beginning. We are reminded of Ahasuerus's powerful deeds and his might. What powerful deeds? What might? With regard to his "greatest deed," losing Persia's most prodigious war and sending the empire into terminal decline, the author is understandably silent; it is imprudent to publicize defeats in an autocracy. Interestingly, the author is also silent on the one great accomplishment of the king, his construction of the great palace of Persepolis, one of the wonders of the ancient world. So what have we left? The Book began with a whopper of a party; it concludes with a whopper of a tax.[38] If this be progress we would prefer to see less of it.

> Now King Ahasuerus levied a tax on the mainland and on the isles of the sea. As for all his powerful deeds and his might, as well as for a full account of the greatness of Mordecai to which the king had promoted him, are they not written in the Book of the Chronicles of the Kings of Media and Persia? (10:1–2).

That comment about the "isles of the sea" is probably an oblique (and nasty) reference to Ahasuerus's mightiest "powerful deed," his naval defeat at Salamis. As a result of Salamis the Persians lost control of the Aegean and most of the Greek islands.[39] There are now precious few islands left to tax. As to Mordecai's greatness, while it is true that he is the CEO of the Persian Empire with full responsibility for the chancellery[40] and with oversight of all the main offices of state, he is the chief officer of a wounded ship. True, like the *Titanic* it will take a long time for this huge "ship of state" to go down, but when it finally disappears little will be left to salvage.[41] Mordecai's brief is one of a holding action. The tone of the ending, like that of the Book's beginning, is one of ironic detachment.

The story has been a wild ride and the author is afraid that there will be readers who doubt the veracity of the tale. In this the author is right; most modern scholars treat it as fiction. So

[38]The various districts of the empire were already subject to an annual tax (see Chapter 12, note 10). This is a special super-tax imposed on top of the regular tax burden, which was not inconsiderable.

[39]A year after Salamis, following the Greek victories at Plataea and Mycale, all Ionia rose in successful revolt against Persia. For all practical purposes the Aegean became a Greek lake.

[40]"Mordecai's position may be that of the Persian *hazarapatish*, rendered by the Greeks as chiliarch. This official was second to the king in rank and was chief of the central state chancellery" (Berlin, *JPSCB Esther*, p. 95).

[41]Following the final disastrous defeat by Alexander the Great at the Battle of Arbela (331 BCE) and the death of her last king, Darius III, the Persian Empire ceased to exist. At first incorporated as a province into the Macedonian Empire by Alexander, upon his death it became the spoils of his generals. They fought over it, looted it, vandalized it and repeatedly carved and recarved the remains into a varying series of Hellenistic kingdoms. After several centuries of this treatment so little was left of Persia that we now have to rely on her enemies, the Greeks, for much of what we know of her greatest era, the Achaemenian Age.

the author covers himself: if you don't believe me you can always check up on me. All the main facts can be found in the official sources, most notably in the Official and Approved Government Record of the Reign of King Ahasuerus, as published in the *Book of the Chronicles of the Kings of Media and Persia*. Most modern scholars, wedded to the conviction that the Book of Esther is historical fiction, dismiss the reference as mere bombast. They may be right, but then they may be wrong. We have no way of knowing. The official government history of the successive reigns of the Persian emperors existing at the time *Esther* was written (all ancient regimes produced such official government histories), perished like so much else with the destruction and dismemberment of the empire by the Greeks.

After this gesture in the direction of authenticity and veracity, the author closes on a positive note with a summation of the role of Mordecai and, by implication, of the situation of world Jewry of those days:

> For Mordecai the Jew was next to King Ahasuerus and great among the Jews, and accepted by most[42] of his brethren; seeking the good of his people and speaking peace to all his seed (10:3).[43]

In other words, as long as Mordecai would remain vizier the Jews would have someone at court to whom they could turn to look after their interests. With him they would be safe, and could look to their own prosperities. Of course Mordecai would not last forever; no one does. Well before the end of the reign of Ahasuerus Mordecai will have been replaced.[44] There will be many ups and down in times to come, but the author wants to end on a note of hope. The position of the Jew in an, at best, indifferent world, will remain precarious, but we have seen the worst and weathered it. The Jew can expect good times as well as bad. So the author chooses to end upbeat with an echo of the words of the Psalm: "Peace be upon Israel!" (Psalm 128:6).

[42]The Hebrew *rov* has the meaning of "multitude," but as the rabbis of the Talmud astutely point out, also the meaning of "majority" (Megillah 16b). Since the author chose to use this term, I have chosen to stress this second sense of the word, a sense that would not be lost on the Book's original audience. The implication of course is that no matter how good you are you can not please everyone; or as the saying goes: "Where there are two Jews there are three opinions."

[43]"Speaking peace to all his seed" is an idiom meaning roughly "seeking the welfare of all his kindred." In some such manner the phrase is usually rendered, but since the author went out of his way to end the Book on a note of "*Shalom*" — "peace" — I have preferred to preserve this resonance by translating the phrase literally.

[44]Mordecai's replacement, or perhaps his replacement's replacement, will be the one who assassinates Ahasuerus. Perhaps he would have done better to stick with Mordecai.

Conclusion

CHAPTER 20

The Dark Vision

> God is dead! Heaven is empty —
> Weep children, you no longer have a father.
> — Gerard de Nerval, "Le Christ aux Oliviers"

As we intimated in Chapter 8, to say that the Book of Esther has been from earliest times controversial is an understatement. Despite early canonization, for centuries its place in the Bible was repeatedly called into question.[1] Even in more recent times there have been those who deeply regretted that it ever was admitted into the sacred precincts of Holy Scripture, as well as those who have called for its excision.[2] Moreover, among those mainstream Jews and Christians who have accepted Esther's place in the Bible, there have always been some who have viewed the Book as problematic and seriously deficient. It is this that led to a unique phenomenon: of all the Books of the Bible only Esther lacks a literal translation into Greek. The Greek renditions are not translations but rather "improved versions," self-consciously doctoring the text to overcome its perceived "deficiencies" and "problematic aspects." The Aramaic versions do likewise.[3]

The assessment of Esther as a problematic book continues to this day. Of the many issues raised by the work no agreement has coalesced among biblical scholars with regard to its composition, purpose or meaning.[4] About the only consensus seems to be that most scholars don't

---

[1]The Jewish sect of Essenes, to whom we are indebted for the Dead Sea Scrolls, apparently never accepted Esther (see Chapter 8, note 36). And as late as the third or fourth centuries CE Rabbis Levi ben Samuel and Huna ben Hiyya doubted Esther's canonicity.

[2]The case of Martin Luther has already been noted (see Chapter 8, note 37). Within Jewish circles we may cite Rabbi Samuel Sandmel who claimed that he "should not be grieved if the Book of Esther were somehow dropped out of Scripture" (Sandmel, *The Enjoyment of Scripture*, p. 44), while Shalom Ben-Chorin actually advocated that "the holiday of Purim be dropped from the Jewish calendar and the Book of Esther expelled from the canon of Holy Writ" as "unworthy" (Ben-Chorin, *Kritik des Estherbuches*, p. 5).

[3]There are no less than two separate Greek versions; they are discussed in Appendix III: It's Greek to Me. The two Aramaic renditions (the *Targumim*) expand the Hebrew text (MT) with large amounts of homiletical (Midrashic) material. Only the Syriac version (the *Peshitta*) and the Latin *Vulgate* of St. Jerome are more or less literal translations of the Hebrew (MT).

[4]Many historians of the Biblical Era have refused even to relate to these issues: John Bright contents himself with three sparse references to the Book's name, but avoids all discussion of the events related therein (Bright, *A History of Ancient Israel*, pp. 432, 434, 444), while Martin Noth (Noth, *The History of Israel*) does not even condescend to mention Esther.

like the Book very much. Most treatments are either apologetic or openly hostile. As in so many aspects of the current study of Esther, L.B. Paton set the trend a century ago when he insisted:

> There is not one noble character in this book.... Morally Est. falls far below the general level of the OT, and even of the Apocrypha.[5]

He then quotes with approval Luther's extreme hostility to Esther and his wish that the Book did not exist. He continues:

> In significant contrast ... stands the high esteem of this book in later Judaism.... With this verdict of late Judaism modern Christians cannot agree. The book is so conspicuously lacking in religion that it should never have been included in the Canon of the OT.[6]

Only the conviction that the events portrayed in the Book are not true makes it somewhat palatable to these critics.[7]

Nor has the person of Esther been shown much courtesy. The reviews she has received are overwhelmingly negative.[8] Linda Day summarizes the bad press Esther has garnered:

> Scholars tend to interpret Esther as weak, immoral or unreligious, selfish, passively obedient, manipulative, and who only gets ahead by using her beauty and "feminine charms." She has also been compared [negatively] with other characters in the story who act in a more exemplary manner: Mordecai and Vashti. And some of those scholars working from a feminist perspective find in Esther a woman who acts in compliance with a patriarchal system, as a stereotypical woman and hence one who should not be emulated.[9]

This last point needs a word of elaboration. There has been a tendency to see the author of Esther as a misogynist, and the Book as systematically belittling and denigrating women. Even as balanced a scholar as Carey Moore takes the position that "Between Mordecai and Esther the greater hero ... is Mordecai, who supplied the brains while Esther simply followed his directions."[10] The Assyriologist William Hallo is among the very small minority who has stood up to the prevailing opinion, insisting that Esther is presented by the author as a strong female protagonist who develops

> by stages from a mere beauty queen to a veritable sage in her own right, outwitting Haman and outstripping even Mordecai, until at the end it is she who dominates the story ... so far from being a woman-hater, the author of Esther could, for all we know, have been a woman! The author was not, at any rate, a male chauvinist.[11]

In sum, my willingness to see Esther in an unabashedly positive light, as well as the favorable treatment of the Book you have just read, while not unique, are far from usual.

Yet despite the "problematic nature" of the Book, despite its many "deficiencies" and the relentless bad press, Esther did succeed in being accepted into the Bible and has remained popular over the years. And despite the vilification of her character Esther herself has been viewed

---

[5]Paton, *ICC Esther*, p. 96.

[6]*Ibid.*, pp. 96–97.

[7]One example among many: "The reader whose ethical sensibilities are offended by the killings must remember the fictional character of the book; there is no record of such slaughters, and it is most unlikely that they ever happened" (Fuerst, *The Books of Ruth, Esther etc.*, p. 82).

[8]We have already quoted some of the negative assessments of her actions. See Chapter 18.

[9]Day, *Three Faces of a Queen*, p. 12. In her exhaustive documentation of these charges Linda Day names the overwhelming majority of treatments of the Book of Esther.

[10]Moore, *AB Esther*, p. lii.

[11]Hallo, "The First Purim," pp. 24–25. See also Appendix V: But Could She Read?

by most readers as a hero, and she has been looked up to as a figure to emulate. Among Jews, Esther has consistently remained one of the most popular names bestowed by parents upon their daughters. One of the purposes of this summing-up will be an attempt to understand why, despite all the opposition and denigration, Esther has won through over its critics.

Why Was Esther Written?

Having become familiar with the Book, the time has come to consider the question of why it was ever written. One of the most popular theories current today is that its primary purpose is simply to entertain. Now it is certainly true that Esther is entertaining: it has an exotic setting, a dramatic plot and is well written and paced. The treatment is humorous; at times it becomes hilariously funny. All in all, the Book is a very good read. But if this were all we would be faced with a very serious problem: how did "mere entertainment" ever make it into the Bible?

I think that we are faced here with the common confusion of means and ends. Of course the Book is a good read; if it weren't, no one would ever read it. Any author who has something to say knows that he has to package his message attractively to get the public to buy the book, because in most cases it is the packaging that sells the product. And while there is little doubt that Esther makes a very attractive package,[12] our interest goes beyond the wrapping to its contents.

For those who go beyond the entertainment value of the Book, perhaps the majority think that its purpose is to legitimize the celebration of a preexisting holiday. The theory runs as follows: as a consequence of the Jews having become a dispersed minority in a Gentile environment, they became acquainted with an annual Mardi Gras–like festival celebrated by their pagan neighbors and accustomed themselves to join in its revels. Once the celebrations had become entrenched, some sort of story or reason had to be invented to justify Jews in observing them. This led to the Book of Esther being written to obscure the pagan origins of the holiday and legitimize Jews in celebrating it.

Despite the long popularity of this theory (it has its roots in the 19th century), and the lengthy list of its proponents, it remains to this day long on theory and extremely short on fact. Carey Moore, despite his tendency to accept some version of this hypothesis, is forced to admit:

> Scholars have suggested much but proven very little about the probable origins of the festival of Purim, the major reason for this being the inadequacies of our present sources.[13]

Over a century of effort has not succeeded in unearthing a single pagan festival that can convincingly serve as a model for Purim.[14] There is a further objection that has been leveled against this theory:

---

[12]While there are some critics who stuffily assert that Esther is not well written at all, its perennial popularity with the public effectively makes such evaluations academic.

[13]Moore, *AB Esther,* p. xlix.

[14]W.W. Hallo, after reviewing the list of the various pagan holidays proposed, finds the biblical explanation of the origins of Purim the most credible.

> That explanation will have to do for us too, for none of the many alternatives offered during a century of the most ingenious scholarly detective work is more convincing…. The problem is that each of these alleged precedents rests on little more than a dubious assonance, and none of them has anything in the least to do with the casting of lots (Hallo, "The First Purim," p. 22).

If the story was intended to explain and legitimate Purim, the narrator devotes a surprisingly small effort toward his task. The festival is mentioned specifically only in Esther 9:28–32, and alluded to only in Esther 3:7 and 9:24.[15]

Berg then turns the argument on its head, showing that contrary to making the assumption that the holiday existed first and the Book was written to justify its observance, one can equally claim the Book to have been written first, and then the references to Purim to have been tacked on later. She concludes by dismissing the entire discussion as unprofitable:

> In effect, we are left with the proverbial problem of the chicken and the egg: we know that they [the story of Esther and Purim] go together, but we cannot decide which came first.[16]

More to the point, Purim is not central to the story. Esther is mainly about the struggle between Haman and Mordecai and how Esther saved the Jews. Far from being central to the narrative, Purim is almost an afterthought. Claiming that the victory celebration is the reason for inventing a victory to justify it seems to be putting the cart before the horse.

A third possible reason would be that the Book was written to commemorate an historic event. This thesis, of course, gets little attention today inasmuch as most scholars take the events portrayed to be pure fiction.[17] But what if, as we have postulated, the story is essentially true? This still does not really explain the Book. Biblical writers did not simply commemorate historical events. They were neither chroniclers nor historians. They were concerned with issues and values, and selectively used historical events to raise these issues and to illustrate them. So the factual veracity of the tale is essentially tangential to our inquiry. Rather, the question is what issue the author of Esther was attempting to raise.

The most obvious answer is the central preoccupation of Esther: the genocidal attempt to wipe out the Jews and how it was thwarted. As we have already noted, at that time anti–Semitism was a new phenomenon, and in this Book the author is attempting to grapple with this unprecedented occurrence and to make some sense of it. My own view is that this is the primary reason why the Book was written, and all the other factors we have mentioned, to the extent that they have a bearing on the purpose of Esther, are either subsidiary or tangential, serving the central theme.

The classic treatments of Esther have tended to play down and marginalize the issue of anti–Semitism, attempting somehow to reduce the central conflict of the Book to an ancient family grudge between Haman and Mordecai or to a power struggle between two courtiers.[18] The genocidal plot has been taken to be no more than an unfortunate spin-off of an essentially private conflict between two individuals. Anti-Semitism is a daemon best left in the closet and not too closely examined. These treatments trivialize the central concern of the Book and, in my opinion, deeply falsify its message. We are seeing less avoidance of the issue in the more recent treatments of Esther: the shadow of the Holocaust hangs too heavily over the world to

---

[15]Berg, *The Book of Esther*, p. 3.

[16]*Ibid.*, p. 4.

[17]"Most recent studies of Esther accept its familiarity with a Persian setting as authentic, yet at the same time they deny the historicity of the account" (*ibid.*, p. 2). Karen Jobes is one of the few who take seriously the events presented in the narrative as a portrayal of real happenings, albeit selected and arranged for literary effect (Jobes, *Esther*, pp. 30–37). Distancing himself from accepting the story of Esther as historical, Moore employs the simile of a pearl: he admits the possibility of some hard grain of fact at the core of the Book, around which "successive layers of colorful foreign substance have accumulated," namely, "legendary and fictional elements" (Moore, *AB Esther*, p. liii). Berlin is far more representative of the current mainstream when she defines Esther as a "historical novel, or historical fiction"—that is, fiction placed in a historical setting—and calls it "a form of imaginative storytelling" (Berlin, *JPSBC Esther*, p. xvii).

[18]See Chapter 12.

ignore. Haman's program of genocide was, this time, not frustrated but successfully implemented; six million Jews were successfully "wiped out, slaughtered and destroyed." Esther is
once again, as it was when it was written, the most relevant of books.[19]

The Eclipse of God

But all that we have said so far does not even begin to explain the most remarkable feature of Esther: the blatant absence of God. We have already become acquainted with the phenomenon of God "not appearing on the stage" as a "player" in the tales of Ruth and Tamar.[20]
We have termed these accounts as effectively secular. However, the radical excision of every ves-
tige of God's presence from a biblical narrative is unprecedented. His name is on no one's lips;
He is unmentioned and unmentionable. Religion in all its forms has been banished. The few
poor vestiges of religious practice that have been allowed to remain, such as fasting, have been
desacralized and turned into secular activities. We have already pointed out that this treatment
is an entirely unhistorical portrayal of that era; it is more than fiction, it is a fantasy. What could
have induced our author to script the story in so radical a fashion?[21]

The first stage of our investigation calls for us to turn back the clock one hundred years,
to the principle event that frames our tale, and indeed everything that is to come in the history
of the Jews. In the year 586 BCE, the Kingdom of Judah was destroyed. The Holy City of
Jerusalem and God's Holy Temple were burned to the ground; the land was depopulated and
the surviving Israelites were driven into exile. The way of life the Children of Israel[22] had known
for over six hundred years — that of God's people living as an independent nation under His
providence in the land He had given them — had come to an end. The survivors of this catastrophe found themselves living as a widely dispersed minority in a Gentile world; the Israelites
had been transformed into the Jews we know today. How did these Jews make sense of what
had happened to them?

The usual answer to this question is that the Jews accepted the catastrophe as their just
punishment at the Hand of a righteous God for the great sin of betraying Him and His Covenant

---

[19]Johanna W.H. Bos, one of the more outspoken Christian exemplars of this new trend, insists "It [the Book]
has something to say to our guilt in the face of centuries of persecution and hatred of the Jewish people." And
further: "We, the Christian church, have played in regard to the Jews the part of Haman, or the king; either
we wove the tissue of lies ourselves and plotted their destruction, or we allowed the destruction to take
place until the tide of hatred became so strong that there was no stopping it" (Bos, *Ruth, Esther, Jonah*, pp. 42,
51).

[20]More significant than God not actively involving Himself in the human activities portrayed in the tales, is the
fact that the players don't take Him into account. While they often speak *about* God they never speak *to* Him,
and in practical terms act as though He does not exist.

[21]There has been a tendency to avoid the seriousness of the question by trivializing it. L.B. Paton is of the opinion that God is not mentioned in Esther in order to prevent the name of God being profaned by drunken revelers in the Carnival-like atmosphere of Purim (Paton, *ICC Esther*, p. 95), a view that continues influential to
this day despite the fact that it really explains nothing. The problem is not that the *name* of God is not mentioned but that all reference to God, even indirect, is missing, and that all references to *religion* are purged.
Jews have always been very sensitive on the issue of not taking God's name in vain, yet have had no hesitation
in preceding and concluding the public reading of the Book of Esther on Purim with benedictions that explicitly contain the name of God. The authors of the Greek versions of Esther (which were also designed for liturgical use), and who were certainly as sensitive to the dangers of blasphemy as the author of MT, have no
hesitation about referring to God.

[22]That is, the descendants of Israel, the alternate name of the Patriarch Jacob.

by repeated lapses into idolatry.[23] The entire First Commonwealth Period — (from the Settlement in the Land of Canaan — the Promised Land — until the Destruction in 586 BCE) — is viewed by the Bible as one long struggle between monotheism and idolatry. Final victory in this life-or-death struggle for the faith of Israel only came after the Destruction. It was only in exile, reeling from the shock of the disaster that they had experienced, that the survivors finally internalized the lesson of the consequences of unfaithfulness to God and turned their backs forever on idolatry. Out of the suffering of exile was born an unwavering faith in God. And this answer is true: this is the way the Bible interprets the catastrophe, and this became the central understanding of Judaism to this day. But this is not the only way of looking at things.

In the chaotic aftermath of the tragedy there was more than one interpretation of the terrible events. We must not make the mistake of assuming that the understanding eventually accepted by the majority of Jews was the only way the disaster was construed. Of the undoubtedly many views contesting the field we know of at least one other. Because this conflicting view is so underrepresented, and so widely ignored, it is important that we digress to explore it. It will become extremely important to our understanding of Esther.

The destruction of Judah and Jerusalem, and the forced deportation of the survivors to Babylon by the conqueror, King Nebuchadnezzar, looms so large in the Bible and in subsequent history that it tends to obscure the creation of another exile. One of the aftermaths of the Destruction was the flight of a large body of Israelites to Egypt — (an enemy of Babylon) — and their taking refuge there.[24] Once more-or-less settled, these people relapsed into idolatry. The main form that their idolatry took was the revival of the ancient cult of the worship of the Queen of Heaven.[25] The worship of the Queen of Heaven had been outlawed in Judah by King Josiah,[26] driving its practice underground. Now in Egypt it re-emerges to prominence among the survivors.

The prophet Jeremiah[27] vigorously denounces the people, insisting that it was this very idolatry that was the cause of the Disaster. The people, however, reject his argument in favor of a different understanding of the events:

> Then ... all the people that dwelt in the land of Egypt, in Pathros, answered Jeremiah, saying: "As for the word that you have spoken to us in the name of the Lord, we will not listen to you! [On the contrary] we will scrupulously perform everything we have vowed to do:[28] to offer unto the Queen of Heaven,[29] and to pour out libations to her, just as we, our fathers, our kings and our princes used to do in the cities of Judah and the streets of Jerusalem; [for then we had] plenty to eat, were prosperous and saw no evil. But ever since we ceased to offer to the Queen

---

[23]The classical prophets added ethical and moral sins to the roster of the crimes for which the Israelites were to be held accountable.

[24]We are informed that the survivors settled in Migdol and Tahpanhes in the Eastern Delta, the region closest to Judea. We also hear of a community at Noph (Memphis, near present day Cairo) and of settlement in the district of Pathros in Upper Egypt (near present day Aswan). Thus Jewish settlement spanned the entire length of Egypt.

[25]Probably the Assyrian-Babylonian goddess Ishtar, possibly identified with the planet Venus. Her worship involved, beyond the usual sacrificial offerings, the pouring out of special libations and the making of cakes (for offerings?) (Jeremiah 7:18, 44:17–19).

[26]See *Josianic Reform* in Glossary.

[27]Jeremiah was in Egypt against his will. He had been opposed to fleeing the land of Judah but had been forcibly abducted by the refugees when they fled. See Jeremiah 42–43.

[28]Literally, "every word that has gone forth out of our mouth."

[29]Reading with LXX; MT reads "the work of heaven."

of Heaven[30] and to pour out libations to her we have lacked everything, and have been consumed by the sword and by famine (Jeremiah 44:15–18).

The people's take on the situation is as follows: far from their idolatry being the cause of the disaster, it was the abandonment of it that was the cause. As long as they worshiped the Queen of Heaven things went well. But when King Josiah forced them to cease worshiping her, she became angry with them; the Disaster was her punishment, and the Lord God of Israel was powerless to prevent it. The conclusion of this line of reasoning is inevitable: abandon the worship of God and worship the Queen of Heaven. While for some the Disaster led to a strengthening of their faith in God, turning them finally into true monotheists, for others it rather strengthened their idolatry and polytheism.

Though we lack specific evidence, we can suggest the possibility of still another reaction to the disaster. Among those who were already convinced monotheists (and there were such), those that firmly believed that the God of Israel was the only God, and all the other so-called "gods" really didn't exist — there were those who lost their faith in God, who felt that God had abandoned them, and that they had no alternative deities to fall back on. The God Who had failed was the only God there was. To lose faith in God meant for them a world without God. And if there is no God, then there is no religion, for religion is but the framework by means of which we relate to God.[31]

We are familiar with this phenomenon; it was common in the mid-twentieth century in the wake of the Holocaust. People who previously had believed in God had their faith broken by the horrors they had undergone, and were left in a Godless universe. In its heyday, this phenomenon was called the "Death of God"[32] This is the world portrayed in Esther. Besides being the first portrayal and exploration of anti–Semitism, this remarkable Book is also, to the best of my knowledge, the first depiction of what the world would be like if "God were dead." Unless the author knew such people who had lost their faith (or knew of them), and had thus become acquainted with the bleak universe of their spirit, the leap of imagination evidenced by its portrayal in Esther is astonishing.

Of course we are here assuming that this dark vision is not autobiographical: that the author is not reflecting his own loss of faith. This assumption remains to be explored, and the next chapter will be devoted to an attempt to determine exactly what the author does believe. For the present, I suggest that perhaps the shock of being the target of a program of genocide only narrowly averted, coming on top of a pervasive and increasingly overt anti–Semitism have reawakened the memory of the great Catastrophe of a century before. The terrible questions of the previous century have returned, possessed with an alarming urgency: Where is God? Has He abandoned us? Is there a God? And if so why can't we perceive His presence?

These are the terrifying questions that lie, I believe, behind the Book and explain why the author crafted it as he did. In portraying the Jew alone in a hostile world with no God, able to rely only on his own meager resources for survival, the author is addressing some of the deepest anxieties and fears of many of his contemporaries. He is taking the doubts and questionings that lie behind Ruth and Tamar[33] to a horrifying extreme, for it is one thing to find a way out

[30]See previous note.

[31]This would explain why Persian religion is also absent from the Book. From the monotheist's point of view, the gods of the nations are no-gods; Ahura Mazda is not real. Zoroastrian religion is relegated to the same void as the faith of Israel.

[32]The "Death of God" phenomenon, of course, long predates the Holocaust, and refers to people who lose their faith (or never had any) for a wide variety of reasons, not just personal or as a result of massive tragedy. But it appears in its most acute form in the case of firm believers whose faith is shattered by personal trauma.

[33]Just as we use "Ruth" as shorthand for her entire story as related in the Book of Ruth, so will we use "Tamar" as a shorthand way of referring to the story of Judah and Tamar as related in Genesis 38.

of a personal crisis in a normal world; it is quite another to be on your own in a world that wants to kill you. The author seems to be taking the reader on a walk through the Valley of the Shadow of Death. Only if one can emerge from under the shadow of this nightmare vision of a Godless universe into the light of faith, he is implying, can a Jew cope with the world in which he now finds himself. But is there an exit from this dark valley? Does the author believe that there is a possibility of seeing God's presence in the world he has painted? Discovering what the author really believes now becomes our focus.

CHAPTER 21

The Hidden Hand

Nam homo proponit, sed Deus disponit.
(Man proposes but God disposes)
— Thomas à Kempis, *Imitatio Christi*

The Ghost of Joseph

We have said that our author is picking up on the theme that we have already explored in Ruth and Tamar, that of a seemingly secular world, in which God's presence cannot be perceived, and people find themselves on their own. But did he know Ruth and Tamar?[1] We have already shown that the author knew the Joseph story: he quotes it[2] (and he expects his audience to be familiar with it as well). Tamar is an integral part of the Joseph saga. While we have no direct proof that he knew Ruth, we have every reason to assume that he did. The Book had, by that time, been "in print" for almost five hundred years, and it had always been a highly popular work.[3] But in Ruth and Tamar the world only seems secular. In each case an Epilogue provides us with a new perspective that shows God as the director of a drama whose plot and outcome are beyond the ken of the actors. To them the world may appear secular. We, the readers, are in on the secret: it is God Who is really steering the ship.

In saying that the Book of Esther, in adopting the theme of Ruth and Tamar, transferring it from the personal to the national stage, and raising the stakes from personal misery to genocidal terror, are we implying that our author also believes that it is God who is stage-managing the tragic scenario? I believe this to be so. But on what basis do I say this? With Ruth and Tamar I could point to evidence. Both narratives contain the Epilogues that put the stories into a historical perspective. It is this historical perspective that illuminates the tales by revealing their long-range purpose: these were the events that brought King David into being, with all that implies. In retrospect we can see the Hand of God implicitly represented in what first appeared to be secular narratives.

But is there a similar shift of perspective in Esther? The narrative covers a mere dozen years. While it is true that Esther also contains an Epilogue, its sardonic message is no vast sweep of

[1]See Chapter 20, note 33.

[2]See Chapter 12.

[3]We have dated the writing of Ruth to the last decade or two of David's reign, or perhaps to the days of the so-called "Solomonic Enlightenment." See Chapter 1, especially note 35.

history bringing us to a glorious and preordained conclusion, as in Ruth and Tamar.[4] While the main message of Esther, I think, is the same as that of Ruth and the story of Tamar, the techniques employed in achieving the results are very different. Our author has a great advantage over his predecessors: writing five hundred years after them he has an old and established literary tradition as part of his repertoire. Let us see how he exploits this tradition.

We have several times noted that the author is well acquainted with Genesis.[5] He weaves quotes and allusions from that work into his narrative to enrich and illuminate aspects of his tale.[6] That there is a clear connection between Esther and the Joseph narrative (Genesis 37–50) has been recognized for some time. As early as 1895 Ludwig Rosenthal convincingly demonstrated a series of striking literary similarities between the Joseph saga and the Book of Esther, similarities that often approach an identity in wording.[7] In addition to the examples we have already noted in our analysis of the text, Rosenthal points out that the verbs used to describe Mordecai's elevation to vizier of Persia are the same ones used to describe Joseph's elevation to Viceroy of Egypt. Esther 8:6 echoes Genesis 44:34; Esther 4:16 echoes the construction of Genesis 43:14, and there is much more of the same.

In a recent study, Moshe Gan has strengthened Rosenthal's case by uncovering yet more linguistic correspondences. He also clearly demonstrates that beyond linguistic similarities there are also similarities in settings and events: briefly, both tales tell of Jewish heroes that rise from humble beginnings to positions of power in Gentile courts, and use their new power and influence to save their people.[8] The usual explanation for this phenomenon is that Esther is modeled on the Joseph Story, but all attempts to apply this theory to the actual narratives break down. While there are certain points of similarity, the stories are fundamentally different in plot and theme. Sandra Berg sums up the puzzling situation: "The Book of Esther appears to rely on the Joseph traditions, but the reasons for this dependence are not clear."[9]

There can be little doubt that Esther, despite the striking similarities, is not modeled on the Joseph narrative. I think that the author is not basing his narrative on the Joseph story so much as recalling it. He knows the Joseph narrative and expects his readers to be equally familiar with it, so that by using some similar language and parallel settings he will be able to recall it to their minds and keep it there while they read his Book. In a word, he is ensuring that his Book will not be read in a vacuum but rather in a specific context. "Meaning depends on context,"[10] so by designing his tale to be read with the Joseph story in mind he is determining how his readers will understand it.

---

[4]Indeed, if we are correct in our dating, Ruth was written more than a century after the events portrayed in the Book, and Tamar as much as half a millennium after the events it describes. By contrast, Esther is almost contemporaneous with the events depicted, having been written at most several decades later.

[5]Many scholars are of the opinion that Genesis, in pretty much the form we know it, was in existence well before our author's time in the fifth century BCE. Others, mostly proponents of the Documentary Hypothesis (see Glossary), agree that the so-called "J source," one of the components from which Genesis is hypothetically constructed, was certainly in existence hundreds of years before our author's lifetime. It is the "J source" that contains the stories, especially the Joseph saga, to which Esther refers.

[6]See Chapters 12 and 14.

[7]Rosenthal, "The Joseph Story Compared with the Books of Esther and Daniel" (German), pp. 278–284. See also Rosenthal, "Once Again the Comparison of Esther, Joseph-Daniel" (German), pp. 125–128.

[8]Gan, "The Book of Esther in the Light of the Story of Joseph in Egypt" (Hebrew), pp. 144–149.

[9]Berg, *The Book of Esther*, p. 128.

[10]Fox, *Character and Ideology in the Book of Esther*, p. 238. It is only fair to point out that the context to which Fox is referring is that of the Bible as a whole in which Esther is embedded, and as Esther was not a part of the Bible when originally written he rejects this context. But the principle itself is valid, and if it can be shown from internal evidence that the author placed the Book within a given literary setting, that context should be taken into account when attempting to determine the Book's meaning.

In this the author has proved surprisingly successful for, as we shall show, his intended audience and their descendents took the hint. To the present day Jews have unfailingly seen the spirit of Joseph hovering over the tale of Esther, and have read Esther with the Joseph saga in mind. Let us follow up this line of reasoning and rethink Esther in the light of Joseph.

The Technicolor Dream Coat

While the story of Joseph and his brothers, probably the most popular of all Bible tales, will be familiar to many readers, it is important to review it briefly. Joseph is the son of the last of the Patriarchs, Jacob, and of his favorite wife, Rachel. Upon her untimely death Joseph becomes Jacob's favorite son, and he is remorselessly spoiled. He spies on his older brothers and reports their misdeeds to his father, dreams of the day when he will lord it over them and when they will grovel at his feet, and then flaunts these expectations to his brothers. Adding insult to injury, their father presents Joseph with a "coat of many colors" that not only sets him apart from the others, but probably designates him as Jacob's heir and ultimate head of the family.[11] All this becomes more than the brothers can bear, and prompts their collective decision to be rid of him. Catching him away from home they seize him and sell him into slavery. They then convey his coat of many colors, torn and bloodstained, to their father who, not unreasonably, draws the conclusion that Joseph has been killed by some wild beast.

The merchants who purchase Joseph resell him in Egypt. He becomes the property of one Potiphar, a high government official, and is put to work on his estate. Quickly mastering the language and lifestyle of his new surroundings, Joseph proves himself both intelligent and competent. His talent and motivation recognized and appreciated, Joseph rises rapidly in the ranks, ultimately becoming Steward, holding full executive authority over the estate and its workforce. His duties bring him into the mansion on a daily basis, and he inevitably comes into frequent contact with his master's wife, who falls in love with him. She makes advances, to no avail. Increasingly desperate, she attempts to seduce him. When he decisively rejects her, she revenges herself upon him by denouncing him to her husband as an attempted rapist. Joseph is stripped of his office and thrown into prison.

Joseph refuses to be broken by repeated catastrophe. Once again his talent and resilience are rewarded. He becomes a prison trustee. His duties bring him into contact with two new prisoners, the chief butler and chief baker of the royal court. Interpreting the dreams they relate to him, he predicts that the butler will be pardoned and will return to his former position while the baker will be executed; and so it comes to pass.

Two years later, the pharaoh, ruler of Egypt, has a dream of which none of his court advisors can make sense. The butler, remembering his experience in prison, recommends Joseph as a skilled and successful interpreter of dreams. Summoned from prison, Joseph seizes the chance of a lifetime. He not only makes sense of the pharaoh's dreams, but brilliantly promotes himself into the position of chief executive officer (CEO) of Egypt.

The dreams, according to Joseph, are an agricultural forecast: seven years of bumper crops to be followed by seven years of consecutive crop failure. Having proposed a master plan to res-

---

[11]The Hebrew term *ketonet passim* is unclear and has been rendered several ways: a long robe with sleeves, an ornamented tunic, and so on. The term literally means a striped tunic or a garment made out of colored panels. We possess Egyptian pictures dating from this period showing Semites wearing robes made of colored longitudinal panels sewn together. Because of the traditional resonance of the phrase we have retained the King James rendition: a coat of many colors. The only other use of the term in the Bible is in 2 Samuel 13:18, where we are informed that the unmarried daughters of King David wore "coats of many colors" to designate them as princesses. What is clear from both references is that the garment was a very special status symbol.

cue the Egyptian economy from disaster (and incidentally to save a large part of the Egyptian population from starvation), Joseph now uses his authority to stockpile the surplus of the seven bumper-crop years against the coming shortfall. He is then in a position to sell the stockpiled grain back to the Egyptians during the lean years.

In the meantime, in Canaan, as drought and crop failure strike the entire region, Joseph's family finds itself *in extremis*. Learning that Egypt has large reserves, the brothers are sent there to purchase grain. They find themselves standing in front of Joseph, whom they do not recognize. He, however, recognizes them. He toys with them, accuses them of being spies, allows himself to be partially persuaded as to their bona fides, permits them to purchase grain but imprisons one of them as a hostage for the good behavior of the rest. Then he insists that they bring back "proof" of the truth of the story they have told him — their youngest brother, Benjamin — when they return. The one brother who did not accompany them, he is the second child of Jacob's beloved Rachel, and the one with whom his father could not bear to part.

The famine persists, and starvation forces old Jacob to permit Benjamin to accompany his brothers on their second trip to Egypt. Joseph continues to play with them, planting his silver cup in Benjamin's sack and then accusing him of robbery. When he announces Benjamin's sentence for his "crime" — enslavement — Judah boldly intercedes for his little brother and offers himself in his place. At this point, realizing that things have gone far enough, Joseph calls off the charade and reveals who he is. After a tearful reunion and reconciliation, Joseph sends for their father and the entire family resettles in Egypt under his protection. The early dreams of Joseph have come true; his status as the person who controls the family, presaged by the coat of many colors, has become reality.

This, in very sketchy outline and omitting much detail and subplot,[12] is the gist of the story. It is a tale of incompetent parenting and family mismanagement, of youthful arrogance leading to sibling hatred and violent revenge, of resilience in the face of disastrous calamities and heroic courage and perseverance despite seemingly insurmountable odds. It is a tale of ability overcoming great odds and winning through to spectacular success, and finally of reconciliation and happy ending. It is a story easy to understand because, unusual and unlikely as some of the episodes may seem, the action develops naturally from the motives of the various characters. And the motives themselves are thoroughly understandable and familiar. It is a very human drama, one with which it is easy to identify. In fact, it is very similar in this respect to Ruth and Tamar. Like them it is the tale of a hero battling against grim circumstance, and by courage, daring, and ability winning through to a happy ending.

It is like those stories in another respect: the story of Joseph is also secular. Taken at face value it is a purely human tale. God plays no part in it. He never appears, never intervenes and the protagonists of the saga do what they do on the basis of their own considerations and emotions, with God playing no part in their calculations.[13] Some of the actors in this drama, most

---

[12]The entire story of Tamar, for example, or the way Joseph exploits the crisis to reorganize Egypt into a command economy are omitted from this synopsis, as are many lesser points.

[13]The one exception is Genesis 46:1–4 in which old Jacob, on the way with his family to be rejoined with his son Joseph in Egypt, breaks his journey in Beer-sheba to turn to God in worship. God responds by appearing to him in a dream, stilling his fear that he is sinning in leaving the Promised Land and assuring him that He, God, will be with him and his descendants in Egypt and will bring them back to the Promised Land. This divine encounter, the last in his life, has no influence on Jacob's actions. The decision to go to Egypt and be reunited with his son before he dies has already been made and without reference to God's directives. Indeed, it is the fear that his decision may have been the wrong one that is the cause of God's speaking to him to reassure him that all will be for the best. This episode is really not a part of the Joseph saga, but rather the conclusion of the epic of the last of the Patriarchs. In this vision the life-long "wrestling-match" of Jacob with his God finds its closure. But the fact that this episode is not an integral part of the Joseph saga does not mean it is irrelevant to it. Its significance will become evident in the next section.

notably Joseph, talk a lot *about* God; they never talk to Him, turn to Him, or pray to Him. And even more notably God never speaks to Joseph or any of the brothers as he regularly did to their ancestors. Everybody is on his own. Like Ruth and Tamar, Joseph is a hero because his success is due solely to his own abilities and efforts.

Eternal Artistries in Circumstances

So far we have looked at the tale of Joseph and his brothers as a humanistic drama, and so it is. But it is also something more, much more. To understand this we must examine the climax when Joseph reveals himself to his brothers.

> Then Joseph said to his brothers: "Come closer to me." And they came close. And he said: "I am Joseph your brother, whom you sold into Egypt. And now, do not be grieved nor angry with yourselves that you sold me here, for God sent me before you to preserve life. For these two years has there been famine in the land, and there are yet five years in which there shall be neither plowing nor harvest. So God has sent me before you, to ensure you a remnant upon the earth, and to save you alive for a great deliverance. So now it was not you who sent me here, but God" (Genesis 45:4–8).

This declaration does more than simply lighten the terrible burden of guilt the brothers bear for the appalling act of selling one of their own into slavery. These words constitute a moment of shocking self-understanding on the part of Joseph. His little speech functions in the same way as do the Epilogues to Ruth and Tamar. It takes what has been a secular story and suddenly shifts the perspective; by showing the entire series of events in a radically different light, it forces us to rethink the story.

We have been looking at the Joseph narrative from a human perspective, the "worm's eye" view as it were. Now the time has come for the "bird's eye" view: God's perspective. God faces a problem: He has chosen Abraham and promised him that his descendants will become a great people who are to be a blessing to all mankind.

> And I will bless those that bless you, and those who damn you will I curse, and through you shall all the families of the earth be blessed (Genesis 12:3).

Subsequently Abraham fathers Isaac, and Isaac fathers Jacob, and Jacob fathers twelve sons and a daughter. The future of the Promise would seem assured but for one fatal flaw: in the natural order of things there is a catastrophic drought in the offing, and in the course of the ensuing famine Jacob and all his children will inevitably starve to death. What then will become of the Promise?

Why doesn't God just, in the words of that old Broadway play, "pass a miracle?" But that is not the way the Bible sees things. God seems to prefer to work through the natural order, rather than to abolish or circumvent it. God achieves His purposes through the natural interplay of human motives and human activity. Joseph struts, brags, and infuriates his brothers. Jacob pampers and spoils his son and marks him out with a coat of many colors. Goaded beyond all endurance, the brothers get rid of Joseph by selling him into slavery. The first move in God's chess game has been concluded: the pawn (the most brilliant of Jacob's sons) has been moved out of the backwater of Canaan onto the big board — Egypt.

Move two: Joseph is resold to Potiphar and employed on his estate. Or to look at it from God's perspective, he has been sent to training school. Here he will master the Egyptian language and Egyptian customs. As he works his way up, his drive and ability earning him regular promotion, he gets training in administration (which includes reading, writing and accountancy, all of which were prerequisites in administering a large Egyptian estate). He learns acceptable manners by constant contact with the aristocratic family he serves. Once his training is complete it becomes time for move number three.

Move three is from CEO of Potiphar's estate to prison. To Joseph, of course, it is disaster. How is he to know that it is in prison he will make the critical contact with the person whose recommendation, years later, will catapult him to greatness: the royal butler? The contact made, Joseph is once again put in a holding pattern until the time comes for the next move.

Move number four on God's chess board: from prison to the Royal Palace. Fully prepared, Joseph is able to seize the opportunity and become CEO of Egypt. More, he has the tools to make good in this unprecedented position. And, in saving Egypt from disaster, he has the possibility of saving his family. This leads directly to move number five: his brothers inevitably show up, driven by famine to the only place in the region with surplus food. When Joseph accepts his familial responsibilities, and invites his family to the safety of Egypt, God's game plan has been successfully concluded.

It is at this point that Joseph attains spiritual greatness. We normally focus on the courage, talent, brilliance and spectacular flair that the story highlights. But in the Bible's view what sets Joseph head and shoulders above most of humanity is that he grasps his role in the divine drama. He realizes that he has been God's pawn who, throughout a turbulent life of trying to keep his head above water and make a success of himself, he has unknowingly been serving a greater purpose than himself. In retrospect, he grasps the greater meaning of his life, and so in revealing himself to his brothers he is not mouthing pious platitudes, but telling the stark truth when he says:

> "Do not be grieved, nor angry with yourselves that you sold me here, for God sent me before you to preserve life.... So now it was not you who sent me here, but God"[14] (Genesis 45:5, 8).

Like Ruth and Tamar, though far more direct and explicit than they in pointing up the "moral," and despite its secular appearance, the Joseph story is revealed at its climax to be a drama of God's governance of human affairs. It is the Hand of the Hidden God that is the force shaping the destiny of mankind.

Nezah Yisrael Lo Yishaker: The Eternal of Israel Does Not Lie

> The Eternal of Israel does not lie neither does He
> repent; for He is not a man that He should repent.
> —1 Samuel 15:29

Now we can understand the author's purpose in writing Esther in such a way as to continuously remind us of the Joseph saga. By writing Esther in the light of Joseph, and constantly referring back to the tale, the author is creating the context in which he wants us to understand his story. Esther may seem secular. So does the story of Joseph until the shocking dénouement, when we are informed that appearances are deceitful; that it is God, hidden behind the seemingly secular façade of events, Who is directing the action and determining the outcomes. The story of Esther, we are being led to infer, should be viewed in just the same manner.

---

[14]This point, the moral of the whole story, is driven home by Jacob's dream on the road to Egypt, when God informs the aged Patriarch that all this is His doing (Genesis 46:1–4, see the previous note).

We return to the concluding portion of Esther shortly before the Epilogue (10:1–3) where, with the initiation of the holiday of Purim, a brief summary of the storyline of the Book is given:

> For Haman, son of Hammedatha the Agagite, enemy of all the Jews, *plotted* against the Jews to destroy them, and he cast a Pur (that is the lot) to crush and destroy them. But when she [Esther] came before the king he decreed in writing that his [Haman's] evil *plot* which he had *plotted* against the Jews should recoil on his own head; so he and his sons were hanged on the gallows (9:24–25).

In Chapter 19 we noted, in passing, that in the three-fold use of the word *hashav* (here rendered as "plotted") our attention is being drawn the very same word, also repeated for emphasis, in Genesis 50:20.[15] With this reference we are drawn to the family crisis precipitated by the death of father Jacob. The brothers are terrified that because their father's restraining presence has been removed, there is nothing standing between them and Joseph's revenge for their ancient betrayal. Joseph reassures them that he bears no grudge. While fully realizing that their motives had been reprehensible, the sting has been taken out of the memory of those events by the stunning realization that it was God Who had been directing the drama of his life with a greater purpose in mind.

> "You *intended* me harm, but God *intended* it for good, in order to save many people alive, even as at this present day" (Genesis 50:20).

The word that, due to context, we have rendered as "intended" is the same term that we encountered in Esther 9:24–25, *hashav*.[16] By using the same word and in a similar context the author of Esther is asking us to read the conclusion of his Book in the same way that we read the conclusion of the Joseph saga: Haman intended the Jews harm, to destroy them, but God intended the outcome to be good (that Haman's evil plot should recoil on his own head). And God's intentions trump human intentions. Human beings strive and struggle to achieve their ambitions and fulfill their destinies, as they understand them, while all the time it is God's purposes that are being realized.

What are these purposes? In the story of Joseph, God's immediate aim is to save alive the family of Jacob. The larger context of Genesis brings God's overall purpose into focus. God had promised Abraham that his descendants would become a great people who would prove a blessing to all humanity. God does not promise idly. His Promise will be kept, and this requires that the seed of Abraham be preserved. And so Jacob's family does not die in Canaan, but descends to Egypt where Joseph fulfills his function of saving them. The destiny of Jacob's descendants, the Children of Israel, which would appear to be the task of bringing God's word to the world, remains open before them. It is on this note that Genesis concludes.

But what is God's purpose that moves behind the story of Esther? By putting this chronicle of thwarted genocide within the context of the story of Joseph the author seems to be suggesting to his readers a similar purpose. The Jews, despite exile and dispersion, are the descendants of the Israelites. They remain the seed of Abraham, inheritors of God's Promise that through them "shall all the families of the earth be blessed." God's Hand still rests upon His people and His Promise still remains in force. Despite the destruction of Judea, despite exile

---

[15]See Chapter 19, note 11.

[16]The basic meaning of the word *hashav* is "to think." From this are derived the secondary meanings of "to plan," "to devise," "to intend," "to plot," "to reckon," and so on. The way the term is translated into English depends upon the given context, but in the original Hebrew the word itself is immediately recognizable in both Genesis and Esther as the same word.

and dispersion, despite the nightmare hatred of anti–Semitism that daily threatens the very existence of the Jew, God's purpose holds. The Jewish people will endure, for it is part of a larger destiny and a larger purpose.

In this sense the Greek versions (and the Aramaic versions — the Targumim — as well) got it right. They correctly saw through the secular façade of Esther, and by emphasizing God and religion they made explicit the underlying theology of the Book. But in so doing they eviscerated its metaphysical and existential dimensions.

By making God's Providence explicit they miss the point that Esther is more than a celebration of God's direction of history for His own purposes. Esther is simultaneously a deep meditation on what it sees as one of the mysteries of human existence: that while we find ourselves in a world made by God, yet we cannot be sure of finding God. In eschewing a simplistic dogmatic certitude, by, in effect, insisting that human beings, by their very nature, are condemned to live with uncertainty and to be faced in extreme moments with the terrible choice between faith and despair, Esther addresses the universal condition of man. The author of our Book presents the world as we find it: a world containing horrors and beastliness, a world full of stupidity and pomposity that invites us to laugh at its ridiculous aspects, a world that appears secular and ruled by chance yet containing hints that there may be plan and purpose after all. It remains up to us to interpret the world in which we find ourselves; to see it as godless and blind, or to intuit the Hand of God behind the façade. It is in this latter direction that our author is discreetly nudging us.

> When we scrutinize the text of Esther for traces of God's activity we are doing what the author made us do. The author would have us probe the events which we witness in our own lives in the same way. He is teaching a theology of possibility. The willingness to face history with an openness to the possibility of providence — even when history seems to weigh against its likelihood, as it did in the dark days after the issuance of Haman's decree — this is a stance of profound faith. It is the willingness of the Jew to bear the responsibility that a fickle history lays on his or her shoulders, uncertain of the future yet confident that, somehow, *nezah Yisrael lo yishaker.*[17]

---

[17]Fox, *Character and Ideology in the book of Esther*, p. 247. The sense of the quote from 1 Samuel 15:29 ("The Eternal of Israel does not lie") is that God is entirely trustworthy; unlike human beings, when He gives His word He does not go back on it.

PART III

SUMMING UP

CHAPTER 22

Thinking Outside the Box

> It can be very liberating to leave your country, to leave everything
> that's familiar.... It can help you make sense of your past.
> — Deborah Moggach, newspaper interview,
> January 27, 2006[1]

The time has come to sum up. Three tales; what are they telling us? They all begin with one central premise: that we live in a world characterized by uncertainty and mystery. Does God rule this world, His purpose giving order and direction to the universe and our lives? Or does chance rule, there being no God? We cannot tell, for if there is a God He is invisible to us.

We have seen how the tales of Ruth and Tamar address this issue. They imply that God is hidden from us because our lives are too short. We cannot perceive the slow motions of His handiwork.

An analogy might make this central intuition clearer. In prior times the ancients called the stars "the fixed heavenly bodies" because, unlike the planets which could be seen to change their positions relative to each other over the course of time, the heavenly constellations seemed permanent. But the stars do move, absolutely and relatively to each other. Because of the interstellar distances that separate us from them, this movement is not perceptible to the naked eye over the course of a lifetime, or even several dozen lifetimes. It would take millennia for an observer to begin to perceive a shift, while over a span of millions of years the movement of the stars would be dramatically evident. During the Jurassic Age, 160 million years ago, the heavens looked very different from the way they appear to us today.

This, in essence, is what the authors of Ruth and Tamar (Genesis 38) are suggesting: just as our lives are too short to perceive the movement of the stars, so are they too brief to discern God's activities, because, to us, He is moving far too slowly to be observed. Only in retrospect — perhaps with the hindsight of a lifetime, more often over the sweep of centuries — does the pattern of His handiwork become evident. It is because of this view of the nature of our relationship with God that the ancient Israelites focused on the study of history as a way of understanding His ways and purposes. Unlike the holy books and scriptures of all other religions, the Bible is largely composed of historical works and narratives.

---

[1]Deborah Moggach, a popular novelist and screenwriter, is here reminiscing on the consequences of her prolonged residence as a young mother in Pakistan more than thirty years previously.

But humans do not live in retrospect, and we cannot wait until our lives — and history — are over before we make our choices. (As Hegel famously put it, the Owl of Minerva spreads its wings only with the falling of the dusk[2] — but we live our lives during the day.) So we are not in a position to see the large-scale pattern that God is imposing on history, or even be sure that there is one. God's face is hidden from us, and we wonder whether there is a God. The Book of Esther is addressing itself to what, at major turning points or crises in one's life can become urgent personal concerns.

What the Book of Esther is saying is that in the welter of our lives, short of a direct revelation from God — and don't count on it — we can never be certain if God or chance rules our world. We are left on our own to do our best. But we do have one choice: we can choose to see ourselves as living in a Godless universe — the world depicted in Esther — or we can choose to understand that our daily struggles are guided by a divine Providence[3] — the situation hinted at in Esther. In this view, behind apparent chance and the clash of human motives and actions an uncontrollable Purpose is operating; events and acts are not what they seem. We are all bit actors in a cosmic drama working to unimaginable ends.

On what basis can we choose? Taken in and of itself, no life has any certainty. The evidence of our senses remains ambiguous, even as the Book of Esther by itself leaves the question open. Only in the context of the Bible as a whole, of which it is a part, can Esther be read (as it was read from the beginning) as a Book that indicates that the Hand of God is operating providentially, even when we behave as if there is no such thing.[4]

So Why Not Say So?

But if this is what the authors of our three tales were driving at, why didn't they come right out and say it? The idea of a God Who acts providentially, manipulating pagan kings who "do not know Him," using them as His instruments to accomplish His purposes is familiar to us from the prophets. Isaiah defines Assyria as "the rod of His anger," His instrument by which He punishes nations and peoples who have sinned against Him. Pagan Assyria, of course, has not the slightest notion that it is being so used. It arrogantly thinks that its imperial policy of conquest and genocidal destruction is of its own making. And so it is, but it nonetheless is serving God's purposes and in due time will get its comeuppance, again by an agent unaware that it is also serving a purpose beyond its own.[5] Jeremiah refers to the Babylonian king Nebuchadrezzar as God's servant whom He will send to smite Egypt,[6] while the prophet of the exile calls Cyrus the Great "God's shepherd" and "His anointed" that He has sent to look after the inter-

---

[2]His point being that only as our lives are ending, or as an epoch is ending, and it is too late to do anything about it, do we in retrospect begin to grasp the true nature of reality (Preface to *Hegel's Philosophy of Right*).

[3]"When we speak of God's providence, we mean that God, in some invisible and inscrutable way, governs all creatures, actions, and circumstances through the normal and the ordinary course of human life, without the intervention of the miraculous" (Jobes, *Esther*, p. 43).

[4]As we have noted, the author of Esther consciously casts the Book in the larger context of biblical tradition by continually paraphrasing the narratives of Genesis and the prophets, and framing Esther in such a way as to reflect them (see Chapter 21). It was this larger biblical context that determined, as the author intended it to determine, how the Book was to be understood. In this the author was successful; and it was because the Book was taken from the first as an illustration of the governance of the Hidden God in His world, that the Book was canonized and became part of the Bible.

[5]Isaiah 10:5–15.

[6]Jeremiah 43:10.

ests of the Jews and to rebuild Jerusalem.[7] Needless to say Cyrus, who worships Ahura Mazda and not God, and is busy carving out an enormous empire, has no idea that he is serving any purpose but his own, and that millennia hence he will chiefly be remembered not for his empire but for his liberation of the Jewish captives and his support of their return and rebuilding of Jerusalem. These prophets speak in the name of God. Indeed all the prophets see God as controlling the destiny of the nations, viewing the international arena as one of the many realms of God's Providence, and they proclaim it openly. Why then are the authors of Ruth, Genesis 38, and Esther so reticent, conveying by indirection what the prophets declare directly?

But then how did the prophets know? They claimed to have been told directly by God. Indeed, in all our instances they are speaking in His name and assert that they are quoting His words. Having a direct pipeline to the Almighty gives adequate grounds for certainty. But short of relying blindly on their pronouncements, all the rest of humanity lives in the uncertainty that is the underlying premise of our authors. The authors of Ruth, Tamar, and Esther are speaking of our ambiguous and uncertain world. All we can know about God must be by indirection. Worse, as the author of Esther implies, without the benefit of hindsight even this becomes impossible. We are left with the biblical tradition of prophetic teachings, and with the vicissitudes of faith.

Three Unconventional Tales

We have been analyzing three gripping tales, spaced at five-hundred-year intervals on the more than a thousand year span of the Biblical Age. Three different authors have been grappling, each in his or her own way, with the problem of a world that seems godless. And all three end by hinting that, behind the seemingly secular appearance of our world, it is God Who is really pulling the strings. These are stories that appeal to us, living as we do in the secular twenty-first century; they speak to our condition and to the secular world in which we find ourselves. It would take a real effort of the imagination to realize how bizarre these tales were when they were written thousands of years ago. In the context of the biblical world they are unique.[8]

As we have pointed out at the very beginning of this work, the Books of the Bible portray God as the one and only Hero, the Maker and Master of all things. God is everywhere and His omnipresence is taken for granted. He speaks to patriarchs and prophets alike, and they speak with Him. His Hand is manifest in all that occurs. How, in an age when God's presence was assumed by everyone, and all society was built on this premise, could it ever occur to our three authors to question this consensus? What was it that brought them to feel God's absence in their familiar landscape — to begin the search for the Hidden God? We have been following a revolutionary quest totally out of step with the mainstream of the Bible.

There is another aspect to these stories that sets them apart from the biblical norm: these tales do not have heroes as their protagonists but rather heroines. In a Bible that is male

---

[7]Isaiah 44:28, 45:1. It is generally agreed that the prophet who authored chapters 40–66 of the Book of Isaiah is not Isaiah son of Amoz, author of chapters 1–35, who lived in the 8th century (approximately 740–700 BCE), but rather a prophet who lived and preached in the Babylonian Exile about 200 years later, and returned with the freed exiles to the land of Judah. We do not know why his writings were appended to those of Isaiah son of Amoz. Perhaps his name was also Isaiah. At any rate he is currently known as Deutero-Isaiah or the Second Isaiah, or simply the unknown prophet of the exile.

[8]The only other "secular" narrative in the Bible is the Joseph saga, of which the tale of Tamar is a part. But apart from the story of Tamar, the epic history of Joseph is not secular. It does not hint, but comes right out and insists that it is God Who stage-manages Joseph's entire life, and by implication, the lives of all of us (see Chapter 21).

dominated, with masculine heroes by the score, the very existence of female protagonists is a rarity. Yet of this small handful of female figures scattered throughout the pages of the Bible three of the most notable of them (four if one counts Naomi) are found clustered in just our seemingly secular narratives. This is a strange coincidence. Three narratives in the Bible that hint at a Hidden God concealed in an apparently secular world feature women as the heroines and prime players. This calls for an explanation. What is the connection between women and the search for the Hidden God?[9]

Strangers in a Strange Land

When we step back and consider the Bible as a whole, we cannot but be struck by how marginal the role of women is. Most of the major figures in the Bible, for good or ill, are men; women protagonists are few and far between. In places where the Bible is not talking about God and is dealing with humanity, the humans it portrays are mainly men. From one point of view the Bible can be seen largely as a Book written for men by men. Women are marginal to the male-dominated concerns of the Bible and are treated accordingly. And this is hardly surprising considering the male-oriented culture of the Ancient Near East against whose background the Bible was written.

When we look at our heroines — Ruth, Naomi, Tamar and Esther — we cannot avoid recognizing that, despite their centrality in their stories, they are clearly second-class citizens in the world they inhabit. The lives of Ruth, Naomi and Tamar are blighted by men and they are consigned to the fringes of society. And this is considered by all, the women themselves included, as normal. What makes these women heroes is that they refuse to accept their status, at tremendous risk rebel against their marginal situation, and successfully take control of their lives. Even Esther cannot escape the marginal status of women in Persian society. She is an object, doing what her menfolk tell her. Pushed into a "Miss Persia" contest, she becomes the favorite "playmate" of the king. Once again, what makes her a hero is her refusal to remain an object and her resolution to be a person in her own right, to take charge of her destiny and that of her people. To be a woman in the ancient world was to be a marginal person, outside of the mainstream of male society. What status a woman possessed was by virtue of the man to whom she was connected; first her father, then her husband. Lacking either of these she was nothing in or of herself. A woman could accept this situation or, in rare circumstances, might rebel against it, but her very gender consigned her to the fringes of society.

But oddly, in the case of our four heroines it is not only their gender that consigns them to marginality. And here, in order to proceed, we must define more exactly what we mean when we speak of marginal persons. One can be considered marginal to the world in which one finds oneself if one cannot find a place among the normal and accepted members of society due to some factor considered essential. In such a case one finds oneself in the society but not belonging to it; an outsider, a stranger looking in, excluded from full participation. For much of history women have been consigned to this position.

Other factors can render a person marginal. Physical deformity or other deviations from

[9]In the process of analyzing these narratives we have pointed out that the authors, had they so wished, could have put different spins on their tales, minimizing the roles of the women and highlighting the roles of the men, and this without any violence to the historic facts or to the essential message or "moral" of the works. Indeed, in the case of the Book of Esther, the author (or authors) of the first rendition of the Book into Greek, the Alpha-Text or AT (see Appendix III: It's Greek to Me) did just that, turning the Book of Esther that we know into "The Book of Mordecai."

an accepted norm can render one marginal. In most societies strangers are consigned to a marginal status. Thus mobility is also a prime cause of marginality. Moving from place to place makes a person a stranger in his new social milieu. This is called by sociologists "horizontal mobility." Then there is what is referred to as "vertical mobility," by which is meant changing one's social class. It matters little from the sociological point of view whether one rises above or falls below the class into which one was born; either way one finds oneself in a world in which one does not fully belong and in which one is not fully accepted. The terms *nouveau riche* and *déclassé* come to mind. In all these cases the person so displaced finds himself a stranger.

What is remarkable about our study is that in all three tales we come up against central figures who are not simply marginal but doubly and triply so. As females they are marginal to their world; they are an embodiment of women on their own, without men, in a man's world. All of them are more mobile than most people of their time. Ruth has exchanged the land of her birth for that of Judah; Naomi has left Judah to live in Moab for over a decade, only to return embittered to a Bethlehem that hardly recognizes her and has no place for her; Esther is taken from her neighborhood in Susa to the palace harem; and even Tamar, who suffers the least displacement, undergoes removal from her Canaanite home to a strange non–Canaanite familial environment. They all undergo radical changes of fortune. Naomi drops from the comfortable life of the wife of a landowner into husbandless destitution; Ruth has less far to fall, but to her penniness must be added her status of *ger*, a resident alien. Both widows have fallen into the underclass of Israelite society. Tamar's condition is, if anything, worse. Although grudgingly guaranteed a roof over her head and enough to eat by her parents, as a widow who cannot remarry, she remains under the authority of the father-in-law who expelled her from his home. She has no status at all. Even Esther, whose meteoric rise has elevated her to the top of the socio-economic pyramid in Persia, is equally displaced from her original class, and is laboring under still another marginalizing disability: she belongs to a minority, and an endangered minority at that. Her period of adjustment to the palace finds her not only in the harem but "in the closet," a Jew hiding her Jewishness and pretending to be a Gentile.

In sum, all of our protagonists are depicted, besides having all the disabilities that come as a result of their being women (and in the case of Esther, minority status as well), as being both horizontally and vertically mobile. We have before us narratives that tell of people who find themselves "strangers in a strange land,"[10] outsiders, marginalized. The picture presented by these three stories is so consistent that it would be unreasonable to consider it a coincidence. So our question becomes: what can be the connection between marginalized persons and a search for the Hidden God in a world that seems secular?

The Marginal Man

To answer this question we return to the strangeness of anyone in the Biblical Age even raising the question of the absence of God. People lived in an all-encompassing environment that took for granted the constant presence of God. We have seen how the Book of Ruth, in portraying day to day life in Bethlehem, depicts landowners, farm laborers, elders in the gate

[10]As remarked in Chapter 3, note 19, the expression comes from Moses' self-description while in exile in the land of Midian (Exodus 2:22). Interestingly, Moses himself had undergone both horizontal and vertical displacement shortly before he made this remark: he had been forced to flee Egypt and take refuge in Midian, and simultaneously he had undergone the radical social drop from (adopted) member of the royal family to the status of humble shepherd. It seems that Moses was deeply aware of his marginalization even if he lacked the sociological language to describe it.

and the women of the town — in a word, everyone — constantly and casually referring to God. There is little doubt in my mind that this picture accurately reflects the reality of those days: everyone took God for granted. The vital importance of this fact is brought into focus by Louis Wirth:

> The most important thing that we can know about a man is what he takes for granted, and the most elemental and important facts about a society are those that are seldom debated and generally regarded as settled.... A society is possible in the last analysis because the individuals in it carry around in their heads some sort of picture of that society.[11]

As we leaf through the Bible we can get a very clear idea of the picture that great and small, priest and prophet carried around in their heads: a world in which God walked with man. How could such an all encompassing consensus be challenged? It is only by persons who, though living within the society, are outsiders, not really part of it. The marginal man is the only person sufficiently outside the consensus to be able to challenge it.

The concept of "The Marginal Man" is one that has long preoccupied sociologists. Robert E. Park, the originator of the term, puts the matter thus:

> The marginal man, as here conceived, is one whom fate has condemned to live in two societies, and in two, not merely different but antagonistic, cultures.[12]

In this definition we can at once recognize Esther, a Jewish girl embedded in a Persian palace; Ruth, a Moabite girl residing in Israelite Bethlehem; Tamar, a Canaanite girl recruited into an Israelite family. And when, to this conflicted identity is added the fact that we are dealing not with men but with women, already marginal to a man's world, and subject to the shock of a rapid and radical displacement either from the class into which they had been born or from the locale in which they had been raised, or both at the same time,[13] we realize how extremely marginal our heroines are. Park continues:

> The fate which condemns him to live, at the same time, in two worlds is the same which compels him to assume, in relation to the worlds in which he lives, the role of a cosmopolitan and a stranger. Inevitably he becomes ... the individual with the wider horizon, the keener intelligence, the more detached and rational viewpoint.[14]

To sum up: the thesis of Park, Wirth and Mannheim is that people's home backgrounds, their interests and the society in which they live bind them into an ideological framework that blinds them to alternatives. Only marginal persons, looking in from the outside, have the ability to question the system. Only such triply marginal figures as Ruth, Tamar and Esther could be detached enough to question the certainties of the worlds in which they found themselves, to challenge them and to rebel against the fates to which they had been consigned.

Now, perhaps, we can begin to understand why these marginal women are chosen to be protagonists of tales that raise profoundly disturbing questions: in a world ostensibly created by God, where is He? Why can't we see His Hand? How can a woman, removed from her identifying status and home, make a new place for herself? And by implication: what kind of identity is proper

---

[11]Wirth, Preface to *Ideology and Utopia* by Karl Mannheim, pp. xxii–xxiii.

[12]Park, Introduction to *The Marginal Man* by E.V. Stonequist, p. xv.

[13]Karl Mannheim insists that one displacement is usually not enough to break a person loose from the generally accepted preconceptions of society. Only when horizontal mobility is accompanied by a rapid movement up or down the social scale "is the belief in the eternal validity of one's own thought-forms shaken. Vertical mobility is the decisive factor in making persons uncertain and skeptical of their traditional view of the world" (Mannheim, *Ideology and Utopia*, p. 7).

[14]Park, Introduction to *The Marginal Man*, p. xvii–xviii.

for a woman? Seen from this perspective we will have to reexamine the way these issues were faced, and explore the possibility that we have here not three isolated bits of answers but rather an ongoing project, each tale taking the issues one step further. But before we can commence our reexamination of these narratives, the time has come to ask ourselves who wrote them. We have reached a point in our analysis where it may be possible to come to some conclusions in the matter.

Who Wrote These Stories?

In the course of our study of Ruth, Tamar and Esther we explored the issue of when these tales were written. Only in the case of Ruth did we speculate on the identity of the author.[15] In order to account for the pervasive feminine perspective that pervades the work we proposed, as a working hypothesis, that the author of Ruth was a woman. In the light of our current analysis this theory makes even better sense. As we have shown, Ruth (and to a lesser extent, Naomi) are marginal persons, and it is marginal persons who are at a sufficient remove from the mainstream culture to have the perspective that enables them to set aside assumptions that underlie societal norms. But while Ruth and Naomi are indeed the ideal persons to challenge the social conventions of their times, they are only characters in a story. They did not write the tale in which they appear. But if it was indeed a woman who wrote the Book then we can suggest that it was her own marginalized status as a woman, and perhaps other factors as well,[16] that led her to question the cultural consensus. This would explain her choice of marginalized women as her protagonists.

What this line of reasoning implies is that, in a spiritual sense, the Book of Ruth, is autobiographical. In other words, the author chose these specific episodes in the lives of Ruth, Naomi, and Boaz not only because of their intrinsic appeal to the public of her time, but also as a means of working through her own crisis of identity and theology, giving mouth to her rebellion against the general cultural consensus that she now perceived to be fatally flawed. By giving this historical episode the literary form we know as the Book of Ruth, with its surprise shock ending, she was sharing with her readership the new understanding of the way God interacts with humanity that her own alienated situation had forced upon her. This unconventional conception of a God Who, by His very nature, is hidden to the direct perceptions of human beings, was destined to have immense impact upon the developing consciousness of Israel, and ultimately of mankind, leading to a theology of Providence — God's hidden yet all-pervasive direction of human affairs — that has become central to current Judaism and Christianity. If we are correct in our conclusions, this was to prove to be a great conceptual breakthrough.

As we will attempt to show, the author of Ruth was also involved in a radical reevaluation of the role of women in society. This will have to wait until the next section. Before we discuss this we must extend our exploration of the question of authorship to the stories of Tamar and Esther, the other two tales that concern themselves with the mystery of the Hidden God. What can we determine with regard to their authorship, and what relationship, if any beyond that of theme, exists between these three narratives?

We have already suggested that both Ruth and the Joseph epic, within which the Tale of Tamar is embedded, are products of something we have referred to as "The Solomonic Enlight-

---

[15] Chapter 1, "A Woman's Tale." For the dating of Tamar see Chapter 7, especially note 49; for Esther see Chapter 8.

[16] The author's depiction of the factors that combined to further marginalize her heroines — horizontal and vertical mobility — suggest a more than passing personal acquaintance with them.

[17] See Chapter 1, note 30.

enment."[17] It has become time to gain a more comprehensive understanding of the historical period that saw the birth of some of the most brilliant and profound parts of the Bible.[18] The significance of this period was first highlighted by Gehard von Rad:

> Certain eras can be discerned which were particularly vital and productive spiritually, and which stand out in clear contrast to periods of a more conservative or stagnant character. We find the early monarchial period was supremely an era of this kind, when there was an intellectual creative upsurge which opened the way to completely new dimensions of life.... David's empire was, after the union of North and South, a state with immense possibilities of expansion ... there was a brilliant court which, for its time, stood at the zenith in the cultivation of the things of the mind. All these were factors which could not but have their effect on the innermost center of a people's life — indeed, they compelled Israel to come to a completely new understanding of herself. Now as always, she sought this understanding by way of her reflection on her historical origin.... The most important prerequisite for this new way of seeing and presenting history was a certain detachment from it ... that is, the ability to make herself the object of consideration.... The strangely remote distance at which the storytellers stand from their subjects ... is a characteristic of practically all the traditions which date from this era or which received their stamp in it.[19]

Van Rad is keenly aware of the ripple effects of David's consolidation of the loose confederation of Israelite tribes into a unified and centralized state, and the subsequent creation of an extensive empire: the progressive weakening of the clan as the base of Israelite life, urbanization and the rise of an urban elite possessing ever increasing levels of sophistication, and the wealth that permitted previously undreamed of standards of living for this new elite. All these provided a market for literary works that previously didn't exist, and a readership increasingly open to new ideas and hungry for an understanding of themselves in this dazzling new world in which they now found themselves.[20] Not being a sociologist, Von Rad either was unaware or underestimated the force of the radically increased mobility that the transition to the new age promoted, with its great increase of displaced individuals. Also not considered by Von Rad was the radical alteration in the status of women wrought by urbanization. We have called attention to the fact that prior to the age of the monarchy, in a rural society made up almost totally of peasant farmers and pastoralists, women were all part of the workforce, providing about forty percent of the labor that powered society.[21] Urbanization created a new phenomenon in Israel: a female leisure class. Adapting to the upper class norms that prevailed in the Ancient Near East, women in Jerusalem and other Israelite urban centers were increasingly segregated in women's quarters and denied occupational access. Time hung heavy on their hands. It seems reasonable to assume that, like their middle-class sisters in the recent Victorian Age, who similarly had leisure-class status forced upon them, they filled many of the empty hours with reading, and thus became a major market for literature.[22] And just as the enforced leisure of middle class Victorian women resulted in a sizeable crop of female

[18]Besides Ruth and the Joseph Epic we can with fair confidence claim that the Book of Samuel and the final form of most of the Patriarchal narratives first saw the light of day at this time. We can also connect much of the *Wisdom Literature* (see Glossary) in the Bible to this era.

[19]Rad, *Old Testament Theology*, pp. 48–50.

[20]As in all new urban elites, there also appeared a tendency to view nostalgically the simpler rural life of their fathers and grandfathers, and the pastoral life of their forefathers. This can help us understand why, despite the many harsh facts depicted in Ruth and Tamar, a rosy and semi-romantic haze hovers over both these tales.

[21]See Chapter 1.

[22]In the past it was blithely assumed that as a "primitive society," the ancient Israelites were mostly illiterate, and that women were universally so. While this attitude persists in certain circles, it is now increasingly realized that literacy was far more widespread than previously suspected, and that in upper class urban circles it was probably universal. There is no reason to exempt women from this generalization. See Appendix V: But Could She Read?

authors — writing being tolerated as a woman's pastime whereas participation in "serious" professions such as medicine or law was considered unacceptable — we suggest that during the affluent era of the United Monarchy there similarly were some leisure class women who turned their hands to writing, the author of Ruth being one of them. With this background in mind we now turn to the Joseph Epic and its "Tale of Tamar," probably a product of this same era.

In our discussion of Genesis 38 we pointed out that while the story of Tamar is woven linguistically and thematically into the larger Joseph narrative, it nonetheless forms an independent self-contained unit. The story of Joseph pauses at the end of Genesis 37, and picks up again with Genesis 39. The story of Tamar is clearly a digression from the main narrative.[23] The question that needs to be answered is: what caused the author to insert Tamar into the Joseph story? Tamar seems almost an afterthought. The oral traditions of ancient Israel stemming from the Patriarchal Age were many. Not all were used when Genesis came to be composed. If leaving Tamar out loses you little, why did the author of the Joseph narrative feel the need to preserve the story of Tamar and to include it in his carefully crafted epic?

We have already indicated that the stories of Ruth and Tamar are clearly connected, and have discussed the reasons why Ruth was probably written first.[24] One reason that springs to mind for introducing Tamar into the Joseph Epic is that the author was inspired by the appearance of the Book of Ruth to resurrect the ancient story of another "gutsy female" and tell her tale in such a way as to emphasize the long range implications of the "secular" story. By so doing the author endorses the revolutionary doctrine of a Hidden God Who achieves His ends by working through the day to day lives of the least as well as the greatest of humanity.

But this answer is not fully satisfactory. In the first place, the entire Joseph narrative is overtly "secular"; in addition to the stories of Ruth, Tamar and Esther, it is the only other overtly "secular" narrative in the Bible. Given the increasingly male dominated world of the late Solomonic era, a man would be the logical choice for the hero of any historical drama, the "precedent" of Ruth notwithstanding. Joseph, the quintessential hero obviously fitted the bill, and the message of Genesis 38 could have easily been conveyed by him. Why should an author who has already created one of the most compelling hero stories ever written decide to dilute the work by intruding the "Tamar incident," thus forcing Joseph to share the spotlight, if only momentarily?[25]

It seems to me that in those days only a woman would have ever thought of making a female the central figure of a tale. This leads me to consider the possibility that a woman, writing from a similar sense of alienation and marginality as the author of Ruth, picked on Tamar

[23]Indeed, until the linguistic evidence for "Tamar" being part of the original "Joseph" composition became overwhelming, it was commonly assumed that Genesis 38 wasn't a part of the Joseph Epic at all, and had been inserted there by a later editor, simply because he didn't know where else he could put the chapter.

[24]See Chapter 7. Von Rad considers the "J" source, which includes the Joseph epic, as having been written toward the end of the "Solomonic Enlightenment" age; or at any rate later than the cluster of narratives that relate to the rise of David (which include Ruth) (Rad, *Old Testament Theology,* p. 49, note 25).

[25]For a synopsis of the Joseph Epic and a short discussion of its significance refer to Chapter 21. We have not included a detailed analysis of Joseph in this work because, unlike the authors of the stories of Ruth, Tamar and Esther, whose strategy is to *indirectly hint* at the Hidden God's direction of human affairs and to let the reader come to his or her own conclusions, the author of the Joseph story has the hero boldly state the "moral" of the story. Additionally, it is my opinion that his purpose is not to focus on the question of where God is in a seemingly secular world — the hiddenness of God is more or less taken for granted in the story — but rather on the question of free will: in a world ruled by Providence to what extent are we free and to what extent can we call our actions our own? I hope to deal with Joseph, and the complex of issues surrounding that wonderful narrative, in a future work.

as a quintessentially marginal figure and inserted her into the epic.[26] While this line of reasoning may seem likely, it remains purely speculative. Nonetheless I feel justified in suggesting that "Tamar" may have been authored by a woman.

When we come to Esther we are on different grounds entirely. We are facing a completely different social context of authorship, at a remove of about five hundred years from that of the "Solomonic Enlightenment." In our discussion of the Book we have suggested that it was written shortly after the events it portrays, that is roughly between 470 and 420 BCE, and thus most probably during the reign of Artaxerxes I (465–424 BCE).[27]

If anything, the Persian world was far more male-dominated than that of biblical Israel. The Book of Esther has made us very aware that in Persian eyes a woman was seen not as a person but as an object. Her worth was dependent on how pleasing or useful she could be to the men who dominated her. In this kind of environment, the appearance of a book whose central figure is a woman, and moreover a book that portrays the heroine's progressive emergence from the Persian stereotype of a subservient plaything into an autonomous person, is a phenomenon that is radically out of step with its cultural milieu.

In a Persian context we would expect a hero and not a heroine. We have already suggested how easy it would have been to make Boaz the hero of the Book of Ruth[28]; it would have been equally simple to so construct The Book of Esther as to portray Mordecai as the hero, and to relegate Esther to a secondary (and subservient) status. Indeed, the Greek version of Esther known as the Alpha-Text does just this.[29] Once again we are pressed to explain why the author of the Book chose to swim against the cultural currents of the times and write the Book in such a way that a woman emerges as hero and not a man. We suspect that had a man written the Book the natural tendency would have been to make a man the hero. Only a woman would have thought of making a woman the pivot around which the Book turns. And the fact that a major subtext of the Book follows the self-transformation of Esther from a subservient object into the predominant figure, into the prime initiator, to whom everyone reacts, merely strengthens the suspicion. In those days who but a woman would have thought to deal with such a theme, much less to portray it so well from a women's point of view?

What we are suggesting is that it seems highly probable that Ruth was written by a woman, that the author of Esther was likely a woman, and also that the author of Genesis 38 was possibly a woman, though the evidence here is less compelling. This thesis does more than merely explain the anomaly of works featuring women in the lead roles appearing in a world where male heroes were the norm, but also accounts for the link between heroines and the radical theology of a Hidden God. Only marginalized persons would be able to question and challenge the accepted consensus of the societies in which they dwelt. And women, marginalized by virtue of their gender, possibly doubly or even triply marginal as were the heroines they wrote of, were natural candidates to "think out of the box." They could see issues everyone else unconsciously swept under the rug and propose new approaches to the human condition. Seen from this per-

---

[26]In this context it may be of interest to call attention to the noted literary critic, Harold Bloom, who in *The Book of J*, a work co-authored with David Rosenberg, has suggested that the entire "J" source (which includes the Joseph narrative) was authored by a woman (Bloom, *The Book of J*, pp. 9–10, 19). For the history of the suggestion that "J" may have been authored by a woman, see the conclusion of Appendix V.

[27]Chapter 8.

[28]Chapter 1, "A Woman's Tale."

[29]See note 8 above. It would appear that the prejudice against a woman assuming a leading role was so strong in some circles that despite the fact that the Book was named the Book of Esther (or in Hebrew *Megillat Esther*— "The scroll of Esther"), in the first surviving extra-biblical reference to the holiday of Purim it is referred to as "The Day of Mordecai!" (2 Maccabees 15:36).

spective one can postulate the existence of an entire tradition of "woman's literature" persisting from the days of Ancient Israel's early monarchy to the very end of the Biblical Period, the three works we have been studying being merely the best examples that made it into the Bible.[30] The overwhelming majority of these works authored by women, if they existed, would have been lost, along with the rest of the vast literature produced in the Biblical Age of which we have only tantalizing hints. From the examples we have before us perhaps we can guess at what the general tenor of these lost works may have been.

Pursuing a New Identity

To this point in our investigation of Ruth, Tamar and Esther we have been focusing on an attempt to discover the presence of God in a seemingly secular world, leading to a radical new theology of God's hiddenness. We have seen both secularism and the idea of a Hidden God forced to their furthest logical conclusions: that existence without God results in an irrational, even insane, world; that the concept of a Hidden God leads to the intuition that we are all players in a vast, cosmic drama directed by Providence, toward unimaginable ends. The time has now come to shift our attention to another theme, one to which we have given less than full attention. Beyond their theological preoccupations, these works featuring women as their protagonists are all struggling with the issue of redefining the identity and the self-understanding of women.

The identity of a woman in the ancient world was determined by the society into which she was born: a world made by men and for men. To be sure, no society ever remains static, and so the status of women varied with the shifts in the social system, but it was always the male dominated society that determined how a woman was seen, and, more importantly, how she saw herself. Women accepted their identities from outside themselves, and so lived lives built on models that they themselves had not shaped. The Books are thus proposing a startling departure — and perhaps initially this was an almost unthinkable departure — from these norms: women should take their lives into their own hands and determine for themselves who and what they should be. In these Books we are shown women who find the strength to swim against the current of a male dominated world and to carve out lives for themselves in the light of their own desires. If we are correct that it was women who authored these works, then we may conclude that we are being presented with models to be emulated, and behind these presentations lies an agenda promoting female self-determination.

It is important to view such an agenda within its historical context. As we noted in the first chapter of this book, the economic exigencies of a pre-industrial subsistence peasant society in the first centuries of life in Ancient Israel made the full-time participation of women in the work force a necessity. As Carol Meyers has pointed out, this in turn led to a social structure best described not as a gender hierarchy but as the coexistence of two worlds, a man's world and a woman's world, each with its own structures and institutions.[31] The close cooperation between these two worlds, in the manner of two horses hitched to a wagon, was what made economic survival possible.[32] We have seen in the Book of Ruth an example of this symbiotic relationship: the men in Bethlehem find their voice in the "elders in the gate," while the women of Bethlehem find theirs in the "women's chorus," each voice predominant in its own sphere. When the Book of Ruth was written, this early semi-egalitarian world that is depicted was already in an advanced

---

[30]This "woman's literature" would be far from unique in the Ancient Near East, which possessed a tradition of female authorship dating back some 1400 years before the age of the "Solomonic Enlightenment." See Appendix V: But Could She Read?

[31]Meyers, "Returning Home," pp. 98–99.

[32]See Chapter 1, "Life as It Was Really Lived."

stage of dissolution.[33] David's startling achievement of a unified state and empire had led inevitably to a new socio-economic configuration: urbanization, a new role for commerce and finance, the rise of a military hierarchy and much more. In this new world, which overshadowed and dominated the rural countryside, woman's role deteriorated from that of a valued economic partner to that of a progenitor of children and a plaything of men. In this, the imported social norms of the Ancient Near East increasingly replaced the more egalitarian norms of ancient Israel.[34]

It is against this background that one must view the aura of nostalgia that pervades the Book of Ruth. The author, writing in the context of a declining female status, is not only promoting a model of female autonomy but also idealizing a lost past when that goal had been at least partly achieved. In this sense Ruth can be viewed as a species of protest literature. For women, the Age of Ruth was, comparatively speaking, a golden age, the likes of which would not be seen again for the remainder of the Biblical Era.

The significant rise in living standards and sophistication that the urban revolution engendered, and the new leisure status afforded to upper class women, made both high literature and women's authorship possible. These possibilities came, however, at a price: the concomitant increasing irrelevance of women to economic productivity which brought with it increasing marginalization.

In Ruth's days women circulated freely, gleaning and working in the fields side by side with men. The story of Tamar, written perhaps a generation or two after Ruth, depicts the brutal victimization of a child bride by the men in her life. Although the narrative is set in a much earlier social milieu, I take the tone of the narrative to reflect an even later stage than Ruth in the marginalization of women during the "Solomonic Enlightenment." The energy and courage necessary to take charge of one's life has become infinitely greater.

If we see Ruth and Tamar as points on a curve of ever increasing marginalization, we reach the outer limits in Esther. Here woman has been reduced by Persian warrior society to the status of a soft porn fantasy: beautiful, sexy, docile and subservient. Imprisoned in a harem, permanently on call (but forever forbidden to initiate), Esther is even pressured by the man who has dominated her life to conceal her identity as a Jew. Yet even here, the author insists it is possible for a woman to take control of her life and forge for herself an inner identity worthy of the name.

In sum, through the heroines they hold up for acclaim, all these works agree on an ideal of an autonomous woman: she should be self-reliant rather than dependent on others, inner-directed rather than outer-directed, active as opposed to passive.

Beyond the progression of ever-increasing marginalization depicted in these works, which call for ever-increasing levels of effort and courage to counter it, they also chart a widening of the goals a woman should set for herself. Ruth and Tamar assert themselves not only in order to rebuild their own lives but also to promote a larger issue: that of assuring the future of their respective families. For them the family was their horizon. With Esther we encounter a sudden broadening of perspective. In widening her horizon to encompass her entire people, and by asserting herself to save them, she becomes their leader. Esther established the role of public figure as a legitimate ideal for women. At the culminating stages of the Biblical Age a woman is no longer pictured as confined to family concerns but is portrayed on the national stage, the traditional arena of men, competing and succeeding. By portraying a woman successfully manipulating the levers of power of the Persian Empire, the author of Esther is insisting that there are

[33]At least one hundred years separate the time of Ruth and Naomi depicted in the Book from the "Solomonic Enlightenment" that is the probable period in which Ruth was written.

[34]This was far less true of farm life as lived by the overwhelming majority of the population. Rural life proved resistant to change, but even in the countryside the changes in women's status was felt; it is the city that sets the style for the rural hinterland, and not the other way around.

women who can function on the big stage at parity with the best of men. It is also assumed that it is legitimate that they should do so.[35]

For two thousand years, ever since the Bible was canonized, myriads of people have been reading these Books, but the clear — even blatant — message of these role models has been lost on most of them. As in the days of the Bible, the accepted norms of society and the conventional way of seeing things form barriers to understanding life from a different point of view. Even today, with all the changes in social norms and the widening of horizons typical in the Western World, most men and women have not as yet internalized the role models presented by the remarkable authors of Genesis 38, the Book of Ruth and the Book of Esther.

One last and speculative thought: could it be that the women's issues so manifest in our texts are meant to serve as a symbol for a larger issue? The thought is worth entertaining. Both *Ruth* and "Tamar" are focused on what are often termed "domestic issues": getting a husband, bringing forth children, continuing family lines. Even *Esther* begins in an atmosphere of domesticity — attracting a man's attention, becoming his mate and keeping his interest and affection (only inadvertently does Esther get drawn into the man's world of power politics). As we have seen, our narratives are insisting that the Hand of God is at work even in these small, very human affairs — invisible because of the temporal scale of God's designs.

The idea that God's Hand invisibly directs human affairs is a familiar idea in the Bible, but with our cases being the prime exceptions, it is through power politics that the Hidden Hand is mostly seen to manifest Itself. We tend to see politics and power — the man's world — as important, and domesticity as trivial and unworthy of attention; this was almost certainly even more the case in the Ancient Near East. Against this male-oriented bias, our texts insist that in the long view, in God's view, these domestic trivialities are the raw material out of which God engineers His far-reaching designs. In the long view, what in our eyes are the vastly different concerns of women and men dwindle to an equal significance, both meaningful in the larger picture only in their utility in achieving God's ends. Putting the matter slightly differently, what I am suggesting is that women and "domestic affairs" are being used to represent *all* human activity: in the long term, we are being told, all of humanity's concerns — power, dominance and wars included — are no more than domestic affairs, mere grist for God's mill.

As in every age, even now, the Bible is the most modern and most relevant of books.

The End of the Matter

We have come to some startling conclusions in this book: possible female authorship of three biblical narratives, an ancient reevaluation, revolutionary for its time, of the status and the role of women in the world, and, of the highest significance, a new way of looking at the relationship between man and God. And while the idea of women as authors and female autonomy is increasingly acceptable nowadays (though some may find it hard to accept that these stances could have been proposed in antiquity), it is with the concept of a Hidden God Who providentially governs the world that many readers may find their real difficulty. For secular readers a theological revolution may seem to be at the most a historical curiosity, and it is to these readers that the following paragraphs are primarily directed.

Whether or not you, the reader, accept the theological conclusions proposed by the authors of Ruth, Esther, and Genesis 38, the insight that underwrote them is of independent — and contemporary — interest: to wit, that a radical disproportion between time-scales results in slower-paced events being invisible to short-lived creatures. Much of our world is invisible to

[35]The ideal portrayed is not new. It is merely a return to the earliest days of the First Commonwealth. Several generations prior to Ruth, at the height of the Age of the Judges, a woman, Deborah, combined in her person the role of both political and spiritual leader of all Israel. She was also, incidentally, a superb poet (see Judges 4–5).

us, simply because of our short life-span, and the ungraspable structures of time that encompass us of necessity escape our understanding. That should be a humbling thought and one that merits our serious consideration. We have also suggested that the texts that developed this thesis were women's texts: narratives written by women, and presumably with a female audience in mind. If we are correct, then it was a literature of feminine provenance that first advanced the idea that our knowledge of and engagement with our world is startlingly limited, due to the shortness and pace of human life.

In my view, the question of why it was women who first put forth this idea is also a problem deserving serious thought. These are issues that readers who do not share a religious point of view with the ancient thinkers who authored these narratives can yet appreciate.

To return to the religious issue, I began this work by promising to remain neutral. I have thus attempted to analyze three ancient texts from a literary and historical point of view, and have attempted to elucidate what they were trying to say and what possible significance their message might have. In so doing I treated these texts as works written by human authors, and scrupulously avoided any speculation as to divine influence or inspiration. Having identified myself as a religious person, you may have wondered how I personally see these works. Do I consider them as purely human works, or do I see them as the Word of God?

I would like to address this question by returning to a central insight embedded in the texts themselves: the question of scale. Taken by itself, any given text looks like the product of a specific place and a specific period, one whose literary strategies are to be accounted for in terms of the background and aims of its author. What such a text has to say is strictly limited by its provenance. Yet when we widen our perspective, and view these narratives as making up a literary tradition extending over some hundreds of years, they turn out to advance a unified, coherent and increasingly sophisticated theological proposal — and approach to history.

Once taken together, these texts begin to speak to us in a different voice. They are telling us that we are to see them as they tell us that we are to see history. Just as the Hidden God in history only becomes visible when we shift our perspective, looking back over the span of generations, even centuries, in much the same manner, only when we move to a perspective from which we can see the centuries-long tradition all at once does the religious point of view become visible.

I would like to suggest that we are being provided with more than the theories that we have been recapitulating. We are being provided as well with reading instructions for these works and for the Bible as a whole. Like many other sophisticated artifacts, these texts tell the reader how they are intended to be read. And I propose that they were incorporated into canon because, among other reasons, the canonizers meant to endorse those reading instructions.

In the case of Esther we have spent much time making these instructions explicit. Although we have not gone into the same detail with Ruth and the story of Tamar, they too have imbedded instructions as to how they should be read. Only if we follow these instructions does the full picture they present rise into view, and the picture they present to us is a religious picture.

The final suggestion that I want to leave with the reader is that the issue at hand is not whether the reader is approaching these writings from a religious or from a secular point of view. It is rather an issue of biblical literacy. If one is to navigate the Books of the Bible competently, one requires an awareness of the self-understanding of the texts. The texts not only contain messages, but also tell you how they want you to figure out what they are. Not understanding this, or willfully disregarding the instructions, will lead to a misreading of the text or texts in question. These texts demand that you take the long perspective, see them within the context of the centuries-long tradition of which they are a part and read them as religious texts. Once read this way the secular person will understand the content of the message; the religious person will hear in it echoes of the Word of God.

From Whom Did Boaz Buy the Field?

The resolution of the drama of Ruth revolves around the question of who is willing to "redeem" a field that had once belonged to Elimelech. This confrontation in front of a convened court and a large assembly of lookers-on at the gate of Bethlehem can only be understood within the context of the laws of land ownership and the laws of inheritance in Ancient Israel; issues that the author could take for granted and that readers of the Book understood perfectly. We, on the other hand, are faced with an alien milieu that our backgrounds ill equip us to understand. To further muddy the waters, I believe that the way the "confrontation at the gate" has been worded has led to almost universal misunderstanding, not only of the specific scene depicted but also of its implications which reverberate backward to the very opening lines of the Book. The seemingly obscure question of who held title to the field that Boaz ultimately "redeems" thus demands serious scrutiny.

We begin our analysis by stating the problem. The verses in question, as we have them, translated literally, read:

> Then he [Boaz] said to the Redeemer [the next-in-kin to Elimelech]: "The portion of the field that belonged to our brother, Elimelech, was sold by Naomi, she who has returned from the land of Moab. Now I said [to myself] that I will lay it open to you,[1] saying: 'Buy it in the presence of those sitting here, and in the presence of the elders of my people.' If you will Redeem it, Redeem it; but if you will not Redeem it, tell me, that I may know; for there is no one else to Redeem it but you, and I come after you." And he said: "I will Redeem it" (4:3–4).

Most scholars understand this to mean that Naomi holds title to the land that had belonged to her late husband, Elimelech, and wants to sell it, or is offering it up for sale, and thus they render the verse. But this violates the plain sense of the statement. The verb *sell* in the Hebrew text is in the perfect tense, which designates an action already completed. In English this is rendered as the past tense: "was sold."[2] To render it as "is selling," "has put up for sale," or "wants to sell" and so forth is a real stretch.

Leaving the question of grammar aside, the real problem lies in the question: does Naomi really have any land to sell? And if so, where did she get it? Starting with the statement that the

---

[1] Literally, "unstop your ears."

[2] Another way to render the verse, in poorer English but perhaps greater accuracy would be: "The portion of the field that belonged to our brother, Elimelech, has Naomi sold, she who has returned from the land of Moab."

land had belonged to her late husband, Elimelech, (and indeed it must have, otherwise what is the whole business of *Redeeming* about?) we face a basic problem: in Ancient Israel *widows did not inherit from their husbands*. The laws of inheritance were very clear: a man's property was inherited by his sons (and if there were no sons, by his daughters). If he had no offspring, then his oldest living brother inherited from him, and lacking a brother then the inheritance passed to the nearest male blood relative.[3] That this was very unfair to the widow is patently true, but that is the way the law was: widows did not inherit. Could Elimelech have willed his field to her? He could not; the field was entailed. This means that the owner had no discretion as to who would inherit the field upon his death; the field had to pass by the strict laws of inheritance.[4]

This leads us to a further problem. Elimelech did not die without heirs. He had two sons who survived him. At his death any property that he possessed automatically passed to Machlon and Chilion.[5] Upon their childless deaths, the land would have passed to their nearest male relative, "Mr. So-and-so."[6] This leads us to the absurdity that Boaz is proposing to this relative of the late Elimelech that he buy a piece of property that *by law he already owns*!

There remains yet a further impediment to the assumption that Naomi has legal title to a piece of land that she is now offering for sale. Setting aside the question of what has happened to the land in the twelve years or more that they have been out of the country (did it lie fallow? was someone farming it?), we find Naomi and Ruth in abject poverty upon their return to Bethlehem, living off what Ruth can bring in by gleaning. If Naomi holds title to the land, and this is the harvest season, why doesn't she claim the produce of her land rather than scrounging from strangers?

---

[3]Numbers 27:8–11 defines nearest male relative as uncles (the brothers of his father), and lacking these "you shall assign his inheritance to the nearest relative in his own clan, and he shall inherit it" (Numbers 27:11).

[4]Various scholars attempt to avoid this conclusion by adopting one of three strategies. (1) They assume that the Book of Ruth was written at a late date, in the Persian period (538–330 BCE), and by that time the strict laws of inheritance, current during the First Commonwealth, had been relaxed to allow a childless widow to inherit her husband. This late legal situation was then, most unhistorically, read back into the Age of the Judges for the purposes of the story (which, needless to say, has little historical basis according to this school of thought). (2) Another school of thought proposes the exact opposite: it holds that the Book of Ruth was written early (during the Early or the Middle Monarchy, 1000–720 BCE), while the laws of inheritance in Numbers (which belong to the hypothetical P Document) were codified and promulgated in the post-exilic age (after 538 BCE). This scenario assumes that in the age of the Judges widows did inherit, and only later did reactionary legislation deprive them of their rights. For neither of these scenarios is there any evidence. (3) And lastly some, again against all the evidence, simply *assume* that widows *must have* inherited or that, in the specific case of Naomi, she *must have been* appointed (by whom?) as guardian of the property until such time as it could be transferred to a hypothetical unborn heir.

The source of all the above speculation is the problem that the text seems to clearly state that it was Naomi that sold the land; that Naomi, despite having sold, still holds title to the land, and that Boaz acquired either the land or the right to redeem it from Naomi. I admit this basic difficulty, but contend that in the light of the compounded difficulties to the entire structure and meaning of the Book as a whole entailed in accepting any of the above positions, overlooking the text's statements that it is from Naomi that Boaz acquires the land (or more likely the rights of *Redemption*) is by far the lesser of the evils. I think that it is wiser to admit that, at the present stage of our knowledge the text as it stands is incomprehensible, and that we have no alternative but to opt for the understanding, however imperfect, that does the least violence to the thrust of the Book as a whole and the evidence of the Bible as a whole. (For a fuller discussion of entailed estates in Ancient Israel, and the rationale that lay behind this institution, see Chapter 1.)

[5]Even if we are content to overlook the laws of inheritance that stipulate that only males inherit, as do various scholars, we still face the problem that the property would still not have passed to Naomi but to Ruth and Orpah, the widows of Machlon and Chilion.

[6]The *"Redeemer"* who is the object of Boaz's proposal.

All this leads me to conclude that the assumption that Naomi somehow held title to a field that her late husband had possessed is a gross error. I accept the picture the entire Book presents: Naomi and Ruth, after having lost everything in Moab, return penniless to the Land of Judah to live in penury from Ruth's gleanings.

So what happened to Elimelech's field? We are told. If we are willing to accept the plain meaning of the word, it had been *sold* (obviously by Elimelech, the only person who had the legal right to sell it), and this obviously prior to his death, and almost certainly before his departure.[7] The field is in the hands of some stranger, and has been so for a dozen years or more.

[7]In the conditions of those days it would be hard to see how he could have sold it in absentia.

APPENDIX II

Can Judah and Tamar Be Fitted into the Joseph Narrative?

In many ways Genesis 38, the story of Judah and Tamar, seems an artificial intrusion into the Joseph saga. It breaks the flow of the narrative, as Genesis 39 (Joseph's travails beginning with his arrival in Egypt) follows directly upon Genesis 37 (the tale of Joseph's betrayal by his brothers and his sale to slave dealers who take him to Egypt). But while the various strands of the larger narrative may have been transmitted orally for centuries as separate stories, it has been demonstrated conclusively that the Saga of Joseph and his Brothers as we know it today (Genesis 37–50) is the work of a single author, and that the story of Judah and Tamar fits in seamlessly as an integral part of the greater literary masterpiece.[1] This unity, however, poses a serious problem of chronology: too much seems to be packed into too few years.

Simply stated the problem is as follows: Joseph is declared to be 17 years of age at the time of his betrayal by his brothers (Genesis 37:2), and 30 years old when he becomes viceroy of Egypt (Genesis 41:46). As the descent of Jacob into Egypt and the reunification of the family there takes place after two years of famine (Genesis 45:11), to the 13 years of Joseph's rise to power must be added the "Seven Years of Plenty" and the first two years of the famine, making a total of 22 years from the time Judah initiated Joseph's sale into slavery and the descent of the family, including Judah, into Egypt. Can all the events related in Genesis 38 — Judah's marriage, the birth of his three sons, their growth to maturity, the marriage of two of them to Tamar, their deaths, Tamar's return to her parent's home, her gradual discovery that she had been abandoned, her subsequent seduction of Judah, her pregnancy and the birth of her twin sons — can all this somehow be fitted into a mere 22 years? And if this were not difficult enough, we are informed that when the family migrated to Egypt, not only were Tamar's sons Perez and Zerah listed as part of the company, but her grandsons, Hezron and Hamul, are included in the list of the migrants as well (Genesis 46:12)! This would seem to imply the passage of yet another generation before the descent into Egypt.

The real question here is: how could the author of the Joseph Saga not be cognizant of

[1]"Many readers have sensed this tale of Judah and Tamar as an 'interruption' of the Joseph story, or, at best, as a means of building suspense about Joseph's fate in Egypt. In fact, there is an intricate network of connections with what precedes and what follows" (Alter, *Genesis*, p. 217). "This digression heightens the reader's suspense at a critical moment in the Joseph narrative, but the skillful blending of the chapter into the larger story shows that the digression is deliberate and the result of careful literary design.... The present chapter, then, provides a foil to the Joseph-centered episodes" (Sarna, *Genesis*, pp. 263–64). See also Chapter 7, note 6.

the impossibility of this simple calculation from the data that he himself has so carefully supplied? Or perhaps a better way of phrasing the question would be: how did he view the events so as to make it credible in his eyes to present the events he relates within the time frame he provides?[2]

Let us begin with the biggest problem: the inclusion of Tamar's grandsons, Hezron and Hamul, in the list of the migrants to Egypt. But wait a moment, *is* the list of names in Genesis 46:8–27 really a list of the persons who migrated with Jacob from Canaan to Egypt? It includes the names of Er and Onan who died in Canaan (Genesis 46:12 admits this fact). The list also includes Joseph's sons, Manasseh and Ephraim, who were born in Egypt and so were never part of the group that came to Egypt (46:20, 27). What we have here is not a list of migrants but a list of the sons of Jacob who founded the tribes of Israel, and of their descendents who founded the clans that made up those tribes.[3] U. Cassuto has pointed out that the terminology used to introduce the names of Tamar's grandchildren is unlike that used to introduce everyone else except the sons of Joseph. His conclusion is that just as Joseph's sons were born in Egypt, so were Hezron and Hamul.[4]

Having disposed of Tamar's grandchildren in Genesis 46:12, we return to the events related in Genesis 38. Can all these events be credibly confined within the compass of twenty-two years? Both Cassuto and N. Sarna show that they can.[5] If Judah separated from his brothers, moved to Adulam and married in the same year that Joseph was sold into Egypt, and if his three sons were then born in rapid succession, then four years would more than suffice for this section of our chapter. Another fourteen years would be sufficient to bring Er to the marriageable age of sixteen. Assuming Er dies shortly after marriage, and Onan then married the widow, only to quickly follow his brother to the grave, we are talking of less than a year. If Tamar then waited two years until Selah reached 16 years of age before realizing that she had been hung out to dry, we have covered a total of twenty years from the start of our tale. This leaves two years for Tamar to seduce Judah, give birth to twins, and they to be brought down to Egypt as infants.

The timing is tight but certainly possible. The author of the sagas, as able to do the calculation as we, would know that the narrative as he penned it contained no inherent chronological impossibilities. Whether the events actually occurred as he described them is another matter, one that we have no way of knowing. Writing a minimum of six hundred years after

---

[2]We have to remember that the author was under no compulsion to set up a 22-year time frame. He could simply have kept quiet about how old Joseph was at each stage of the narrative, and so conceal the very existence of a problem. To go out of his way to give the relevant chronological information means that he saw no inherent difficulty in fitting the events he relates into the time frame he himself created.

[3]Numbers 26:5–51 makes all this specific. The tribe of Judah is listed as made up of five clans. The first three are familiar to us: the clans founded by Shelah, Perez and Zerah, the three surviving sons of Judah. But then, strangely, Er and Onan are also listed as sons of Judah. By rights they too should have founded clans, but "Er and Onan died in the land of Canaan" (26:19). Who then takes their place? Judah's grandsons, the sons of Perez: Hezron and Hamul. They founded the clans of the Hezronites and the Hamulites (26:21), thus insuring that Judah does not end up short two clans.

[4]"The meaning of the passage in Genesis xlvi 12 ... now becomes self-evident in all its details: '*The sons of Judah: Er, Onan, Shelah, Perez and Zerah,*' that is to say, these five were born to Judah before he went down to Egypt; '*but Er and Onan died in the land of Canaan,*' that is, although these two sons were not among those who emigrated to Egypt, nevertheless, '*there were the sons of Perez, Hezron and Hamul,*' who represented Er and Onan, and consequently retained their place among the sons of Judah. [Thus we] come to the conclusion that Hezron and Hamul did not emigrate to Egypt" (Cassuto, "The Story of Judah and Tamar," pp. 38–39. The lengthy analysis that leads to this conclusion begins on p. 35. Italics indicating biblical quotation added).

[5]*Ibid.*, pp. 39–40; Sarna, *Genesis*, pp. 264–65.

the events he is depicting, he also would have had no way of knowing. All he could do was to rely on his sources[6] and so shape his narrative as to embody the messages he was trying to convey in the most elegant manner possible while avoiding internal contradictions and blatant impossibilities. In this he was brilliantly successful.

[6]"There is much in the narrative that testifies to great antiquity. Judah's wanderings take place in the border regions of the future tribe, not in its main area of settlement. He is not portrayed as a conqueror or even as a settler. He is still a pastoral nomad, not a city dweller. There is no hostility or tension between him and the Canaanites; later tradition would hardly have invented the uncomfortable account of a marriage to one. Thus the image of the tribe of Judah reflected here is, in general, not that of the post-conquest situation.... Finally, both the fact that no stigma is attached to what would, in later times, be the offspring of an incestuous marriage and the Narrator's need to offer an apologia for Judah's behavior ... combine to confirm an early date for the details of the action" (Sarna, *Genesis*, p. 264).

APPENDIX III

It's Greek to Me:
The Greek Versions of Esther

The Greek versions of Esther are very different than the Greek versions with which we have become slightly acquainted in our perusal of the tales of Ruth and Tamar. The Septuagint (LXX) of both Ruth and Genesis are quite literal translations of the Hebrew text. Such is not the case when we come to Esther.

In the first place, there are two separate and distinct Greek versions of Esther, not one: the Septuagint and the Alpha- (or A-) Text. Beyond being in Greek, they are united in that neither of them is a literal translation of the Hebrew; they both are "literary translations." By this I mean that while they render the surface meaning of the Hebrew text, verse by verse, they make no attempt to preserve the word order, or even use the exact wording and idiom of the Hebrew original. They do not so much as translate as they paraphrase. They are also united in currently containing six blocks of text (called Additions A–F) which are totally alien to the Hebrew text. More on these Additions later. Beyond this, the two versions are very different.

They differ in length, the A-Text (AT) being shorter than the Masoretic or Hebrew text (MT), while the Septuagint (LXX) is much longer than the A-Text, and even MT. This is due to different evaluations with regard to exactly where the Hebrew text is "deficient." The A-Text (AT) finds the Hebrew text it sets out to translate as seriously deficient in style. There are, for example, numerous repetitions in the Hebrew. Not recognizing the role repetition plays in biblical Hebrew, it treats repetitions as redundancies and, in the interest of good (Hellenistic Greek) literary style, deletes them. (This fault is also characteristic of LXX.) In addition, its authors do not understand the use of repeated words that are used sometimes for emphasis, sometimes as key words to clue the reader into a theme, sometimes as connectives to tie the narrative to some other part of the Book or of the Bible. The AT routinely replaces them with synonyms.[1] Further, the AT frequently omits personal names, numbers and dates. In sum, partially due to an insensitivity to the nuances of biblical Hebrew, and partially due to what amounts to oversensitivity to the niceties of Greek style, the A-Text heavily edits the Hebrew text, and not only edits, but radically cuts. For example, most of the material in chapters 8–9 of Esther is omitted. The result is a much shorter and tighter version of Esther that is literarily more elegant in terms of Greek style, and, while rendering the story line, misses much of what makes Esther

---

[1]See Introduction, "Conventions and Context," for the signals conveyed by the biblical literary convention of repetition.

more than just a "good read." In other words, the AT sacrifices depth and subtlety for a smooth, elegant style.

But more significantly, the focus of AT differs from that of the Masoretic Text. As Karen Jobes puts it:

> As it now stands, the AT is a version of the Esther story that, in comparison to the MT, magnifies Mordecai's role and minimizes Esther's. Instead of highlighting the origin of Purim, it amplifies the political dynamics of the Jews in relationship to a pagan empire powerful enough to threaten their very existence.... [T]he AT emphasizes that Jews in positions of political power benefit not only the Jewish community, but the king and the empire as well.[2]

The AT was almost certainly the first Greek version of Esther, speaking to the issues of Hellenization during the chaotic period following Alexander's conquests. The Septuagint (LXX), a later and more authoritative translation, then supplanted it. AT then fell into disuse, and today is known only through four medieval manuscripts.

The LXX is a different matter entirely. It sees the "fundamental failures" of the Hebrew Esther in that it is not "sufficiently religious" and that it lacks dramatic verve and colorful detail. It sets out to remedy these "deficiencies" by means of additions. God is inserted into Esther, as are the religious practices of prayer, circumcision, and kashrut (the Jewish dietary laws). This "improvement" is achieved through tinkering here and there with the text (an example: by inserting the words "were circumcised"[3] into 8:17, LXX injects religion), and by means of grafting six large blocks of text (known as Additions A–F)[4] into MT.

These additions serve several purposes: they transform the heroes of the Book from secular, marginal Jews (as they are portrayed in MT) into pious, God-fearing and religiously observant Jews (Addition C: "The Prayers of Mordecai and Esther" and, to a lesser degree, Addition F: "The Interpretation of Mordecai's Dream"). They add "dramatic color" (Addition D: "Esther Appears Before the King Un-summoned"). They provide motivations where in MT these are lacking, being left for the reader to ponder (Addition C: why Mordecai won't bow to Haman). They provide "official documentation" to underwrite the historicity of the tale (Additions B and E: "The First and Second Letters of the King"). And finally, they transmute the natural, secular background into a supernatural setting (Additions A and F: "Mordecai's Dream" and "The Interpretation of the Dream").

The sum of these changes, both small (adding a word here, a phrase there) and large, is to create a very different book than the biblical Esther. A secular work has been turned into a religious one brimming with God-fearing heroes and pious platitudes. A lean and focused drama has been turned into a draggy[5] Hellenistic romantic melodrama. All the big issues have either been papered over (the absence of God by superimposing Him everywhere) or trivialized (the central issue of anti–Semitism is reduced to an old grudge between the families of Mordecai and Haman). Finally the text has been doctored so as to "Biblicise" it; that is to make it artificially

---

[2]Jobes, *The Alpha-Text of Esther*, p. 225.

[3]MT reads literally: "And many from among the peoples of the land became Jews." LXX alters this to read: "And many of the Gentiles were circumcised and became Jews." While *Gentiles* may be considered a legitimate paraphrase of "peoples of the land," the words "were circumcised" are a blatant insertion whose purpose is not to translate the text but rather to "improve it."

[4]Moore thinks that these additions are original to LXX and were copied from there into AT (Moore, "Esther, Additions to," p. 630). On the other hand, Jobes believes that they were not original to LXX (excepting possibly Additions B and E), but were copied from AT, then altered to bring them into line with the ideological perceptions of LXX (Jobes, *The Alpha Text of Esther*, p. 232).

[5]All this padding adds 40 percent to the size of LXX as compared to MT: an additional 107 verses!

resemble the late biblical Books of Daniel, Ezra, and Nehemiah. The "Dream of Mordecai" and its interpretation are in clear imitation of the dreams and visions of Daniel and, to a lesser extent, those of the Book of Zechariah. The "Letters of the King" are designed to make Esther resemble Ezra and Nehemiah, which include summaries and direct quotations from Persian official documents. The inclusion of these last additions (which really add nothing to the narrative) seems to be deserving of nothing so much as the classic remark of Pooh-Bah: "Merely corroborative detail, intended to give artistic verisimilitude to an otherwise bald and unconvincing narrative."[6]

While Judaism canonized the version of the Hebrew text we know as MT (probably very close, if not virtually identical, to the original version of Esther) and which we find in the Hebrew Bible today, the early Church adopted LXX as its canonical version. It remains so in the Eastern Church to this day. And it was LXX that formed the basis of the Old Latin translation (OL) that was the first official version of the Western or Catholic Church.

It is to the credit of St Jerome that, when he undertook his translation of the Bible into Latin,[7] he became deeply uneasy upon comparing the LXX with the Hebrew MT that, as he knew, was the Jewish canonical version of Esther. Not only were the sections that are today called Additions A–F not to be found in the Hebrew, but also, as he was quick to note, actually contradicted MT. His solution was to remove them from the text, and tack them on as appendices to Esther, counting them as Chapters 11–16. Jerome's translation (known as the Vulgate) became the official Bible of the Catholic Church, and as such these Additions, while still considered canonical by the Church, remained an appendage to the Book of Esther proper. The Protestant Churches, when they arose, rejected the Additions as non-canonical and removed them to the Apocrypha.

It is the Hebrew version of Esther, the Masoretic Text (MT), which is the text used for this book.

---

[6]Gilbert, *The Mikado*, Act II.

[7]Jerome translated the Hebrew Bible into Latin in Bethlehem between the years 390 and 405 CE.

Mordecai's Decree:
A Technical Interlude

In Chapter 17 we have drawn attention to the uncertainties surrounding our understanding of the decree issued by Mordecai to counter Haman's edict. The ambiguity of the text (8:11–13) proceeds directly from a difficult sentence structure that creates grammatical confusion. We tried to account for this strange example of bad writing in an otherwise well written work by citing three factors. In the first place, the decree was originally written in Persian; what we have before us is a Hebrew translation of the original, and one that is quite possibly not a particularly good translation, but one that slavishly copies the word order of the original. Second, the decree was written in the bureaucratic jargon of the government service. Either or both of these factors could account for the poor and confusing style.

But even without these two factors there is a third that would ensure confusion. It was Robert Gordis who pointed out that Mordecai's decree contains quotations from the previous edict of Haman.[1] I have attempted to show that Mordecai's decree is largely composed of phrases cut out of Haman's edict, rearranged, and embedded in the new "composition." No wonder the end result is not only stylistically poor but also confusing. But for whatever the reasons, this is the version of Mordecai's decree that we have before us,[2] and it is our business to make sense of it.

In dealing with the ambiguous grammatical construction of the decree, the agenda for modern commentators was set, as in so many of the issues pertaining to Esther, by L.B. Paton. Almost a hundred years ago, in trying to determine the subject of the decree and the object, he reached the following conclusions:

---

[1]Gordis, "Studies in the Esther Narrative," p. 52. That the decree contains quotations is not immediately evident since ancient Hebrew possessed neither quotation marks nor any other means to mark a passage as a quotation. Gordis, in a series of studies that he cites in the above article, has demonstrated that quoting (without any formal indication that one is doing so), besides being a regular occurrence in biblical and rabbinic literature, was also standard practice in the literatures of the Ancient Near East; he cites Sumerian, Akkadian, Egyptian and Ugaritic examples.

[2]LXX contains another version of the decree in Addition E, but this long and rambling composition has no intrinsic relation to the Hebrew text ("Modern scholars agree that ... Additions B and E are too florid and rhetorical to be anything but Greek in origin" Moore, *AB Esther*, p. LXIII–LXIV). Its purpose is to "improve" and "clarify" our text. See Appendix III: It's Greek to Me.

Children and women might grammatically be the subject of the preceding infinitives, but this gives no good sense.[3]

In other words, Paton refused to read the text as if it says:

The king's edict granted the Jews in every city the right to assemble and protect themselves, to destroy, kill, and annihilate any armed force of any nationality or province that might attack them and their women and children.[4]

because, though perfectly possible grammatically, it doesn't make "good sense." However, he refrained from explaining exactly why this doesn't make "good sense." Paton then went on to say:

Accordingly, in spite of the absence of a conj[unctive] we must regard *children and women*, like *armed force*, as objects to *kill, slay, and annihilate*.[5]

In other words, while admitting that the grammar is questionable, he preferred to read the verse as if it says:

the king allowed the Jews who were in every city to gather and defend their lives, to destroy, to slay, and to annihilate any armed force of any people or province that might attack them, with their children and women.[6]

The difference is that in following the grammatical reading that Paton rejects, the decree says that the Jews have the right to defend themselves against anyone who comes to kill them, their wives and their children. The grammatically questionable reading that Paton prefers says that the Jews are given the right to kill the wives and children of anyone who attacks them. Or to quote a recent (1997) commentary: "The substance of the new edict is that the Jews are now permitted to gather in self-defense, to slay the women and children of any that attack them."[7] This has become the preferred understanding of the passage for the entire twentieth century.

This understanding has not gone unquestioned. Joyce Baldwin, a Christian scholar, in rejecting this interpretation, sees behind it an overtly Christian agenda of promoting the New Testament at the expense of the Old. She claims that most scholars have misunderstood the Hebrew text because of a predisposition to read into the Book of Esther what they take to be the "bloodthirsty" vengeance theology of the Old Testament, "an eye for an eye and a tooth for a tooth" (an old standby of anti–Jewish polemics), thus "proving its barbarity" by comparison with the New Testament's theology of love.[8] It is this inbred bias, she avers, that leads them to misunderstand "the plain sense of the text," whose meaning is correctly reflected in the NIV (New International Version) translation:

---

[3]Paton, *ICC Esther*, p. 274.

[4]This is how the *New International Version* Bible (*NIV*) renders verse 11.

[5]Paton, *ICC Esther*, p. 274.

[6]This is how the *Revised Standard Version* Bible (*RSV*) following Paton, renders verse 11.

[7]Levenson, *Esther*, p. 110. Levenson attempts to explain what could possibly have motivated Mordecai to propose massacring women and children as follows: "The killing of women and children, offensive to any decent moral sensibility today, is dictated by the symmetry of the two decrees" (*ibid.*). In other words, since Haman specifically proposes that the Gentiles massacre the children and wives of the Jews, "symmetry" "dictates" that Mordecai should mandate that the Jews massacre the children and wives of the Gentiles. We shall return to this supposed "symmetry" later.

[8]Or to put it in Baldwin's own words: "The thought is that this Esther story works out the retribution theme of the Old Testament by permitting, and even glorying in, the outworking of 'an eye for an eye and a tooth for a tooth' (Ex. 21:23–25), so proving its barbarity by comparison with the New" (Baldwin, *Esther*, p. 97).

"The king's edict granted the Jews in every city the right to assemble and protect themselves, to destroy, kill and annihilate any armed force of any nationality or province that might attack them and their women and children."

Without necessarily subscribing to Baldwin's thesis as to the reasons lying behind the general misunderstanding of Mordecai's decree, I most emphatically agree with her understanding of the text, as well as with that of the NIV.[9] My agreement is also based on the analysis of Robert Gordis, the primary challenger of the majority view. He makes three main points:

1. He rejects an assumed parallelism or "symmetry" between Haman's edict (3:13) and Mordecai's decree (8:11). He faults the various commentators in that "They all regard this passage (8:11) as patterned after the earlier text in 3:13 ... because of the superficial resemblance between the two passages."[10] On the contrary, while in Haman's edict the words "to wipe out, to slaughter and to destroy" are immediately followed by the words "all the Jews, young and old, [their] children and their wives" ("so that it is clear that the phrase is in the accusative and the object of the verbs"),[11] in Mordecai's decree the phrase "to wipe out, to slaughter and to destroy" is immediately followed by "any armed force of a people or a province," which is the direct object of the verbs "to wipe out," and so on. The two decrees are in no way grammatically similar.

2. Citing numerous biblical examples, Gordis shows that the term "children" never occurs with "wives" alone. The phrase "children and wives" (or "children and women") is invariably preceded by a term referring to adult males. Thus the term "them" in "them [their] children and wives" must refer to "the Jews in every city" mentioned earlier in the verse.

3. Gordis further calls attention to a point that has been overlooked by all commentators on the verse: The Masorites[12] who are responsible for the text we possess (MT) understood the words "that would attack [them], their children and their wives" not as two separate phrases but as one, and accent accordingly, linking them together.[13]

All these points lead Gordis to read our text: "the king permitted the Jews in every city to gather and defend themselves, to destroy, kill, and wipe out every armed force of a people or a province attacking 'them, their children and their wives, with their goods as booty.' The last five words in the Hebrew text of 8:11 are not a *paraphrase* of 3:13, giving the Jews permission to retaliate in precisely the manner planned by Haman, but a *citation* of Haman's original edict, against which his intended victims may now protect themselves. In accordance with modern usage, the citation should be placed in quotation marks."[14]

As Baldwin, I find the case Gordis makes persuasive, and therefore in the main body of the book I have rendered these verses accordingly: that the Jews now have the right to defend themselves against anyone who comes to attack, to loot and despoil them (i.e., Jewish men, Jewish women and Jewish children).

---

[9]After insisting that the object of the verb "attack" is "them, with their children and women," that is, Jewish men along with their children and women, Baldwin continues: "This is the way in which NIV interprets the meaning, and indeed it is the plain sense of the text. Whatever ethical objection may be raised against the actions of the Jews as recorded in this book, at least they should not be based on this verse, misunderstood as it has commonly been" (*ibid.*, p. 98).

[10]Gordis, "Studies in the Esther Narrative," pp. 50–51.

[11]*Ibid.*

[12]See Glossary.

[13]Gordis, "Studies in the Esther Narrative," p. 51. "The accents are respectively *merkah, tiphah, munah, etnahtah.*"

[14]*Ibid.*, p. 52–53.

But Could She Read?
The Question of Literacy
in Ancient Israel

Having proposed that some, if not all, of the works investigated in this book were authored by women, and probably written in large measure for a female audience, it becomes necessary to examine if this was indeed a possibility in the Ancient Near East or whether we are simply being captivated by current feminist issues and are anachronistically projecting them back into the distant past where they have no place. But before we enquire into this matter we need to address a prior question: that of literacy in the Ancient World in general, and in Ancient Israel in particular. Were there indeed enough persons who knew how to read and write in those days to create the necessary mass for what we would call "a reading public"?[1]

Until recently it has been universally assumed that during the Biblical Age virtually all Israelites were illiterate. Such literacy as did exist (and that mainly only from the eighth century) was believed to have been confined to a very small class of professional scribes who performed such reading and writing activities as were necessary for rulers and the elite. As was the case in other illiterate societies, it was taken as a given that most "compositions" and "traditions" were oral, and were transmitted by bards and "story-tellers" who wandered from village to village and from tribe to tribe.[2]

This portrayal rests upon the 19th century thesis, popularized by the German scholar Julius Wellhausen, that Israel had its origins in a conglomeration of primitive desert tribes.[3] It was taken for granted that the invasion of these "primitive" Israelite tribes into "civilized" Canaan

---

[1]This is especially necessary as we have provisionally dated both Ruth and the 38th chapter of Genesis as written at an early stage of the First Commonwealth; in the 10th century BCE.

[2]With regard to the classical prophets, "schools" of "disciples" were postulated who memorized the words of their masters, and then passed them down from generation to generation until they were committed to writing sometime in the post-exilic age.

[3]Wellhausen categorically dismissed everything the Bible has to say about Israelite origins — specifically almost everything reported from Genesis through Joshua — as fictions invented by post-exilic Jews. "We attain [in Genesis] to no historical knowledge of the patriarchs, but only of the time when the stories about them arose in the Israelite people; this later age is here unconsciously projected, in its inner and its outward features into hoar antiquity, and is reflected there like a glorified mirage" (Wellhausen, *Prolegomena*, pp. 318–19).

produced results similar to those of the Doric invasions of Mycenaean Greece at roughly about the same time: a dark age of barbarian illiteracy that lasted for centuries.[4]

The problems with this point of view are twofold. In the first place, the theoretical basis of a barbarian invasion on the model of the Doric invasion of Greece, followed by a "dark age" lasting centuries, has collapsed. As with so many 19th century theories constructed in a time when virtually nothing was known of the Ancient Near East, the explosion of knowledge produced by twentieth century discoveries — especially the vast libraries and archives of ancient Ugarit, Mari and Ebla to name but a few — have rendered most of the views of Wellhausen and his school obsolete.[5] Ancient Israel did not exist in a vacuum. It was irrevocably part of its world, and could no more isolate itself from the major currents of its times than Belgium could remove itself from the events of Europe over the last several hundred years. We now have a picture of the larger context of which Ancient Israel was a part, and as more and more of that larger picture is filled in we gain a correspondingly better understanding of what really went on in that small part of the whole that was Israel. One thing can now be said with certainty: the entire idea of a primitive "dark age" was never anything more than a figment of 19th century imaginations.

The second major problem with centuries of illiteracy in Ancient Israel is that we possess a large body of literature from those very centuries: the majority of the Books of the Bible. If virtually no one could read, then for whom were the Books written? This problem was "solved" by summarily moving the dates of their composition to the post-exilic age when the "primitive Israelites," having been transformed into the presumably less primitive Jews, now possessed a sizable reading public.[6] This arbitrary tactic, feasible when next to nothing was known of the Ancient Near East, has been undone by the same avalanche of knowledge to which we have already alluded. The consensus view has now returned the composition of most of the biblical Books to the time when almost everyone was supposedly illiterate. The problem returns with full force: literary composition presupposes a reading public. While there may be an odd eccentric here and there who writes simply to amuse himself/herself, the experience of humanity is that writers generally write so that people can read what they have written.

In sum, what we have been arguing is that the presumption of near total illiteracy is a holdover from discredited 19th century theories, and can be classed as more a blind faith than an item of historical knowledge based on fact. Or as K.A. Kitchen puts it:

> [It is] the persistence of long-outdated philosophical and literary theories (especially of the 19th century stamp), and ... wholly inadequate use of first-hand sources in appreciating the earlier periods of the Old Testament story.[7]

---

[4]The Dorian conquest of Greece took place at approximately the midpoint of the Age of the Judges in Israel (about 1100 BCE). The oldest Greek inscriptions date only from the eighth and seventh centuries. Homer flourished in the ninth century; the masterpiece attributed to him, *The Iliad*, was transmitted orally by wandering bards and by guilds of "rhapsodes" (from *raptein*, to stitch together, and *oide*, a song) until finally being reduced to written form in Athens under the dictatorship of Pisistratus (died 527 BCE, and thus a contemporary of the Babylonian Exile). The illiteracy of Greece during almost the entire First Commonwealth period was naively taken as a model for Israelite society just across the Mediterranean.

[5]Wellhausen used primitive pre–Islamic Arab tribes as his models for what the earliest Israelites were like. We now recognize this model as pure anachronism.

[6]We have seen this strategy employed with the Books discussed in this study: how until recently scholarly opinion has held Ruth to be a product of the post-exilic period, Genesis likewise, while Esther (obviously a post-exilic work) was held to be a product of the (supposedly more cultured, hence more literate) Greek period. In each case we have been constrained to argue for a revision of these datings on the basis of more up-to-date scholarship.

[7]Kitchen, *The Bible in Its World*, p. 7.

The question now is: beyond the logical inference that as books were written from at least the early monarchic period (the days of David and Solomon) there must have been a reading public to read them, is there any *evidence* of a literate population in the period of the First Commonwealth? Before we attempt to answer this question we need a little background with regard to the history of writing in the Ancient Near East and the revolutionary impact of the invention of the alphabet.

The earliest form of writing, invented in Sumer in a long series of stages and reaching maturity about five thousand years ago, was a very complicated mixture of hundreds of signs representing whole words (logograms), signs for syllables or parts of words (syllabaries) and unpronounced signs used to indicate to which category of things a phonetic sign belonged (determinatives).[8] As such knowledge of writing was very hard to master, it was mainly confined to professional scribes in the employ of the king or of a temple. Writing was mostly used for clerical purposes: keeping records of goods collected as taxes, rations paid to workers as wages and so on. Only slowly did the writing, by becoming even more complicated, become sufficiently flexible to be able to be used for such purposes as state propaganda and the recording of myths. From the beginning writing was designed to facilitate the functioning of the centralized state (which included the state religion); its effective restriction to state-employed professionals was seen as a plus.

The invention of the alphabet, sometimes around 1700 BCE by Canaanites somewhere in Southern Syria-Palestine, changed everything.[9] Using a mere 22 signs to represent the consonants any word could be constructed. It was so simple that virtually anyone could easily master it. Writing ceased to be the monopoly of professionals. We can get some idea of the revolutionary impact of alphabetic writing from the history of its introduction into Greece. The Greeks got their alphabet from the Phoenicians,[10] and from the moment of its appearance it was a private vehicle used for private purposes, and so the first example of Greek alphabetic writing we possess appears scratched onto an Athenian jug from about 740 BCE, and is an announcement of a dancing contest: "Whoever of all the dancers performs most nimbly will win this vase as a prize." The very next example is three lines of poetry scratched onto a drinking cup: "I am Nestor's delicious drinking cup. Whoever drinks from this cup, swiftly will the desire of the fair-crowned Aphrodite seize him."

> The earliest preserved examples of the Etruscan and Roman alphabets are also inscriptions on drinking cups and wine containers. Only later did the alphabet's easily learned vehicle of private communication become co-opted for public and bureaucratic purposes. Thus, the developmental sequence of uses for alphabetic writing was the reverse of that for the earlier systems of logograms and syllabaries.[11]

---

[8]Egyptian Hieroglyphic writing, equally complicated, emerged also about 3,000 BCE, but apparently without the long period of experimental development that preceded Sumerian cuneiform. This leads some scholars to conclude that the Egyptians did not invent hieroglyphic writing from scratch, but got the original idea of writing from the Sumerians and then proceeded to develop their own system of writing based on the same principles.

[9]The alphabet was the invention of those Semitic-speaking peoples who used what we currently call Western Semitic languages. Hebrew, Phoenician and Aramaic, which are part of this language group and are closely related, were all soon using the alphabet. (By the thirteenth century BCE the original 27 letters representing consonants had been reduced to 22.) To the best of our knowledge, this discovery was unique in human history. All alphabets, past and present, derive from this original alphabet.

[10]A Semitic people located in what is now western Lebanon, who specialized in sea-born commerce. They were the Semites with whom the Greeks were in contact, and it is from them that the Greeks borrowed the Phoenician-Hebrew alphabet, even retaining the Semitic names of the letters.

[11]Diamond, *Guns, Germs and Steel*, p. 236. The Greek examples are also taken from this book.

With this background in mind, we now return to that area of the Ancient Near East where the alphabet had been invented more than half a millennium before it was introduced into a Greece just beginning to emerge from its dark age. Commenting on the impact of the invention of the alphabet, and the way in which it simplified to an amazing extent the art of reading and writing, K.A. Kitchen has this to say:

> With this limited set of simple signs [letters] to spell any word by its consonantal framework, literacy steadily became possible for a far greater number of people.... We have ... private letters (ostraca, Hebrew and Aramaic), some papyri (mostly Aramaic), and innumerable personal stamp-seals bearing the name of their owners (practically all dialects), use of which presupposes that many people could read enough to distinguish between them. There are inscribed arrow heads, notations of person, place, or capacity on jar handles — the list of everyday uses is quite varied. Thus certainly from 1100 BC (and probably rather earlier), writing in Canaan, then in Israel, Phoenicia, and round about was clearly part of everyday life and not restricted solely to a special scribal elite.[12]

In a later work Kitchen provides numerous examples taken from archeological discoveries in pre–Israelite Canaan, from Israel's immediate neighbors and from a site bearing both Israelite and non–Israelite remains, of a literacy not confined to elite and scribal circles. In a description of the Fosse Temple III in Lachish (late 13th century Canaanite) he comments:

> Finally, the locals could write. A splendid two-foot-high ewer was decorated in deep red paint with a series of animals, over which the artist had jotted, very informally, a dedication:
>
> > Gift (of) an oblation, O my [lad]y Goddess [? and Reshe]ph!
>
> This is only one of several fragmentary inscriptions from thirteenth-century Lachish, all informal such that any reasonably intelligent Canaanite might have inked them onto bowls and basins — and did.[13]

Here we see shades of the Greek vases and drinking cups yet to come over five hundred years later.

Next, from the Transjordan shortly before 800 BCE, we have the Tell Deir Alla Text entitled "The Book of the Afflictions of Balaam, Son of Beor," written out on the white-plastered surface of a wall. Kitchen points out that this was not a temple inscription but was written on the wall of a private home, most probably by the owner, giving a dramatic account of events that had taken place hundreds of years before.

> There is nothing "religious" about this room in a ninth-century dwelling; benches against the other walls may have served readers of the texts as seats.[14]

The assumption here is that there was a stream of people who came to read the inscription which was on public display.

For yet another example we turn to northeast Sinai, to Kuntillet Ajrud, thirty miles south of Kadesh-Barnea. This was a caravanserai, a fortified stopping-off place for caravans and merchants located near a junction of two international trade routes (Kitchen refers to it as a "high security motel"), that was active from the late ninth through part of the eighth century. It is rich in crude sketches and jottings in both the Hebrew and the Phoenician languages such as

---

[12]Kitchen, *The Bible in Its World*, p. 18. This was written before 1977. Since then further data has strengthened this evaluation. A survey of some of the more recent data can be found in Kitchen's 2003 book, *On the Reliability of the Old Testament*.

[13]Kitchen, *On the Reliability of the Old Testament*, p. 407.

[14]*Ibid.*, pp. 412–13.

"I [have] bless[ed] you by YHWH of Samaria and by Asherat." This graffiti is the work of travelers, merchants and common soldiers.[15]

Finally, it is significant that the three earliest Israelite inscriptions yet discovered are abecedaries (schoolboy pads for practicing the writing of the alphabet); the earliest, from the little farming village of Izbet Sartah,[16] dates from the 12th century BCE. If tiny farm towns, some like Izbet Sartah numbering less that two dozen houses total, had schoolchildren occupied with practicing their ABC's, this argues a much wider distribution of literacy at this early period than had previously been suspected.[17]

Hopefully, by this point we have established a strong presumption that literacy was sufficiently widespread by the 10th century BCE to create the basis of a reading public for whom authors could write.[18] Our task now becomes to dispel the belief that whatever literacy did exist was restricted solely to males. The strongly held conviction that women in the Biblical Age were held in ignorance and illiteracy, unquestioned in many circles, needs to be set against what we know of the larger picture of the Ancient Near East.

The first point that has to be made is that the Ancient Near East has a long proven record of female literacy going back to the beginning of writing in ancient Sumer. All through the centuries when the complicated cuneiform system of writing restricted literacy almost wholly to a small professional elite, we possess ample evidence that women were part of this elite. Indeed, the Mesopotamian patron deity of scribes was the goddess Nisaba, "chief scribe of heaven, record-keeper of Enlil, all knowing sage of the gods." She was to serve as model to women professionals for well over a millennium. The first scribes to be specifically identified as females are two women in an Ur III text.[19] At Mari, in Old Babylonian times, one text alone names nine female scribes.[20] In one site in Sippur, at least a dozen are known by name.[21] In the late Assyrian period, Asshurbanipal informs us in two letters addressed to the gods that the scribes writing the letters were women.[22] And as late as neo–Assyrian times there were female scribes employed in the queen's palace both at Kalah and at Nineveh.[23]

---

[15]*Ibid.*, pp. 413–15.

[16]Izbet Sartah is the name of an archaeological site in the foothills of Samaria named after the adjacent Arab village. We currently are unsure what its original biblical (Hebrew) name was.

[17]I append here from personal observation an example of my own: a recently discovered tomb from the early monarchic period cut into bedrock in the Kidron Valley opposite the Temple Mount of Jerusalem, bears an inscription advising potential grave robbers that it will be unprofitable for them to break into the tomb as there is nothing there to take. But should you disregard this advisory, the inscription continues, and do break in, may a curse fall upon you and all your descendants. Just as today we post "Beware of the Dog" signs with the expectation that potential trespassers will be able to read the sign and be warned off, so does the ancient inscription presuppose the ability of the grave robbers of those days to be able to read and so be deterred.

[18]This does not in any way imply that one could make a living by writing literature. Writing was an avocation, not a paying proposition. But for one who had something to say, one could write knowing that there were people able and willing to read what one had written. More: the extraordinary levels of sophistication and artistry of biblical Books (we have repeatedly commented on such even though this was not always germane to our line of inquiry) implies that there were readers out there who could appreciate this high level of literature, even demand it. We have no way of estimating the size of the reading public at any given period; we can only suggest that it was sufficiently rooted to have developed good taste.

[19]Hallo, *Origins*, p. 262.

[20]*Ibid.*

[21]*Ibid.*

[22]*Ibid.* The scribes are not named, but from analysis of the handwriting we know that both letters were not written by the same woman.

[23]*Ibid.*, p. 263. These women scribes were bilingual, being proficient in both cuneiform and alphabetic (Aramaic) writing! Aramaic was used by the neo–Assyrian Empire as their official language in administering their western provinces, while they retained Akkadian (written in cuneiform) for homeland use.

Not only were there women who made their living from their literacy, but the Ancient Near East had a long tradition of female authors. The first on record was Princess Enheduanna, daughter of King Sargon of Akkad, c. 2360 BCE. Her surviving works include a cycle of short hymns apostrophizing the temples of Sumer and Akkad, and a cycle of three lengthy hymns celebrating the military triumphs of her father, Sargon.[24] We actually have a full-figure portrait of her making an offering at an altar (she had her father appoint her priestess to the moon-god of Ur). Because she prefaced one of her hymns with a detailed autobiography we know quite a bit about her. She has the distinction of being not only the first woman author on record, but also the very first author known by name. "On present evidence, Enheduanna is the first non-anonymous, non-fictitious author in world history — and a woman."[25]

She was far from the last. Hallo lists a series of woman authors. There was Watartum, widow of King Ur-Nammu of Ur (c. 2094 BCE), who composed a plaintive lamentation for her husband, slain in battle. Then there was Queen Abi-simti, wife of Shulgi, who composed a beautiful lullaby for her son Shu-Sin.[26] When Shu-Sin grew up a whole series of erotic love songs were composed for him, one by the priestess Kubatum and one by an anonymous barmaid (a bawdy drinking song), perhaps one Il-ummiya. Finally we have the case of Nin-shatapada, daughter of King Sin-kashid (c. 1800 BCE). When their kingdom was conquered by King Rim-Sin of Larsa, she composed a letter-prayer in poetry to him pleading to spare her and to restore her to her position as high priestess of the city of Durum. It seems that she was successful.[27]

Was it only queens and princesses who wrote in ancient Mesopotamia? Hallo suggests that "the answer to this question is complicated by the noted reticence of the sources to identify authors altogether."[28] It is persons with royal connections who tend to get their compositions preserved along with their names in the days before the invention of the alphabet.

With a documented long-standing tradition of female literacy in the Ancient Near East, and a tradition of female authorship, we should not be surprised that, as a part of the Ancient Near East, Israel should also have its share of poetic compositions attributed to women authors, "The Song of Deborah" (Judges 5) and "Hannah's Prayer" (1 Samuel 2:1–10) being the outstanding examples. Nor should we find it improbable that, with the creation of narrative prose as the preferred form for biography and historiography in Ancient Israel, women should take a hand in its composition.

A Short Note on Suggestions of Female Authorship for Biblical Works

In the main body of the book we have explained the reasons that have prompted us to propose female authorship for the Books under discussion. We have made no pretense of being the first to hold such an opinion. Over the years various scholars and critics have suggested that several Books of the Bible, or parts thereof, can best be understood as having been written by

---

[24]These are all stylized and elevated compositions. Several of them are included in the anthologies *Women Poets of the World*, edited by Joanna Bankier and Deirdre Lashgari, and *A Book of Women Poetry from Antiquity to Now*, edited by Aliki and Willis Barnstone.

[25]Hallo, *Origins*, pp. 265–66.

[26]We are not absolutely certain that Abi-simti was the author. It could have been one of Shugli's other wives.

[27]*Ibid.*, p. 267. All the above compositions are in poetry, the sole literary form employed for "literature" in ancient Sumer and Akkad. Prose was only used for accounting in those days.

[28]*Ibid.*

women. In our discussion of Ruth we listed several scholars who are of the opinion that the Book is clearly a work authored by a woman, while others, though having suspicions of possible female authorship, are not willing to commit themselves.[29] In our summation of Esther we quoted William Hallo's suggestion that the Book was authored by a woman.[30] Thirteen years later he returned to this opinion, enlarging on his reasons.[31]

Far less straightforward is the case of the 38th chapter of Genesis. The story of Tamar is embedded in the saga of Joseph. Most of the scholars who accept the documentary hypothesis (see Glossary) consider the Joseph Saga part of the strand of the Bible (or "document") that is labeled "J."

In his 1987 book *Who Wrote the Bible?* Richard Friedman suggested that a woman may have been the author of the "J document."[32] Three years later, the well known literary critic Harold Bloom, in far more definitive terms, assigned the "J document" to a woman, possibly a princess who was the granddaughter of King David![33] Bloom's proposal generated extensive controversy.[34]

The bottom line is that while each of the three works treated in this book has, in varying degree, been attributed to female authorship by respectable scholars, these proposals remain very much in the minority. The current general consensus of scholarly opinion is not yet ready to entertain the suggestion of female authorship for Books of the Bible.

[29]See "A Woman's Tale" in Chapter 1.

[30]Hallo, "The First Purim," p. 25.

[31]Hallo, *Origins*, p. 269.

[32]Friedman, *Who Wrote the Bible?*, p. 86.

[33]Bloom, *The Book of J*, pp. 9–10, 19.

[34]Even Richard Friedman, besides resenting the discourtesy of not being given credit by Bloom for the original suggestion, strongly insisted that Bloom's elaboration went far beyond the available evidence and was thus seriously flawed (Freedman, "Is Everybody a Bible Expert?" pp. 16–18, 50–51).

Timeline:
Putting Things in Perspective

This chronology is based on the dating of K.A. Kitchen and is approximate, give or take about 10 years for the more exact dates.

Date (BCE)	Events in the History of Israel	Events in World History
1900–1600	The Patriarchal Age (including Joseph); *Tamar* circa 1690 ?	Code of Hammurabi
1690/80– 1400	Israel in Egypt	Hyksos expelled from Egypt; New Empire begins
1400–1300	Israel in Egypt	Egypt rules Canaan; Amenophis IV (Akhnaten) fails in attempt to reform Egyptian religion
1300–1210	Israel Exits Egypt; Entry into Canaan[1]	The Minoan Empire collapses; the Peoples of the Sea invade Egypt and are repulsed; New Empire disintegrates; Egypt loses control of Canaan; the Trojan War
1210–1032	Age of the Judges (*Ruth* circa 1100); Age of Samuel; Destruction of Shiloh	Dorian invasions of Greece; Philistines arrive in Canaan; Arameans establish states in Syria
1032–1010	Saul king of Israel	
1010–970	David rules the kingdoms of Judah and Israel; makes Jerusalem his capital around 1003, conquers all the states between Egypt and Mesopotamia	

[1]Sinai Covenant no earlier than 1400, no later than 1200–1180; the female tavern keeper phenomenon (cf. Rahab, *Joshua* 2) is valid down to circa 1100, after which customs changed.

Date (BCE)	Events in the History of Israel	Events in World History
970–930	Age of Solomon; Temple built in Jerusalem; Davidic Empire begins to disintegrate.	Beginning of Egyptian and Assyrian resurgence
928–875	The kingdom of Israel successfully revolts against the House of David; the United Kingdoms permanently separate and the Davidic Empire collapses; Judah unsuccessfully attempts to reconquer Israel.	Egypt invades the region, then collapses. Rise of Damascus as the major power in Syria; rise of Assyria.
875–740	Judah and Israel learn to live together and cooperate; continual war with Syria; Ahab, Jezebel and the struggle with Elijah over the faith of Israel. The beginning of the age of Classical Prophecy: Amos and Hosea.	Assyrian attempt to conquer Western Asia checked at Battle of Qarqar (853); Carthage founded as a Phoenician colony in North Africa.
740–721	Decline of Israel and final destruction by Assyria (721); Judah survives as a vassal of the Assyrians. Prophets: Isaiah, Micah.	Damascus falls (732); Assyria rules all Western Asia.
721–586	Judah subject to Assyria. King Josiah implements a major religious reform (622), canonizing the Book of Deuteronomy. Judah, now subject to Babylonia, rebels. In 586 Jerusalem falls, the Temple is destroyed, and much of the surviving population is exiled to Babylon. Prophets: Nahum and Jeremiah.	Assyria conquers Egypt. With the death of Asshurbanapal the Assyrian Empire begins to disintegrate: Assyria is expelled from Egypt; Babylonia rebels; Nineveh falls (612). The Assyrian Empire is divided between the Babylonians and the Medes. Solon reforms Athens's laws.
586–538	Babylonian Exile; Cyrus frees the Jews (538) and permits them to return and rebuild their Temple in Jerusalem. Prophets: Ezekiel and Deutero-Isaiah.	Cyrus the Great unites the Medes and the Persians, conquers Lydia (547) and captures Babylon (539) thus creating the greatest empire the world had known. Pisistratus seizes power in Athens.
538–430	42,000 Jews return to Jerusalem, rebuild the Temple (515) and re-found the commonwealth of Judea. *Esther* (483–465). Ezra and Nehemiah rebuild the walls of Jerusalem, canonize the Torah and institute it as the law of the land (430). Prophets: Haggai, Zechariah and Malachi.	Persia conquers Egypt and the Greek states of Asia Minor, invades Greece and is defeated at Marathon and Salamis. The Greeks now start fighting among themselves (the Peloponnesian Wars between Athens and Sparta). The Age of Pericles and the Athenian Empire, Aeschylus and Sophocles.

The Biblical Age Comes to a Close.

Date (BCE)	Events in the History of Israel	Events in World History
431–404		The Great Peloponnesian War. Athens loses. Plays of Euripides and Aristophanes.
404–338		Continual warfare in Greece and major social change. Macedonia consolidates as a major state; Philip of Macedon conquers Greece at the battle of Chaeronea. Plato.
338–323		Philip assassinated (336); Alexander the Great conquers the Persian Empire (334–323) and dies in Babylon. Aristotle.
323–200	Judea becomes part of the Ptolemaic Empire. Antiochus III (the Great) pushes the Ptolemaic Empire back to the border of Egypt; Judea becomes part of the Seleucid Empire.	The Era of the Diadochi (the successors of Alexander) who battle for the succession, and end by dividing it among the survivors of the wars, Seleucus getting Syria and Mesopotamia and Ptolemy getting Egypt. First Punic War (264–241) Rome defeats Carthage and occupies Sicily. Second Punic War (218–201) sees total defeat of Carthage. Rome now master of the Western Mediterranean.
199–165	Decree of Antiochus IV outlaws practice of Judaism; Temple profaned Dec. 168. Revolt of Judas Maccabeus and his brothers. Temple rededicated Dec. 165.	Rome defeats Philip V (199) and Greece becomes a protectorate of Rome. At Magnesia Rome defeats Antiochus III (190) and detaches Asia Minor from the Seleucid Empire. Rome is now the sole superpower.
164–63	Judah dies and his brothers continue the struggle against the Seleucid Empire. Judea declared an independent state by Simon (143). He and his successors (the Hasmoneans) are both kings and High Priests. Independence ends with the capture of Jerusalem by Pompey (63). Judea now a vassal of Rome.	Social and civil war in Rome: the Gracchi, Marius and Sulla; Pompey defeats the pirates, Mithradates and Tigranes (66), and annexes Syria. Rome now effectively rules the entire Hellenistic world to the Euphrates.
63 BCE– 70 CE	Herod declared king of Judea by Rome (40), rebuilds the Temple. Upon his death Rome assumes direct rule of Judea (4). The Jews revolt against Rome (66–70 CE); Jerusalem and the Temple both destroyed.	Julius Caesar defeats Pompey but is assassinated. In the resulting civil war Octavian defeats Antony, becoming the first Emperor of Rome. Persecutions of Christians begin in Rome. Nero, last of the Caesars, dies in Greece. General Vespasian declared emperor of Rome.

Glossary of Terms, Place Names, and Persons

Achaemenian (or **Achaemenid**) Referring to the dynasty that ruled the **Persian Empire** from **Cyrus the Great** (enthroned 559 BCE) until the death of Darius III (in 330 BCE). The Persian Empire is thus often known as the **Achaemenian** Empire.

Adulam A Canaanite city about 13 miles southwest of **Bethlehem**.

Ahasuerus The Persian king of the Book of Esther, usually known by his Greek name of **Xerxes I** (reigned 486–465 BCE). Aside from his fame as **Esther's** royal husband, he is chiefly remembered for his failure to conquer Greece.

Akkadian A language spoken in ancient **Mesopotamia**.

Amphictyony The Greek term for an association of neighboring communities having one central shrine sacred to them all. In the Age of the **Judges** the tribes of Israel formed an amphictyony.

Anshan A province (also city) in the ancient Empire of **Elam** in modern southwest Iran. Under **Cyrus I** it became a mini-kingdom, destined to be the kernel from which the **Persian Empire** was to grow.

Apocrypha A body of works, dating primarily from the period of the **Second Commonwealth**, not included in the canon of the Hebrew Bible (although they are included in the canon of the Roman Catholic and Greek Orthodox Churches). The Protestant Church also denied them sanctity.

Arabah The below-sea-level trench stretching North-South from the Sea of Galilee to Akabah. The portion north of the **Dead Sea** is known as the **Jordan** Valley.

Aramaic A Semitic language close to Hebrew, and sharing with Hebrew the same alphabet. The **Persian Empire** used **Aramaic** as its lingua franca to facilitate communication between the various peoples in its polyglot empire.

Arnon River A river in the **Transjordan** flowing from east to west, and emptying into the **Dead Sea**; the border between the Israelite tribe of **Reuben** and the Kingdom of **Moab** to its south.

Asshurbanapal Last of the great **Assyrian** conquers; see **Assyrians**.

Assyrians A people centered in upper **Mesopotamia** who were among the most single-minded militarists in history. Totally ruthless, they built up one of the most fearsome military machines the world has ever known, destroyed their many competitors and, for the first time, unified the entire **Fertile Crescent** under one rule. Their final crowning military achievement was the conquest of Egypt by the last of their great warlords, **Asshurbanapal**. Upon his death Egypt's successful revolt signaled the beginning of the end for the **Assyrians**. Bled white by their exertions, their empire imploded within a generation. The end came when their capital, **Nineveh**, was stormed and its population put to the sword in 612 BCE by the joint forces of the **Medes** and the **Babylonians**.

243

Babylonian Exile (Sometimes known as the Babylonian Captivity.) The historical period following the destruction of the Kingdom of **Judah** (586 BCE) during which the remainder of its population was removed from the land by the victorious **Babylonians** and resettled in **Mesopotamia**.
This period is deemed to end with the proclamation of **Cyrus the Great** (538 BCE) allowing the
Jews to return to their homeland.

Babylonians An ancient people centered in southern **Mesopotamia**. Their greatest city, **Babylon**,
was sited close to the present Baghdad. After throwing off the **Assyrian** yoke, they inherited the
Western portion of the now defunct **Assyrian** Empire. They also inherited the **Assyrian** practice
of breaking the spirit of peoples who revolted against them by first crushing them militarily, then
deporting the survivors to distant lands; the fate meted out by their greatest ruler, **Nebuchadnezzar**, to the unhappy residents of **Judah** in 586 BCE. Their short-lived rule of **Mesopotamia**
and Western Asia (73 years, from 612 till 539 BCE) was ended by the **Persians** under **Cyrus II
(The Great)**.

BCE (Abr.) Before the Common Era.

Benjamin The tribe of Saul, occupying the area between **Jerusalem** and Beth-El; also **Jacob's**
youngest son.

Benjamite A member of the Tribe of **Benjamin**.

Bethlehem A **Judean** town about five miles south of **Jerusalem**, the birthplace of **David**; revered
by Christianity as the birthplace of Jesus.

Bigthan Eunuch bodyguard of King **Ahasuerus**, executed for high treason.

Boaz Husband of **Ruth** and great-grandfather of **David**.

Cambyses II A son of **Cyrus the Great**, he succeeded his father to become the second ruler of the
Persian Empire, reigning from 530 to 522 BCE.

Canaan The name given by the Egyptians to the geographical region of their empire that eventually became the Land of Israel. Prior to the Israelite conquest it was inhabited by various peoples
and ethnic groups, and organized into independent city-states.

Canaanites One of the largest of the ethnic groups inhabiting the Promised Land prior to the
Israelite conquest of the Land. Sometimes used collectively for all the pre–Conquest peoples.

Canonization The process by which the various Books that now make up the Bible were accepted
and certified as genuine and inspired Holy Scripture.

CE (Abr.) The common era.

Chilion Son of **Elimelech** and **Naomi**.

Chronicles, Book of The final Book of the Hebrew Bible (in Christian Bibles it the eleventh Book),
currently divided into two Books, namely, **1 Chronicles** and **2 Chronicles**. Written in the Persian era, it is basically a religious history of **David** and his dynasty.

Commonwealth, First The historical period from the Conquest and Settlement of the Land of
Israel until the destruction of **Judah** and the exile of its surviving inhabitants in 586 BCE; a period
comprising over six centuries. This period is the heart of the Biblical Age.

Commonwealth, Second The historical period beginning with the return from the **Babylonian
Exile**, starting in 538 BCE, until the destruction of **Jerusalem** by the Romans in 70 CE; a span
of almost six centuries. The first part of this period brings the Biblical Age to a close.

Cubit a measure of length; originally the distance between an average man's elbow and the tip of
his middle finger, later standardized to a bit under eighteen inches.

Cyrus I Grandfather of **Cyrus the Great**, founder of the **Achaemenian** dynasty.

Cyrus II (The Great) The founder of the **Persian** or **Achaemenian** Empire who ruled from 559 to
530 BCE. One of the greatest conquerors and rulers in recorded history; he is famous for having freed the Jews from the **Babylonian Exile**.

Darius I (The Great) Reigned from 522 to 486 BCE; father of **Xerxes I (Ahasuerus)**. It was he
who established **Susa (Shushan)** as a capital of the **Persian Empire**.

David Israel's greatest King. Successor to King Saul, he reigned from 1010 to 970 BCE, creating an empire stretching from the border of **Egypt** to the **Euphrates River**. Capturing **Jerusalem**, he both made it his capital and turned it into a holy city.

Dead Sea Sometimes called "The Salt Sea." Over 1275 feet below sea level, this stagnant body of water is the lowest body of water on the earth's surface. The water is much more saline than seawater; fish cannot live in it. It is approximately fifty miles in length and ten miles wide at En-gedi.

Dead Sea Documents (Q) Scrolls and Scroll fragments of various biblical and extra-biblical Books found in caves at **Qumran** near the **Dead Sea**. They are the oldest extant versions of biblical Books, some dating from as early as the 3rd century BCE.

Diaspora Jews living in the "dispersion" outside of the Land of Israel; sometimes the term refers to the area of Jewish settlement outside the Land of Israel.

Documentary Hypothesis A theory, popularized by the 19th century scholar Julius Wellhausen, that Genesis-Deuteronomy should be read, not as five discrete books, but as an interweaving of four separate older sources (called "documents" and labeled J, E, D and P). These "documents" were held to have been redacted, or edited, into the Pentateuch that we currently know after the **Babylonian Exile** during the **Second Commonwealth**.

Ecbatana The current Hamadan. Originally capital of **Media**, it was conquered by **Cyrus the Great** in 550 BCE. The city served as the summer residence of the **Persian** kings, and thus was one of the four capital cities of the **Achaemenian Empire**.

Edom A Hebrew-speaking kingdom located on the **Transjordanian** plateau south of the Kingdom of **Moab**. Its people were known as **Edomites**.

Edomites see **Edom**

Egypt An ancient African kingdom and Great Power, separated by the Sinai from the South of **Judah.**

Elam An ancient empire in southwest Persia (originally centered in the modern Iranian province of Khuzistan). At its height **Susa** was its capital. Incorporated into the **Persian Empire** it was governed as a satrapy, while **Susa** became one of the capitals of the Persian Kings.

Elder Usually a senior member of a community; a member of its governing body.

Elephantine A fortress city on a small island in the middle of the Nile River a few miles north of the First Cataract, opposite the present day Aswan, which served to guard the southern gateway to **Egypt** from Nubian incursions. It was garrisoned by regiments of Jewish mercenaries and their families, the male children of each succeeding generation taking up the profession of their fathers. Founded by the **Assyrians** when they ruled **Egypt** in the seventh century BCE, the military colony survived the expulsion of the **Assyrians** by the Egyptians, the **Persian** conquest, and ultimately the Greek conquest under Alexander the Great. Its importance lies in the discovery, at the beginning of the twentieth century, of a hoard of documents in the **Aramaic** language that became known as the Elephantine Papyri. These shed light on historical situations that were previously either unknown or shrouded in obscurity.

Elimelech **Bethlehemite** expatriate, husband to **Naomi.**

Ephah A measure of dry volume approximately equal to a bushel.

Er Oldest son of **Judah**, first husband of **Tamar.**

Esther Hebrew name: Hadassah bat Abihail. Consort of King **Ahasuerus** and hero of the Book of Esther.

Euphrates (River) One of the two mighty rivers that flow through **Mesopotamia**; at one point in history it marked the northern border of the Davidic Empire; the distance between Tipshah, the closest point on the **Euphrates**, and **Jerusalem** is approximately 340 miles.

Fear of God A common biblical phrase meaning something akin to "common decency."

Fertile Crescent The fertile area curving from the river valleys of Mesopotamia through Syria and ending in the Land of Israel, bounded on all sides by either arid regions or the sea. It was in the **Fertile Crescent** that organized agriculture and animal husbandry first came into being about ten thousand years ago.

Ger A non–**Israelite** who held the status of permanent resident within the land of Israel, and who enjoyed equal protection with **Israelites** under law.

Geulah "Redemption"; the responsibility imposed by customary law in Ancient Israel on blood relatives to provide redeeming succor, under certain circumstances, to their kinsmen in distress. See Chapter 1 for details.

Goel Hebrew for "Redeemer." The person responsible for "Redemption." See **Geulah**.

Haman, son of Hammedatha The anti–Semitic Vizier in the Book of Esther who attempts to annihilate the Jews of the **Persian Empire**.

Harbonah Eunuch official, probably one of king **Ahasuerus**'s bodyguards.

Hathach Eunuch major-domo of **Esther**.

Hebron An ancient city about 19 miles South of **Jerusalem**.

Hegai Eunuch in charge of preparing girls for the bed of **Xerxes** (**Ahasuerus**).

Herodotus The first major Greek historian, author of *The Persian Wars*. Though often inaccurate and even misleading, he is our main source of information concerning the early period of the **Persian Empire**.

Hesed (Hebr.) Compassion, mercy, kindness, faithfulness, loyalty and grace are all meanings of this important term in the biblical lexicon. It usually refers to some act of generosity unmerited by the recipient.

Hirah Resident of **Adulam**, close friend of **Judah**.

Holocaust The name given to the genocidal murder of over six million Jews by the Nazis (1933–1945) as part of their attempt to annihilate world Jewry.

Ibn Ezra, Abraham (1089–1164). Poet, grammarian, philosopher and one of the greatest Jewish medieval commentators on the Bible.

Ionia The western portion of Asia Minor (present-day Turkey) that comprised the heartland of the Greek civilization prior to its conquest, first by **Lydia**, then **Persia**.

Israel, Kingdom of The Northern Kingdom comprising ten of the tribes of Israel, in contradistinction to the Southern Kingdom, **Judah**. The **Kingdom of Israel** was destroyed by the **Assyrians** in 721 BCE.

Israelites The People of Israel (synonym for the Children of Israel).

Jacob the last of the **Patriarchs**.

Jerusalem An ancient city in the central highlands of Palestine. Known as Jebus (after the Jebusites who ruled it) during the latter Bronze Age until its conquest by **David**, it then reverted to its ancient name of **Jerusalem**. It served as the capital, first of the **Israelite** kingdom, and then of one of its successor states, **Judah**. Destroyed by **Nebuchadnezzar**, it was rebuilt after the return from the **Babylonian Exile** to become the capital of **Judea**.

Jordan River The main river of the land of Israel, running from the Sea of Galilee down to the **Dead Sea**, a distance of about seventy miles. See **Arabah**.

Joseph Eleventh son of **Jacob**. He is the subject of the brilliant epic to be found in Genesis 37–50.

Josephus Flavius (c. 38–100 CE) Jewish historian and apologist. Born into an aristocratic priestly family he was appointed a general in the Great Revolt against Rome (66–70 CE) and given command of the Galilee. Bungling the campaign and decisively defeated, he surrendered to the Romans and spent the remainder of his life as a pensioner of the Roman Emperors whom he served with his writings. Despite their selective and propagandist nature, his major works, *The Jewish War*, *Jewish Antiquities* and *Contra Apion*, form the best sources we possess today for the era of the **Second Commonwealth**.

Josiah (640–609 BCE) The last ruler of **Judah** as an independent kingdom, he is mainly remembered as the originator of the major religious reform that goes by his name.

Josianic Reform A major religious reform implemented in **Judah** by King **Josiah** in 622 BCE based on the Book of Deuteronomy. Various idolatrous practices that had flourished under his grandfather, King Manasseh, were made illegal and all rural shrines were abolished, the formal worship of God being centralized in **Jerusalem**.

Judah (1) The fourth son of the patriarch Jacob, and the father-in-law of **Tamar**, (2) The southernmost tribe in the land of Israel, (3) Kingdom of: the Southern Kingdom ruled by **David** and his descendents from 1002 to 586 BCE. After the **Babylonian Exile** the kingdom was reconstituted under the name of **Judea**.

Judea The name by which the reconstituted Kingdom of **Judah** was known during the **Second Commonwealth**.

Judges (1) The name given to the charismatic leaders of the **Israelites** in the period prior to the establishment of the monarchy (approximately 1200–1020 BCE), (2) the biblical Book that deals with this period.

Kadesh-Barnea An oasis, rich in springs, at the southern edge of the Land of **Canaan**, about ninety-five miles southwest of **Jerusalem**. This oasis was the center of **Israelite** settlement in the wilderness, prior to the conquest of **Canaan**.

Kafka, Franz (1883–1924) A Jewish novelist whose tragic vision of the human condition has had enormous impact on Western art and literature.

Ketib The Hebrew consonantal text of the Bible (see **Qeri**).

Ketubim The third division of the Hebrew Bible (see **Wisdom Literature**).

Kish Father of King Saul, ancestor of **Mordecai**.

Levirate Marriage Literally "Brother Marriage"; the institution whereby a childless widow is compelled to marry the brother of her deceased husband for the purpose of producing children who will legally be the heirs of the dead husband.

LXX (Abr. for The **Septuagint**) The earliest Greek translation of the Bible, made in Alexandria, Egypt, from the third to the first centuries BCE.

Lydia An empire that covered the western half of Asia Minor (present-day Turkey). Its capital, **Sardis**, was located roughly 45 miles due east of modern Izmir. Its western provinces contained many Greek city-states. Its last king, Croesus, was reputed the richest man in the world. Lydia fell to **Cyrus the Great** in 547 BCE.

Maccabees, Books of Two Books included in the **Apocrypha**. **1 Maccabees** is the historical account of the family of the **Maccabees** or Hasmoneans, from the beginning of the uprising against the Hellenistic Greeks to the death of Simon who established the independence of **Judea** (168–135 BCE). **2 Maccabees** confines itself to the wars of Judah the **Maccabee**, dealing with them in greater detail.

Mahlon Son of **Naomi** and **Elimelech**, first husband of **Ruth**.

Marathon The site near Athens where the first **Persian** attempt to conquer Greece was repulsed (491 BCE).

Mari One of the principal cities of **Mesopotamia** during the third and early second millennia BCE. First excavated in 1933, its hoard of some 20,000 documents (tablets) dating from the 18th century BCE has thrown much light on West Semitic affairs in general and on the early stages of the Biblical Age in particular.

Masorites The term for those persons who, over the generations, were concerned with the precise preservation and transmission of the holy text of the Bible. The end product of the millennia-long endeavor is the current definitive text of the Hebrew Bible, known as the **Masoretic Text (MT)**.

Medes First mentioned by the **Assyrians** in the ninth century BCE, like the **Persians** they were an Iranian-speaking people of mountain tribes. The **Assyrians** during their ascendancy managed to keep the **Median** tribes from uniting, but as their power declined Cyaxares succeeded in bringing them together under his rule. This was the birth of **Media**. Some time after 625 BCE they rose in rebellion against **Assyria** and, in 612, together with the **Babylonians** they took **Nineveh** and dismembered the **Assyrian Empire**, inheriting its eastern provinces. It was the son of Cyaxares, Astyages, whom **Cyrus II** defeated in 550 BCE. Made subject to the **Persians**, the **Medes** nonetheless formed, with the **Persians**, the core of the **Persian** War Machine and were accorded equal honor.

Media Land of the **Medes**, later the Empire of the **Medes.**

Memucan Advisor to the king, and member of the Imperial Advisory Council of Persia.

Mesopotamia the name given to the region watered by the **Euphrates** and **Tigris** Rivers. The region today goes by the name Iraq.

Midianites A nomadic people whose range extended from the rim of the Arabian Desert to the Sinai Wilderness.

Moab **Transjordanian** kingdom often hostile to Israel; bordered on the north by the tribe of **Reuben**, on the south by the kingdom of **Edom** and on the west by the **Dead Sea.**

Mordecai High official, ultimately Vizier, in the **Persian** government; cousin and guardian of **Esther.**

MT (Abr.) The **Masoretic Text**; the standard version of the Hebrew Bible. See **Masorite.**

Mycale, Battle of The naval victory of the Greeks over the **Persian** fleet that freed the Greek cities of **Ionia** from Persian rule (August 479).

Naomi Widow of **Elimelech** and mother-in-law of **Ruth.**

Nebuchadnezzar **Babylonian** king who destroyed **Jerusalem** and exiled the surviving **Judean** population to **Babylon.** See **Babylonian Exile.**

Nineveh Capital of **Assyria.**

Obed Son of **Ruth** and **Boaz**, grandfather of **David.**

Onan Second son of **Judah**, **Tamar**'s second husband.

Orpah Widow of **Chilion**, sister-in-law of **Ruth.**

Papyrus A kind of paper made from the stem of the papyrus plant, manufactured in Egypt.

Parchment The skin of a sheep, goat or other animal prepared to be written on.

Patriarchs The name used to designate the fathers of the Jewish people — Abraham, Isaac, and **Jacob.** If we include **Joseph**, the **Patriarchal Age** encompasses approximately 1900–1600 BCE.

Pentateuch The "Five Books of Moses" (Genesis, Exodus, Leviticus, Numbers and Deuteronomy). See **Torah.**

Perez Son of **Tamar** and **Judah**, distant ancestor of **David.**

Persian Empire (559–330 BCE) Created by **Cyrus the Great**, this miraculous political entity encompassed most of the known world of its day.

Persians The Aryan warrior people who created the **Persian Empire.**

Plataea The site in Northern Greece where, in August 479 BCE, the Greeks followed up their naval victory at **Salamis** by destroying the **Persian** army sent to conquer them, thus signaling the beginning of the end of the **Persian Empire.**

Plutarch (46 to sometime after 119 CE). A Greek writer whose fame rests chiefly upon his *Lives*, a series of biographies of pairs of outstanding Greek and Roman figures.

Pogrom A Russian term meaning a state-organized massacre of helpless people (originally of Russian Jews).

Polytheism The belief in, and the worship of, many gods.

Q (Abr. for Qumran) See **Dead Sea Documents.**

Qeri ("read thus"); the text as it is read according to the **Masorites.** See **Ketib.**

RASHI Acronym of Rabbi **Sh**lomo **I**tzhaki (Solomon ben Isaac), 1040–1105 CE. One of the greatest medieval Jewish commentators on the Bible.

Redemption *see* **Geulah**

Reuben (1) The oldest of the twelve sons of the **Patriarch Jacob**, (2) **Israelite** tribe, settled in the **TransJordan**, its borders the Kingdom of **Moab** to the south, the **Dead Sea** to the west, and the tribe of Gad to the north.

Ruth **Moabite** daughter-in-law of **Naomi**, great-grandmother of **David** and heroine of the Book of Ruth.

Salamis, Battle of The decisive naval battle fought in the Bay of Salamis in September, 480 BCE, between the **Persian** and Greek fleets. The **Persian** defeat proved the turning point of the war, and ended the invasion of Greece.

Sardis *see* **Lydia**

Septuagint *see* **LXX**

Shekel A unit of weight amounting to approximately 11.33 grams.

Shelah Third son of **Judah**; prospective husband of **Tamar**.

Shofar A ram's horn, used in biblical times primarily to sound a warning of danger, or for military signaling in the field, and as a means of rallying the public.

Shua Father of **Judah's** wife.

Shushan *see* **Susa**

Solomonic Enlightenment The literary renaissance which G. von Rad proposed; beginning during the last years of the reign of **David**, and peaking during the reign of his successor, Solomon. Several the Books of the Bible are presumed to have been written during this period.

Sumer The earliest known name of the land corresponding roughly to the southern half of present-day Iraq. It was the earliest known civilization, flourishing from before 3500 till 1750 BCE, when its remains were incorporated into the **Babylonian** empire by Hammurabi. The greatest accomplishment of **Sumerian** civilization was the invention of writing.

Susa The Biblical **Shushan**. Former capital city of **Elam**, it served from the days of **Darius I** as the central administrative hub of the **Persian Empire**.

Syr. (Abr. for Syriac) The Peshitta; a translation of the Bible into **Syriac** (a late form of the **Aramaic** language) possibly dating to the 1st century CE.

Talent The basic unit of weight in the Ancient Near East (amounting to 3,000 **shekels**), equivalent to approximately 66 pounds.

Tamar Daughter-in-law of **Judah** and distant ancestress of **David**. Heroine of Genesis 38.

TANACH The Hebrew Bible; an acronym designating the three divisions into which the Hebrew Bible is organized.

Targ. (Abr. for Targum) One of several translations of the Bible into **Aramaic**, at one time the lingua franca of the Near East. **Aramaic** is a sister language to Hebrew.

Teresh Eunuch bodyguard of King **Ahasuerus**, executed for high treason.

Thrace The ancient name of the area in Europe west and south of the Black Sea, currently shared by the Greek province of Thrace and southern Bulgaria.

Thucydides A general and the greatest of the Greek historians who lived in the second half of the 5th century BCE. He is famous for his masterpiece *The History of the Peloponnesian War*.

Tigris (River) One of the two mighty rivers that flow through **Mesopotamia**. It is to the east and roughly parallel to the **Euphrates. Nineveh,** capital of **Assyria**, was situated on the **Tigris.**

Timnah A Canaanite town southeast of **Hebron**.

Torah Literally "teaching," "instruction"; used as a synonym for the word of God; more narrowly the **Pentateuch**, the Bible, and ultimately the entire religious tradition of Judaism.

Transjordan The area east of the **Jordan River**.

Ugarit An ancient metropolis and trading hub destroyed about 1195 BCE. It was located on the Syrian coast about seven miles north of the present Latakia. Important for the vast library discovered in its ruins. (See **Ugaritic**.)

Ugaritic The language spoken and written by the inhabitants of **Ugarit** is a language very similar to Biblical Hebrew, and the literature written in it has helped illuminate much that was obscure in the Bible. **Ugaritic** poetry in particular has proved to be one of the models upon which biblical poetry is based.

Vashti Queen, wife of King **Ahasuerus** in the Book of Esther.

Vul. (Abr. for Vulgate) *see* **Vulgate**

Vulgate The translation of the Bible from Hebrew into Latin made by St. Jerome in the last quarter of the 4th century BCE.

Wisdom Literature The literary category that predominates in the Books of the **Ketubim** or Writings, the third division of the Hebrew Bible. This was a broad literary genre common to the main cultures of the Ancient Near East. It embodied a way of thinking and an attitude to life emphasizing experience, reason, morality and the life concerns of human beings. See **Ketubim**.

Xerxes I *see* **Ahasuerus.**

Yehud The name by which the province comprised of **Jerusalem** and its surrounding region was known during the Persian period. See also **Commonwealth, Second**.

Zerah Son of **Tamar** and **Judah**.

Zeresh Wife of **Haman**.

Selected Bibliography

Albright, William Foxwell. "The Lachish Cosmetic Burner and Esther 2: 12." In *A Light unto My Path: Old Testament Studies in Honor of Jacob M. Meyers*, edited by H.N. Bream, R.D. Heim and C.A. Moore, pp. 25–32. Philadelphia: Temple University Press, 1974.

Alter, Robert. *Genesis*. New York: W.W. Norton, 1996.

_____. "A Literary Approach to the Bible." *Commentary*, vol. 60, no. 6 (1975): 70–77.

Anderson, B.W. *The Book of Esther, Introduction and Exegesis*. New York: Abington Press, 1954.

Anderson, Francis I. "Israelite Kinship Terminology and Social Structure." *The Bible Translator*, vol. 20 (1969): 29–39.

Baldwin, Joyce G. *Esther: An Introduction and Commentary*. Tyndale Old Testament Commentary. Leicester, UK: Intervarsity, 1984.

Bankier, Joanna, and Deirdre Lashgari (editors). *Women Poets of the World*. New York: MacMillan, 1983.

Barnstone, Aliki, and Willis Barnstone (editors). *A Book of Women Poets: From Antiquity to Now*. New York: Schocken, 1990.

Barzun, Jacques. *From Dawn to Decadence: 500 Years of Western Cultural Life, 1500 to the Present*. New York: HarperCollins, 2000.

Ben-Chorin, Shalom. *Kritik des Estherbuches: Eine theologische Streitschrift*. Jerusalem: "Heatid" Salingre, 1938. (In German)

Berg, Sandra Beth. *The Book of Esther: Motifs, Themes and Structure*. Missoula, MT: Scholars Press, 1979.

Berlin, Adele. *JPS Bible Commentary: Esther*. Philadelphia: Jewish Publication Society, 2001.

Berman, Joshua A. "Hadassah bat Abihail: The Evolution from Object to Subject in the Character of Esther." *Journal of Biblical Literature*, vol. 120, no. 4 (2001): 647–669.

Bickerman, Elias. *Four Strange Books of the Bible*. New York: Schocken, 1967.

Bloom, Harold and David Rosenberg. *The Book of J*. New York: Grove, Weidenfeld, 1990.

Bos, Johanna W.H. *Ruth, Esther, Jonah*. Atlanta: Knox Press, 1986.

Breneman, Marvin. *Ezra, Nehemiah, Esther*. Nashville: Broadman & Holman, 1993.

Brenner, Athalya. "Female Social Behavior: Two Descriptive Patterns within the 'Birth of a Hero' Paradigm." *Vetus Testamentum*, vol. 36 (1986): 257–273.

Briant, Pierre. "Persian Empire." Translated by S. Rosoff. *Anchor Bible Dictionary*, Vol. 5, p. 241. Garden City, NY: Doubleday, 1992.

Brichto, H.C. "Kin, Cult, Land, and Afterlife — A Biblical Complex." *Hebrew Union College Annual*, vol. 44 (1973): 1–54.

Bright, John. *A History of Ancient Israel*. Third edition. Philadelphia: Westminster Press, 1981.

Bury, J.B. *The Ancient Greek Historians*. New York: Dover Publications, 1958.

Campbell, E.F.C. *The Anchor Bible: Ruth*. Garden City, NY: Doubleday, 1975.

Cassuto, Umberto. "The Story of Tamar and Judah." *Biblical and Oriental Studies*, Vol. 1, pp. 29–40. Jerusalem: Magnes Press, 1973.

Cooke, G.A. *The Book of Ruth: The Cambridge Bible for Schools and Colleges*. Cambridge: Cambridge University Press, 1918.

Crenshaw, James Lee. *The Anchor Bible: Joel*. New York: Doubleday, 1995.

Dahood, M.J. "Northwest Semitic Notes on Genesis." *Biblica*, vol. 55 (1974): 76–82.

Daube, David. "The Last Chapter of Esther." *Jewish Quarterly Review*, vol. 37 (1946–47): 139–147.

Day, Linda. *Three Faces of a Queen: Characterization in the Books of Esther*. Sheffield, UK: Academic Press, 1995.

Diamond, Jared. *Guns, Germs and Steel: The Fates of Human Societies*. New York: W.W. Norton, 1999.

Dommershausen, Werner. *Den Estherrole: Stil und Zeil einer alttestamentlichten Schrift*. Stuttgarter Biblische Monographien 6. Stuttgart: Katholisches Bibelwerk, 1968. (In German)

Durant, Will. *Our Oriental Heritage*. New York: Simon & Schuster, 1954.

Eissfeldt, Otto. *The Old Testament: An Introduction*. Translated by Peter R. Ackroyd. New York: Harper & Row, 1965.

Fisch, Harold. *Poetry with a Purpose: Biblical Poetics and Interpretation*. Bloomington: Indiana University Press, 1988.

Fox, Michael V. *Character and Ideology in the Book of Esther*. Columbia: University of South Carolina Press, 1991.

Freedman, David Noel. "The Chronicler's Purpose." *Catholic Bible Quarterly*, vol. 23 (1961): 436–442.

Friedberg, Albert D., and Vincent Decan. "Dating the Composition of the Book of Esther: A Response to Larsson." *Vetus Testamentum*, vol. 53, no. 3 (2003): 427–429.

Friedman, Richard. "Is Everybody a Bible Expert?" *Biblical Research*, vol. 7, no. 2 (1991): 16–18, 50–51.
_____. *Who Wrote the Bible?* New York: Harper & Row, 1989.

Fuerst, Wesley J. *The Books of Ruth, Esther, Ecclesiastes, The Song of Songs, Lamentations*. Cambridge: Cambridge University Press, 1977.

Gan, Moshe. "The Book of Esther in the Light of the Story of Joseph in Egypt." *Tarbiz*, vol. 31 (1961–1962): 144–149. (In Hebrew)

Gifford, Thomas. *The Assassini*. New York, Bantam Books, 1991.

Gilbert, Martin. *The Holocaust: The Jewish Tragedy*. Glasgow, UK: Fontana/Collins, 1987.

Gilbert, W.S. *Iolanthe*, 1882.

Gilbert, W.S. *The Mikado,* 1885.

Goitein, S.D. "Women as Creators of Biblical Genres." Translated by Michael Carasik. *Prooftexts*, vol. 8, no. 1 (1988): 1–33.

Gordis, Robert. "Love, Marriage, and Business in the Book of Ruth: A Chapter in Hebrew Customary Law." In *A Light unto My Path: Old Testament Studies in Honor of Jacob M. Meyers*, edited by Howard N. Bream, Ralph D. Heim and Carey A. Moore, pp. 241–264. Philadelphia: Temple University Press, 1974.
_____. *Megillat Esther with Introduction, New Translation and Commentary*. New York: Rabbinical Assembly, 1974.
_____. "Religion, Wisdom and History in the Book of Esther: A New Solution to an Ancient Crux." *Journal of Biblical Literature*, vol. 100 (1981): 359–388.
_____. "Studies in the Esther Narrative." *Journal of Biblical Literature*, vol. 95 (1976): 43–58.

Gottwald, Norman K. *The Hebrew Bible — A Socio-Literary Introduction*. Philadelphia: Fortress Press, 1985.

Hallo, William W. "The First Purim." *Biblical Archaeologist*, vol. 46 (1983): 19–29.
_____. *Origins: The Ancient Near Eastern Background of Some Modern Western Institutions*. Leiden, The Netherlands: Brill, 1996.

Hals, R.M. *The Theology of the Book of Ruth*. Philadelphia: Fortress Press, 1969.

Hamilton, Victor P. *The Book of Genesis: Chapters 18–50*. Grand Rapids, MI: Eerdmans, 1995.

Hazony, Yoram. *The Dawn: Political Teachings of the Book of Esther*. Jerusalem: Genesis Jerusalem Press, 1995.

Hegel, Georg Wilhelm Friedrich. *Hegel's Philosophy of Right*. Translated by T.M. Knox. Oxford: Oxford University Press, 1967.

Herodotus. *Histories*. 2 vols. Translated by George Rawlinson. London: Dent & Sons, 1964.

Hubbard, Robert L., Jr. *The Book of Ruth*. Grand Rapids, MI: Eerdmans, 1988.

Hume, David. *The History of England*. 6 vols. Indianapolis: Liberty Fund, 1983.

Jobes, Karen H. *The Alpha-Text of Esther: Its Character and Relationship to the Masoretic Text*. Atlanta: Scholars Press, 1996.
_____. *Esther*. Grand Rapids, MI: Zondervan, 1999.

Jones, B.W. "The So-called Appendix to the Book of Esther." *Semitics*, vol. 6 (1978): 36–43.
_____. "Two Misconceptions about the Book of Esther." *Catholic Biblical Quarterly*, vol. 39 (1977): 171–181.

Josephus, Flavus. *Against Apion*. Translated by H.St.J. Thackeray. Loeb Classical Library, Vol. 1, pp. 162–411. Cambridge, MA: Harvard University Press, 1956.

Kass, Leon R. *The Beginning of Wisdom: Reading Genesis*. New York: Free Press, 2003.

Kaufmann, Yehezkel. *History of the Religion of Israel*, Vol. 4. New York: Ktav Publishing House, 1977.
_____. *Toldot Ha'emunah Ha'yisraelit Meyime Kedem Ad Sof Bayit Sheni*. 8 vols. Tel Aviv: Devir, 1953–1956. (In Hebrew)

Keil, C. F. *Esther*. Grand Rapids, MI: Eerdmans, 1980.

Kitchen, Kenneth Andrew. *The Bible in Its World: The Bible and Archaeology Today*. Eugene, OR: Wipf & Stock, 2004.
_____. *On the Reliability of the Old Testament*. Grand Rapids, MI: Eerdmans, 2003.

Kuhrt, Amelie. *The Ancient Near East, 3000–330 BC*. 2 vols. London: Routledge, 1995.

Lacocque, Andre. *The Feminine Unconventional: Four Subversive Figures in Israel's Tradition*. Minneapolis: Fortress Press, 1990.

Laffey, A. *An Introduction to the Old Testament: A Feminist Perspective*. Philadelphia: Fortress Press, 1988.

Levenson, Jon D. *Esther: A Commentary*. Louisville, KY: Westminster John Knox, 1997.

Levine, Baruch A. *JPS Torah Commentary: Leviticus*. Philadelphia: Jewish Publication Society, 1989.

Luther, Martin. *The Table Talk of Martin Luther*. Translated by William Hazlitt. Philadelphia: United Lutheran Publication House, n.d.

Mannheim, Karl. *Ideology and Utopia: An Introduction to the Sociology of Knowledge*. Translated from the German by Louis Wirth and Edward Shils. New York: Harcourt, Brace & World, 1936.

Maspero, Gaston Camille Charles. *The Passing of Empires*. London, 1899.

Menn, Esther Marie. *Judah and Tamar (Genesis 38) in Ancient Jewish Exegesis: Studies in Literary Form and Hermeneutics*. New York: Brill, 1997.

Meyers, Carol. "Returning Home: Ruth 1: 18 and the Gendering of the Book of Ruth." In *A Feminist Companion for Ruth*, edited by Athalya Brenner, pp. 85–114. Sheffield, UK: Sheffield Academic Press, 1993.

_____. "'Women of the Neighborhood' (Ruth 4: 17): Informal Female Networks in Ancient Israel." In *Ruth and Esther: A Feminist Companion to the Bible* (Second Series), edited by Athalya Brenner, pp. 110–127. Sheffield, UK: Sheffield Academic Press, 1999.

Meyers, Jacob. *The Linguistic and Literary Form of the Book of Ruth*. Leiden, the Netherlands: Brill, 1955.

Milgrom, Jacob. *Anchor Bible: Leviticus*. 3 vols. New York: Doubleday, 1991, 2000, 2001.

_____. *JPS Torah Commentary: Numbers*. Philadelphia: Jewish Publication Society, 1990.

Mills, Robert. *Space, Time and Quanta: An Introduction to Contemporary Physics*. New York: Freedman, 1994.

Moore, Carey A. *Anchor Bible: Daniel, Esther and Jeremiah: The Additions*. Garden City, NY: Doubleday, 1977.

_____. *Anchor Bible: Esther*. Garden City, NY: Doubleday, 1971.

_____. "Archaeology and the Book of Esther." *Biblical Archaeologist*, vol. 38 (1975): 60–79.

_____. "Esther, Additions to." *Anchor Biblical Dictionary*, Vol. 2, pp. 626–633. New York: Doubleday, 1992.

Munn-Ranken, Joan Margaret. "Persian History." *Encyclopedia Britannica*, Vol. 17, pp. 652–662. Chicago: Benton, 1972.

Noth, Martin. *The History of Israel*. Second edition. Translated by Stanley Godman. London: Black, 1958.

Openheim, A. Leo. "On Royal Gardens in Mesopotamia." *Journal of Near Eastern Studies*, vol. 24 (1965): 328–333.

Orlinsky, H.M. "The Canonization of the Hebrew Bible and the Exclusion of the Apocrypha." In *Essays in Biblical Culture and Bible Translation*, pp. 257–286. New York: Ktav, 1974.

Park, Robert E. "Introduction." In E.V. Stonequist, *The Marginal Man*, pp. xiii–xviii. New York: Scribner's Sons, 1937.

Paton, Lewis Bayles. *ICC: A Critical and Exegetical Commentary on the Book of Esther*. New York: Scribner's Sons, 1908.

Plutarch. *Plutarch's Lives*, Vol. 11. Translated by Bernadotte Perrin. Loeb Classical Library, London: Heinemann, 1959.

Podhoretz, Norman. *The Prophets: Who They Were, What They Are*. New York: Free Press, 2002.

Porten, Bezalel. "The Scroll of Ruth: A Rhetorical Study." *Gratz College Annual*, vol. 7 (1978): 23–49.

Prouser, Joseph H. "As Is the Practice of Women: The Practice of Birth Control in the Book of Esther." *Conservative Judaism*, vol. 53, no. 2 (2001): 51–59.

Rad, Gerhard Von. *Old Testament Theology*. Vol. 1. Translated by D.M.G. Stalker. London: Oliver & Boyd, 1962.

Rauber, D.F. "Literary Values in the Bible: The Book of Ruth." *Journal of Biblical Literature*, vol. 89 (1970): 27–37.

Rendsburg, Gary A. "Biblical Literature as Politics: The Case of Genesis." In *Religion and Politics in the Ancient Near East*, edited by Adele Berlin, pp. 47–70. Bethesda: University Press of Maryland, 1996.

Riddle, John M. *Contraception and Abortion from the Ancient World to the Renaissance*. Cambridge, MA: Harvard University Press, 1992.

Riddle J.M., J.W. Estes, and J.C. Russell. "Ever Since Eve: Birth Control in the Ancient World." *Archaeology*, vol. 47 (March/April 1994): 29–35.

Robinson, Ira. "*bepetah enayim* in Genesis 38: 14." *Journal of Biblical Literature*, vol. 96 (1977): 569.

Rosenthal, Ludwig A. "Die Josephegeschichte mit den Buchern Ester und Daniel verglichen." *Zeitschrift fur die alttestamentliche Wissenschaft*, vol. 15 (1895): 278–284. (In German)

_____. "Nochmals der Vergleich Ester, Joseph-Daniel." *Zeitschrift fur die alttestamentliche Wissenschaft*, vol. 17 (1897): 125–128. (In German)

Rowley, H.H. "The Marriage of Ruth." In *The Servant of the Lord and Other Essays on the Old Testament*, pp. 161–186. London: Lutterworth Press, 1954.

Samuel, Maurice. *Certain People of the Book*. New York: Knopf, 1958.

Sandmel, Samuel. *The Enjoyment of Scripture: The Law, the Prophets, and the Writings*. London: Oxford University Press, 1979.

Sarna, Nahum M. *The JPS Torah Commentary: Genesis*. Philadelphia: Jewish Publication Society, 1989.

Slotki, Judah J. "Ruth: Introduction and Commentary." In *The Five Megilloth*, edited by A. Cohen, pp. 36–65. London: Soncino Press, 1952.

Smith, Louise Pettibone. "The Book of Ruth." In *The Interpreter's Bible*, Vol. 2, pp. 829–852. New York: Abingdon Press, 1953.

Speiser, E. A. *Anchor Bible: Genesis*. Garden City, NY: Doubleday, 1964.

Sternberg, Meir. *The Poetics of Biblical Narrative*. Bloomington: Indiana University Press, 1987.

Talmon, Shemaryahu. "Wisdom in the Book of Esther." *Vetus Testamentum*, vol. 13 (1963): 419–455.

Tigay, Jeffrey H. *The JPS Torah Commentary: Deuteronomy*. Philadelphia: Jewish Publication Society, 1996.

Torrey, C.C. "The Older Book of Esther." *Harvard Theological Review*, vol. 37 (1944): 1–40.

Trible, Phyllis. "Two Women in a Man's World." *Soundings,* vol. 59 (1977): 251–279. Reprinted as "A Human Comedy." In *God and the Rhetoric of Sexuality: Overtures to Biblical Theology*, pp. 166–199. Philadelphia: Fortress Press, 1978.

Ungnad, Arthur. "Keilinschriftliche Beitrage zum Buch Esra und Ester." *Zeitschrift fur die alttestamentliche Wissenschaft*, vol. 58 (1941): 240–244. (In German)

Weinfeld, Moshe. "The Book of Ruth." *Encyclopedia Judaica*, Vol. 14, pp. 518–522. Jerusalem: Keter Publishing House, 1971.

Wellhausen, Julius. *Prolegomena to the History of Ancient Israel.* Translated from the German edition of 1878 into English in 1885 by Mr. Menzies and Mr. Black. Reprint. New York: Meridian Books, 1957.

Wirth, Louis. "Preface." In Karl Manheim. *Ideology and Utopia.* New York: Harcourt, Brace & World, 1936.

Xenophon. *Cyropaedia.* 2 vols. Translated by Walter Miller. Loeb Classical Library. London: Heinemann, 1943.

Zeitlin, Solomon. "The Books of Esther and Judith: A Parallel." In M.S. Enslin (editor), *The Book of Judith*, pp. 1–37. Leiden, The Netherlands: Brill, 1972.

Biblical Verses Index

This book contains the entire text of Ruth in chapters 2–5, Genesis 38 in chapter 7, and Esther in chapters 9–19. Specific verses can be located in their sequential order. All other references to biblical verses, including those additional citations from Ruth, Esther and Genesis 38 that are not in sequential order, are listed below. The order of the books follows that of the Hebrew Bible.

Genesis 12:1 49
Genesis 12:3 200
Genesis 14:22–23 177
Genesis 17:1–2 41
Genesis 17:6 86
Genesis 18:16 38
Genesis 19:30–38 36
Genesis 20:35
Genesis 23:7 128
Genesis 23:8 40
Genesis 24:3–4 79
Genesis 26:1–6 35
Genesis 26:2–3 35
Genesis 27:1–34 142
Genesis 27:34 142, 145
Genesis 28:1–2 79
Genesis 28:3 41
Genesis 32:23–33 3
Genesis 33:3 128
Genesis 35:11 41
Genesis 36:35 35
Genesis 37 79
Genesis 37:2 224
Genesis 37:14 78
Genesis 37:26–7 85
Genesis 37:29 141
Genesis 37:35 79
Genesis 38 23
Genesis 38:11 11
Genesis 38:29–30 66
Genesis 39:1 79
Genesis 39:8 129
Genesis 39:8–9 129
Genesis 39:10 129
Genesis 41:45 115
Genesis 41:46 224
Genesis 41:54–46:27 35
Genesis 43:14 41, 193

Genesis 43:28 128
Genesis 44:34 162, 197
Genesis 45:4–8 200
Genesis 45:5 201
Genesis 45:8 201
Genesis 45:11 224
Genesis 46:1–4 199, 201
Genesis 46:2–4 35
Genesis 46:8–27 225
Genesis 46:12 89, 224, 225
Genesis 46:20 225
Genesis 46:27 225
Genesis 48:3–4 41
Genesis 49:25 41
Genesis 50:20 180, 202

Exodus 1:15–22 134
Exodus 1:17 131
Exodus 2:1–2 71
Exodus 2:22 48, 211
Exodus 2:23 143
Exodus 17:8–13 130
Exodus 17:14–16 130
Exodus 18:7 128
Exodus 22:20 130
Exodus 23:9 130

Leviticus 18 33
Leviticus 18:9–10 45
Leviticus 19:14 132
Leviticus 19:32 132
Leviticus 19:33 130
Leviticus 20 53
Leviticus 20:10 85
Leviticus 25:8–10 22
Leviticus 25:14–16 22
Leviticus 25:17 132

Leviticus 25:23–24 21
Leviticus 25:25 22, 23
Leviticus 25:35–38 130
Leviticus 25:36 132
Leviticus 25:43 132

Numbers 21:20 35
Numbers 22–24 36
Numbers 26:5–51 225
Numbers 26:19 225
Numbers 26:21 225
Numbers 27:1–11 20
Numbers 27:8–11 20, 222
Numbers 27:11 222
Numbers 32 21
Numbers 33:50–56 21
Numbers 33:54 21
Numbers 34:1—35:8 21
Numbers 35:16–29 19
Numbers 35:47–55 23
Numbers 36 21

Deuteronomy 10:17–19 130
Deuteronomy 11:16–17 71
Deuteronomy 15:12–15 130
Deuteronomy 21:15–17 21
Deuteronomy 22:21 85
Deuteronomy 23:1 58
Deuteronomy 24:17–22 130
Deuteronomy 24:19 45
Deuteronomy 25:5–6 23
Deuteronomy 25:5–10 87
Deuteronomy 25:7–10 80
Deuteronomy 25:17–19 130

Deuteronomy 26:5–10 73
Deuteronomy 27:20 58
Deuteronomy 30:11–14 9
Deuteronomy 31:11–12 9

Joshua 2 240
Joshua 8:34–35 9
Joshua 14–19 21
Joshua 15:44 77
Joshua 15:57 81

Judges 3:11 28
Judges 3:12 28
Judges 3:12–14 132
Judges 3:12–30 36
Judges 3:30 28
Judges 4–5 28, 219
Judges 5 238
Judges 5:31 28
Judges 6:1–6 132
Judges 11:17 36

1 Samuel 1–2 32
1 Samuel 2:1–10 238
1 Samuel 7:2 81
1 Samuel 15 128, 132
1 Samuel 15:29 201, 202
1 Samuel 17:42 11
1 Samuel 17:55 19
1 Samuel 22:3–4 26
1 Samuel 24:9 128
1 Samuel 25:36 57
1 Samuel 25:41 57
1 Samuel 26:19 34

2 Samuel 13:18 198
2 Samuel 13:19 141
2 Samuel 14:4 128

1 Kings 1:16 128
1 Kings 2:22–23 254
1 Kings 3:16–28 32
1 Kings 6:1 101
1 Kings 19:2 40
1 Kings 21:3 22

2 Kings 18:37 141
2 Kings 24:6–17 114
2 Kings 25:1 179
2 Kings 25:3–4 179
2 Kings 25:25 179

Isaiah 10:5–15 208
Isaiah 44:28 209
Isaiah 45:1 209
Isaiah 45:15 68

Jeremiah 7:18 193
Jeremiah 32 64
Jeremiah 32:11ff 64
Jeremiah 42–43 193
Jeremiah 43:10 208
Jeremiah 44:15–18 194
Jeremiah 44:17–19 193

Ezekiel 16:8 58

Joel 2:12 145
Joel 2:13–14 146
Joel 2:15–17 147

Micah 1:14 77

Haggai 2:1–10 99

Zechariah 1:7 101
Zechariah 7:1 99

Zechariah 8:9 99
Zechariah 8:19 179, 181

Psalms 23:4 141
Psalms 53:2 72
Psalms 83:1–8 132
Psalms 119:105 x
Psalms 128:6 xix

Proverbs 12:4 58
Proverbs 31:10 v
Proverbs 31:10–31 58

Ruth 1:1 18, 70
Ruth 1:2 44
Ruth 1:6 69, 70, 71
Ruth 2:4 61
Ruth 2:11–12 40
Ruth 2:13 57
Ruth 3:9 57
Ruth 3:10 65
Ruth 3:11 64, 65
Ruth 3:13 60
Ruth 4:3 33
Ruth 4:3–4 221
Ruth 4:7 24
Ruth 4:10 23
Ruth 4:12 86
Ruth 4:13 69, 71, 72
Ruth 4:14 72
Ruth 4:17 72
Ruth 4:18–22 86

Ecclesiastes 12:12 x

Esther 1:9 163
Esther 1:10 57
Esther 1:11 167

Esther 2:5 185
Esther 2:11 182
Esther 2:17 167
Esther 2:20 182
Esther 2:22 182
Esther 2:23 153
Esther 3:4 127
Esther 3:6 134
Esther 3:7 100, 144, 191
Esther 3:8 135, 184
Esther 3:8–9 166
Esther 3:13 135, 232
Esther 3:15 167
Esther 4:1 179
Esther 4:4 182
Esther 4:7 138
Esther 4:8–10 183
Esther 4:13 166
Esther 4:15 183
Esther 4:16 183, 184, 197
Esther 5:12–13 166
Esther 6:7–9 166
Esther 6:10 143
Esther 6:18 167
Esther 7:4 138, 139, 184
Esther 8:1 184
Esther 8:2 128
Esther 8:3 128
Esther 8:6 197
Esther 8:7 197
Esther 8:8 176
Esther 8:9 173
Esther 8:10–14 139
Esther 8:11 232
Esther 8:15 167
Esther 8:17 172, 173, 228

Esther 8–9 227
Esther 9:2 173
Esther 9:3 173
Esther 9:13 177
Esther 9:17–19 185
Esther 9:20–10:3 178
Esther 9:24 191
Esther 9:24–25 180
Esther 9:24–25 202
Esther 9:28–32 191
Esther 10:3 128

Daniel 1:7 115
Daniel 5 163
Daniel 6:9 163
Daniel 6:13 163

Ezra 2:2 114
Ezra 2:64 114
Ezra 4:4–24 177
Ezra 4:6 99

Nehemiah 1:1 99
Nehemiah 2:1 101
Nehemiah 7:7 114
Nehemiah 7:66 114
Nehemiah 13:23–24 110

1 Chronicles 1:46 35
1 Chronicles 4:41–3 132
1 Chronicles 8:8 35

1 Maccabees (Apocrypha) 216
2 Maccabees 103

General Index

A-text *see* Alpha-text
abecedaries 237
Abihail 119, 148, 181, 183f
Abishag 154
Abi-simti, Queen 238
Abraham 1f, 31, 35f, 38, 49, 72, 76, 79, 85, 130, 177, 200, 202
Achaemenes 94
Achaemenian Empire *see* Persia
Acropolis 95, 105, 112, 114f, 122, 128, 140, 143f, 147, 174, 185
Adam 2
Adar, month of 136, 140, 166, 173, 177–81, 185
Additions (to LXX) A–F 227–29
Adonijah 154
adoption 67, 115
Adullam 76–78, 225
adultery 23, 82, 85, 129, 132
Advisory Council 108f, 125, 138, 145
Aegaleos, Mount 97
Aegean Sea 96
Aeneas 31
Agag, King 128, 130
Agagite 124, 128, 130, 132, 138, 161, 180, 202
Ahab 22
Ahasuerus 95–98, 100, 103, 105–13, 116, 118–22, 124–28, 133f, 136–40, 143, 147–50, 152f, 159f, 159, 162, 165f, 173, 180–84, 186f; *see also* Xerxes I
Ahura Mazda 99, 118, 164, 194, 196, 210
Akkadian 136f, 168, 237
Albright, William Foxwell 118
Alexander the Great 97, 102, 113, 118, 186
alien 32, 36f, 43, 45, 48, 100, 102, 142, 211, 221, 227
Alpha-Text 127, 211, 217, 227f
alphabet 6, 95, 235–38
Alter, Robert xi, 77, 83, 224
Amalek, Amalekites 130f
Ancient Near East 1, 17f, 37, 46,

61, 67, 80, 84, 93, 113, 121, 129, 156, 184, 210, 214, 217–19, 230, 233–38
ancient versions *see* Bible, ancient versions
Anderson, B.W. 176
Anderson, Francis I. 44, 115
Antiochan Persecutions 101
anti-Semitism 98, 99f, 100, 101, 102, 116, 133, 135, 137, 139, 151, 155, 156, 166, 168–70, 173f, 176, 178, 180, 184, 185, 191, 194, 197, 229
Apadana *see* court, inner
Apocrypha 147f, 189, 229
apostasy 34
Aramaisms 3, 5, 24, 110, 188, 203, 235–37
Arbela, Battle of 186
Arnon River 36
Artabanus 97, 122
Artaxerxes 95, 97–99, 101, 113, 122, 155, 216
assassination 28, 122, 126, 145, 153, 179, 182
Asshurbanapal 159, 237
assimilation 100, 114
Assyria 126, 158, 208
Athens 96–98, 234
Atossa 113
Austen, Jane 20, 53, 111
Av, 9th of 179

Babylon 96, 98f, 105, 113f, 124, 135f, 142, 163, 193; Babylonia 93, 114, 126, 158; Babylonian Empire 94; Babylonians 93, 115, 139, 179
Babylonian Exile 9, 24, 100, 102, 114f, 137, 209
Bactria 94, 96, 135
Baker, Sir S.W. 118
Balaam, son of Beor 236
Baldwin, Joyce G. 167, 230–32
Bankier, Joanna 238
Barak 28

Bardiya 96, 122
barley 42, 44f, 50, 52, 55, 59f
Barnstone, Aliki & Willis 238
Barzun, Jacques 14
Bathsheba 1
beauty: contest 115, 118, 120, 151, 182; cosmetic fumigation 118; treatments 112
Beer-sheba 199
Belshazzar 163
Belteshazzar 115
ben-Asher text 4
ben Chayyim text 4
Ben-Chorin, Shalom 188
Benjamin son of Jacob 199; tribe 115
Berg, Sandra Beth 191, 197
Berlin, Adele 103, 121, 128, 133, 137, 140, 142, 186, 191
Berman, Joshua A. 148, 183–85
Bethlehem 18f, 31–37, 41–46, 51, 53–56, 59–62, 64f, 71, 73, 76, 99, 211f, 217, 221f, 299
Bible: admitting unrighteousness in 86; ancient versions of 5f, 48, 57; antecedents of Israelites 113; arrangement of Books in 29, 103; artistry of 237; authors of 3; background necessary 10; barriers to reading 11f; beauty in 43; begins with creation 21; Books of 3; bowing to humans in 127f; bread in 37; brevity in 18; "brother" in 62; canonization 103, 111; Christian 29, 58, 72, 103f; common decency in 131; composed in different periods 3; context of 198, 208; esoteric 8; *Esther*, place in 188f; evidence of 222f; "foolproof composition" 9; God as Maker and Master in 209; God not mentioned in 98f; Greek translators/translations of 129, 188; Hebrew 3; hidden in narratives 210; historical narratives largely composed of 207;

historicity of 12–14; inclusion of *Ruth* in 68; "in former times" as used in 64; *Kadeshah* in 84; King James 6; known as OT 3; literacy Biblical 220; literary conventions of 11f, 227; male dominated 209, 215; Masoretic Text of 5 102; modern and relevant 219; motives in 80f; mourning signs in 143; names in 114f; names of months in 136; naming children in 66; narrative Books in 70; narratives with heroines 210; National Charter 9; natural order preference for 200; not Scripture when written 7; presumes clan structure 23; protection of *ger* in 36; reading instructions for 220; redemption in *see* redemption; religious work 27; *Ruth* anomaly in 69; scholarship of 8; secular seeming 2, 89f; secret codes 9; "Solomonic Enlightenment" in 213f; sources of understanding 18f; struggle against idolatry in 193; tone of solemn antiquity 6; Torah first part of 5; translation by St. Jerome 229; transparency 9; treats leaving Promised Land 35; *tzom behi* and *misped* in 146; unified picture of history in 70; Venice first printed in 4; view of Joseph 201; "women's literature" in 217; written by women 238; written for its time 10; written for whom? 235
Biblia Hebraica 4
Biblical Age 3f, 10, 24, 28f, 72, 79, 91, 210, 218, 220, 235
Biblical Era *see* Biblical Age
Bickerman, Elias 128, 163f
Bigthan 122, 126, 153
Bigthana 153
birth control 119
bless 45, 49, 200, 237
Bloom, Harold 216, 239
Boaz 12, 17, 40, 44–71, 86, 88f, 213, 216, 221–23
Bomberg, Daniel 4
Book of Records 122f, 153
Bos, Johanna W.H. 192
Brenerman, Marvin 95, 159, 163
Brenner, Athalya 26f
Briant, Pierre 163f
Brichtto, Herbert C. 33
Bright, John 188
Bury, J.B. 13

Cambyses II 94, 96
Campbell, E.F.C. 24, 26, 57, 64
Canaanite 24, 28, 76–79, 81, 83, 85–87, 101, 211f, 226, 235f
Candaules, King of Lydia; 108
canonization 5, 7f, 8, 103f, 188, 208, 219, 229
Canticles see Song of Songs

Cassuto, Umberto 79f, 225
CEO 125f, 132, 186, 198, 201
Chedorlaomer, King 177
Chemosh *see* god
Children of Israel *see* Israel
chiliarch 186
Chilion 35, 37, 63f, 71, 222, 236
Christian Bible *see* Bible, Christian
Christianity 3, 29, 58, 63, 72, 101–4, 175, 213; church 135
circumcision 103
cities of refuge 19
clan: Boaz and Elimelech from same 46; centralized state weakens 214; Elimelech cuts loose from 32; of Ephrath 35; folklore of 88; founders of 225; inheritance in 222; land alienated from 62; *mishpaha* defined as 44; Perez founder of 87, 89; person defined by 19, 46; responsibilities to 22f, 55, 58f; women responsible for cohesiveness of 66; world depicted in *Ruth* based on 25
coat of many colors 198f, 200
Columbus, Christopher ix, xi
concubines 108, 113, 118
Contra Apion 102
conversion 169
Cooke, G.A. 28, 68
Council of Jamnia 103
court: of David 214; of Egypt 198; inner (the Apadana) 144, 147; of law 20, 61, 65, 221; of Persia 97ff, 103, 106, 117, 182, 187
courtyard: of palace 106, 153; of Women's Quarters 115, 121f
Covenant 27, 192
Crenshaw, James Lee 145
Croesus, King 181
cuneiform 235, 237
Cyrenaica 94
Cyrus I 94
Cyrus II (the Great) 94–96, 99, 103, 105, 113f, 125, 174, 179, 181, 208; Proclamation of 114

Dahood, M.J. 81
Darius I 94–99, 101, 113, 115, 122, 124f, 137, 191
Darius III 186
Daube, David 132
David 1, 11, 17, 19, 25, 34, 66f, 70–75, 86, 88f, 93, 100, 132, 154, 175, 196, 198, 214f, 218, 235
Day, Linda 156, 161, 189, 216
Dead Sea 36, 100, 188
"Death of God" 194
Deborah 28, 207, 219
DeCaen, Vincent 101
decree 21, 103, 109f, 112, 125f, 140, 142–48, 155f, 158, 161–84, 203, 230–32; Royal 111f, 164
Delphi 181
Diamond, Jared 235

Diaspora 103, 115, 146
dietary laws 103, 229
divination 136
Documentary Hypothesis 89, 197
Dommershausen, Werner 113, 147
Doric invasions 234
Dostoyevsky, Fyodor 12
drinking 55f, 57, 105–12, 116, 119, 140, 149–51, 158, 160, 177, 185, 236–38
Durant, Will 125, 164

Eber Nahara 95
Ebla 234
Ecbatana 105, 135, 160
Egypt 5, 35f, 67, 72, 73, 76–78, 88–98, 102, 115f, 126, 129–31, 135, 139, 140, 143, 162, 179, 193, 197–202, 208, 211, 224f, 235
Ehud 36
Einstein, Albert, 74
Eissfeldt, Otto 178
Elam 105
elders 31, 61, 64f, 87, 147, 211, 217, 221
Elephantine 102, 172; Papyri 116
Elijah 40
Elimelech 32–37, 44–46, 51, 58, 62–66, 69f, 76, 221–23
Elizabeth I 175
Enayim 81f
Enheduanna, Princess 237
entailment 20; estates 62, 79, 222
entertainment 150, 161, 190
ephah 50, 59
Ephraim 225
Ephrath 35
Er 65, 76–82, 88f, 225
Eretria 96
Esau 142f
Essenes 102, 188
"*Esther the queen*" 112, 122, 147, 181
Esther's decree 181
Ethiopia 94, 105, 110f, 135, 165
Ethiopian Jews 53
The Eyes and Ears of the King 176

famine: begin with a 42; cause of departure 32; consumed by 194; creating a 71; Egyptian 199–201; ended 37; in the land 35, 70; in lives of Patriarchs 35; two years after 224
farce 98, 111, 156
fast 57, 63, 93, 103, 140, 142f, 146–49, 179, 184, 192
fear 31, 54, 58, 130–32, 141, 147, 151, 169f, 172–76, 199
feasting 57, 169, 172
feminine provenance 219
feminism 26f, 109f, 189, 233
fiction: dramatic 161; *Esther* as a work of 165, 176, 186; historical 24, 25, 191; indicators of 11; irrevocable decrees as 164; more than 192; treat works as 12

Final Solution 100, 133f, 141
First Commonwealth 101, 192, 219, 222, 233–35
first fruit 72
Fisch, Harold 43f
fool 71, 98, 111, 116, 151, 178
"for who knows" 145f
Fox, Michael 197, 203
Freedman, David Noel 101
Friedberg, Albert D. 101
Friedman, Richard 239
Fuerst, Wesley 175, 189

gallows 122, 152–54, 160, 162, 175, 180, 202
Gan, Moshe 197
Gandhi, Indira 122
garden of Eden 2
gate: of Bethlehem 221; city 58f, 61, 85; elders in the 211, 217; fortified complex 61; King's 121, 127, 141, 143, 151f, 155f, 167, 182; of his place 64; of my people 58, 65; of Sardis 108; seating accommodations in 61; site of courts 61; town 41
gender: balance 29; hierarchy 217
genealogy 17, 26, 66f, 88f, 114
Genesis: author of 197, 209, 219, 220; Book of 3, 84f; calling God Shadai 41; canonized 5; conclusion 202; dependence of *Esther* on 129; language of *Ruth* resembles 24; LXX of 227; Northwest Semitic Notes on 81; oral traditions used 215; paraphrasing 208; post-exilic product 235; RASHI comments 21; recounts beginning of world 2; reference to Amalek in 130; Wellhausen dismissed 233
Genesis 38 86, 207; as artificial intrusion 224; comparison with *Ruth* 77, 106; connections between *Ruth* and 87; discussion of 215; events depicted in 87; female authorship of 216, 239; full text 6; and "moral" 88; not part of Joseph Epic 215; part of larger literary unit 88; provisionally dated 233; redemption alluded to 23; in saga of Joseph 76; subject of inquiry 4; "Tamar" as shorthand for 194; theological conclusions proposed 220; translation of 5
genocide 132, 133, 150, 162, 176, 191, 194; attempt 98; chronicle of 202; critical mass necessary for 169; Haman's decree 179
Gentiles 99f, 116f, 169, 182, 190, 192, 197, 211, 228, 231
ger 32, 36, 45, 211
Gerar 35
Gestapo 140
gibor hayil 44
Gifford, Thomas xii

Gilbert, Martin 133, 140
Gilbert, Sir W.S. 56, 228
Ginsberg, H.L. 181
glean 44–48, 50f, 53f
God: abandon worship of 194; absence of 2, 13, 70, 74, 89, 172, 192, 207, 209, 211, 228; acceptance of 72f; activity of 203, 207; angry with 39; Bible the story of 70; bless in the Name of 73; bringing the word of 202; call of 49; cannot be found 74; Central Figure in Bible 2, 12; chess game, board, plan of 200f; commits herself to 54, 69; conception, author of 71; covertly present 72; Creator of universe 2, 21, 74; cry rise up to 143; death of 188, 196; did her dirty 42; did not fear 133; Director of drama 196, 202; earth, God of 79; *elohim* rendered as 6; emphasis on 203; family God possessed 87; famine, author of 71; fear of 132; finding 202; God-fearing Jews 228; God Most High 177; Godless universe 144, 152, 162, 194f, 209, 217; Godless world 147, 209; Hand of 39, 71, 75, 201f, 208; heavens of 79; Hero 209; Hidden 46, 72, 74, 89, 196, 207, 209f, 211, 213, 215f, 220; holidays ordained by 179; Holy Temple of 99; humanity's relationship with 68; instructs Moses 130; intended 202; invisible 207; of Israel 38, 41, 50, 54, 58, 73, 131; Israelite's relations with 3; justified in the sight of 14; knows nothing about 40; land given by 21; leaving Promised Land sanctioned by 35; Lord your God 130, 146; manifestation of 69; master 209; mentioned 70; Mordecai explains behavior to 127; never mentioned 98, 103, 146, 169; never speaks/acts 70, 200; to "pass a miracle" 200; pattern imposed on history 208; pawn of 201; people of 35, 192; perspective of 200; plays no part 88, 199; pray to, doesn't 146; presence of 185, 192, 194f, 209, 211, 217; promise of 79, 202; pronouncing the Name of 6; Providence of 203, 208; Purpose(s) of 27, 75, 89, 202, 208; reconstructing personal name of 6; reference to as a cliché 88; relationship with humanity 12, 219; removed from tale 151; rod of 130; sacred obligation to 24; *sent me before you* 200f; *Shadai* appellation of 41; shepherd of 209; silent 70; sin against 129, 132; speak in the name of 209;

take for granted 211; talking about 210; term *goel* used to describe 19; terrifying presence of 72; thanksgiving to 51, 175; there is no 72; thought of no 146; trustworthy 203; turn to 143; walks with man 212; ways with humankind 2; what has done 41; where is 152, 212; Who acts 2, 69, 73; Word of 220; works through the natural order 200; world made by 203, 212; world without 88, 172, 199; Your God my God 40; *see also* the Lord
god/ess: Chemosh 34, 38; Ishtar 114, 193; moon-god of Ur 238; Nisaba 237; not regarded as a 164; Queen of Heaven 193ff
gods: all knowing sage of 237; didn't really exist 194; images of 102; imitated the 163; Jewish rejection of "the gods" 102; letters addressed to 237; may the gods do to me 40; Nisaba 237; Oriental 163; season when gather 136; serve other 71
goel 19
Goethe, Johan Wolfgang von 68
Goitein, S.D. 27
Goliath 19
Gordis, Robert 33, 98, 110, 119, 165, 177, 181, 185, 230, 231
Göring, Hermann 121, 133
Gottwald, Norman K. 27
governors 32, 95, 106, 124, 126, 132, 140, 165f, 172–74, 179
grace 69, 118f; *see also hesed*
Grand Viziers *see* vizier
"great and bitter cry" 141–43, 146, 179
Greece 96f, 106, 108, 118–20, 122, 138, 234–36
Greek 3, 5, 13, 29, 61, 71, 95–97, 101–4, 112, 118, 122, 126f, 129, 139, 146, 159, 186, 188, 192, 203, 210, 216, 227, 230, 234, 236; versions 103, 227
Guards of the Threshold 122, 153

Habakkuk 18
Hadassah 114f, 148, 183f
Haggai 18
Hallo, William W. 189f, 237–39
Hals, R.M. 25
Haman 98, 100–2, 117, 124–28, 132–41, 143, 147–62, 165–77, 179–85, 189, 191, 202f, 228–32
Hamilton, Victor P. 84f
Hammedatha 124f, 128, 138, 162, 179, 202
Hamul 224f
Hannah 32
Hanukkah 103
Harbona 107, 159
harem 97, 107, 110, 112, 117, 119, 121, 144, 160, 211, 218

harvest 22, 42–45, 47, 52–56, 59, 62, 72f, 200, 222
hashav see "plotted"
Hathach 143, 145, 183
Hazony, Yoram 128, 158, 168f, 171
Hebrew: alphabet 236; Bible 3–5, 12, 29, 48, 70, 102f, 146, 229; language 5–7, 11, 24, 34, 49, 78, 100, 136, 148, 165, 197, 216, 230, 235; name 115, 124, 237; term 19, 32, 36f, 39–41, 44, 49f, 55–58, 84f, 106, 115, 130, 143, 159, 169, 175, 180, 185, 187, 198; text 46, 112, 127, 137, 148f, 165, 181, 188, 202, 222, 227–29, 231f; usages 67
Hebron 76, 78, 81
Hegai 112, 116–21
Hegel, Georg W.F. 208
Hellenism 101f, 147, 169, 186, 227f
Herodotus 95–97, 106, 108, 111–13, 121, 126, 128, 137f, 141, 145, 160, 163
heroine 17, 27, 43, 87, 103, 216
hesed 49, 69, 116; *see also* grace
Heydrich, Reinhard 140
Hezekiah 114, 132
Hezron 67, 86, 224f
Hidden God 72f, 201, 209f, 216, 219
The Hidden Hand 46
hieroglyphic writing 98, 235
Hindu 112, 139
Hirah 76, 78, 81f, 84,
historian 13f, 96f, 98
historicity 12f, 17, 26f, 95, 98, 163f, 191, 229
history: Amalekites in 130; of Biblical Age 29; detachment from 214; discipline of 12; dramatic form 13, 215; first attempted extermination of Jews in 139; first named author in 237; focus of 28; God's direction of 203; of God's relationship with Israel 27; of hostility 36; of the Jews 192f; marginality in 210; meta-71; narrative 3; official 187; Persian 94, 97, 113, 125; perspective 220; study of 207; subjects of 1; Wannsee Conference in 140; work of 96; of the world 70; of writing 235f
Hitler, Adolph 134, 161, 176
holiday 103, 140, 169, 172, 177, 179–81, 185, 188, 190, 202, 216
Holocaust 133f, 140, 191, 194
Homer 234
horizontal mobility 211f
Hubbard, Robert L. 24, 40, 51, 71
Huguenots 161
Hume, David 175
humor 98f, 111, 167, 185
Huna ben Hiyya 188

Ibn Ezra, Abraham 181
ideals 171

idolatry 39, 114, 192f, 194
Iliad 234
India 94, 105, 110f, 122, 126, 135f, 165
inheritance 18, 20–23, 51, 62–64, 79, 130, 221–23; of the fathers 22
intimidation 173f
Ionia 96, 186
irrational 108, 151, 156, 172, 217
Isaac 1, 31, 35, 79, 142, 200
Isaiah: prophet 25
Ishtar *see* god/ess
Islam 3
Israel: alternate name of Jacob 191; Ancient 19f, 22, 33, 49f, 53, 66, 217, 221–23; Biblical 216; children of 3, 69, 113, 131, 192, 202; customary practice in 51; definition of 31; Eternal 201, 203; faith of 193f; God of 34, 38, 40, 48, 54, 58, 68, 131; House of 64, 219; kingdom of 93, 115; land of 26, 31f, 36, 45f, 56, 65, 72, 93, 99, 131, 236; language 44; people of 1, 9, 12, 21, 23, 25, 27, 31, 49, 51, 65f, 70, 73, 76, 99, 127, 130, 187, 214, 234; pre-monarchic 11, 41; society 17, 64, 67, 214; tribes of 75, 225
Israelites 2f, 21, 24, 27, 34, 36, 40, 72, 76, 79, 89, 99–101, 113, 128f, 131, 136, 143, 192f, 202, 207, 214, 233–35
Izbet Sartah 237

J document *see* J source
J source 89, 197, 215, 239
Jacob 1, 3f, 24, 31, 35, 72, 76, 78f, 86, 89, 93, 142, 192, 198–202, 224; ben Chayyim 4
Jael 28
Jeconiah *see* Jehoiachin
Jehoiachin 114
Jerome *see* St. Jerome
Jerusalem 1, 5, 34, 75, 78, 93, 99, 103, 113–15, 135, 142, 146, 178, 181, 185, 192f, 209, 214, 237
Jesse 66f, 72, 86
Jewish Problem 99, 101, 132f, 134, 141f
Jew(s) 3f, 6, 53, 95, 98–103, 110, 113–15, 121, 127f, 131–36, 138–48, 152, 154–57, 160–70, 172–75, 176–81, 183–85, 187–94, 198, 202f, 209, 211, 228, 231f, 234f
Jezebel 40
Jobes, Karen H. 128, 147, 175, 191, 208, 228
Joel 18, 145–47
Jonah 18
Jones, Bruce W. 118, 178
Jordan River 35
Joseph 76–78, 85, 88–89, 115, 130, 132, 140, 162, 196f, 209, 214f, 224f

Josephus, Flavius 102
Josiah 9, 193
Jubilee Year 22, 63
Judah: King of 144; Kingdom of 100, 113f, 179, 192f; Land of 70, 193; Persian Provence of 95, 114, 209; son of Jacob 11, 65–67, 76–89, 93, 162, 199, 224–26; Tribe of 18, 32f, 35–37, 211
Judaism 3, 102–4, 117, 169, 189, 193, 213, 229
Judges 28

Kabul 135
Kadesh-barnea 130
Kafka, Franz 172
Kahle, Paul 5
Kalah 237
Kass, Leon R. 24, 80, 86
Kaufmann, Yehezkel 101
Keil, C.F. 146
Ketubim see Writings
Khshathra 125
Kidron Valley 237
King's Gate *see* gate, King's
kinsman 44, 46, 51, 55, 58, 62, 66; blood kinship, 19
Kipling, Rudyard 105
Kish 114, 128
Kitchen, Kenneth Andrew 31, 67, 76, 80, 89, 235f
Kittel, Rudolph 5
Kohn, Hans xi
Kubatum, Princess 238
Kuhrt, Amelie 113
Kuntillet Ajrud 236

LaCocque, Andre 26
Laffey, A. 26
land ownership 18, 21, 23, 63, 221
Lashgari, Deirdre 238
Leah 1, 64f
leisure class 111, 214
Leningrad Manuscript *see Biblia Hebraica*
Levenson, Jon D. 231
Levi ben Samuel 188
Levine, Baruch A. 22
Levirate Marriage 23, 39, 79, 81, 87
Liberum veto 163
literacy 214, 220, 233, 236–39
literature: academic 7; of the Ancient Near East 230; Canaanite 24; of feminine provenance 220; guileless 68; historical fiction 25; making a living by writing 237; male roles in 17, 26; market for 220; protest 218; second century BCE 100; signals to readers 11; of Sumer and Akkad 238; of the time 7; Western 11; woman's 217; women in 26f
the Lord 21f, 37f, 40f, 45f, 48f, 51, 58–60, 64–66, 69–72, 79f, 101, 130, 146f, 155, 169, 177, 193
Lot 36, 177

lucky days 135
Luther, Martin 103, 188

Macbeth 61, 181
Macedonia 96
Mahlon 35, 37, 49, 52, 54, 58, 63–69, 71, 222, 236
male-dominated 1, 13, 210, 215
Manasseh 225
Mannheim, Karl 212
Marathon, Battle of 96
Marduka 115
marginal: factors that render one, 210f; Jews, 228; "Marginal Man," 211f; notes, 4; questioning consensus, 216; role of woman, 209f; woman, 89, 213, 215f
marginalization 211, 218
Mari 51, 234, 237
marriage 17, 23f, 36, 38f, 52, 54, 58f, 63, 65, 69, 78f, 81, 87f, 110, 136, 154, 224f; customs, 53
Masoretic Text 4–7, 29, 127, 227, 229
Maspero, Gaston C.C. 116
massacre 130f, 134f, 136–38, 140, 142, 151, 159, 161, 168f, 180, 184, 231
Medes 94, 105, 109, 137, 156; Media 105, 108–10, 163, 186
Memucan 108–10
Menn, Esther M. 85, 89
Mesopotamia 67, 106, 158, 238
Messiah 19, 87
Meyers, Carol 26, 29, 44, 66, 217
Meyers, Jacob 25, 137
Midian 48, 131, 211
Migdol 193
Milgrom, Jacob 21, 23
Millgram, Elijah xi, 163
Mills, Eric 133
Mills, Robert 74
mishteh 106, 149
Moab 26, 32–38, 42, 46f, 47, 51, 62, 69–71, 73, 78, 99, 131
molestation 45
monarchy 1, 20, 24, 64, 89, 93, 125, 163, 214
monotheist 34, 194
Moore, Carey A. 95, 99, 101, 103, 116, 128, 137, 141f, 167, 175, 181, 189f, 228, 230
moral principle 130
Mordecai 98, 103, 114–17, 119–22, 124, 126–30, 132–34, 141–47, 151–74, 176, 178–89, 191, 197, 210, 216, 228–32; the Jew 155, 181, 184
Moses 5, 9, 20, 29, 48, 70f, 130f, 135, 211
Munn-Ranken, Joan Margaret 163
Mycale, Battle of 186
myrrh 118

Naboth 22
Nahum 18
Naomi 1, 27, 31, 33, 35–47, 49,

51f, 54–67, 69–73, 75f, 88, 210f, 213, 218, 221–23
narrative 1, 3, 11, 17–19, 27, 35, 60, 64, 68–74, 85, 87–89, 98f, 129, 144, 150f, 180, 191, 196, 200, 209, 214, 218, 224–29
Nazis 96, 100, 132–34, 140, 185
Nebuchadnezzar 98, 114, 193
need to know 106
Neff, Emery xi
Nehemiah: active in reign of Artaxerxes 98; Book of 9, 24, 98f, 101, 110, 114, 229; high official 99
New Testament 3, 231
Nineveh 158, 237
Nin-shatapada, Princess 238
Nippur 135
Nisaba *see* god
Nisan 101, 136, 140, 179
Noah 2
Noph 193
Noth, Martin 188
Numbers 2, 4, 222

oath 40, 130, 154
Obadiah 18
Obed 66f, 71f, 86
Old Testament 3, 24–26, 29, 31, 67, 76, 80, 178, 214f, 231, 235f; *see also* Bible
Onan 77, 80, 81, 88, 225
Oppenheim, A. Leo 106, 158
Orlinsky, H.M. 104
Orpah 35, 38–40, 51, 222
Owl of Minerva 208

P Document 222
pagan 65, 69, 75, 84, 99, 103, 114, 190, 208, 228
Park, Robert E. 212
parties 57, 64, 105–8, 112, 119, 123, 131, 148–52, 154, 156–59, 177, 184f
partying 106, 112, 122, 177, 180, 185
Passover 140, 179
Pathros 193
Paton, Lewis Bayles 118, 161, 175f, 178, 189, 192, 231
Patriarchal Age 76, 130, 215
Patriarchal structure 20
Patriarchs 3, 31, 35, 76, 170, 198f
pavilion 106, 158f
Pentecost 30
People of Israel *see* Israel, People of
Perez 65–67, 86, 88f, 224f
perfume 118
Persepolis 97, 99, 105, 135, 138, 186
Persia (also Persian Empire) 93–98, 102, 106, 108–11, 113f, 116, 118, 120–23, 125, 132–37, 145, 151f, 156, 159–61, 163f, 167, 175f, 178, 181f, 186, 197, 210, 219; court, 97; period, 24, 102, 115, 118, 132, 172, 222; world, 11, 98f, 143, 180, 216; Persians, 94,

96f, 109, 111, 113f, 118, 122, 126, 142, 157, 163, 174, 176, 180, 186
Peshitta 5, 188
Pharaoh 131, 198
Pharisees 102
Phoenician/s 235f
Pisistratus 234
Plataea, Battle of 97, 120, 186
playmate 182f, 210
"plotted" 122, 153, 161, 180, 191
plunder 132, 135, 140, 166, 174, 177
Plutarch 113, 155
Podhoretz, Norman x, 6
poetry 3, 18, 70, 93, 99, 236
pogrom 102, 135f, 155, 161, 168, 176
polygamy 55, 81, 113
polytheist 34
Porten, Bezalel 46, 64
Porter, Judith xi
Potiphar 129, 140, 142
power: absolute 125; base of 126; concentrated 30; display of 169; Esther who has the 176; fitful 172; in his hands 164; land 120; leap to 155; levers of 219; logic of 171; masters 141; military 131; no 40; of Persian government 182; pinnacle of 132; political 228; politics 168; position of 175, 197; power attracts 168, 171; rise to 224; seize 123; structure 160; threats of 173; to transform 69
practice 103, 192
prayer 52, 103, 127, 143, 146, 184, 228, 238; of Esther 147; of Mordecai 147
Promised Land 1, 31, 34f, 39, 73, 76, 93, 193, 199
Prophets: books of 70; third division of Hebrew Bible 29
prostitute 82, 84f
Prouser, Joseph H. 119
Providence: guided by divine 208; hint that 145; making explicit 203; many realms of 209; possibility of 203; theology of 213; under God's 192; we mean by 208; world ruled by 215
province(s) all the 109f, 112; anti-Semitism in 176; armed force of 231f; cities and 168; compact governmental units 95; dwellers of 135; each of 112; from every 97; governor of 126, 132, 139; in every 141, 145, 169; incorporated in 186; Jews in 162, 177, 180; of King Ahasuerus 166, 173f; the king's 174; observed in every 181; officials of 173; one hundred and twenty seven 96, 105, 165, 181; people of the king's 144; people scattered throughout all 137f; remission of taxes 119; unruly 124; western Assyrian 237

Psalm(s) 8, 70, 143, 187
Ptolemy VII: 104
public reading 9, 185, 192
Pur 136, 180, 202
Purim 30, 103, 177, 180–82, 185,
    188–92, 202, 216, 228
Pythius 108

Queen of Heaven *see* god
Qumran 100, 102

rabbis 103, 128f, 187
Rachel 1, 64, 198f
racism 100, 102
Rad, Gerhard von 25, 213–15
Ranke, Leopold von 14
Rashi (Rabbi Shlomo Itzhaki) 12, 51
Rauber, D.F. 8, 30
reading public 4, 233, 235, 237
reapers 44–48, 50
Rebecca 1
Redeemer 18f, 22–24, 51, 55, 57f,
    61–66, 71, 79, 221f; of the Blood
    20
Redemption 19, 22f, 62, 65f, 79,
    82, 97, 222
religion 2, 5, 13, 27, 31, 34, 37,
    40, 53, 68, 83, 74f, 75, 98f,
    102f, 115, 117, 122, 127, 128f, 135,
    139, 141, 146, 147, 151, 163, 169,
    172, 179, 185, 189, 192, 194, 203,
    219f, 228, 236
Rendsberg, Gary A. 89
Riddle, John M. 119
ridicule 98
Robinson, Ira 82
Roman alphabet 236
Rosenberg, David 216
Rosenthal, Ludwig A. 129, 197
Rowley, H.H. 18, 28
Royal Decree *see* Decree, Royal
royal gardens 106, 158
RSV 180, 231
Rubin, Yitzhak xi
Ruth 1, 12, 76, 87, 93, 170, 200,
    210–13, 218f, 222; age of 24;
    author of 215f; drama of 221;
    Ruth 3–6, 8, 11, 77, 79, 82, 87–
    89, 93, 98f, 106, 122, 194–96,
    209, 211, 213, 215–21, 233, 235,
    238; tale of 192, 199, 201, 207,
    213f, 215f, 227

Sabbath 103, 114, 117
sackcloth 142f, 145f, 179
sacrifice 53, 80, 103, 137
Saducees 102
St. Jerome 5, 188
Salamis, Battle of 97, 119f, 186
Samuel 2, 24, 29, 214; prophet 128
Samuel, Maurice 118, 145, 148, 154
Sandmel, Samuel 188
Sarah 1
Sardis 108
Sargon of Akkad 237
Sarna, Nahum M. 36, 224f
Satire 98f, 106, 112f

satraps 66, 95, 126, 132, 134, 165f,
    172–74
Saul 19, 26, 93, 115, 128, 130f
Scribes 3, 233, 235, 237
Scripture 5, 7, 9, 103, 146, 179, 185,
    188
scrolls 4
seah 59
Second Temple 1101f, 146
secularism 103, 217
Sennacherib 114
Septuagint 5, 29, 104, 127, 227f
settlement 1, 19, 21, 31, 192
Shaashgaz 119
Shadai 41
Shakespeare, William 46, 61, 131,
    138, 161, 171, 181
shalom 187f
sheaves 45–48, 50, 54
Shelah 11, 77, 80–82, 85f, 225
shoe 23, 64
Shua 76, 81
Shushan 95, 105f, 112, 114–16, 124,
    128, 132, 140, 143, 147, 167, 169,
    172, 174–77, 179, 183, 185; *see*
    Susa
Shu-Sin, Prince 238
signet 83, 138, 160
Sikh 122
Simon 132
Sisera 28
Slotki, Judah 28, 68
Smith, Louise P. 68
Sodom 177
Sogdiana 94, 135
Solomon 25, 32, 74, 89, 93, 101,
    154, 173
Solomonic Enlightenment 25, 89,
    196, 213, 215–18
Song of Songs 29, 99, 175
Spartans 96
Speiser, E.A. 40
Spiegel, Shalom xi
staff 37, 47, 50, 54, 83–85, 130,
    141, 153, 183
Sternberg, Meir 9
Stonequist, E.V. 212
Sumerian 230, 235
Susa 95–99, 105, 113, 115, 120f,
    133, 135, 140, 147f, 158, 160, 211;
    see also Shushan
Synagogue 30, 98, 147, 185f

Tabernacles 9
Tahpanhes 193
Talmon, Shemaryahu 165
Tamar: drama of 199; mother of
    Perez 65f; the person 1, 11, 65f,
    75, 78–89, 170, 196, 200, 210–
    17, 224f; shorthand for story of
    194; tale of 11, 89, 192, 201, 207,
    209, 213–16, 218, 220, 227, 239;
    world of, 93, 98
Tammuz, 9th of 179
Targum 5
Tekoa 19
Tell Deir Alla 236

Temple 5, 99, 103, 179, 237
Teresh 122, 126, 153
Thermopylae 96, 98
Thrace 96f
threshing 47, 50, 55–57, 59, 61
Thucydides xi, 13
Tigay, Jeffrey H. 84
Timnah 81f, 84
Tishre, 3rd of 179
Torah 4f, 9, 29, 103, 185
Torrey, C.C. 160
tragedy 3, 14, 34f, 42, 138, 151,
    167, 193f
transparency 9
Trible, Phyllis 17, 26f

Ugarit 81, 172, 230
uncertainty 172, 203, 207, 209
Ungand, Arthur 115
Ur 237f
urbanization 25, 214, 218

Vashti 106–9, 112f, 119, 125, 145,
    149, 151, 160, 189
vertical mobility 211, 213
Victorian women 214
vizier 105, 122, 125–27, 132, 152,
    155, 160, 167, 187
Voltaire, Francois Mari xi
Vulgate 5, 188, 229

Wannsee Conference 140
Watartum, Queen 238
Weinfeld, Moshe 64, 66
Wellhausen, Julius 232f
Western Civilization 3
Western Semitic languages 24, 235
wheat 42, 52
widow: bound by no restrictions
    24; childless 63, 79; did not
    inherit 222; dutifully residing
    with parents 84; duty to marry
    the 23; fallen into the underclass
    of society 211; free to choose
    53; garments of 82f; of King
    Ur-Nammu 238; knows Tamar
    only as 85; of Mahlon 63; not
    free to marry 23, 81; of one of
    his relatives 17; Onen married
    the 225; penniless 45; poor,
    orphan, alien and 45
wine 50, 53, 57, 106f, 149, 151,
    158f, 236
wing 48, 57f, 115
winnowing 50, 55
Wirth, Louis 212
Wisdom Literature 214
women: ability to inherit 20;
    appearance 115; as author 27,
    213, 216, 218, 233, 237–39;
    autonomous 218; bad breath 118;
    beautiful 123; of Bethlehem 41,
    66, 71, 217; Biblical 1; blood-
    thirsty 175; Book written by 27;
    Canaanite 86; in Canaanite
    world 81; chores before dawn 59;
    chorus 218; conceived 71;

confidently at home 27; cosmetic fumigation of 118; cosmetics 118; danger to unconnected 49; denigrating 189; desirable 53; disabilities of 211; expected to understand Scripture 9; focused on own concerns 28; grown 83; hero figures 2, 210, 216; Herodotus claims 96; hold leading roles 13; identity of 217; illustrious 65; as Judges 32; leisure class 214, 218; legitimate ideal for 219; lessons applicable to 12; literate 214, 237–39; literature 27, 217; loved her more than 119; make things happen 27; manager of 117; marginal 149, 212f, 218; marry only from seven families 113; minimizing the roles of 210; narratives featuring 1; narratives written by 220; of the neighborhood 66, 72; outsider 87; on own 211; pagan 71; at parity with men 219; part of the work force 214, 217; party for 107; point of view of 17; pretty 111; private story of 66; proper identity 212; quarters 107, 110, 116f; redefining identity of 217; reevaluation of role of 12; role of 2, 213, 218; safe with 52; segregated 215; to slaughter 135; status 210, 214, 218; stereotypical 189; take initiative 110; tale of 17, 26, 68f; textbook for intelligent 162; that approaches king 144; their children and 231f; of the town 44; treat husbands with respect 109; two beloved 38; two remarkable 14; unbecoming to a 175; wages at Mari for 51; who but a 216; to whom all others react, 183; work contributed by 29; of worth 58, 65; writer 27; writing tolerated 215; young 55, 65

Writings 5f, 30, 103

Xenophon 111, 121, 122
Xerxes I 95–97, 98, 101, 108, 111f, 115–17, 122, 127, 138; *see also* Ahasuerus
Xerxes II 96

Yahweh 6, 71
Yehud 95
young virgins 112, 115

Zebulon 35
Zechariah 101, 229; prophet 101, 179
Zedekiah 114
Zeitlin, Solomon 104
Zelophehad 20
Zephaniah 18
Zerah 86, 88, 224f
Zeresh 152f, 156
Zion 99, 147
Zoroastrian religion 98, 102, 117, 194